# forgive me no longer

## THE LIBERATION OF MARTHA

by

esther fibush

and martha morgan

FAMILY SERVICE ASSOCIATION OF AMERICA
NEW YORK

Library of Congress Cataloging in Publication Data

Fibush, Esther, 1913–
    Forgive me no longer.
1. Psychotherapy—Cases, clinical reports, statistics.
2. Psychotherapy patients—United States—Biography.
3. Morgan, Martha, 1932–    4. Women—Mental Health.
5. Feminism. I. Morgan, Martha, 1932–   joint author.
II. Title.
RC465.F49      616.8′914′0926      [B]      75–27965
ISBN 0–87304–148–8

Designed by Joan Stoliar

Printed in the United States of America

# CONTENTS

# INTRODUCTION

This is a book written by two women, a social worker and her client, about the shared experience of therapy. It tells the story of a woman's liberation from old, unhappy patterns of living as she risks herself in the new patterns emerging from her relationship with her therapist. Both client and therapist discover parallels between the course of therapy and the process of liberation that so many women are currently going through in their lives.

A woman's problems almost always reflect in some way the relationships between men and women, and a woman's therapy must take those relationships into account. As the story of this particular woman's therapy unfolds, it becomes a testimony to the far-reaching implications of the feminist cause.

Women have a special stake in therapy because it has been one of the ways by which masculine opinion and masculine domination have been reinforced in recent years. A number of women have started to raise some serious questions about psychotherapy, and the subject has been drawn into the battle for women's liberation.

There are many different kinds of therapy, and it would be a tedious, perhaps impossible, task simply to list them. Each person's therapy is different from every other person's, even with the same therapist, for the therapist responds in different ways to different people. There is one kind of therapy, however, that is especially in tune with the needs of women; it was originated by women and has been practiced predominantly by women. This is the therapy developed by the social work profession. It arose from a concern for people and the realities with which they have to contend. Practiced under a variety of names—social casework, family casework, psychiatric social work, psychosocial therapy, and clinical social work—it remains humanitarian in conception and equalitarian in conviction. Its basic principles are those of democracy: the dignity of the human being, the right of self-determination, the acceptance of individual and group differences, the freedom to seek and to speak one's own truth. It is grounded in a profound respect for the wisdom of intuition as well as for the findings of research. It stands midway between science and art and draws on both.

Social workers have had a bad press. From the early years, theirs was a woman's profession in a man's world; they were cast in a traditional woman's role: to serve others and—without much in the way of power, prestige, or money of their own—to find ways of making everything right for everybody. Social workers have been associated with and blamed for the failures of a public welfare program that was a political product not of their making and that could not, in any case, solve the economic ills or the social woes of the nation.

All the while, however, social workers in every setting—family service agencies, clinics, schools, hospitals, and a variety of community organizations and institutions—were helping people in whatever ways they could devise. Because social workers often found they could help with the psychological part of a problem, they developed their own kind of psychotherapy. Borrowing from any and every source, they put together a psychosocial therapy that had its roots in a recognition of the intractable realities of human existence, its source of inspiration in the humanistic strivings and creative productions of human beings, and its theoretical framework from the findings and formulations of social and behavioral sciences. This book is about that kind of therapy.

As a social worker who is a therapist, I write about therapy from my own experience, both on the giving and the receiving sides of the desk. I look on therapy as a second chance, an opportunity for human beings to come closer to what they want themselves and their lives to be. The medium through which such change takes place is the relationship between client and therapist. The method is communication. The therapist is responsible not for answers but for seeing that the interaction—the exchange of ideas and emotions—is as helpful to the client as possible. Therapy is an intensely personal relationship for the therapist as well as for client, but it is disciplined by the professional purpose for which it is undertaken.

This book is not a story of bizarre pathology or sensational events. It is about an ordinary human life, with its share of drudgery and dullness as well as drama. Nor is it a story of therapy proceeding at breakneck pace to a miraculous conclusion. It is simply a report of therapy as it actually happened, told as honestly as two human beings have been able to tell it.

People often say, "You can't really understand therapy unless you have been in it yourself." Perhaps this is so, but I hope not. I hope that this story of one woman's therapy, with the personal thoughts, memories, and feelings that I as the therapist have brought to it, will convey to others some understanding of what therapy is, and what it can do.

Esther Fibush
*Licensed Clinical Social Worker*
*Bethel Island, California*
*July 1975*

# PROLOGUE
## esther

The art teacher glanced at my watercolor and pronounced sentence on it: hopelessly derivative. I looked at it and saw a pattern of shapes, vaguely rectangular and triangular, that had given me pleasure first to draw, then to fill in, as a child colors in his coloring book. I had superimposed upon this pattern some wavering lines that became, without my having planned it, what seemed to be a picture of a mother embracing her young son against the background of a stained-glass window. I found that I liked to look at it very much.

But it wouldn't do. We must be authentic, express our "real" selves. I assumed that the teacher had taken my measure, for she suggested that I start with a self-portrait. Because she didn't make this suggestion to anyone else in the class, I felt that I had been found out. When I was a child, I liked to look at myself in the mirror and was told that I was vain. I knew this was a bad thing to be, but it didn't feel bad; it felt good. Later, when I began to grow up and no longer found myself beautiful, I would sometimes try to recapture that feeling of pleasure in myself. I could not; it eluded me. It was somewhere within me still, but I could not find it.

So now I would do a self-portrait. I sat down with paper and charcoal—snowy, textured paper, lovely random charcoal sticks. Surely with such equipment one should be able to produce a not unbeautiful self. I could not, but neither could I bear to leave that sheet of paper blank. The face of a child came to me, a little girl three years old, the daughter of friends, a child who for some reason liked me, so I liked her. I quickly outlined her face, no detail, just a face with sad eyes but a sturdy look. Not a self-portrait, but it would do.

I took it to the next meeting of the class. The teacher smiled but accepted it. When I showed it to my small friend, she liked it so well that I gave it to her. I could do another one for myself. I tried, and it was almost the same, but somehow the child looked older. Although I soon dropped out of the class, every once in a while during the next few months I would take paper and charcoal and try again. Each time the child looked a good deal older than in the previous sketch. I found this very strange and a little frightening, and I finally gave up. I kept one picture and framed it, the one in which the child looked about five years old. But many times I wished I had the first sketch back again.

A few years later I became familiar with the work of Klee and saw immediately that my watercolor of mother and son could be considered a poor imitation. I have several books of Klee's pictures now, and I look at them often; they tell me that the world is full of wonder and beauty, sadness and terror, which I know to be true. But I still keep my watercolor on my wall, for it speaks to me of love, and I know this to be true, too.

I have been a therapist for over twenty years, and I am aware that the foregoing is open to a variety of interpretations, depending on one's school of thought, one's life experience, and one's personal idiosyncracies. I myself have interpreted it in different ways at different times and will no doubt continue to do so. At the moment, it symbolizes for me this joint venture, Martha's and mine, to combine therapy with the writing of a book. This is not my story, or Martha's story, or just our joint story either. It is the story of many women seeking to discover who they are and why they are and where they are going from here, women who still believe in the possibility of a human relationship in which no one exploits or is exploited.

It seems to me that women have been making a tremendous gain in the use of their intelligence in the past few years. At the family counseling agency where I work, the change appears dramatic. Women now have a different starting point; their horizons are broader, their goals are more advanced; they are further along in their understanding of themselves and the world in which they live. Not all women have progressed to the same place, of course, but whatever their color or ethnic background, whatever their differences in economic and social circumstances, all seem to share in some of the factors that are stimulating women's growth and development.

These factors are so numerous and varied and the impact of each is so impossible to measure that an attempt to focus attention on any single one would inevitably be misleading. Nevertheless, one in particular seems to have an especially liberating effect on the intelligence: the questioning of traditional answers. It is as though women were only going through their own renaissance now. Just as men led the revolt against the "revealed truths" of the medieval world, in which the church arrogated to itself the right to define reality for all human beings, so women are revolting against a variety of "truths" evolved to define the nature of reality for women and to dictate to them what the relationships between men and women are to be.

Each time a woman asks "But why?" she is questioning the validity not only of men's assumptions about women but also of women's assumptions about women. Thus she is beginning to revolt against accepting anyone's definition of herself but her own. In doing so, she is opening her mind to the possibilities of change—not only for herself but also for men—that may yet enable human beings to survive as a species despite their attempts to wipe one another out.

It may seem a little absurd to make so great a claim for the power of questions, even those with the scope and significance raised by outstanding women today. Yet, over the long run I find I have equal or even greater faith in the impact of simple questions asked by ordinary women about everyday matters of living. As a therapist in an agency to which women often come with questions and problems about their marriages, or their relationships with men in general, I am impressed by the nature and value of all the concerns they raise. Whether the matter is as seemingly trivial as who is to do the dishes or as crucial as whether to marry or to divorce, the fact that women are raising questions instead of accepting traditional answers means that they are opening themselves to new ideas, new attitudes, new ways of arranging their relationships and their lives.

Basically, they are questioning a view of man-woman relationships that has dominated the scene, in one version or another, for centuries. Though times are certainly changing, I still hear echoes of this theme in my office, both from men and from women, almost every day.

It is a theme that children learn early. The little girl is everything nice, but the little boy is full of fight. The girl child, whatever her advantages or disadvantages from birth, must be loving and giving as she goes through life. If she is to find happiness, it must be in a feminine manner, that is, by being good. She must never fight directly for what she needs or wants on penalty of being found unfeminine and thus forever unlovable. However, because a woman's drives and disposition are those of a human being and not of an angel, someone inevitably pays a price somewhere along the line.

At the other end of the scale, the boy child, if not born to wealth or privilege, is expected to go out into the world to seek his fortune through pluck and luck, sheer grit, fair means or foul. No matter what he may have lacked in early advantages or later opportunities, he is expected to climb the ladder of success. He must present himself to his children, his wife, his world, as a model of the dominant and superior male. He may act out his notion of this role at home and on the job by bullying or boasting, or he may resign himself to a life of quiet desperation that takes its toll, directly and indirectly, not only of himself but of the whole family.

The theme that begins as a charming myth often ends in an ugly reality, with men and women feeling and being exploited by one another. This myth is at the root of much marital conflict and, because it extends itself to the children, of much mental and emotional illness. If, as some authorities hold, this is a myth that symbolizes the true nature of men and women, then human mentality has been shockingly deficient in its failure to devise a world in which that nature can be more readily fulfilled.

There have always been exceptions to the established scheme of masculinity and femininity, of course. The young people today seem to be modifying it beyond recognition, but the psychological casualties continue to present themselves at the doors of clinics and agencies and to a variety of therapeutic practitioners. Women come in far greater numbers than men, though therapists (except in social work circles) are far more likely to be male than female. No doubt the myth is at work here, too. The therapist-client relationship is often seen, at least initially, as a superior-inferior status situation and therefore is apt to be looked at according to prescribed male-female attitudes. At any rate, for better or for worse, women seem more predisposed to request help with emotional and mental problems.

Although there can be little doubt of the intellectual advantage of the open mind over the closed one, from the standpoint of emotional comfort it often seems that the advantage lies with the closed mind, at least in the short run. Both the rate of divorce and the incidence of mental illness seem to increase as the questioning of old values and standards increases. Certainly in my work I find that some women are as disturbed by the unsettling implications of the women's movement as others are by their own unliberated status. Many women, of course, find ways of dealing with these matters without coming to a counseling agency for help, and no doubt they are doing their own growing in their own way. There are as many roads toward intellectual enlightenment as there are women to travel them, and there are sources of emotional insight other than therapy.

The women who have chosen to come for therapy are the women I have had the opportunity to know best. Although they are not necessarily the most troubled ones, they are usually more aware of their troubles and more willing and able to put them into words. Often their experiences, past or present, have been somewhat more disturbing or damaging, or perhaps just more confusing, than those of other women. Their need to make some kind of sense out of their lives has brought them to a recourse that requires them to reveal more of themselves than would be likely in ordinary social or academic conversation. In so doing, they bring out problems common to many women and ask questions relevant to man-woman relationships in general.

Because the search for understanding through therapy is necessarily an emotional as well as an intellectual process, it usually has a personal meaning beyond that which may be gained from reading books or taking courses. It is the relationship between therapist and client that contributes the emotional meaning, and it is through this relationship, with its mingling of the personal and the professional, that Martha and I propose to describe this process of therapy.

Martha is a real person, though Martha Morgan is not her real name, and her story is a true story, though it has been somewhat disguised. Martha and I have sat across the desk from each other for many hours—I on the therapist's side, she on the client's. More and more as her story developed, it seemed connected with the old myth: a woman should be like this, a man should be like that, and they should relate to each other in such and such a way; if they cannot, or do not, one or the other must surely be to blame. Yet therapy was becoming for Martha, as for so many other women, a matter of revising—if not entirely discarding—the traditional view.

I remarked to her one day that I wished I could write a book about all the women who have struggled with this problem in my office, including me.

"Why don't you?" Martha asked.

"If I were to write about them as real human beings, not just unidentifiable case examples," I answered, "I would need their permission, and because there are so many, I could never reach them all."

The next week Martha came in and said, "Let's try to write that kind of book together."

I said, "Okay." To be exact, I said, "Okay, if you'll do the hard work. I'm lazy."

"I'm a hard worker," Martha replied. (As it turned out, so was I—otherwise, no book!)

A few months earlier, another client had suggested collaborating with me and I had made the same response. She had laughed and said she was lazy, too, and would just go on writing poetry, which for her is a labor of love and thus not quite labor at all. So it happens that I have written a book with Martha instead of with —or about—one or more of the other women I have come to know in therapy, but I hope they will recognize something of themselves in it. I hope, too, that all the clients, men as well as women, who have contributed to my thinking will recognize their influence—even, perhaps, their very words—in my parts of the book.

In deciding to expand our therapeutic collaboration into a literary one, Martha and I did not deliberately plan to add to the growing literature on the plight of women. We were not unwilling, however, when it seemed possible that our book might tend to go in that direction. We were eager to establish our concern for women's liberation within the context of our concern for human liberation. Though men are in a position of power or advantage over women in some respects, they also share the powerlessness of most human beings in the face of life's circumstances.

In assessing the nature of any one woman's private troubles, the backdrop of socioeconomic and political discrimination against which she is operating must always be taken into account. A woman's individual functioning in her family, her marriage, or her career is necessarily affected by cultural expectations and limitations that place her at a considerable disadvantage. However, to ascribe all of a woman's woes to the second-class position of women in our society would not only be false but would also invite attack by those who are only too glad for an excuse to discredit the true and legitimate complaints of women. In any case, we would not take pleasure in making a point for women's liberation by slanting our material, though we would be delighted if our unslanted material should happen to speak to that point.

We are concerned, too, that those troubles that are one woman's own neurotic burden, or the product of neurotic interaction between one man and one woman, should not be confused with those common to all women. It would be unwise, and certainly untherapeutic, not to give sufficient weight to those problems unique to the specific man-woman combination. Men and women have individual problems long before they have marital ones. They are likely to continue to have their difficulties long after they have divorced themselves from the problems of their spouses, though what has gone on in the marriage may make a great deal of difference in the subsequent psychological history of each partner.

Martha's experience cannot be equated exactly with any other woman's experience; it resembles the "average" in some ways but is more extreme in others. From early childhood Martha had serious problems for which she received no therapy of any kind. Her effort to escape through a sexual relationship locked her into a marriage that made matters considerably worse. She did not get the kind of help she needed for a long time, and some of the therapy she was offered was based on inadequate information or false assumptions.

Martha had no firmly established conviction of her own worth and no solid sense of herself as a person, let alone as a woman. She saw herself as other people seemed to see her. So when her husband and her therapists seemed to see her as "crazy," who was she to say they were wrong? Of course, she had to fight back in any way she could, and her battle to survive became the story of her marriage, her divorce, and much of her previous therapy.

When I first saw Martha, this was all behind her chronologically but still very much with her emotionally. Our first work together was a holding action to help her retain any ground she had gained in her previous therapy while repairing some of the damage that had compounded the original, still unresolved problems. Most of our discussions during this first contact were on a practical, realistic level or on a theoretical, intellectual level. Martha was not ready to look at the emotion-laden past; it was enough to have survived it.

Recently, almost five years after our earlier contact, I saw Martha again. During those years she had handled a job as well as her home and children. When Martha came back, she was strong enough to look at some of the things she had avoided before. It was as if she had had to test herself in the world in order to arrive at sufficient faith in her own perception of reality, as if she had needed sufficient distance from the disturbing events of the past in order to examine them more closely and evaluate their meaning in her life. Little by little, as we talked about these things, we began to see that some of Martha's problems were very much like other women's problems, though often greatly intensified and sometimes distorted beyond easy recognition. I think it was this realization—that she was, after all, not so different from other women—that eventually gave Martha the courage to look at how bad her situation had actually been. But it was a very slow and fearsome process.

In turning our therapeutic venture into a writing venture as well, we were aware that there would be both dangers and advantages. Martha was still in therapy, with much in her life remaining to be understood and dealt with. Neither she nor I would be willing to sacrifice her progress for the sake of a book. Our relationship had never had the parent-child flavor, even at the beginning. Although a peer relationship would include the possibility of considerable rivalry, Martha and I had apparently stimulated the growing edge in one another rather than a cutting one. Because we had been operating on a basis of personal equality, each autonomous within her own sphere, it seemed to us that we would find ways of continuing a favorable balance. In any case, I have never written from the sheer joy of writing, and if it would take some competition to stimulate my production, so be it. As Martha put it, we would probably kick each other along enough to keep ourselves going.

Not only is each therapy different from every other therapy, each differs in its own way. Martha's therapy, of course, differs most radically because it incorporates and revolves around the writing of a book. It is paradoxical that we should be trying to tell what therapy is like through a therapeutic endeavor that departs so radically from the common experience. But life is full of paradoxes, and I see no reason why therapy should not be one of them. Of course, Martha's therapy was immediately and continually affected by the fact that we were writing a book. To the extent that we are aware of the effects, we say so, but we must always keep in the back of our minds the fact that effects are taking place whether we are aware of them or not. And, paradox or not, we believe that therapy may be presented more accurately in this fashion than in some more systematic, objective textbook style.

In writing the story of her earlier experiences with therapy, which Martha was proposing to do, there was a special danger for her. She would be writing from the standpoint of how things felt to her at the time, thus exposing herself to the judgment of anyone who cared to find her unreasonable, unfair, "bad," or "crazy." * [See Notes, page 427.] Yet she had to pour out all the thoughts and feelings that she had tried for so long to hold back—the resentment and bitterness a good woman is not supposed to have, the complaints a woman is not supposed to make, the anger she is not supposed to express—for fear of earning herself such labels as "fishwife," "nag," "hysterical," and, at the very least, "unwomanly." Perhaps if Martha could now express her anger in some creative fashion, she could rid herself of the constant burden of potentially destructive rage, the impotent rage that a woman experiences when her anger is driven underground.

No one person can tell the whole story of a marriage, Martha no more than her husband. Individual troubles arise from a multiplicity of factors, and marital troubles grow out of such multiplicities in geometric progression and in infinite variety. The task of therapy is not to establish an official version of the story, but to discover and sort out pertinent material in order to understand and to deal with what is going on. There is no way to recapture in retrospect material that was perhaps not even available during Martha's therapy. There is, for example, no certain knowledge of what Martha's husband was feeling and thinking beneath the behavior that Martha reports, or what the emotional dynamics of his behavior and attitudes might have been, or even exactly what the patterns of interaction were in the marriage. Without such material, neither Martha nor I can expect to do justice to Martha's husband, and we can in no way claim to be telling his story as well as hers. But as in any therapy conducted without the participation of the significant others in the client's life, I must make the best educated guess I can, based on what is necessarily only part of the story.

My guesses are not to be taken as the closest possible approximation of what the facts actually were (though I would hope that I am not very wide of the mark), but as hypothetical constructs derived from a number of sources, all with some relevance. These sources include my background in social and psychological theories, my many years of practice with other clients, personal experiences in the course of my own life, and acquaintance with a wide range of literature—drama, poetry, novels, biography, and autobiography—as well as with professional writing. I shall apply such guesses to Martha's material not only from the standpoint of our concern with the general subject of women's problems and man-woman relationships in our society, but also from the standpoint of my concern for the progress of Martha's therapy. If my interpretations sometimes differ from Martha's or from those of the lay or professional reader, so be it. Each may have its own validity and none is sacred.

There was another difficulty for me with regard to Martha's story. Until we actually began writing, I had not realized how much of Martha's anger was directed at previous therapists for their readiness to accept "the man's point of view." Because I have all the advantages of hindsight as well as the obvious one of being a woman, I could easily appear to be casting myself in the role of a know-it-all, passing judgment on Martha's earlier experiences in therapy as though my own work were immune to confusions and conflicts and errors. The score would be evened, of course, by the fact that my work would be open to scrutiny. Just as in my everyday conduct of therapy my clients see me as the fallible human being that I am, so would I no doubt reveal myself in my writing.

Thus there were dangers for me as well as for Martha. There is no question, however, that the advantages are definitely mine. One of the most important realities of therapy is that the professional, by reason of being the professional, has the advantage over the client. That is why the therapist must have a commitment not only to a professional code of ethics but also to the kind of self-knowledge and self-discipline necessary for carrying out the commitment.

Martha's writing represented a significant new step for her in therapy. She writes her story the way a client is likely to present material at the beginning of therapy, when the client fears above all the possibility of being judged and found "to blame." It is only sensible to be cautious about what one says until some confidence in being understood and accepted has been established. Clients are also likely to seem protective about important matters, not intentionally but because the material is so fraught with anxiety that they cannot yet present it clearly. Problems may be described in such broad, general terms that one cannot quite be sure what actually has been going on. If, as in Martha's case, there are factors operating in the situation itself that obscure the client's awareness of what actually *is* going on, the story is bound to contain confusions and contradictions. The reader may wonder what lies behind all this confusion but, like the therapist, will have to wait until therapy has progressed far enough for the story behind the story to emerge. Therapy must begin where the client is able to make a beginning.

Some of the facts and their significance do not emerge until well along in the second period of Martha's therapy with me. The reader will see how therapeutic understanding develops gradually—on both sides of the desk. When we come to this phase of our work together, Martha and I supplement our writing with some tape-recorded material. What is actually said in interviews, however, is, to borrow a famous analogy, just the tip of the iceberg, not because so much remains unconscious in both participants (true though this may be), but because so much that is conscious goes unsaid. I am inclined to think that the most important part of therapy goes on below that visible tip, and no tape recording or videotape can reveal it. For this reason my written comments include some of my own story—not only those experiences that have a direct bearing on my professional work but also some of those in my more remote background from which my attitudes and opinions derive.

Early in our writing experiment, Martha started a notebook to capture some of the thoughts and feelings below that tip of the iceberg. I was keeping notes, as I always do, of themes that come up during therapy hours and that seem significant to my client's questions and to my own. It occurred to me that I might follow Martha's example. I began to include in my notebook not only professional associations with what was happening in Martha's therapy hours but also associations ranging more widely over time and space, even when I saw no immediate connection with our work together. Perhaps through material in both our notebooks, we could provide some notion of what the hidden part of therapy may be. All the while, of course, we recognized that the course of the therapy was affected by everything we were doing.

Martha and I both had qualms about revealing ourselves in the way we were planning, but we thought it was worth a try. Martha added, "And if we find we can't do it, then we'll talk about that." This is the saving grace in therapy: Anything that happens, whether for good or for ill, can be discussed and so can serve the purpose of therapy.

O    MARTHA'S STORY

was twenty-six years old. I was expecting my fourth child; my oldest was a first-grader. Whatever charm this northwestern city might have had for me when I first came here had long since dissolved in the perpetual rain. Although I denied it resolutely, my marriage was in extremely serious trouble. Also, I was beginning to develop a set of symptoms that frightened me. I began to feel that the mundane unrelated facts of the world around me must have a special significance if only I could puzzle it out. It seemed portentous and mysteriously important that there were exactly three trees growing in front of the house, no more and no less. I felt the universe was trying to convey a message to me that was very important but just out of my grasp.

I couldn't sleep, or even rest. My body was rigid with tension day and night. I felt trapped and desperate. Past and present were without pleasure, the future was hopeless. Most of all, I felt utterly inadequate for the job of raising four children. These years now, while they were small, would set the pattern for their whole lives. Once past these formative years, their lives would be determined irrevocably, forever. What right did I have to saddle the children with existence at all? And granted that, how could I morally expect them to have even half a chance at any sort of happy life with me as their mother?

My death seemed the only hope for any of us. I prayed for death daily, devoutly and with bitter tears. It seemed so unfair that so many people who wanted to live died every day, and I, who wanted so badly to die, couldn't manage it.

My mind went round and round with a dozen plans for suicide but always came to a stop at the same place: the unborn baby. To kill myself was wrong, I thought, and would separate me from God forever. Being the person I thought myself to be, I considered that as a foregone conclusion anyhow. At any rate, suicide was my own choice, to make or not as I decided, but I couldn't face killing the helpless child I carried. That was wrong in a totally different sense and nearly unthinkable.

In those desperate years, I think that pregnancy was my only

24

means of expressing hope in the future. It was certainly, for a long time, the key to my survival. Even though I felt that my own existence had nothing to offer but isolation and pain, my instinct to preserve that child's life proved stronger than my own desperation.

In moments of some detachment I surveyed the wreckage of my feelings and summed it up: These are signs of real and serious mental illness.

I don't think anyone else noticed a change in my behavior at that time. My relationship with my husband, Scott, was such that he would never have noticed nor would he have shown much interest if he had. My function was to deal with *his* illness, not to start a competing illness of my own.

Although as a couple we had a circle of friends, my relationships with all of them were in some way odd, almost impersonal. We visited other couples and they visited us. We went to their parties and gave parties of our own. I liked them and had no reason to think they didn't like me. But I didn't know how to talk to them. Scott was so brilliant, never without something witty and relevant and sardonic to say. Whenever I tried to say what I thought, it came out sounding strange and unrelated, even to my own ears. Everyone would be respectfully silent for a second or two and then go on just as though I hadn't spoken. I didn't know how to convey what I was thinking and consequently doubted that I was in fact thinking anything at all. At parties or when friends visited, I was glad to bustle around making sure everyone had coffee or a glass of wine, glad to listen to the conversation, glad to welcome them to our house. I loved and valued them, but I couldn't make vital contact with them. I talked "strange." There must be something very wrong with me indeed. Who could value an oddity like me? There was no one, then, to whom I could turn for advice or comfort.

I was aware of community resources for therapy available to low-income families. When I had previously hoped to get Scott into therapy, I had called the City Mental Hygiene Clinic to ask if he could be taken as a patient. The clinic refused unless Scott himself was willing to call and make the arrangements, which he was not.

The staff member to whom I spoke had seemed to me fairly kind and supportive, so I phoned the clinic again, this time to ask for an appointment for myself.* I told no one. I left the children with a neighbor when I went to see the intake worker.

I outlined my situation as honestly as I could and said I really didn't know how much longer I would be able to go on. I was a little startled to have the problem taken seriously.

The interviewer agreed that the problem sounded very serious. The agency had a very long waiting list, he said, but he felt that I presented a real emergency and arrangements might be made for me to begin therapy at once. A staff meeting was scheduled for that afternoon, and he would bring it up. Could I come back tomorrow for the decision?

"Do you think they'll take me?" I asked him. "I just want to know whether to start giving up."

He grinned at me. "Don't give up," he said.

I was overwhelmed by hope and fear. Somebody had heard my call for help. That was an enormous relief. But did it mean that I really was just another worthless, crazy woman?

The next day I returned. Yes, the clinic would accept me. First appointment three days away, appointments either once or twice a week, depending on the arrangements made between the therapist and me.

I was very lucky to have Dorothy Jackson assigned as my therapist. She was a psychiatric social worker with years of experience on the clinic staff, a warm, comfortable sort of person. She took time to listen to me carefully and seemed alarmed at my depression. I really shouldn't have tried to cope with anything this serious alone, she said. There was no mistaking her genuine concern, and I came to respect her professional judgment greatly.

Once I was in therapy the suicidal impulses and fantasies I had been having seemed to double. Miss Jackson tried to get me to commit myself to the state hospital, but I declined. I didn't want to have the baby in a madhouse. It would have been a confession of worthlessness on my part that I could never have survived. I finally did agree to carry in my purse a letter of introduction to the hospital that Miss Jackson had written for me. She urged me not to hesitate to make a run for it if at any time I felt the suicidal push too strong for me.

Quite early in the short period of our work together, Miss Jackson demanded that my husband come in for an interview apart from me. He refused at first, but finally, reluctantly, he went. Neither of them ever told me what they talked about. A couple of days later Scott did say to me, more or less in passing, "There's really nothing wrong with you, is there? You're still just trying to get me to a shrink."

Miss Jackson had also insisted I tell my husband that the possibility of my being hospitalized was a real one. At first I refused to discuss it with him. I knew how seriously that would rock our already shaky marriage. She was adamant. It was a matter of justice, she said. It would not be fair for him to come home from work some day and find me gone, leaving him with the total care of three small children. When she put it that way, I agreed.

I left a note for Scott to read when he came home from work, saying I wanted to talk to him about something important in the morning. (He was working a swing shift, as he continued to do during most of our marriage.) In the morning he asked me what was on my mind. I repeated the therapist's comments verbatim, telling him that I hated to upset him but it seemed only fair that he should know. Scott left the room in a cold fury. It was three days before he would speak to me or even remain in the same room with me.

I was able to continue in therapy with Dorothy Jackson for only two months. Then she was called for jury duty and the judge refused to excuse her. I was assigned to another therapist, which turned out to be a disaster.

In justice to the City Mental Hygiene Clinic, I must admit I told the therapists as little as I possibly could about Scott and his problems. Looking back, I can see that they really could not have had a complete picture of our marriage because I told them so little. It seemed to me an unforgivable offense to rat on your husband: that's what makes you a castrating bitch. And I also carried over, quite unconsciously, the instructions I had been given for the confessional: "Don't go on and on about extenuating circumstances—just tell us what *you've* done that's wrong." A great deal of harm came of that.

I had, in all, three more therapists after Dorothy Jackson, but I retain a clear picture of none of them, nor do I think anything happened in the treatment proceedings that was of any further use to me. By shifting me from worker to worker, the clinic seemed to be telling me that a personal relationship with the therapist was not the way to accomplish anything, that I was a patient of the clinic and not of any one person in particular, and that one combination of patient and therapist was as good as another.

In addition, the clinic at that time was manned almost entirely by young psychiatric residents. All the therapists I saw were very inexperienced, very orthodox, not at all inclined to risk any departure from approved technique (what would their supervisor say?). I can't recall any of those men now except for Dr. Jamison, who later became locally known for his stance as an administrative rebel. I do not remember clearly who they were or what they looked like, or any of the details of the work we did or tried to do together. I do remember a Dr. Kelly who used to tell me that I must be very angry at the Church for making me have so many babies—so little did he grasp that my faith and my love for my children were the only positive experiences in my life. He used to exhort me to tell him how angry I was. I didn't feel angry at all. What would have been the use? I felt drained, hopeless, worthless, but I couldn't seem to make him understand.

These visits went on for about two years. I didn't feel I was getting anywhere. One afternoon each week Scott took care of the children for an hour while I went to therapy. It did get me out of the house and away from the family once a week, and it gave me a sort of rudimentary contact with somebody who was, as it were, duty bound to take a personal interest in me. Someone sat across the desk from me once a week and said, "Yes, go on," or "And how do you feel about that?" But the sessions didn't add up to much that was helpful to me.

I had no idea that I might try to find better help elsewhere. Spending money on myself for medical care would have been unthinkable even if we had had the money to spend, which we did not. But mostly, I just didn't know there was anything better. The thought that I might ever be happy, that I myself could change, or that I could change my circumstances so that things would ever be better never crossed my mind. My one idea in living was reduced to grim stoicism: do your duty and bear it to the end.

I had not fallen into a bad and isolated time from a happier one—I had always been isolated and unhappy; I simply took care that no one ever knew it. I thought that everyone was as unhappy as myself but that they were stronger and therefore better at hiding the pain. If I formulated any goal for treatment at all, it was to become strong enough again to bear my pain without showing it. These cold and businesslike men showed me little that could help me achieve that. The clinic had a good reputation. There was no reason to think that the therapists were not technically proficient at their job. Why go elsewhere?

Nevertheless, I continued to survive. It was touch and go for quite a while. The pressures at home continued. It rained and rained. The children were in the house and under my feet constantly. Scott's symptoms, which seemed to me indicative of an illness even more serious than my own, recurred constantly. There was never enough money.

I don't have any clear recollection of why I finally left therapy at City Mental Hygiene. It wasn't discouragement with the treatment. I had no expectations of what treatment was supposed to accomplish, no hopes to be disappointed. It was fairly well established all around that I was mentally ill and not expected to get much better. I do remember that my leaving had something to do with Dr. Kelly and his efforts to get me to express my (actually his) anger at the Church. But there wasn't a big blow-up or confrontation scene. I just said I was leaving therapy and didn't go back.

I felt, however, that I ought to go on receiving treatment of some kind. Crazy people are supposed to have psychiatrists. A friend made arrangements for me to be seen by Dr. Knight, a Jungian therapist, in private practice, and I continued to see him for a little over a year.

I had been reading Jung—as had all our circle of friends—and had found his geography of the psyche, so to speak, more convincing and more hopeful than any of the Freudian-oriented work I had encountered. Jung's view seemed to me to be directed more toward possibilities that the individual had not yet explored and developed than toward irremediable hurts he had sustained.

I liked Dr. Knight very much. He was kind and generous and supportive, enthusiastic about my progress, and pleased with my insights into dreams and symbols. He helped me a great deal to see how the unconscious and irrational in myself (and in all of us) manifest themselves in daily life, and he helped me begin to understand how to live with them.

He also tried valiantly to get me to see how irrational my view of my husband was. (He had never met him.) So far as Dr. Knight knew, Scott did not behave in a bizarre fashion; he did not have a cruel or rejecting attitude toward the children or me. My illness was distorting my perception of the emotional climate around me; when I had made a little more progress in therapy, things would be much better. I tried and tried.

Yet in some subtle way I felt the problem of "progress" repeated much of my experience at City Mental Hygiene. With Dr. Knight there were valuable differences, of course. He was manifestly pleased with my insight into many of the problems we talked about. Jung's writings and their impact on my experience were both fascinating and useful. Still, there always seemed to be something I was expected to do, something I just couldn't catch on to. If only I could grasp this "something," the implication seemed to be, my life would quickly become much happier. It had to do with my marriage, of course. Was it that I should see my marriage the way Dr. Knight saw it?

The therapeutic balance finally broke down over another issue. I fell in love. It was ironic that Scott's needs brought another man into my life, yet that was what happened.

At that time, Scott's suicide threats were at their most urgent. A week almost never went by without a bitter farewell, hints that I'd soon understand what I had done to him. As I had in past years, I ruled out committing him to a state hospital against his will. Our state hospitals were not known for their successful cures, I could not see him cooperating with treatment in any way, and I feared the consequences for myself if I forced the issue and he escaped or was released. Most of all, I didn't (and still don't) believe in taking away somebody else's freedom.

One spring Sunday night Scott began to describe his approaching suicide in graphic detail, in a way I had never really heard him talk before. I knew he was serious, and I knew that if I didn't act, he might very well die. Under pretense of taking out the garbage, I raced up the street to the nearest telephone at the Johnson's, friends and neighbors. It was late in the evening, but I knocked on the door till Edith answered.

"I need help quickly," I said to her. "Please call Father Michaelson at St. John's and ask him for emergency help. Give him ten minutes to get here and then call the police."

I raced back home again, dumped the garbage, and tried to look as though nothing had happened. Father Michaelson arrived ten minutes later. (The police never did come, although I kept expecting them all night. Edith had misunderstood my message.)

When Father Michaelson walked into the room at eleven thirty on a Sunday night and asked what was the matter, there was no way to make it look like a coincidence. Scott blew his social cover, one of the few times I ever saw him do so. He let out a blast of invective at me and went on and on, telling me he would make me suffer every day of my life for what I had done. I was drained and shaking. All I could say was, "I know, but I couldn't let you kill yourself."

Father Michaelson didn't say much. He listened a lot and smoothed things over as much as he could. He stayed a couple of hours till things were calmer. As he was leaving, I silently motioned to him to stay on—I still thought that the police might arrive at any minute—but he just shook his head at me and left.

And then what happened? I don't know. Father Michaelson came around fairly often, occasionally to dinner. He and I never talked together much. I rarely spoke much in those days, especially with people I didn't know well. Everything I said seemed so odd to other people. But I listened to him talk, brought him coffee, sat in the room. I got to know him and like him a little. He was a midwesterner like myself and quite reticent, intelligent, kind. I went to see him at St. John's to ask his advice a couple of times. He offered rather diffidently to hear my confession. (I was having trouble getting through to my regular confessor; he knew I was seeing a psychiatrist and felt this meant he should handle me like a moron.) I thought it over for a few weeks and then asked Father Michaelson if he would be willing to be my regular confessor. I never felt then and have never felt since that our personal feelings for each other ever altered the disinterestedness of his judgment in the confessional.

After that, I saw him by appointment once a week. Everything was friendly and simple. The memory of one encounter stands out in my mind, though. It was when Jim Anderson, a friend of ours, was staying with us at the time he first came to the area. We were sitting up late, talking and waiting for Scott to come home from work. Father Michaelson came by on his way back from somewhere and, knowing Scott would be home soon, he stopped in for a short visit. The three of us were sitting around the kitchen table, talking and drinking wine. Jim and I were speaking about Bob Jones, another friend, who had said something outrageously unpleasant to me that day.

"I can't think why he's like that," I said; "I really haven't done anything to him."

"Maybe," said Father Michaelson, "he's secretly in love with you."

I saw Father Michaelson once a week, in one of the visitors' parlors at St. John's. Quite early in these meetings, something happened that revolutionized my life. He taught me to talk. It began when we were discussing a point of doctrine. I had an intuition on the subject I wanted to communicate and couldn't. After one or two lame starts, I gave up, saying that I wasn't making any sense and guessed it wasn't a very good idea anyway.

"I can hear that you're trying to say something really valuable," said Father Michaelson, "but I can't quite get clear what it is. Start again, but start with the idea *before* the idea you were telling me."

Somewhat startled, I did so.

"Not back far enough," he said, "and what fact or observation are you basing it on?"

More and more bemused, I told him.

"Okay," he said, "now just start one more move back. I think I see what you mean."

It was a conversation in reverse, always moving backward to the previous premise. Finally we turned it around and had the conversation going forward, so to speak. Then, by George, he had it! He really understood my idea and saw how it related to what we had been saying, and he was pleased.

"But that's a very subtle idea," he said, "and it was based on a lot of things I either didn't know or didn't see were connected to the subject. How come you assumed I knew them?"

I was absolutely thunderstruck. I had grown up in a family where I was the only child among four adults. I was the last one to learn or know or think of anything. All my major discoveries about the world had been greeted with "Did you just find that out? Why, everybody knows that!" My extreme shyness had made everything much worse. I was so unable to articulate what I wanted to say in the presence of strangers (and eventually, if you're that shy, everybody is a stranger) that I had collected years and years of negative feedback, which had reinforced the original pattern. I had it firmly stuck in my mind that whatever I knew, everybody else had known years before me.

Father Michaelson persisted. "I think you must do that all the time. You start at the end of a very complicated idea, just as if people will know what you're talking about without your telling them. Instead, start as far back as you can and lead up to it, the way you did it in your mind when you first had the idea. You make perfectly good sense. It's just not coming out."

And that is how I learned to talk. I was terrified, but it was very exciting. I found myself trying it out on all kinds of people—friends, strangers, everybody. I found I could risk trying to say what I meant. I had lots of failures. I still got the "she must be crazy" response from plenty of people, but I was elated to be able to make a point at all.

I never got the "crazy" response from Father Michaelson. I trusted him more and more. As I became more and more articulate, we talked more and more. We must have covered every subject known to man. Never once did I feel that the territory between us was booby-trapped, the way the ground between men and women of reasonably good will can be, with the land mines that the sexes so often set for each other. I never felt that there was anything in his feelings he would be reluctant to have me know. I never felt that he was setting out to triumph over me or to prove anything at my expense. I felt that he accepted me as I was.

I know that our relationship in the confessional hastened that feeling a good deal. Both of us took an extremely serious view of our religious duties. In confession, the penitent is supposed to state matters as clearly and forthrightly as he can, aware that plenty about himself is repugnant and, yes, even bad. Usually, large-scale, grandiose actions are what most of us think of when the word "sin" comes to mind. Yet, it's the pettiness of day-to-day living, the small misuses of the humanity of the people around us, the mistakes we make over and over again, that are so hard to face in ourselves. What with my rigorous conscience and Father Michaelson's general stance of leaning over backward not to be lenient to me, we very quickly got down to business on whatever nasty attitudes I had to examine.

Father Michaelson once remarked to me, after we had known each other for a long time and he had spent many, many hours with me and my family, "I don't think there's anything bad about yourself that you don't know." I was enormously comforted. My greatest terror at the time was of the disparity between the evil I saw people do and the evil those same people thought they did. We are all so blind to our own faults and I can see so much evil in myself, so many instances when the way I am and the things I do damage the people around me. If the disparity between how I regard what I do and the harm I actually do is of the same degree in me as in others, what must I in reality be? That thought still haunted my days with an overpowering dread.

It was clear to me that Father Michaelson didn't agree. Not that he said so, over and over; he simply kept treating me with solid respect and approval. I realized he knew the worst there was to know about me, but he didn't go away, didn't change. I began to feel as though I had room to breathe a little. I wasn't dramatically and radically rescued from my illness; I don't mean that. I was still very hard pressed indeed. I had to cope with my husband, no money, and the physical and emotional burdens of trying to raise—and, in difficult circumstances, to reassure—four tiny children. Had the choice been put before me, I still would have chosen death over life. But a new piece of information was gathering somewhere inside me: I wasn't automatically and totally cut off from the other people in the world.

I could talk when anyone was willing to listen. I had the means of transmitting questions, answers, values, and feelings, at least some of the time. I was beginning to learn that it was possible for someone to know, really know, the worst about me that I knew about myself and still not abandon me. I was still strung up by my thumbs, but no longer was I hanging over the void. Somewhere there might be solid ground. So things went on unmarked by incident for perhaps six months. I was comforted very greatly by my friendship with Father Michaelson. I didn't reflect on it particularly; it was just there. Then everything changed dramatically in the course of a day.

At that time Scott and I moved in a small, rather tightly knit circle of friends who had met one another largely through our contacts with the Catholic Worker movement. We were a fairly like-minded lot, liberal in our politics, devout but liberal in our religion, distinctly maverick in our life-styles. We formed for each other a supportive community the like of which I have never seen and which I probably never shall see again.

Several of the marriages were in disastrous shape. (Almost all of these troubled couples eventually separated or divorced, but that's another and different long story.) At the time of which I'm speaking, Robert and Ellen Jones had just separated. Ellen was trying to make it on her own on welfare with a large family of small children, and she was deeply worried and deeply troubled. That summer I decided I really would feel better if I got out of the house once in a while and did something not concerned exclusively with my family. I enrolled in a course at a local junior college summer school, with classes every morning but Thursday. Ellen lived at the end of the block. I asked her if she could watch the kids for me in the mornings, and she said she would. We had often exchanged baby-sitting, so things ran smoothly for a few weeks.

Then one day when I showed up for my weekly appointment with Father Michaelson, I found him looking concerned and upset. He told me that he had received a letter from Ellen. "I think you'd better read it," he said.

The letter was a passionate denunciation of me. I had been led astray by worldly friends into forsaking my vocation as a wife and mother. My school project was an obvious threat to my salvation, and if he as my confessor could not or would not put a stop to it, she at least would not be a party to it. She would do no more baby-sitting.

I was furious, speechless. I knew Ellen was having a hard time, but the whole attack on me was so grossly irrational! Furthermore, why did Father Michaelson have to show me the letter? If he had just told me about it, maybe softening it a little bit, it might have been another story. But to make me read the precise phraseology, to see that Ellen had written those exact words about me and no others, seemed unforgivable.

Instantly we found ourselves in the middle of a roaring fight. We were normally the most pacific of persons; I had never heard him say an angry word before, to me or anyone else. In those days I never raised my voice to anyone, ever, yet here we were yelling at each other with anger uncontrolled. After a while we fell silent.

"Why are we doing this?" I asked. "Of course it's maddening, this whole situation, but we're reacting to it all out of proportion. Why?"

A long silence. Then he said, "Because I'm in love with you. I have been for a long time."

Longer silence. All the pieces fell quietly into place. Some very big things that I had been trying so hard not to name or recognize announced their inescapable identity. Time to face the facts.

"I know it," I said; "I know you are. I've known it for a long time. I love you, too."

"I think," he said, "we'd better talk about this." We talked for a very long time.

Late that evening, he phoned me at home. "I just wanted to make sure you're okay," he said.

"I'm fine," I replied, "in fact, happier than I can ever remember. I've got the migraine of my life, though. How are you?"

"Fine," he said, "and very happy. But I've got the migraine of my life!"

I'm very doubtful about the wisdom of hindsight. I know that our views of the emotional crises in our lives are obscured at the time by the very needs, tensions, and prejudices that bring the crises into being. But I also think that our afterthoughts are apt to be tailored as much to the needs and prejudices of the present as our feelings then were to those of the past. Looking back now over the years that separate that time from this, I can see many things: transference and countertransference, of course, the frustrations of celibacy, and a bad marriage. I can also see that each of us, for separate but similar reasons, harbored a massive fear of the opposite sex. Choosing someone "unavailable" meant never having to face that fear squarely. In remembering all the complexities of that most tangled of relationships, it would be simple now to look back and say, "After all, it was nothing but sexual frustration . . . nothing but a desire to get even with my husband . . . just trying to prove something, that's all."

But of all the things that had attracted me to Jung's writings, perhaps the most lasting piece of wisdom was in his admonition to his students to beware of *nicht als*—"nothing but." This is nothing but that; it can all be reduced to. . . . Rarely can any relationship or any real situation be reduced to merely "this" or "that." It is the nature of life and of all relationships to be complex, contradictory, overdetermined, rich with meaning, and in this relationship most of all, *nicht als* has no place.

I certainly know that Father Michaelson and I were extremely foolish from almost any standpoint. That we never slept together or tried to maintain a home together, though plentifully painful in the obvious sense, meant we never had to face many of the issues on which real relationships often founder. Things between us could stay in a fairly idealized state. I also believe that his guilt toward my husband kept Father Michaelson from allowing me to examine separation or divorce as a possible solution to the problems of an impossible marriage. I know now that he was in a crisis in his own vocation. The fact that leaving his job was unthinkable for him seemed almost automatically to make leaving my marriage unthinkable for me.

But, looking backward, I know this incontrovertibly: Father Michaelson saved my life. I was twenty-seven years old. I was swamped with suicidal impulses, paralyzed by despair. I had the total care of dependent and helpless children. That my marriage was insane had at that time not yet occurred to me. Scott and I concealed our misery cleverly enough. I assumed all marriages were as bad as mine and all couples as clever as we. I had always been isolated, alone. I did not question the lack of love in my life. I did not believe that anyone would ever love me, or that anyone could or should.

(That was God's job, of course, and one could rely on Him to do His duty.) I had carried my burden alone to the last limits of my endurance. Somehow Father Michaelson convinced me that he did indeed love me, and for no other reason than that I was myself. Had he not loved me, not changed my life, had he not made room for hope when there simply was no hope, I know I could not have survived the next year. The suicidal urge would have pulled me under.

Since then, I have seen people stand where I then stood and I marvel that he accomplished it. The drowning victim pulling the lifeguard under is a pale simile for the actual course of events. I was often threatened to the point of panic, desperately frightened, guilty, and not at all a terribly attractive or easy-to-deal-with proposition. Yet somehow he managed to make me certain with an absolute certainty. I knew then and still know it: He loved me. I had never been important in anyone's life before. It was a revelation. So *that's* what everybody has been talking about! I'd been in love before, but never with somebody who loved me in return. The whole world was new overnight.

But what were we going to do? Elope to Samoa? Renounce each other nobly? First elope and then renounce? What?

We found a fairly simple solution. No changes. We both knew that Samoa would have defeated us. Apart from our very real responsibilities to other people, there is a limit to what one can pile on a midwestern Puritan conscience and expect the creature who owns it to function. Renunciation has its charms, but not really very many of them. I'd like to say here that, surprisingly, I did not then and do not now think there was anything wrong in our relationship. Whether this is common sense or a classic example of "strain at a gnat and swallow a camel," I will leave to the reader to decide privately.

I had been seeing Father Michaelson for an appointment once a week. He often came to dinner or did various Sunday-afternoon-type things with my whole family. None of that changed. By silent agreement, we never touched each other, even to shake hands or to give one another something. We had been talking fairly frequently on the telephone. Now we talked nonstop every evening after I got the children into bed. And talked and talked. And grew closer and closer. And I became saner and saner.

All this could hardly go on without affecting my therapy with Dr. Knight. I knew he was a very devout (and, I thought privately, a very conventional) Catholic. I also knew that believing a priest to be in love with them secretly is a common fantasy among Catholic ladies, especially those who have marriage problems of one sort or another. I was beginning to realize that Dr. Knight had some doubts about my ability to distinguish fantasy from reality. Altogether, the subject of Father Michaelson was a sticky one, but I brought it up in due course. The results were just about what I would have predicted. To his question, "What makes you think he's in love with you?" my answer, "He says so at least five times a day," was probably not quite the answer he expected to hear. Dr. Knight was admirably tactful and nonjudgmental, but the therapy wasn't really viable from that point on. It was clear to both of us that the therapy transference was not the operative one. Dr. Knight felt my other attachment was certain disaster on psychological grounds, if not on moral ones (to which he certainly never referred, though it was a bit thick in the atmosphere). We struggled on for another month or so and then gave it up more or less by mutual consent.

And then for about two years, although I kept my "crazy" status, I didn't have a psychiatrist at all. I felt perhaps a little better. The marriage fared perhaps a little worse. The children grew, bringing satisfactions and problems. Peter's school recommended that we seek psychiatric care for him; his school adjustment was not at all satisfactory. It recommended the Child Guidance Clinic as a possibility. Because we didn't have the money for private care, Child Guidance referred us to its Family Counseling Division, but added that Peter would be accepted only if the whole family agreed to participate in the treatment. All the family but one agreed. Finally, under pressure, even Scott said he would go with me, at least for the intake interview.

Scott's performance that morning was memorable and brilliant, if a trifle savage. He talked for almost forty-five minutes straight. I hardly said a word, nor did the social worker, who seemed a bit stunned. It must have been totally unintelligible to anyone who didn't know what was going on. The object of Scott's monologue was to parody, nonstop, just about every serious or intimate thing I'd said in the last few months. By changing a word here or there and standing them on their heads once in a while, everything—from what I'd said in bed last night to my worries about Peter's school problems to whatever serious remarks I might ever have made—became neatly, coherently, and uniformly slanted. See the unfortunate woman I'm married to, he said in effect. After ten minutes I was crying uncontrollably. There wasn't anything he wasn't willing to twist.

"He really made me feel threatened," Scott said casually when we left the office. "I thought I'd better keep his attention away from me. You're not going to start *crying*, are you?"*

No, Scott was not interested in participating in therapy for Peter. What do those people know anyhow? No, there were no other clinics that might accept Peter if just part of the family participated. No, they had no advice as to how to handle the boy's school problems if no therapy situation could be found for him. No.

## esther comments

I am breaking into Martha's story at this point with some personal and professional comments. Martha has chosen to begin her story not with her childhood nor even with the early years of her marriage, but with her first efforts to seek help as a young wife and mother. She has presented what is essentially raw data, the feelings and thoughts she experienced at the time, without editing and without the kind of evaluation and revision she might be inclined to do later on, as her therapy progresses. She has, in essence, revealed herself to the reader the way a client does to the therapist.

This is definitely a one-sided openness. Even though the therapist may reveal some personal history, as I shall do in my narrative here, what the therapist chooses to reveal is by no means raw data. It is as thoroughly finished a product as years of education and training, of professional experience and judgment, can make it. This one-sidedness is inherent in the client-therapist relationship. If it did not exist, the therapist would have little to offer the client except sympathy and identification, and it would be pretty much a case of the blind leading the blind.

It is this built-in inequality in the relationship that keeps many people from seeking and using therapy. This inequality is particularly unacceptable, I think, to those who always feel compelled to maintain a stance of adequacy, self-reliance, and strength. Martha is, of course, experiencing that inequality twice: first by being the client in therapy and again in writing and being written about as the client. Although I shall attempt to balance things out somewhat in the course of my comments, there is no way I can really even the score. Whatever I reveal of myself and my personal history will necessarily be from the vantage point of the therapist, the professional person in the relationship.

Martha has written about a period in her life that has remained so vivid in her memory it could have been only yesterday, yet it was actually some fifteen years ago. I am starting my own narrative from the same period in my life, early adulthood, but for me this dates back almost thirty-five years. It is interesting to me that Martha's choice for the starting point of her story seems a safe and appropriate place to start my story, too. And of course I wonder how many women in early adulthood today are beginning to confront, if not similar circumstances, at least similar questions.

When I was twenty-six—Martha's age on first seeking psychiatric help—I was becoming increasingly aware of my own psychological problems, but I would almost literally have had to be crazy to get any help, since very little was available outside of mental hospitals. I was not one of the sophisticated individuals who were beginning to go into psychoanalysis at that time. In fact, I knew little of Freud and could not possibly have paid for such treatment even if I had known it existed.

My husband had returned to school to get a teaching credential, having discovered that a master's degree in economics got him no kind of job whatsoever (though the government had been claiming for some time that the depression was over). It was all we could do to keep afloat on my earnings from a job I did not want but was desperately glad to have. The university placement service had turned me away, making me feel I was presumptuous even to apply for work when men were unemployed; why wasn't my husband supporting me? Since I didn't quite understand all this, I was doubly humiliated—for my husband and for myself. When I finally did get a job, I was both grateful and apprehensive.

This was not at all what I had expected life to be. I had had some academic exposure to the economic facts of the time, and I had voted for Norman Thomas, the Socialist candidate, as soon as I was old enough to do so. But I was not at all prepared to be personally affected by the economic situation. I was sure that somehow my husband would find suitable employment whatever the state of the world, and I would pursue my own feminine interests within the home. Instead, it was I who managed to get a job, which paid only fifty dollars a month, and our "home" was a couple of furnished rooms converted to purposes of housekeeping solely by virtue of an electric plate. There was very little satisfaction and even less success in this way of life for either one of us. Still, I continued to believe that our future would be assured once my husband obtained his teaching credential, a faith that later proved unduly optimistic.

About the middle of that struggling year, I began to develop some very distressing physical symptoms. I would suddenly find I could hardly breathe and my heart would pound like a hammer, sometimes for hours on end and very often in the middle of the night. The doctor found nothing physically wrong with me and suggested

I have my tonsils out, perhaps because I complained of frequent colds or, more likely, simply because tonsillectomies were the fashion of the day. As I lacked the money for such experimental surgery, I was left with the feeling that something was terribly wrong with me, the nature of which was completely unknown and for which I could have no treatment, if indeed any appropriate treatment existed. I had a vague notion that my symptoms were somehow related to the fact that my life was not going the way I had expected, but because I believed it was just a matter of time before it would, I assumed that the thing to do was to carry on with as little fuss as possible.

I placed our son, who was only eighteen months old, in a public nursery school, which I was grateful was available without cost. He cried his heart out every morning when I left him there on my way to work. The teacher assured me that as soon as I was gone, he followed her around quite happily. He was content until I came to take him home, when he again cried his heart out, this time with relief at seeing me. The teacher was a warm, patient, motherly sort of person, and I didn't doubt that she was giving my son a superior quality of attention and care, but I suffered agonies of guilt each day. I have always been perfectly capable of blaming myself for circumstances beyond my control, and it was only long years afterward that I began to learn not to do so.

My guilt was compounded by my conviction that I was a failure as a mother. I had followed the "baby book" to the letter. I had had no previous experience with babies to enable me to make my own decisions, and I apparently had not come equipped with natural maternal instincts to guide me. In any case, I was inclined at the time to accept the word of someone who appeared qualified as an expert: He was able to state so exactly not only what a mother should do and when she should do it but also what she should never do—such as pick up a baby when he cries.

The trouble with the baby book was that although I could follow it, my son could not. As I conscientiously continued to obey its rules, he registered his protests more and more vocally. Most of his first year or so was spent crying, and I often cried with him. Finally there came a day when I realized—I'm sure with relief—that he had won, and I threw the baby book away.*

Only a few years later, the rule books on babies began swinging to the opposite extreme. They advised mothers to fit their schedules entirely to the baby's demands and to meet all his needs as they arose. These rules seemed much more likely to please the baby, but they would have been no help to me, because I could not have afforded the luxury of following them. If I had not worked, we would not have been able to eat or pay the rent.

At the time my only consolation for my maternal failings was that I had some kind of faith in my son—in his strength, his intelligence, his ability to grow and to do and to be. Once I had thrown away the baby book, I discovered I could learn a great deal from observing and listening to him. As he became more and more a person in his own right, I began to love him as a fellow human being with his own way of going about the business of living. Although I agree that love is not enough, I am convinced that it makes up for a good deal of human error, folly, and bad temper. If this were not so, we would all be in far worse shape than we are. Although I have spelled out my philosophy of therapy in some detail in the professional statement at the back of this book (see Appendix), I suspect that my recognition at age twenty-six of the drive within each human being to live his life as best he can—and the power of love to help him do so—is at the core of the matter.

I was, however, slow to come to any understanding of my own difficulties. I began to suspect more and more that the seemingly physical symptoms I suffered were psychological in origin, yet there seemed nothing for me to do but to go on suffering them. Because I had found the books on child care of so little use, I did not turn to the psychological or psychiatric books of the day for help with my own problems. I thought that an upswing in our economic circumstances would do more for me than anything else, but it took a number of years before there was any real improvement on that score. When it did come, it provided the essential base upon which I would build some emotional security, but it did not do much to alleviate my symptoms.

Finally, in sheer desperation I began to read anything that came to hand, ranging from the sedate academic theories familiar to me from undergraduate psychology to the exciting and rapidly proliferating varieties of psychoanalytic thought. There seemed to be not just one set of rules but many, so that I did not need to try to fit myself, as I had tried to fit my son, to a ready-made rule book. Instead, I could hope to put together a set of rules of my own, ones that would fit my own individual measure.

It was probably fortunate that I came across Karen Horney, who was unwilling to settle obediently for a masculine view of feminine psychology, before I encountered Helene Deutsch, who accepted for women all that the most chauvinistic of men might choose to put upon them—and more.* I am glad, too, that I read the modifiers and deviationists before I read Sigmund Freud himself. The tone of his writing is of such a sweet and humorous reasonableness that I would surely have been persuaded beyond the merits of his argument had I not had some acquaintance with alternative theories. This is not to disparage the Freudian contribution—indeed, others have built upon what is valid in its base—but I needed to come to it with a recognition of its limitations and an awareness of the improbability of some of its doctrines.

I saw that there could be a diversity of theories, each with its own validity and not necessarily cancelling out another. When theories were contradictory rather than complementary or interchangeable, I was free to make my own choices; I was beholden to no academic curriculum nor to any school of therapy. I soon realized that my suffering was by no means unique, that its nature could be understood, and that there might be more than one appropriate method of treatment. How much I could do for myself, how much I would need in the way of help, I could only guess, but in the absence of money for any kind of treatment at all, I was obviously going to have to do as much on my own as possible. Although my reading proved to be somewhat more educational than therapeutic, it opened so many mental doors that some emotional ones came open as well, and I dared to hope that I might work out my problems without formal psychotherapy.

Meanwhile, because I could pick and choose among theoretical concepts according to their usefulness to me, it did not occur to me that I had to make some kind of once-and-for-all choice among them. It was not until I reached graduate school, a good many years later, that I experienced such pressure. By that time I was hardly a candidate for conversion to any one school of thought. My efforts at self-help proved to have been a mixed blessing. I found I had already done most of the required reading and much specialized reading besides, but in the process I had become a confirmed maverick.

In those days, the academic program and most of the field placements for social work students were strongly Freudian. My first year of fieldwork was at a family service agency, where I was able to feel very much at home: Its Freudian orientation was outweighed by its commitment to social work principles and by the personal qualities of its staff. But like many of my fellow students, I found my anxieties mounting under the impact of work that activated and reactivated every personal problem I had ever had. My efforts to help myself had carried me this far, but I had had no actual therapy and I became increasingly aware that I could not go on without it. So I followed my friends to the university psychiatric clinic, not knowing at the time I applied for help that it was to be the scene of my second-year field placement.

The university clinic was one of the few exceptions at that time to the Freudian dominion. It was known as an eclectic clinic because it had on its staff representatives of many different theoretical orientations. Freudian though she was, my first-year supervisor, who valued quality of therapy above all else, congratulated me on being offered this placement because the university clinic was famous for the excellence of its work. She nevertheless expressed considerable concern for my personal psychological security in a setting that would expose me to so many conflicting points of view—unaware that I had long since lost that kind of security, if indeed I had ever possessed it.

It was at the clinic that I had the advantage of seeing therapy from the standpoint of both patient and therapist at the same time. There, too, I developed the profound conviction that although some theoretical concepts were more useful and adequate than others, what mattered most was the way they were used and the people who used them. My psychiatric consultant at the clinic was a Jungian, but he made no attempt to convert me to his doctrine. He treated me as he did the rest of the staff and, I am sure, his patients—as a human being with gifts of my own, equal though different from his. My therapist at the clinic was a psychiatrist with a Freudian orientation. Although I felt less compatibility with him, I found him a man of integrity and reliability with whom I could safely disagree. With him, too, I eventually became able to communicate on a basis of equality.

The clinic staff seemed quite comfortable in tolerating one another's differences of opinion, and I found much to be learned from all of them. I was nevertheless something of an outsider, as I was not a follower or member of any of their theoretical groupings. In social work school, I felt considerable compulsion to conform to the majority position. Freudian thought, except for a minor dissenting voice or two, was definitely dominant. Adherence to its tenets, although not exactly mandatory, was by far the most practical course, at least from the standpoint of knowing on which side one's academic bread was buttered. To have been psychoanalyzed, if possible by a well-known Freudian, bestowed great prestige. Not to have been psychoanalyzed at all, I was told by one of my faculty advisors, would make it impossible for me ever to work in a psychiatric clinic.

Fortunately, my supervisor at the university clinic was a woman whose simple, natural, open approach to people left me free to be myself, with the knowledge that I would have her support should I need it. Although she was known to have been psychoanalyzed by Erik Erikson, at that time the most prestigious of Freudians, she seemed to subscribe to no school of thought but her own. It was to her and to a few others like her that I owe not only my intellectual but also my emotional survival in a field (then as now) riven by a score of competitive sects. I consider my experience in living through all this to have been part of my therapy at the time, though much of it was never discussed with my psychiatrist.

No therapy comes all in one piece. Even for those fortunate few—usually only patients who can afford private treatment—who happen to find the "right" therapist at the "right" time and are able to continue without transfer to another for as long as may be necessary, therapy comes in bits and pieces, much of it from other people and outside regular therapy hours. Martha's story of her previous therapy is by no means a horror tale. It simply delineates some aspects of human and theoretical frailties and demonstrates how much depends on the individual's determination to get help despite disappointments and obstacles in the course of treatment.

At any clinic or agency there are inevitably students or interns or residents who come and go, and often there is a large turnover of regular staff as well. Sometimes it is an advantage to have more than one therapist. There is some protection for the patient in being exposed to different points of view, assuming, of course, that not all the therapists adhere rigidly to one doctrinal approach and that one does not derogate whatever the patient may have gained from another. Martha's therapists seem to have been people of good will, with enough self-understanding and self-discipline not to ride roughshod over patients for their own unconscious purposes; to encounter a number of such people under one roof is a matter of no small consequence.

It was certainly an important matter for me, both at the family agency and at the clinic. Each was located, as was common at the time, in a remodeled house. Each became a kind of spiritual home for me, so important to me that at one point my psychiatrist protested that I was placing more faith and trust in my colleagues than in him.

"But you can't make a transference to a house!" he said, using the Freudian term for emotional investment in the therapeutic relationship.

"I already have," I said to myself. I first had to develop trust in a whole group of people dedicated to the psychotherapeutic profession before I could trust this specific one.

I have ever since been convinced that the work of volunteers and other lay people in the mental health field needs to be contained, thoughtfully and flexibly, within the professional framework, or at least should have some significant connection with professional people. I feel this way not because the professionals have a monopoly on the ability to help, or necessarily better educational or practical training for the actual purpose at hand, but because of the safeguards provided by professional ethics, by professional associations—both formal and informal—and by the opportunity for review by professional peers.

Nevertheless, it is the quality of people as people that makes the difference in therapy, not their qualifications on paper. From that standpoint, being a member of the staff was a very great advantage for it enabled me to learn to know therapists as human beings. In my own time of need, when the house of cards I had built for myself was falling all about me, acceptance by my colleagues really counted.

I came to the clinic one day in a state that no one could mistake. There is a degree of disturbance so intense that even the lay person usually recognizes it. The psychologist took one look at me and exclaimed, "Welcome to the gang!" The resident threw her arms around me and cried, "My fellow sufferer!" My thesis advisor said, "We've all gone through this in one form or another." My consultant told me, "Anyone who is worth his salt in this work has come to it this way."

When I said I could not go on, my supervisor replied that I must not drop out because I might not be able to come back later. She called the head of the clinic to help her persuade me to stay. "Take a little sick leave," he said. "Your patients will be all right. It's

the therapists we have to worry about—we can't afford to lose any."
So of course I stayed on and was much the better for having done so,
though I still feel with the utmost conviction that there ought to be
an easier way.

The difference between my clinic experience and Martha's
is so great that I am filled with a tangle of emotions: I, to whom so
much was given, must help Martha resolve her feelings about a
situation in which she was given so little. And I, who had needed
everything I could get, might not have survived at all on Martha's
share. Such a combination of emotions in various proportions is not
an uncommon experience on my side of the desk. When I am sure
it will be helpful to the person on the other side, I share some of it.
More often it remains unspoken, but whether I speak or remain
silent, I must handle my own feelings about it. In Martha's case I can
say to myself: At least there was a clinic to turn to, which was not so
for me at her age. And I do not underestimate the advantage of
coming to therapy sooner rather than later.

The original telephone contact with the clinic, when Martha
had called about her husband, had granted her dignity while denying
her request; and Martha had immediately recognized the competence of her first therapist there. The pattern was shattered, however, by a premature interruption: jury duty—still a hazard to clients
in treatment with social workers. Martha experienced the interruption as a disaster. To find someone in whom one has confidence only
to have that person snatched away parallels some of the most painful
experiences of childhood. It can also be a most serious and realistic
loss in one's adult life. Such a loss in the course of therapy draws from
both sets of emotions, the child's and the adult's. And for Martha, the
problem grew in magnitude with each change of therapist. That the
therapists happened to be men, following a premature separation
from a woman, seems of lesser though certainly not negligible consequence. That they were young and no doubt as inexperienced in
marriage as in therapy was surely a greater disadvantage.

To the extent that Martha could experience a disinterested
good will on the part of her therapists, she was getting something

that seems to have been rare in her life. It must have had some value, since her more ominous symptoms diminished during this period. Yet, to the extent that her therapy was conducted according to rule books instead of the needs of people, Martha felt her therapists to be uninterested in her as an individual with something of her own to bring to her treatment. From Martha's report, part of the difficulty was the inability of her therapists to go outside their theoretical frameworks and unbend sufficiently as human beings to learn from Martha what she needed from them.

Unfortunately, Martha herself was not in possession of a vital piece of information: Her emotional condition and state of mind were being directly affected by the most important environmental factor in her life at that time—her marriage. Her feelings of inadequacy and uncertainty were so great, or her fear of rejection and condemnation so overwhelming, that she could not, or dared not, describe to her therapists exactly what was going on in her marriage. Even if she could have brought herself to do so, the rule books in those days did not yet fully recognize the impact of the marital situation on mental health. Therapists tended to dismiss complaints about a spouse as "projection" of responsibility or "resistance" to treatment. The patient was seen as the product of his past and the creator of his present. It was assumed that once he came to understand and handle his own emotions, he would automatically be able to deal with his spouse, his boss, his government, or whatever might be contributing to his current difficulties.

A few years later, the rule books began to change. Therapists not only invited marital partners to participate in therapy but also sometimes refused to see either one alone. Some would not even see a child unless the whole family went into treatment, on the theory that the patient's sickness is always the product of family interaction. Of course, the new rules brought about their own absurdities and injustices along with their important discoveries and improvements, and Martha was caught in the middle.

Martha had originally seen Scott as the one most in need of treatment and had tried to arrange it for him. When her attempt was unsuccessful, she arranged help for herself, not at all an unusual course on the part of a wife and a logical progression of thought: If he won't get help, then I must. In the absence of a therapy that would have taken the marriage into account, what Martha needed most was to build up her self-esteem and develop her own strengths. Instead, what seems to have been built up by her early experience in therapy was primarily frustration. This might have had a strengthening effect could she have expressed it in direct anger at her therapists, but she was not yet able to do that. She would need first the security of an ongoing relationship in which she was understood and valued for what she was and in which she would be helped to grow. The approval by the Jungian therapist of her intellectual insight was a poor substitute; even for his approval, she could not adopt his view of her marriage.

Martha was obviously angry at the way her therapy was going, but if complaining about her husband made a wife a "castrating bitch," complaining about a therapist who was trying to help would make her an ungrateful wretch as well. Had she nevertheless done so, her anger probably would have been viewed as a transference manifestation—a reaction irrationally superimposed on the therapy relationship—rather than a natural response to the frustrating experience of not really being heard, to say nothing of not being understood. But it was clear almost from the beginning that Martha was one of those people who not only survive but somehow persist until, one way or another, they get the help they need.

And she did get help—from someone who was not officially a therapist at all. Yet by reason of his intuitive wisdom, his religious vocation, and his personal love for Martha, he was able not only to listen but also to understand and to help. It is interesting that Father Michaelson taught Martha how to "talk." This was going back to very early days indeed, psychologically and symbolically speaking, and provided Martha with a corrective learning experience essential to all further emotional progress. Her inability to convey thoughts and feelings had cut her off from the process of sharing experiences and ideas with other people and thus from the possibility of developing a sufficiently realistic perspective on human beings. Nor had she learned to make the small automatic adjustments to differences in personality that grow naturally out of the give-and-take of ordinary everyday conversation, so that almost any difference at all would loom very large.

Martha must often have been at a loss to know how to deal with people. She lacked the experience that might have helped her to understand them better or to get them to understand her. That lack made the outside world seem a very dangerous place and too much to cope with alone, no matter how miserable things were at home. (All of this helps to explain why Martha could see her husband as being in dire need of hospitalization yet be unable to say or do anything decisive about it.)

But there is another even more basic kind of communication problem. To be in touch with others, to experience closeness, one must be willing and able to recognize and to name some of those "very big things" that so often go unidentified and unnamed. One cannot communicate about something one has to deny. For many people, it is easier to be aware of anger, fear, envy, jealousy—the negative emotions—while for others it may be exactly the other way around, with only the positive emotions admitted into awareness. I suspect that Martha learned very early not to let herself recognize much of either set of emotions, although they were always there, stirring about in the unconscious depths of her being.

These are the unidentified terrors—terrible exactly because they go unrecognized, unnamed, unexpressed—that are so often at work in the fear of insanity, of falling apart, of being overwhelmed by tides of uncontrollable emotion. These are the monsters within: quite human, understandable, even tamable monsters once they are admitted to their proper place in the total personality. How ironic that loving, sexual feelings can play as terrifying a role when relegated to the murky, monstrous depths of unconsciousness as the most hateful of emotions!

It was of the utmost importance that Martha was not forced by some mistaken moral conception to perpetuate her pattern of denial and repression in the relationship with Father Michaelson. I shudder at the thought of what would have happened to her had he not declared his love. What effort she would have put into blinding herself to the reality, which she could not help sensing on some level, out of fear that even to entertain such a thought for a minute would indeed prove her to be "crazy"! By affirming his love, Father Michaelson gave Martha for the first time the experience of being truly loved by a man. That there was no sexual consummation of that love in no way detracted from the importance of the relationship to her emotional growth. On the contrary, it was just as well that the love experience was not jeopardized by the foreseeable pitfalls.

Martha's afterthoughts are very well taken. The episode with Father Michaelson could, of course, be evaluated and analyzed and interpreted ad infinitum and ad nauseam, in accord with whatever psychological theory one chooses. Its importance for Martha was that it happened at all. Martha finally had the experience of real love between woman and man, not just the show of love. (And if this is the emotion kindled originally in the girl child by her father, and if Father Michaelson was a father figure, so much the better; it was what Martha needed.)

But there are difficult problems for the informal counselor in such a situation. He is without the protection of the professional framework and thus is as vulnerable to out-of-bounds emotional impulses as the client. Father Michaelson was faithful to his religious vocation, but he was inevitably torn between his role as spiritual guide and his feeling for Martha.* In giving Martha what she so desperately needed, it became impossible—if indeed such a possibility ever existed—to reach and help Scott. Without training in pastoral counseling, Father Michaelson was in no position to consider the question of Scott's mental state. And perhaps in his effort to be neutral and not to interfere in any way with the marital relationship, he could not even allow himself to elicit from Martha simple, factual information about Scott. So, once again, there would be no official attention directed toward what was going on with Scott.

The Child Guidance Clinic, of course, was in a position to

give official attention, to explore with Martha not only the nature of Peter's problems but also those problems in the marriage that might be contributing factors. A thorough preliminary inquiry along these lines might have encouraged Martha, uncertain and in conflict though she was, at least to describe the situation as she saw it. There is no reason to think Martha would have misrepresented the facts, although she would naturally present them from her own point of view. That is exactly where therapy often is best begun—with the material brought to it by the client who wants help. From there, the therapist can go on to explore with the client the possible meaning, impact, and implications of the problems for the client himself and for other members of the family. And finally, on the basis of the best evaluation the therapist and client can make together, the most feasible treatment plan can be chosen. A great deal of useful therapy has been conducted in just that way, useful not only to the client but often to the marriage and the family as well.*

Instead, in this case the choice was made to enforce a rigid rule for involving everyone in the family right from the beginning. Scott came for the intake interview against what I shall call his own better judgment, because the upshot of the interview was clearly, as he himself stated, that he felt far too threatened to make any use of the contact except to obscure matters further. There was no opportunity to find out who he was and what he needed and how he could have been helped. So Peter was deprived of treatment; and if Scott was himself a candidate for treatment, he was certainly left more thoroughly frightened of it than ever before.

## martha continues

The next three years passed by without any real change. Father Michaelson and I continued to see each other on pretty much the same basis. My marriage neither improved nor deteriorated.

Our family, however, gained another member, and from an unexpected source. Rosemary Johnson, the fifteen-year-old daughter of our friends and neighbors, was finding her home situation more than she could handle. She began to spend more and more time at our house, occasionally even staying with us for a week or more. Rosemary was friendly and likable, although deep in her struggles with the problems of adolescence. I enjoyed her company, and her help with my children, so much younger than she, was very welcome. One day, she asked Scott and me if she could move in with us to help with the children and to be our foster child as well. Scott and I talked it over, both with Rosemary's parents and with each other, and agreed to give it a try. So it happened that I found myself almost without warning the mother of a teen-age "daughter." It was an exhilarating but confusing experience.

Then came a disaster, a tragedy about which even now it is almost impossible for me to write.

Sunday morning, two days before Christmas. A busy time for me, getting Christmas shopping done, the house cleaned, plans made for the holidays. The children and I had gone to early Mass, come home, had breakfast. They went outside to play and I made a start on the housework. I was in the basement putting dirty clothes into the washing machine when I heard the loud squeal of brakes and a crash. I froze. I did not move a muscle, my mind would not frame a thought. Then Rosemary came running through the house and stood at the top of the basement stairs. "Martha, Martha, Becky's hit!"

I wish I could say that everything that follows is a blur. It isn't. I remember each second with crystal clarity. Sometimes when I least expect it, I will find it all moving through my mind, clearly, clearly, in slow motion. Bending over her in the street. Becky was unconscious, blood running from her mouth. The firemen from the fire-house across the street running out to help with first aid. There was nothing for them to do. The other children standing white-faced in the small crowd at the sidewalk. A friend calling to me, "Martha, is there anything we can do?" Nothing except pray. Scott was still asleep. I sent Rosemary to wake him and he came running out. A priest from St. John's came and stood with the crowd. You don't give the last rites to four-year-olds.

The ambulance at last. Friends gathering up the older children to care for them while we were gone. The firemen helping the ambulance crew to lift Becky onto the stretcher. They asked my permission to tear her little blue sweater to get it off so they could examine the injuries. It's funny how the trivia remain with you forever. In memory the ambulance seemed to crawl through the streets. I knew she was badly injured. How badly I refused to think. Wait until a doctor sees her, I kept saying to myself.

Hospital emergency entrance. A crew of doctors and nurses waiting. Then quickly into one of the examining rooms. Three doctors examining her, dictating phrases to the young pediatrician standing beside me. He wrote them into the record, detached medical phrases, so at odds with the tiny child crumpled on the examining table. She was still unconscious, but she began to gasp for breath. Rapid irregular respiration, said one of the doctors. The pediatrician wrote it down. The neurosurgeon came. "Massive cerebral injuries. We'll do those first if her spleen didn't get it." Then quite suddenly the examination was over. The surgery team filed out to get ready for emergency surgery, and I was left alone with Becky and the pediatrics resident.

Neither of us said anything for a minute. It was desperately difficult to frame the question, but I realized that I simply had to know. "What are the chances she'll die?" I asked.

He looked me over for a minute. Then he said, "Practically certain."

"Thanks," I said and stumbled out into the hall.

I was and still am grateful that he told me the truth. If false hope had been added to my burden, I don't see how I could have survived the days that followed.

Scott was standing in the hall. I went over to him and told him what the doctor had said.

"Don't you say that," he said fiercely. "Don't you ever say that again." I knew he feared my saying it would make it happen.

Father Michaelson had arrived. A couple of neighbors came and sat with us. Someone gave me a tranquilizer and I took it, though I felt tranquil enough. I was more wiped out by shock than hysterical. They wheeled Becky out of the examining room and up to surgery. A nurse came and showed us another room where we could wait during the surgery. Time dragged on. We talked quietly once in a while, but there was literally not much we could say. Mostly we just waited in silence. I remember there was a cut-out cardboard crèche set up at one end of the room. Scott went over and savagely kicked it to the floor.

A very long while passed. Another pediatrician, a young woman, came in to tell us that, contrary to their expectations, Becky had survived the extensive neurosurgery and was making a surprisingly strong fight for her life. If she could pull out of shock. . . . The next twelve hours would tell.

We saw her for a few moments in the intensive care unit. They had shaved her head for the surgery and it was swollen and misshapen. A respirator was breathing for her. There are no words to describe how she looked to me then.

I couldn't face going home. We had friends who lived just around the block. They had come to the hospital to stay with us through the long wait. When we found there was to be no final word on Becky's condition for hours or perhaps even days, they invited us to stay with them for the rest of the day, to let them handle phone calls and other such business. I remember desperately wanting to take a bath and wash my hair, a sort of furious need for purification. Other friends had taken the three older children out for dinner. Afterward, they came and joined us, and we all talked quietly for a while.

"Mom, she's not going to die, is she?" Peter asked.

"Yes, the doctor thinks so."

Scott literally howled me down. That made me furious. Playing with his private superstitions was one thing, but these were real live people, dependent on him and me for their information about what to expect in reality. There was no way to prepare them to face the coming reality except for whatever expectation we could give them. Why tell them or ourselves lies that we knew to be lies? Much better to look at things as they really were and face them all together. Anyway, how could he expect to convince them if he knew it wasn't true? Even so, angry as I was, I held my peace.

Much later, friends told me that on that first day Scott had taken a number of people aside and told them that I had unreasonably formed the fixed idea Becky was going to die. Of course, he explained, my weak mental health could not cope with the strain and he was sure that they would be understanding. I wondered at the time why some of my friends became so pointedly "understanding."

We took the children home at last and put them to bed in some parody of normal routine. The long night began then.

It was the worst time I can ever remember. I was braced for the phone to ring any moment, telling us Becky was dead. Scott sat up talking to a friend. I took a tranquilizer and drank a water glass full of bourbon; with those I slept fitfully, waking every few minutes, waiting for the phone. Every three and a half hours by the clock, the tranquilizer wore off and I became wide awake. I repeated tranquilizer and bourbon, slept and woke again. (I drank quite a bit of bourbon that week.)

It grew light at last and the phone still had not rung. I called the hospital; there was no change. It was Christmas Eve. All of us felt instinctively that we wanted to keep to as much of our normal routine as we could. I felt if that were removed, that whole framework of custom and usual procedure, I would find myself falling through space and the whole of my world would collapse.

We always put up our Christmas tree on Christmas Eve. Now friends helped the children to do it. Hardest of all was to decide whether or not to wrap Becky's presents. I knew that there was no hope that she would ever open them now, but not to wrap them was to admit it, to admit that hope was finally and absolutely dead, to give up whatever hope against hope remained. I felt then it would be throwing in the sponge for her if we did not wrap them. So I wrapped her gifts.

We called the hospital every two hours to see whether there was any change. The twelve hours during which the doctors thought Becky might have rallied went by without a change.

Early in the evening Father Peterson, another friend from St. John's, came in. He had just left the hospital. The doctors had said there was now no hope whatsoever. The respirator was breathing for her; she could not breathe on her own. Now it was just a matter of wearing out her heart. Scott accepted it as inevitable, then. He went into the bedroom, lay down on the floor, and cried in very great agony for a long time. I sat in the room with him and said nothing. Each of us was totally alone.

After a while I went out to say something to Father Peterson. A few minutes later Scott followed me out.

"I want you to drive me to the hospital," he said; "I know you will be skeptical, but it would be wrong for someone with my special powers not to use them for my own daughter. Take me to the hospital. I'm going to raise her from the dead."

Father Peterson was young, newly ordained, and obviously terrified, but he sat with Scott for a long time and helped to calm him down. His main line of approach was, "You've got to stay here with Martha. She needs you."

In bitter retrospect, this seems like a fair paradigm of my entire marriage and how it was regarded by friends. At the moment he was speaking, indeed through the whole of that week, I was calm and reasonable and dealing with reality. Scott seemed to me to be visibly psychotic, however understandably so, yet here was a friend basing his plea on my "madness" and Scott's sanity. Why, I wonder?

At last that day was over. Another night to face. It was a little easier, now that hope was gone.

Daylight again, Christmas day. The family heard Mass together in a small private chapel at the church. Home again, presents opened. All of us were feeling battered by the ordeal. Because the end was inevitable, one hoped it would come soon, and yet I felt a perverse pride that a child of mine should be so hard to kill.

In the early afternoon the hospital called. Becky was beginning to fail. If we wanted to see her alive, we should come now. Scott, Father Michaelson, and I went to the hospital and stood beside her bed. She was deeply unconscious and already seemed very far away from us. I stood and watched her and tried to give her back to God.

One of the intensive care nurses stayed with us (ready to deal with the emergency if one of us collapsed, I think). I remember saying to her, "There's no hope she'll ever recover."

"Her brain is terribly injured." she said. "You don't want her to recover."

That helped me a lot, for when she said it, I saw it was true.

After we left the hospital, Father Michaelson drove Scott and me out into the country, along the Sound, a long ride without a fixed goal. We wanted to be away, away from the telephone and other people, away from the expectation of the news that might come any minute. When we returned, we thought, we'll call the hospital and she'll be dead. The children were safe with friends. We drove for hours.

Home again, the children gathered home again. And Becky was still alive. There was still another night to go through. It was easier, with practice. I felt nothing. My feelings had worn themselves out. I was numb. All during that long wait, we were surrounded by friends and enormously supported by both their practical help and their devoted and genuinely selfless concern. Their love mitigated the nightmare as no other force could possibly have done. They gave more than I can ever thank them for, or repay, or measure. I know that during that ordeal I saw the very best of what people can do when they really mean to help each other.

But deep in myself, in my shock and grief, I felt I was alone.

The fourth day of waiting. Going mechanically through the

motions of normal living, knowing it couldn't go on much longer. Then early in the evening, the hospital called to tell us it was over at last. Becky was dead. I was too exhausted to feel anything but relief.

Both Scott and I had always hated funeral parlors and the whole of the conventional burial business. Becky was buried from home. Dozens of friends came to share our grief with us. Mostly there was just quiet talk and companionship. All night, the night before her burial, friends sat quietly with us. There was a chess game going most of the night in one corner, I remember. I slept part of that night curled up on the living room couch, holding Becky's shoes. Every time I woke up, someone was there to talk to for a minute, and then I slept again.

The brothers from St. John's sang Becky's funeral Mass, the Mass of the day for the Feast of Holy Innocents. We buried her in the churchyard overlooking the Sound.

And so she was gone from our lives, and the business of trying to pick up the pieces began. The children were desperately upset and frightened. Two days after the funeral, Ann tried to run in front of a car. I grabbed her coat just in time to stop her. Peter kept almost completely to himself, saying nothing. Sasha had bouts of hysterical crying. Rosemary kept asking me why did it have to happen, why? Everybody—children, friends—seemed to be looking to me for comfort and reassurance. Mechanically I tried to comfort and reassure. Woman is the heart of the household, after all. It was my job to make everything all right again. I gave away Becky's clothes, burned her coloring books, tidied things up and put them out of sight. I was too numb even to cry.

## esther comments

What does one say in the face of such stark tragedy? I think of the Appalachian couple described by Robert Coles, so grateful to the doctor for telling them their child was doomed. There was no way they could have gone through the financial and emotional drain of long-drawn-out tests, of repeated visits to the hospital, of continually sacrificing the other children in the vain hope of keeping the sick child alive. They literally could not afford the luxury of false hope, nor could Martha. Yet Scott could not afford to face the truth. Each was under a different but equally compelling psychological necessity. Scott's mind literally revolted; it would break before it would bend under the weight of an intolerable truth. Martha would allow her mind neither to break nor to bend but would insist on standing and looking on to the bitter end. How different these two human beings are, how antithetical to one another, and how separate and apart each remains in the midst of a shared tragedy!

## martha continues

In the days and the weeks after Becky's death, I tried hard to get some sort of grip on myself. I couldn't do it. It wasn't a continuation of paralyzing grief; indeed, grief seemed almost absent. But I was frozen, and everyone seemed to want something from me, some sort of reassurance. It was up to me somehow to show them that everything was really all right. I had my position to uphold as the saint of our little circle. It was my job to understand what had happened and make it all plain and meaningful. Hadn't I gone through the whole time of Becky's death and burial as a perfect model of submission to the will of God? Now all I had to do was continue in the same way indefinitely. It was soothing to the people around me. I took on the job as a matter of course.

The children were frightened and clung to me, both literally and figuratively. Rosemary became very dramatic and demanding. I didn't see how I could either help her or handle her. Scott had repeated and violent flashbacks of hallucinations—voices, and hands touching him.

I wanted to turn for help to Father Michaelson. I discovered he was in the midst of his own personal crisis and fighting for his life. He felt that Becky had been struck down instead of us, an innocent victim and perhaps a warning. He did not want to abandon me, that much was clear. But everything between us was irrevocably changed. He was torn with conflict as he never had been before.

And I was frozen. I could get through a day's work, mechanically, but there seemed to be no person alive inside. Every day I seemed more and more ground away by the needs and demands of others. They were needs I meant to answer, demands I had invited, but that made no difference. There was nothing left to answer them with. I wanted to go away somewhere by myself, lie down on the floor, and cry for a year. I couldn't seem to cry at all. I felt choked by my unshed tears. The demands went on and I knew there would be no end to them. I felt as if my skin had been sandpapered all over. Contact with other people, with family, with friends, made me wince with pain. If only I could get away. The demands were changeless and unending.

And then I discovered I was pregnant. It was the ultimate disaster. Scott and I had lived totally apart for several years. One short hysterical turn in bed in the week after Becky was buried (which each of us afterwards, in great bitterness, accused the other of engineering with ulterior motives), and there it was, another baby. Scott was delighted. He went around happily announcing it to all our friends. So good for Martha! I was appalled, but he didn't tell them that.

You can't replace a dead child by having another baby. That I knew in advance. How could there be another Becky? The marriage wasn't functioning. I was resigned to the fact that things would always be as they were now and that I would always be unhappy. I had accepted that for myself and was trying to make some sort of a life for the children as best I could, trying to keep the worst of the conflict away from them. I wanted to make their lives happier than mine could ever be. If they could someday be free and happy, then I would be satisfied. But to bring another child into the situation . . . so much younger than the others. . . . All the isolation of my own childhood came back to me. I didn't love my husband and I didn't want his child, still another visible tie to him. I did love somebody else and I wanted his child very much.

It would have been easy for me to obtain an abortion even in those days on a plea of my endangered mental health, which, God knows, was real enough. I never really considered it, and, were the situation repeated today, I would not consider it now. I know that some people will believe this to be the blind and wicked influence of the Catholic faith, but my convictions about abortion long predate my conversion to the Church and indeed were one of the reasons for that conversion. I experienced each of my children from the very start of pregnancy as a separate person, independent of me, not "belonging" to me in the sense of ownership at all. It wasn't up to me to decide whether the child should live or die. My convenience, even in so desperate a matter as my own sanity, did not seem a consideration equal to its life or death. The unborn child seemed to me the most vulnerable and helpless of human creatures, entirely dependent on me for its very life. I couldn't seriously consider taking that life.

I also didn't see how I was going to make it through another pregnancy. If only I could get away! The world does not abound in refuges for mourning, pregnant, Catholic housewives in precarious mental health, with no money. I was afraid to be alone. I didn't want to be with other people. I was needed where I was. I needed to get away. Where could I go?

I began to consider psychiatric hospitalization. Therapy

hadn't helped me much, but in a hospital I would at least be some-what protected from my renewed suicidal impulses and might con-ceivably get some help in sorting out my feelings about Becky's death. They must have had some experience with that kind of prob-lem in those places, I thought. No money, though, and every place but a state hospital would cost a lot. I asked Scott whether his hospi-talization insurance would cover the cost, and he told me it would not. I knew his answer was a fabrication because he had told me himself not too long before that a friend of his had been in a mental hospital and the company insurance had paid the bills. I called his company's personnel office and was told that it was indeed fully covered.

Casting around for help, I phoned Dorothy Jackson at City Mental Hygiene and told her of Becky's death. She took time to listen to me and sounded really alarmed at my depression. Would I come back to the clinic if any of the therapists had time free? Again there was no mistaking the genuine concern. I had always respected her professional judgment, so I went back.

I was assigned to Malcolm Rogers. We had four or five ses-sions together, a simple fact that was later to provide a turning point in my life, though I had no idea of it then. All that was evident at the time was that I was paralyzed by guilt and depression. Becky had been given to me to care for; I hadn't taken care of her and she was dead. I had already given up hope of ever doing anything in my life except protect my children. Now it was clear that I was disastrously bad even at that. My one life goal was gone. How could I go on?

And what to do about Rosemary? I felt an abject failure. She had come to us in an attempt to get clear of a scrambled family situation, family troubles with which she couldn't deal. Now we had put her in a situation far worse than the one she had left. No wonder she was having trouble. Rosemary was reacting to what had hap-pened as best she could, but I simply couldn't handle her. If I sent her away now, it would seem as if I were rejecting her for the very reasons that had made me willing to take her in the first place. It was grossly unfair, but I had no other choice. I had no hope she would understand my position. Her last state would be far worse than her first, and it would be my fault.

Rosemary would have to leave us, but she didn't want to go back home. A couple we knew offered her a room in exchange for help with their large family of small children, and she moved in with them. I felt an enormous weight of guilt. Every attempt of mine to help others ended in failure for me and misery for them because of the weak and twisted person I was. Self-destruction would be a relief for me and a kindness to my friends.

(When Rosemary emerged from her adolescence, she and I became good friends. She told me then—and I know she was sincere —that she felt only gratitude for the part I had played in her life. My willingness to take her in when she felt so confused and to stand by her was a major factor in her coming to terms with her troubled state of mind. She didn't feel I was wrong to send her away after Becky's death. She saw it as inevitable in the situation, not as a personal failure of mine. She and I remained close, as close as sisters. I had not failed her after all, but I didn't know that at the time.)

I discussed the possibility of psychiatric hospitalization with a friend who had a doctorate in behavioral psychology and was a psychotherapist at the Veterans Hospital in a neighboring city. She and I had an ongoing, frequently hilarious debate about the nature and basis of psychotherapy. Her doctoral dissertation had been on the learning process in rats. My viewpoint was Jungian-based, philosophical, speculative in the extreme. We disagreed radically on theory. Once when I asked her if she trained her patients to run through mazes, she inquired in return whether I was prepared to have them sit around indefinitely waiting for a mystical experience that would make everything plain. I thought she had rather a good point.

She came by one day after I had begun to think about hospitalization and I asked her what she thought. She considered it very carefully for a while.

"You know, it might be a good idea," she replied slowly. "I don't mean that you're 'crazy'. Obviously you're not, and anyhow I'm not even sure just what 'crazy' is. There's nothing the matter with your learning processes, that's for sure. But I have a feeling that you need to hit bottom, to find out just where the limits really are, before you can come back from all this. You can't do that here. You've got too many responsibilities, and too many people around you. In the hospital, you'd have a chance to explore the bottom, if that's what you need to do, and start back up again. I'd say you should consider it seriously."

I broached the subject with Father Michaelson. He had been taking some courses in pastoral counseling and had some idea about inpatient facilities. He volunteered to make inquiries. Presently he reported back: one hospital had no openings; two had said they would take me.

I then broached the subject with Scott. He was furious, but his reaction was quite brief and to the point. If I persisted in trying to commit myself and if I should actually succeed, it would mean I no longer had legal control over what happened to me. He would arrange for me to have shock treatment. (Scott knew that both my sister and a close friend had had shock therapy and regarded it years afterward with helpless terror. I knew he didn't believe in the therapeutic efficacy of electroshock treatment. I had heard him say so plenty of times.) It would undoubtedly kill the unborn child, he said, and I would have to remember all my life that I had chosen to kill it.

But I had to get away. I called Kirkpatrick Hospital, one of the two Father Michaelson had mentioned, to ask whether shock treatment was used and, if so, whether the patient himself had to give consent or if the family could order it. I was assured that it was virtually never used, but that when it was, the decision was made by the therapist and the patient. Families did not direct treatment.

I had to get away. I decided to sign myself into Kirkpatrick if they would take me. It was a Catholic hospital and I thought they'd be less likely to pressure me for an abortion. I called Scott's company and had the insurance forms sent to me. I found families of friends who said they would take the children while I was in the hospital. It

MARTHA'S STORY    69

meant splitting them up, but I couldn't very well ask anyone to take in all three. The children were very frightened. I reassured them as best I could, promising them that they could come and see me and that I'd be in touch by phone. The morning I left, Sasha was running a fever. I took her temperature and arranged with a friend to take her to the doctor if it went up in the afternoon.

Father Michaelson arrived to drive Scott and me to the admissions appointment. "How are you?" he wanted to know.

"Well, I've finally gotten most of the arrangements made," I said. "I feel as if they won't let me lie down and die until I arrange the burial and cook a meal for the wake."

"They'll probably ask you to comfort the mourners, too," he said, and I could see he was close to tears.

So we drove over to Kirkpatrick Hospital to an admissions interview with three of the staff psychiatrists. I told them that I needed help in dealing with my daughter's death and that depression was making it hard for me to function normally. Scott made a dramatic plea for shock therapy to restore me as soon as possible to home and family. He was told quite brusquely that the value of shock was questionable and they rarely used it.

So I was admitted as an inpatient. I was to be there for a little less than six weeks.

Later, much later, several friends told me that Scott had talked to them about how sorry he was to have to commit me. I was behaving so oddly, he said, my bizarre behavior really gave him no choice. I asked with considerable interest if he told them what I had said or done. It seemed he had never been very specific. Too embarrassed, perhaps.

Once inside the hospital I felt a little better at first, then a great deal worse. As my psychotherapist friend had predicted, I had a chance to explore the bottom. I was assigned to a staff psychiatrist whom I liked and basically trusted. His responses, however, were so minimal that I had a hard time figuring out what I was doing, whether I was getting anywhere or, so to speak, just running in place.

(I think this may have been intentional on his part and that perhaps it was a good idea, but at the time it seemed very frustrating.)

Patients slept two to a room in small but pleasant rooms off a main corridor. Outwardly, it was rather like life in a college dormitory. There was a large lounge and recreation room, where it was taken for granted that we would spend most of our time. We were not allowed to stay alone in our rooms for very long or to sleep in the daytime; those retreats from reality were pretty well cut off. Each of us had half an hour a day with our psychiatrist. In addition, every morning there was group therapy conducted in rotation by staff therapists or sometimes by visitors. The whole ward and all the day staff participated. We were also expected to have an occupational therapy project going. Mine was making maternity clothes. I was determined that this time around I was at least going to look decent.

We were allowed out of the building with our doctor's permission (which I had) so that we could walk in the park or go to the museum. There were frequent field trips to places like the zoo and the planetarium, and sometimes there were tickets to afternoon symphony concerts. Occasionally we had cookouts or picnics. We had to be accompanied by staff members on all these outings, but they wore their own clothes, not hospital uniforms, when we went out, so they seemed less like keepers and more like friends. The food was very good. The nurses and technicians, with very few exceptions, were kind and well trained. It was an admirable facility in almost every way.

But it was while I was a patient there that I found out what it's like to hit bottom and how to stay alive there. Upon admission to the hospital, I had a physical examination and was started on a course of medication. I was given large doses of tranquilizers and an anti-depressant, first by injection to build up the level of the drug in my system, then in pill form to maintain that level. My nose-diving spirits were helped somewhat, but the side effects of the drugs gave me additional problems. My mouth was so dry I could hardly speak. My muscles were tense to the point of rigidity—whether from the illness or the cure, I never found out. I was ferociously restless. I couldn't sit still, couldn't rest, read, listen to music. I couldn't even stand still; I paced up and down the corridor endlessly. I had to keep moving.

Katy, a patient whose problems seemed quite similar to mine, sometimes used to pace the floor with me, or we would pass and repass each other in the hallway. We had a series of running jokes that we tossed out to each other as we passed. One was based on a floor wax commercial that we improvised as we went along: "Our product was used on this hall floor, paced by a wardful of certified madwomen for sixty days. See how brightly it still sparkles!"

But I didn't feel I was sparkling very brightly. Away from my home and family, all my morbid shyness returned. I was afraid people would think I was stupid or worthless. When they would eventually tell me so—which I expected to happen at any time—I would see that they were right. Because the hospital was so expensive, I felt that the other patients were all much richer than I and somehow more experienced with the world. (By and large, this was true, but it didn't matter the way I thought it did.) Without my family around me, I was deprived of the only way I knew to relate to other people. When I couldn't say, in effect, "See who I am! I'm the mother of these children, that's who I am!" When I couldn't define my identity in terms of my maternal role, I felt utterly lost and stranded.

Under other circumstances I might have tried my second-string repertoire, that of "Saint," but I wasn't doing too well on that score and I didn't think I could bring it off. I felt adrift, without identity. There were only two things I knew about myself: I was trying to be a "Mother" and trying to be a "Saint." Otherwise, I hadn't the faintest idea who I was. I used to beseech the staff just to tell me who they wanted me to be and what they wanted me to do and I'd do it instantly. This hanging around minus my usual persona and without a new human face to replace it was a source of genuine terror to me. We kidded about it with wry humor, but I know the staff read the real terror within me. Although there are no words that can help with that terror, the staff helped in other ways. I felt in them a wordless understanding of how hard all this could be and a reassurance that it was a problem for which there would be a solution, even if none of us could say at that time what it would be.

Bill, one of the technicians, helped me most. He was almost the first person I talked to when I was left on the ward on the day of my admission, and we hit it off instantly. He was one of those people who doesn't feel embarrassed or apologetic about walking around with their intelligence showing, which reassured me quite a lot. Bill was a premed student at the state university and was planning to specialize in psychiatry. He had seen combat in the Korean War, which made him a bit older than some of the other students. Like myself, Bill was an observant Catholic, which I found very reassuring. Ever since my experience with Dr. Kelly, I've been aware that some people confuse Catholicism with insanity, or at least with sloppy and unrealistic thinking.

It wasn't that Bill helped by uttering great gems of insight, though he sometimes made remarks that indicated other angles from which the problem in hand could be viewed, and that did help. But what helped me most of all was his human concern for me as an individual. He was willing to talk about anything, to examine things the way they really were, with no barriers between what one ought or ought not to say.

And Helen helped a lot, too. Helen was doing her final work before getting her credentials as a psychiatric nurse. Kirkpatrick was her fieldwork placement. She was supposed to choose two patients, work with them intensively, and make her final case report on them. She chose me as one of her cases. But neither with Bill nor with Helen did I ever feel like subject matter or material for a case report. Neither one made me feel that because I was a patient in a psychiatric ward I was just another hopeless nut, or even that they felt it made me in some way different from them, or inferior. Perhaps for no other reasons than those it helped me a lot to have them around.

I also received help from another unexpected source. The one unbreakable rule on the ward was attendance at morning group therapy. Everyone on the ward attended. The staff doctors took turns presiding. One Saturday morning, instead of the doctor who usually led the group, in strode a stranger with an enormous grin on his face.

"Visitor's Day," he announced, as he cleared the ashtrays and coffee cups off the coffee table and put his feet up. "Now, let's see who wants to get well today."

I was really tickled. All the staff doctors seemed to think that they were being overly directive when they merely said "Good morning," and here was this madman offering instant health! I waved my hand in the air like a fourth grader.

"Are those guaranteed results?" I wanted to know.

"No," he said, "but we'll see what we can do. What are you doing here?"

"Running away from a bad marriage and trying to figure out how to have a baby I don't want. And my daughter was killed and I don't know how to handle myself anymore."

We were off. For the next forty-five minutes we hammered away at the problems just about as fast as we could talk. For the most part, the thirty other people in the room just sat and stared at us. Once the doctor broke off. "I wonder if you realize that you and I are the only two people in this room who understand just what the hell we're talking about."

I looked around and everyone nodded. I could see that it was true. "I didn't realize it," I said, "but I can see that you're right. How come?"

"I don't give people answers. I just give them questions," he said. "But you might give the matter some thought. I imagine it happens to you quite a bit."

About the coming baby, he said, "People don't have babies they don't want. Why are you having this one? Maybe if somebody will still give you a baby, it proves you're not such a bad mother after all."

At this point Irene broke in. Irene was a well-to-do middle-aged mother of nine children. She had come to the ward after what had seemed to be a stroke turned out to have no physical basis at all. She had all the symptoms of heart disease without having heart disease. Irene exploded into the conversation. "I think it's just terrible that you don't want that poor little baby. God gave you that baby. You should want it!"

"Just a minute," said the guest artist, turning to her. "Why are you here?"

"I have headaches," she said, "such awful headaches."

I tried to pick up the conversation with Irene. "Look," I said, "I know I'm supposed to say I want this baby, and I'm not going to kill it. But I don't *feel* that I want it one bit."

"I think there's something wrong with you not to want your own baby," said Irene.

"Why are you talking to her?" interrupted the therapist before I could answer.

"I think she's trying to tell me something I don't know," I said. "Lots of people tell me things I didn't know before, and sometimes they help me figure things out."

"She's not trying to help you," he said rather pointedly.

"Well, maybe I can help her then," I said.

"For God's sake, let her sit there with her headache. She deserves it," he said. Then, speaking very seriously to me, "I want you to pay *very* close attention to what just happened. Think about what you just said to each other. And *remember what I just told you*. Time's up."

"Who on earth's that?" I asked Bill, as the guest therapist left the room.

"Oh," he answered, "he's just about the biggest wheel we get around here."

Well, but there I was, still crawling around the bottom of the world. Most of the time I couldn't get my mind together, couldn't think two sensible thoughts in succession, couldn't sit or stand still. Every night I took my sleeping pill as soon as I was allowed to have it and knocked myself out for twelve hours, only to wake up the next day and begin crawling again on the bottom of the world. Therapy didn't bring relief.

My psychiatrist had a few sessions with Scott alone and a few with both of us together. He suggested I consider separation. I was panic-stricken. I couldn't even begin to consider it. How would I live? I was living the only way I knew, now. I refused to make such a choice. Then at the very least, he said, the two of us should be seen in conjoint therapy. When I was discharged, Scott and I should have joint sessions with the same person; I should not go to one therapist and Scott to another. On that point my psychiatrist was adamant, and when I was discharged those were the arrangements we made. But all that came later.

Meanwhile, I didn't feel I was getting anywhere at all. I was very impatient. But little by little, I found I could talk somewhat in the group therapy sessions. Once or twice another patient came to me after a session and told me, "You said just what I wanted to say but was afraid to."

Looking back now, I can see that I accomplished a good deal while I was a patient at Kirkpatrick, though at the time it seemed I was doing nothing at all. I didn't *feel* any better, God knows, but I was slowly learning to relate to other people simply as myself, not in terms of a role I might be playing, like "Mother" or "Saint." I learned that when I could just be myself, people would often accept me simply as I was, not how I thought I ought to be. And for the first time, a therapist had questioned whether going on with my marriage was a good idea. That terrified me beyond measure and I refused to consider it. In fact, the marriage did go on for quite a bit longer; still the new idea had been expressed and now became one of the factors that could be discussed.

I had lots of visitors. In some ways they were a problem. Scott came at least once a week; I didn't want to see him at all. Several times the children came with him. They looked to me desperately for comfort and reassurance, and I had none to give them. I knew that they needed me and that I was failing them, but I couldn't think what to do. I could not sit or stand still and could hardly speak. What had I to give them?

Father Michaelson came often, a couple of times a week. He was so depressed that *he* could hardly speak. He was in therapy now with a psychiatrist and I could see that he was trying to deal with an enormous load of guilt, much of which centered on me. Each of us was carrying a load so heavy that we had very little to give to the other; nevertheless he came, and we sat together, and it helped.

Other friends dropped by. Sometimes they just paced the floor with me, when that was all that I felt I could do. Visits, cards, letters, phone calls, messages—all let me know that friends were thinking of me and would help me if they could. But the struggle to find oneself is a struggle that everyone has to make essentially alone.

I knew that before long I'd have to leave the hospital and go back to the day-to-day struggle. I dreaded it. How I was going to go on with the daily round of housework and family responsibilities, I couldn't imagine, but I knew that I must and somehow would. (I did discover presently that I had been having an adverse reaction to medication. When I changed to a much lighter dosage of a different tranquilizer, I felt a great deal better and life became more manageable. Sometimes it's difficult to tell the difference between the illness and the cure!)

In the week before I left the hospital, I was considerably startled to find myself pointed out by one of the nurses as exemplifying the way to make progress in the hospital. "Look at Martha," she told one of the other patients. "She's really working hard on the problems that brought her here."

Look at me, indeed, I thought—crying, complaining, and pacing the floor. Both the other patient and I thought that the nurse must be crazy.

I had made three weekend visits home as my stay in the hospital drew to a close. I would come home on Friday night and stay until Sunday. The visits were in no way remarkable. Nothing in the household had changed. I was always glad to get back to the hospital. But the day was drawing near for me to return home for good.

Leaving the hospital meant parting from newly made friends. I owed them so much; their help had been so warm and generous, and most likely I would never see them again. Although Helen's project included follow-up contacts with her patients after their hospital discharge, I lived outside the area for which her project had been funded and her supervisors decided against having her follow up on my case. Both of us were disappointed.

One of the things Helen and I had worked on most was my feeling that I had never had the experience of being a cared-for child. It wasn't based on any actual lack; there was nothing that my parents omitted to do, but there was some kind of emotional component missing for me. The movie *David and Lisa*, about the psychiatric treatment of two troubled adolescents, had just been released at that time. I told Helen how moved I had been by the scene in which Lisa runs away from the school to the museum, where she is found curled up in the lap of the large Henry Moore statue of a mother holding a child. I remember telling Helen how it struck so close to where I was hurting. I told her how much it had meant to me when she had washed my hair; it was a kind of mothering that didn't hit home particularly at the time, yet it stayed with me as a simple demonstration of being cared for in two senses—having something done for me and having someone care about how I felt. With Helen I had the feeling I'd been given a chance to do over something that had originally gone wrong for me.

On the day I left, Helen gave me a copy of *The Little Prince* and said, "Read the section about the Little Prince and the fox. It's the closest I can come to telling you what working with you has meant to me." So I read it, and I have reread it many times since. And though I have not seen Helen again, I know she is my friend and thinks of me still, as I do of her.

Bill also came to see me and said, "There's a list they keep of former patients who can sign themselves back into Kirkpatrick when they feel that they need to. Your name's on the list and they'll take you back whenever you feel you need to come. But honestly, I don't expect we'll ever see you back here again."

For a minute I felt as if my retreat had been cut off. Then I realized that he had just told me I was going to make it.

So I went home from the hospital, home to the same situation I had left.

## esther comments

When Martha speaks of hitting bottom, of crawling around on the bottom and learning somehow to live there, she is speaking in metaphor about something that even yet is too disturbing for her to report in complete, grim detail. One has to be a long distance away from such an experience before one is willing to risk any retelling of it vivid enough to convey what it is actually like, for fear of being drawn down into it again.

Like every other human experience, the exact happening is unique to the person who undergoes it. Symptoms vary widely, but I think that an acute and intense struggle for survival of selfhood is usually going on at some level, in the face of conflicting forces both within and outside of the self. There may be a feeling of losing oneself —almost of a dissolving of the self—in a seemingly bottomless pit of unassimilable emotions, of which not even some psychotic kind of sense can be made. Or there may be a state of utter terror as one feels oneself on the brink of such a loss. Sometimes there is a partial, in-and-out-of-touch experience: One never entirely loses hold of oneself or the world, though that hold is extremely precarious. There is the possibility, too, of making the choice to put an end to the agony by putting an end to the self.

Such professional descriptions, however, cannot really describe an experience that is a waking nightmare to the person who undergoes it. Once having lived through it, one may have a need to forget or to repress it, but there also may be a need to incorporate it into one's sense of an ongoing, viable self. Martha has taken the latter course and used a somewhat light touch in the process, which tells me she has found a constructive way of handling it for herself.

Martha's story is no longer essentially raw data, unevaluated and unrevised in the light of later insights. Already there are some important differences in her feelings. In her account of her conversations with her psychologist friend, there is a high level of sophistication and a healthy sense of humor, as well as a kind of psychological astuteness that seemed quite beyond Martha's reach in the earlier part of her story. Her effort at an open-minded attitude toward minimal response from a psychiatrist may have been due to a growing ability at that time to be aware of "good vibes"—or it may be a second thought arising out of her present therapeutic work. And, of course, there is always the possibility that this was the first "silent" psychiatrist who was really hearing Martha. In any case, she was finally experiencing a therapeutic program that met her needs. What begins to come through clearly is that under favorable conditions Martha has a very considerable inner reserve of good will toward both men and women on which to draw.

Martha had to pay a high price for the rigid strength she demanded of herself throughout the period of tragedy. The woman is expected to hold the strands of life together for everyone, to sustain the emotional fabric of existence for the whole family. Martha's recognition of her inability to do so any longer suggested to her that she was falling apart, so closely had she identified herself with her role as a woman.

Martha was bitter, but her bitterness is expressed in an ironic reference to a religious concept (her "perfect model of submission to the will of God"), not in a reference to the man of religion to whom one might have expected it to be directed. In her reaction to Father Michaelson's withdrawal from his previous position, Martha seems to have drawn on every ounce of her capacity for accepting another's need even though it meant her own greater need would go unmet. There had to be considerable residual anger somewhere. Father Michaelson's help in finding a treatment resource must have been very much a bittersweet thing, for it so painfully symbolized his retreat from the untenable role of lover to the tenable one of pastoral counselor. Yet Martha needed whatever Father Michaelson could still give her as a friend, and she was not about to let her disappointment get in the way of that.

Martha's choice to continue to place her faith in Father Michaelson at this point was a choice for love against hate. Whatever the hidden psychological cost to herself, it was a healthy choice.

From the beginning of Martha's story, her marriage sounds as though it had long been dead, if it had ever had viable life at all.

People often stay in dead marriages—dead, that is, from the standpoint of any surviving spark of spontaneous love, passionate or compassionate, sexual or platonic, sibling or companionate. To the extent that such people stay together for truly realistic reasons, are aware of what they are doing, and have no need to punish one another for the demise of the love there had once been, these may be true "marriages of convenience." Such marriages do little harm to either partner, even to the children. When a marriage is dead, however, and the partners do not know it (or cannot face it) but stay together for unconscious neurotic reasons, a great deal of harm may be done, and to everyone concerned.

Martha seems instinctively to have known, however much she must have been reeling from the shift in Father Michaelson's position, that it is better to preserve what is left of a living relationship than to do false obeisance to the remains of a dead one. It was not only that she couldn't get the love and emotional support she needed from Scott—she had obviously long given up on that—it was also that she constantly had to be on guard against him because she feared the power he had been able to wield for so long.

From Martha's description of what actually happened, it appears she was able to insist on the kind of help it seemed to her she needed, whatever Scott said or did. This indicates that she was finally able to bring some anger to bear constructively on her own behalf. As a result, one begins to question whether Scott was as powerful and persuasive as Martha thinks, or as able to control her as he seemed to have been in the past. Certainly, it is clear that the hospital staff was of no mind to depart from its judgment and accept Scott's. As a matter of fact, Scott's need to control the situation seems to have been acute, and one gets the impression of a man who must be desperately afraid of something. Without sufficient facts to understand the basis for such fear, I would guess that it might be related to the prospect of Martha's going away, as though he could not function without her even for a short span of time. If so, it would seem that Scott may have been as dependent on Martha as she was on him. Had she been able to see this, she might have gotten some sense of her own potential power and persuasiveness.

Martha, however, was in no position to recognize her strength at that time. Her willingness to accept two young staff members, both students, as surrogate parents was not only a tribute to them but also a measure of her need to reexperience her beginnings in a different way. Martha describes in such loving detail what the young psychiatric nurse did for her that there can be no question how strong the yearning to be cared for must have been behind the facade of brittle strength she had displayed. Martha was getting a second chance, though a very brief and limited one, to be a child again and to be cared for as a child—but in a new way and with different people. Although Bill and Helen were no doubt younger than Martha, they had personal qualities compatible with her image of what a father and mother should be; thus, they provided a rock-bottom experience of trust that had previously been missing.

The ward as a whole seemed to provide the kind of therapeutic milieu about which one hears a great deal but which is not all that prevalent in actual fact. There seems to have been a genuine camaraderie among the ward patients. Even in the group therapy session with the "big wheel," only one of the patients attacked Martha, though the "prize pupil" role, especially when so openly encouraged by the professor himself, usually doesn't make for much popularity with other group members. That Martha didn't recognize she was being attacked was not surprising (there were so many things Martha didn't recognize in those days), but if you don't know you are being attacked, you are in no position to defend yourself. Martha is well aware of her debt of gratitude to the "big wheel" for rescuing her from this state of danger.

It is interesting to note Martha's panic at the suggestion of separation from Scott. Her reaction is one so prevalent among women, even among those who have had some experience of self-sufficiency, that her panic must be viewed as an entirely "normal" reaction. This is especially so in her case because she had had very little experience on her own, had three young children to care for, was pregnant, and had just gone through a most devastating tragedy. Had she felt no anxiety, she would indeed have been "crazy." But Martha recognized the importance of putting the thought into words: If it could be said, it was obviously no longer unthinkable.

It is only when the possibility of breaking out of a relationship is fully faced that a person can truly make a decision to stay in it. Otherwise, there is no alternative and no choice is actually being made. To consider separation is to see whether there is any reason to stay, which may save a marriage as well as end it. But to consider separation at all seems an enormous risk to any woman who suffers from the conviction that she, not her marriage, is hopeless.

Martha went home from the hospital to the same situation she had left, but with a commitment to look at the marriage in joint sessions with Scott. This prospect could only seem a threatening one to her, for she was not yet aware of the new strength she might be able to bring to bear on the situation.

## martha continues

Nothing had changed, except that I was in some strange way less able to handle things than before. Now I felt saddled with a permanent diagnosis of "crazy." Anything I might do, however reasonable to me or pertinent to the situation I was dealing with, any action not instantly self-explanatory, anything odd, would reinforce that diagnosis. I knew what had happened in the past, and I had a pretty good idea that Scott would be right there to help the situation along. But now it had an official seal of approval on it: "My wife has had some serious emotional problems. She was in a mental hospital, you know." If ever we differed on anything, who would believe me now?

The months after I came out of the hospital were some of the hardest in my life. I don't like to think back on them now. I made it, living not so much one day at a time as one hour at a time. I slept a lot, whenever I could. I looked after the house and the children as best I could. Slowly I prepared for the coming baby. I still felt tense and rigid. Everything was grey, hopeless. I could not imagine the future as happier than the present.

Slowly, I began to be aware of a change in Scott. For the first time in my memory, he seemed to be trying to put some effort into the marriage and the family. Instead of shutting himself in his room on weekends, sometimes he would let the kids come in and talk to him or he would even sit in the living room or at the dining-room table so that he could see them at their normal activities. Sometimes, too, he would sit down and have a cup of coffee with me and carry on a conversation. Instead of going to the movies alone, he would ask if I wanted to come along.

Looking back, I think that Becky's death had shocked him into the realization that the "someday" he had told himself he would get to know his family and participate in our life together might never come, that good intentions can't be left safely for the future. The future is too uncertain for that. Scott's chance to spend time with Becky and know her and love her was gone for good. Good intentions can only count in the here and now. And now he was trying.

I tried, too, tried to accept what he offered, tried to be more open with him, tell him more of what was going on with me. Always in the past, when he had, for instance, taken something I had said seriously and twisted it and ridiculed it and me, he had somehow conveyed that he did it deliberately. Tomorrow he might choose to do differently, or maybe tomorrow I would be more worthy of his respect and he would be more inclined to take me seriously. If I just tried a little harder, tomorrow he might make a different choice. And so I kept trying harder. I had always thought that maybe tomorrow he would come around and everything would get better.

Now Scott had come around, and nothing got better. It was clear that he was aware of what he had been doing and that he meant to quit the sadistic routine he'd been following for so many years. He was trying hard to make personal contact, both with me and with the children, to include himself in our lives. It was then that I realized that he couldn't change. The incidents went on just as they always had. In fact, as we proceeded with the conjoint therapy at City Mental Hygiene, they became crueler and more devious. Now when he tried to relate to all of us, it just didn't work. There was no sense of the person inside the gesture, so to speak. The whole sense of human relationship was just missing.

Most deadly of all, I simply couldn't trust him. Scott and I had been together for fourteen years. Not one day had been free from destructive land mines in the territory between us. How could I trust him? He was making what was clearly a last-ditch attempt to improve things between us. Now or never. We both tried very hard. And nothing changed. Clearly, it was never. This was the gist of what emerged, slowly, in our joint work with Malcolm Rogers at the clinic. And it was I who finally bombed out of therapy there.

Things had begun well enough. I think when we started conjoint therapy Scott's intentions were mainly honest. I was just out of the hospital; Becky's death was still fresh and painful. It was apparent we were going to have to do something with the marriage if we were to have any viable living situation at all. We settled down to weekly sessions with Malcolm Rogers.

To describe Mal is to explain in part what went wrong. A solid, dependable man, intelligent and kind rather than brilliant, with a not too sophisticated sense of humor. Everybody's idea of a nice guy. Predictable. At first, things went smoothly. We were Mal's first clients in the morning. Because mornings were often chilly as well as rainy at that time of the year, Scott and I always stopped on the way and bought three cups of coffee to take out. We'd bring them to the clinic and the three of us had coffee as we talked. Everything was friendly and informal. That phase lasted perhaps a month or six weeks.

Since Mal was not an M.D., my medications were prescribed by one of the doctors on the clinic staff. When my medication level was reduced, I felt a great deal better, more relaxed, less rigid. With a change to a different and much milder tranquilizer, some of the perception problems I'd had—floors slanting uphill, shifting and wobbling walls, and so on—which I'd thought were part of my illness disappeared overnight. As I felt better and more myself, the family began to settle back into its routine again.

In early October Benjy was born. I was so relieved not to have had a daughter. I was still tense and angry about the pregnancy and, to say the least, ambivalent about having another child. I remember saying to myself as the nurse hoisted me onto the delivery table, "If it would do the least bit of good, I'd get up right now and walk out."

The obstetrician did less than nothing to help. This was the fourth child of mine he'd delivered. (Heaven only knows why I went on with him, except that at the time I didn't know there was such a creature as an obstetrician who liked and respected women and the process of birth.) My labor pattern in all four deliveries was identical. Contractions never became regular. I'd just poke on and on for hours and then deliver the baby very suddenly, with only a few minutes of warning. (I had delivered my third child myself in the back seat of the next-door neighbor's car on the way to the hospital, because the same idiot doctor kept saying to me on the phone, "Let's wait and see what happens." We waited, and that's what happened.)

When I arrived at the hospital, I reminded the doctor how the other deliveries had been and how quickly the baby had arrived each time once, so to speak, he'd made up his mind. Yes, yes, he said, and went to sleep in the doctors' quiet room. I had a chance to talk with the anesthetist, a marvelous woman who told me about delivering her first baby herself while walking on the hospital grounds during her residency. I told her I'd watched all my other kids being born and I wanted to watch this one, too. She agreed it would be silly to miss the fun, once I'd gotten this far. A little after midnight she came to tell me she was going to lie down and that the nurse would call her when I came closer to delivery. "Anyhow," she added, "you may not need me."

Just past two, the baby decided it was time. The nurses on

night duty brought me into the delivery room at top speed, but they had a hard time rousing the doctor. Benjy was in the middle of being born when the doctor trotted into the room, calling for the nurses to tell me to hold back so he could get ready. I was furious. This was the fourth time this had happened. I'd reminded him of it just two hours ago. He wasn't exactly donating his services, and I damned well didn't see why I should make myself uncomfortable for his convenience. It wasn't his labor, it was mine, and we were going to do it my way this time.

"She doesn't seem to be holding back, Doctor," said the nurse, understating the matter somewhat.

"Put her out," he said, but the anesthetist was still asleep upstairs.

And suddenly there was Benjy. The doctor reached me in time to catch him. He never did get his hands washed.

Benjy at birth was rather small and severely jaundiced. His liver didn't seem to be functioning and for almost ten days he was kept in the hospital. The pediatric staff watched him closely and made blood tests constantly. If he didn't get better quickly, the doctors were set to do a complete blood change, to exchange all his blood for new blood from a donor. But Benjy held his own, at last turned pink instead of yellow, and began to grow.

I welcomed him as best I could. Despite my confused and conflicted feelings, I couldn't not love him. There he was, a completely new and separate person, a bundle of his own individuality, another fresh start for the human race. So we settled in to begin our journey together. For the two weeks after Benjy was born, before I was really up to my full schedule again, Mal Rogers came to the house and we had our weekly therapy hour there. It was very kind of him to come. We worked diligently, but things were very faintly sour.

I see I'm going to have to stop here and say something about Scott's penchant for manipulating people. It was awesome—and fascinating. He was perfectly capable—I saw him do it once—of privately telling three people, more or less strangers to each other, something rather scandalous and totally imaginary about one another. ("Joe is a homosexual, but he doesn't want anyone to know; I hope you won't mention it to him," or "Jim drinks more than is good for him. We'll have to help him watch it tonight. I know you won't say anything about it.") Then he would sit down together with them and orchestrate the conversation so that each had the illusion that all were agreed on what they were talking about, yet each version of that conversation would have been completely at odds with every other, and each person would have been shocked and horrified at the other versions. In its way, the manipulation was brilliant. Scott thought it was hilarious. To me it seemed like the ultimate betrayal of human communication. It was based on his very considerable ability to predict what anyone would think or say next.

Little by little, the therapy hours began to show signs of Scott's little game. Mal was a man utterly devoid of malice and surely no match for Scott, who at any given time was at least three jumps ahead of him. Slowly but very surely, a picture called *The Trouble with This Marriage* began to emerge during the therapy hours.

One of Scott's most brilliant social accomplishments was his ability to put over a particular kind of straight-faced verbal hoax. It could be hilarious to watch, and it was fascinating to see him do it. It was one of the first things that attracted me to him. In the course of a conversation, without any warning and without the faintest change in his facial expression, Scott would begin to interject details of his fantastical subject, a sort of tall story introduced detail by small detail. Nothing in his face or manner alerted you to the fact that he was putting you on. He would progress earnestly, each detail just faintly more beyond belief than the last. But each detail counterfeited reality so artfully that even when you slowly began to realize that what he was saying couldn't be so, the earnestness of his expression kept you somehow believing him.

Scott would gradually build to his conclusion: In Albania they raise a breed of dog that can fly, or a well-known Japanese painter will paint nothing but black furniture in dark rooms—whatever he had decided to convince you of. Then without a break he would return to rational conversation, with nothing to indicate his humorous intent. If no one stopped him in the course of the conversation, the fact that he was kidding would never be mentioned at all. He was so utterly convincing, his details were so realistic, that I am willing to bet there are to this day a few people walking around who believe in flying Albanian dogs.

Even when we had been married for years, Scott could still string me along for a little way. It was a very long time indeed before I had any confidence in my own ability to tell when he was kidding and when he was not. In the vast majority of cases his intent in this game was innocent. For him, I think, it served as a kind of social testing. It told him what manner of person he was dealing with at the moment, how gullible, how anxious to be convinced. As our relationship over the years grew progressively embittered, this game sometimes came to have aspects that, from my point of view, were considerably less innocent. Friends (mainly those in our circle who were primarily his friends rather than our friends as a couple) began to regard me a bit quizzically and became—how shall I put it?—inordinately supportive but very watchful of my behavior, especially at parties and social gatherings. In conversations with me, one or two referred to my "problem." Well, I thought, that wasn't so unnatural. I was, after all, just out of a mental hospital. Finally somebody spilled the beans: Scott was telling people I was a secret alcoholic.

In therapy hours with Mal Rogers, I faced Scott with it. The result was a disaster beyond my wildest nightmare. Mal, kind and understanding, was also very decidedly serious, hardly the type to be on familiar terms with a Machiavellian sense of humor. Scott turned the situation inside out so skillfully that it took my breath away. Looking back now, I can see that he felt he was fighting for his sanity if not for his life. At the time, all I knew was that he was subverting the therapy to the point where it was much worse than useless.

"She has no sense of reality," he told Mal. "She can't tell what my intentions are. I kid her a little when we're with other people and she immediately jumps to the conclusion that I'm out to get her. I know it's only part of her illness, but it's really hard to live with."

And Scott followed this up with demonstrations in the therapy hours. Mal was so predictable; it was easy for Scott to tell in advance what he would fall for. My religious beliefs, in particular, were my Achilles heel. There is a fairly large body of misconceptions, even among intelligent and well-intentioned people, about Catholic doctrine. Scott knew what in fact I did believe, but he also saw what Mal could easily be convinced of. And he played it both ways, brilliantly. My reactions were, to say the least, not helpful in assuring anyone of my stability. I howled with shock and betrayal. Scott had once believed these things, too. How could he now use them against me?

"Can't you see," I implored Mal, "how he's using your misconceptions of what I believe to prove I'm crazy? Of course I get emotional about it. Can't you see what he's doing?"

Most infuriating of all was that at home Scott admitted it. "For Christ's sake," he said. "It's just a joke. I'm just stringing him along a little—you know I do that all the time. You've always thought it was funny yourself. Why get so upset about it now? Besides, if he can't even see what I'm doing, how can I respect him enough to do serious therapy with him? If he can see it, I'll respect him, but if he can't, then why should I take him seriously?"

"But Scott, Scott, he can't see! He's not a person who *can* see this kind of thing. And this is therapy. He's not just a family friend. This is our last chance to pull the marriage together. Please play it straight, *please.*"

Then Scott would apologize and say he wouldn't do it again. In the next therapy hour, I would turn to him and say, "Tell Mal about the discussion we had when we got home last week, tell him what you said to me then. Mal, he's admitted what he's doing. He said he'd explain it to you and promised not to do it again."

"There she goes again," Scott would say. "She has no sense of my real intentions toward her. She keeps insisting I'm trying to prejudice you against her. I know she can't help it, but I really wish she could take a joke."

Scott held forth one night at a dinner party we gave, demonstrating to the guests what he was up to in therapy. He played all three parts, mimicking Mal and me to the life and improvising a sample dialogue as he went along. It was hilariously funny. The guests laughed till they cried. It was so wickedly accurate that, bitter as I was, even I laughed.

It was only to Mal that he wouldn't admit to his verbal hoaxes, and Mal could never see them for himself. Patiently, he tried to free me of my delusions. Hysterically, I tried to convince him of Scott's game. My very emotional response, of course, counted heavily against me. Scott was so calm, so reasonable. And what therapist wants to be convinced that he's got the picture all wrong?

So, at last I quit. I explained to Mal as straightforwardly as I could that in these circumstances therapy was simply another and very heavy liability to me. There was no way in the world that it could do me any good, and if it continued as it had been going, it was bound to do me great harm. Very simply, my survival was at stake. I had been receiving my medication from a doctor at the clinic, however, and although the therapy had not helped (to say the least), the medication had. I wanted to go on with the tranquilizers if some way could be arranged.

The doctor who had prescribed my medication at City Mental Hygiene Clinic sent a letter of referral to Alfred Williams, a doctor in private practice with a good deal of experience with medication for psychiatric patients. Dr. Williams was, as it happened, a personal friend of Mal Rogers. He continued to prescribe the same medication I had been taking before, and I continued on with my life as best I could, hanging on by the skin of my teeth. Scott stayed on alone in therapy with Mal.

After about six months, Dr. Williams called me in for a medications review and really laid it on the line.

"Now look," he said after he had sat me down in his office. "I just can't go on prescribing this stuff for you. You are taking a very strong medication and it's no joke. The drug is so new we simply do not know what its long-range effects on the human body are. There is a very strong possibility that prolonged use may affect you seriously. We think in particular it may cause severe and irreversible damage to the liver. By no means can I prescribe it lightly. And that's not all.

"You are taking this stuff without any attempt at therapy. I can't have you walking around on the streets, thinking and doing God knows what. According to Mal, you are really a serious nut. I can't, in professional conscience, give tranquilizing drugs to real kooks if they refuse to make some attempt to get better."

Just at that moment the phone rang. "Here," he said, "you may as well read this." And he handed me a letter from the file sitting on his desk. Dr. Williams was on the phone for a while. I had time to read the letter three times. What I read shocked me speechless.

It was the referral letter from City Mental Hygiene Clinic written by the doctor who had prescribed my medication, not even by anyone who had ever seen me in therapy at all. *Diagnosis:* Schizophrenic with paranoid delusions. *Prognosis:* Poor. Constant hallucinations. (I had told him I had visual distortions with the first tranquilizer; they disappeared overnight when my medication was changed.) There were a couple of quotes from things I had said to him in one or another of our three or four meetings, taken so hopelessly out of context that it was impossible to make sense of them. The letter ended with the statement: Discontinued therapy because of inability to deal therapeutically with paranoid delusional system relating to her husband, who remains in therapy.

I was absolutely thunderstruck. I literally saw red. (Interesting to discover that that phrase is not just a figure of speech!)

"Well," Dr. Williams said when he finished his phone conversation and turned back to me, "what about it?"

"Just this," I said. "I never heard such a bunch of bullshit in my life. In the first place, the guy who wrote it knows virtually nothing about me at all. In the second place, everything he says I said is taken so totally out of context that there's no indication of what I really meant at all.

"I have lived with my husband for fifteen years. In all of that time, not one month has passed without his showing overt signs of mental illness. He openly admits to me that he hears voices, feels hands touching him, not just once or twice in his lifetime but often, really often, sometimes almost daily. To this day, he truly believes he can influence the score of a baseball game by listening to it on the radio and exerting his 'special' powers.

"He has threatened the children, he has threatened me. I have seen him do things and heard him say things you would hardly believe—I hardly believe them myself. I have spent all of these years doing my damndest to live with him and protect him and keep everyone outside the family from catching on because I thought that's what a good wife does, and anyway that was the agreement he and I had with each other.

"Sure, I have emotional problems. Do you think if you had taken on the job I've tried to do you wouldn't have problems, too? But that he's sane and I'm crazy is just too bloody much. I won't plead guilty to the garbage in this letter, even if that's the price for the medication that makes me able to hack it from day to day. I will not!

"If my husband is now willing to sell me out completely, which it's beginning to be apparent to me that he is, then I'll be God damned if I'll stand for it. He thinks he has to sink me to save himself. He's said that to me many times. I've always kept my mouth shut because that's what I've always thought a good woman does—it's the price a woman pays for her own self-respect. But I won't stand for what's happening now.

"There's a paranoid schizophrenic involved, all right, but it isn't me. And no matter how you try to get me to say that I'm hopelessly crazy, I won't say it and I won't believe it. Because I know that it simply isn't true. Keep your pills, if that's the price I have to pay to get them!"

And I walked out of the office. It was the first time in my life that I lost my temper and said exactly what I felt. It did me a world of good. That was the day I began to get well.

But I was in turmoil. Dr. Williams had no business calling me a kook and a nut. It struck me as scarcely professional behavior. Well, he could either treat me with respect or not at all, that was for certain. If I had to grovel for my medication, I'd be better off without it. The price was too steep. But since I'd left the hospital, I had never been without tranquilizers. Was I sure that I could do without them?

And there was the whole business of Dr. Williams showing me the letter from City Mental Hygiene Clinic. I couldn't tell whether he had done it on the spur of the moment or had thought it out ahead of time and had done it on purpose. The letter itself infuriated me. It was so glib and half-baked. Of course, if that was all Dr. Williams had to go on, it was no wonder he thought of me as a nut and couldn't bring himself to treat me with any respect.

I had always known the doctor who wrote the letter was a fatuous idiot. Many times I'd thanked my stars I hadn't been assigned to work with *him* at City Mental Hygiene. But the letter appeared to be a report on *all* my therapy at the clinic. The only conclusion I could come to was that it represented the thinking of all the previous workers who had dealt with me. And as I thought it over, things I had never been able to understand about my therapy there began to fall into place.

It now seemed to me pretty clear that all my therapists at the clinic had believed they were hearing a nutty report of a straight marriage. Apparently it had never even occurred to anyone who had worked with me to question whether it might not be a straight report of a nutty marriage. That would explain why they were always seeming to be waiting for me to "get somewhere," while I could never figure out what it was they were waiting to hear me say. Of course! They were waiting for me to discover that Scott was perfectly sane and normal, and that I just imagined his saying and doing all those strange things. That would explain why they always hurriedly shooed me off the subject when I began to talk of how strange the marriage was, and why they had so often praised me and extolled my progress when I took the blame for the trouble in the marriage on myself. That had been my growth in "dealing with reality." It would also explain why in fact I never did make any progress. The therapists were trying to adjust my head to a situation that in *real* reality was nutty in the extreme, and nutty enough to buy that I was not.

But had it never, then, occurred to any of those solemn

gentlemen to say to me instead of "Yes, go on" or "And how do you feel about that?" something like "Pardon my asking, but did that really happen?" or even a nice, flat, honest "Sorry, I don't believe you"? I would have been angry, but it would have cleared the air and let us get on with it. As it was, it certainly was beginning to look as though Dr. Williams, detest him as I might, was the first person who'd had a single straightforward thing to say to me. All that those tactful bastards at City Mental Hygiene had done was waste my precious time. I was furious. And I stayed furious. I walked around for weeks in an exhilarating rage.

The diagnosis of schizophrenia, however, had a totally different effect on me. I fought that tooth and nail, insisted it wasn't— couldn't—be true, but secretly, within myself, I was terrified that it might be true. And to me, to be schizophrenic meant exile from the human race forever. It meant that all those relationships I felt were most real, most comforting, were built on delusion. It meant that I could never hope to know what happened among human beings, meant I could perceive the world around me only in a distorting mirror. I fought against saying that about myself, yet secretly I feared and believed it. And there was always the problem of what I would do when I came to the end of my dwindling supply of tranquilizers.

Then, unexpectedly, Tom Flynn, whom we knew through our contacts with the Catholic Worker movement, asked if we would like to use his place on Atherton Island for a vacation. Tom's dream was to move his family out to the country. Himself a carpenter, he and a couple of helpers were building a house on the island whenever he could find time between jobs and on weekends. He had the roof and walls up, and there was running water and electricity; beyond that, the house had no luxuries, but to me it sounded like heaven. Scott vetoed Tom's idea. Such a vacation wasn't his style, and besides he couldn't get off work right now.

I'd always loved the island. I asked Tom whether he'd mind if the children and I went alone.

"Fine," said Tom.

"Impossible," said Scott. He didn't have time to drive us out.

Anyhow, we'd be stranded there without a car, and he needed the car to get to work.

"Not really a problem," said Tom. "Sally and the kids stay there without a car sometimes for a couple of weeks at a time. It's only about a mile to the village if you really need something, and the beach isn't much of a walk at all."

There was still no way to get out there if Scott declined to take us, but that proved not to be an insoluble problem. A couple of friends agreed to drive us out, along with supplies for a week and a half, and pick us up when we were ready to come back. It was one of the few times in our marriage I can remember presenting Scott with an accomplished fact.

The time the children and I spent on the island that summer stands as a landmark in my life, not so much because anything new or instructive happened there but because while we were there together I became aware of the world in a whole new way. We camped in the house, sleeping bags on the floor, a hot plate for cooking. Sanitation was an outhouse around back—Tom hadn't connected the sewer system yet. The dirt road ran by the front door, but no cars passed in all the time we were there. Benjy was just beginning to walk a bit; he could toddle around to his heart's delight without my having to worry about where he might be. The older kids were free to roam. Once or twice a day we plopped Benjy into the stroller and hiked to the beach. None of us are strong swimmers, but the tidepools were endlessly fascinating. All of us waded and whooped and hollered and built sandcastles, collected shells, sat and watched the ocean. We went to bed tired out each night and woke up in the morning to smell clean country smells. There was no sound all day but the wind in the trees, the birds, and the children playing.

And every day as I woke, I tried to figure out what it was in myself that was so different. Something in me was changing. I didn't know how to name it. I could never remember a time in my life when I wasn't sorry to wake up in the morning and open my eyes to the world. Suddenly, that was gone. I awoke one morning on the front porch, where I had been sleeping. It was barely daylight. The mist was beginning to lift a little. Everything was silent. I lay there quietly and looked at the world and I knew what was different. I was happy! This was how it could be, to wake up in the morning to a world you liked, to go through the day without worry and guilt, to fall asleep at night because you were tired—not just because you couldn't bear the world anymore—and to wake up again in the morning, still happy.

So, after all, it could happen to me, too. I had always thought that some people were not meant to be happy. It was simply their lot in life to suffer; God alone knew why. They were set at cross-purposes with all the world; it was useless for them to seek or expect happiness. For them—for me—it was a waste of time. All the time I'd been in therapy, to posit happiness as a goal seemed out of the question. If it really existed at all, it was meant for The Others. I had no picture in my mind of what I was trying to reach. Now suddenly, living quietly on the island, happiness was simply put into my hand as a gift. I could be happy. I could be free.

(I have, to this day, two strings of shells that the children had strung that summer. They're hanging beside the bathroom mirror; I see them every day. Sasha said to me one day not long ago, "Why don't you take those shells out of the bathroom, Mom? No one really looks at them anymore." But she's wrong. I look at them almost every day, and I never see them without being reminded: I can be happy, too.)

I stopped taking tranquilizers while we were away. My stomach was upset for a couple of days and I felt mildly nauseated, but that was all. I was frightened, braced for a God-knows-what onslaught of depression. I wondered whether my suicidal fantasies would return in force. That was one reason I had wanted to be out there on the island. I thought I couldn't possibly kill myself if I were alone in the country with the children and they were dependent on me. But it was all right. The nausea passed, the days went on, and I was still happy.

Of course, that peaceful time ended at last. We went back to town and to the struggle of getting from day to day. But I've never lost what I gained on the island.

## esther comments

This section of Martha's story begins with the "old" Martha still very much in evidence: feeling helpless in the face of whatever interpretation Scott might choose to put on her hospitalization, despite the utter clarity in her own mind of what had actually been the case. But progress made is rarely completely lost, and with Martha I have every reason to expect, whatever the momentary setbacks, that it will continue.

Until now, I have not come to know Scott very well. Martha has been slow to describe his symptoms, and though I gathered they were very disturbing, I didn't realize how disturbing. I can now understand that day-to-day living in close proximity with such psychotic manifestations would be extremely difficult and would put a tremendous strain on Martha's strength and stability. Just to withstand contamination by proximity to such symptoms is difficult enough for people trained to it; it is no task for the amateur—especially one who is a member of the family—to say nothing of an insecure, emotionally and financially dependent wife.

I have also had glimpses through Martha's eyes that suggest quite different facets of Scott's personality. His intelligence, his wit, his ability to attract people around him and to influence them, all the attributes that must have drawn Martha to him in the first place. Now I begin to get a view of Scott's behavior, both within the home and in therapy hours, that goes a long way toward explaining how Martha could have become confused and why she would have felt so powerless.

Scott seems to be a brilliant man whose gifts, had they been channeled into some creative medium—the theater, for instance, where he could have established a legitimate mastery over his material and made legitimate use of his remarkable talents—might have won him fame and fortune. Instead, he amuses himself by his skillful manipulation of others for purposes ranging from the ostensibly humorous through a variety of probably defensive ploys to a Machiavellian brand of gamesmanship that could easily become a threat to his own sanity as well as to that of his targets. How does one know when such a man is being dangerously destructive or when he is simply indulging a malicious sense of humor?

If the therapist was no match for Scott, it is not surprising that Martha had been unable to hold her own or that she was often caught in the intricate webs he could weave. There is an additional risk in all this, too, far beyond that of the ordinary neurotic games people play. Wit, as Freud pointed out, often has as part of its process the employment of faulty thinking. It can be the faultiness of the thinking that is exactly the cream of the jest. The audience as well as the jester and the butt of the joke all participate in this departure from realistic thinking. Much wit is motivated by hostility and is an indirect form of attack. Scott's wit was so skillfully placed as to prevent effective retaliation by the victim, a situation that made it extremely difficult for Martha to get across to any outsider exactly what was happening.

Martha's material also indicates the existence of competitive behavior in the marriage. Because competition is built into our society, it is often looked upon as simply a fact of life and thus not really examined at all. Competitiveness between husband and wife is not a rare and remarkable occurrence, nor is it necessarily sick. In an atmosphere of mutual respect, with a healthy sense of humor on both sides, it may add spice to a relationship. Where respect is lacking and humor is distorted, however, competitiveness may take a malignant form.

When neither partner has enough self-esteem nor enough outside recognition, which was certainly the case with Martha and no doubt with Scott also, and when both have psychotic symptoms of some sort, competition may come to be expressed by questioning who is the sick one, or who is sicker, or even who is driving the other crazy. This kind of interaction between husband and wife cannot be dismissed as mere game-playing, or simply part of the battle of the sexes, or just a transferred sibling rivalry to be analyzed away. It has within it the seeds of destruction, and the spouse with less ego strength or the poorer defenses is the one in greater danger. It can become a life-and-death struggle, and it must be taken with the utmost seriousness.

I am reminded of the desperate attachment and deadly competitiveness between Zelda and Scott Fitzgerald, the tragic denouement of their marriage, and the fact that only recently have significant voices been raised on Zelda's behalf. A couple need be neither so gifted nor so glamorous to fall into the same trap; given the malignant form of competitiveness between the two, one or the other or both may be in danger of a similar fate.

But Martha is now taking up arms in her own behalf, and once she does so, the outcome seems to be assured. Martha, in the midst of it, cannot feel so certain. She is obviously becoming a "new" Martha, and a very angry one indeed. It was not until her sojourn on Atherton Island that she discovered the other side of the coin, the happy Martha. (Would that every woman could have her own island refuge in time of need!) Martha recognized immediately she had found something there that would always remain with her.

Anger remains, too. Anger is a necessary weapon, but it is a dangerous and deadly one, for it can as easily be turned against oneself as against another.

## martha continues

Just after Thanksgiving, all the kids came down with terrible colds.
It had been an especially cold month; we'd even had a little snow.
The children had been out and around in all the bitter weather, so
it wasn't really surprising that they all had coughs and raw throats.
Peter and Sasha were quickly ready to go back to school and Benjy
was his active self again, but Ann's cold lingered on and turned into
bronchitis. I took her to the clinic. The doctor tapped her chest and
peered down her throat, gave us a prescription for antibiotics, told
me to keep her in bed and not to worry. The inactivity was hard on
Ann's patience. What ten-year-old wants to stay in bed week after
week?

Still she was cooperative, remained quietly indoors, and
took her pills. (She had a terrible time swallowing those enormous
capsules, and we ended up taking them apart and mixing them
with orange juice or sprinkling them over ice cream, anything we
could think of to help get them down.) Then she developed laryngitis. She whispered and squeaked when she tried to talk and
could hardly make us understand what she was trying to say. The
cough and bronchitis slowly retreated, but the laryngitis hung on
and on.

I took Ann back to the clinic. This time the pediatrician
looked really concerned. He gave Ann a very thorough examination
and put her through a series of tests for a wide variety of respiratory
ailments. He asked us to return in two days, with the understanding
that if none of the tests indicated where the trouble lay and if her
condition had not greatly improved he would insist on hospitalizing
her. Scott and I spent the two days in terror. Once you've lost a child,
the natural assumption that your children will always be all right, the
magic sense of invulnerability, vanishes.

We tried hard not to convey our fears to Ann. Scott took her
to the return appointment and phoned me late in the morning to say
she had been admitted to the hospital.

"What do they think the trouble is?" I asked. "Didn't they suggest anything?"

"They can't find anything wrong," he said. "All the tests were completely negative. They're going to give her a complete neurological exam this afternoon. The doctor said you could come in to see him about five o'clock."

Frightened and puzzled, I went to the hospital that afternoon. I visited with Ann for a little while. She was still speechless and obviously apprehensive. The grown-ups were behaving very strangely, and no one would tell her what was wrong with her. I read to her for a little while, and we talked about being in the hospital. Then I had to leave to get dinner for the other children, but I promised to come back during the evening visiting hours.

As I was leaving the hospital, the nurse caught up with me. "Dr. Crosby would like to talk to you," she said.

I turned back to the nursing station on the pediatric ward to talk to the resident who had charge of Ann's case.

"Can't you tell me what's the matter?" I asked. "Did the neurological exam show anything?"

"Mrs. Morgan, all of the tests were completely negative. There is absolutely nothing physically the matter with your daughter."

"But that doesn't make sense," I said. "What about the laryngitis? And if she's not sick, what is she doing in the hospital?"

"I didn't say that nothing was the matter," he replied, "only that nothing is physically wrong. I'm afraid that her illness is emotional. This is what we refer to as hysteria. It doesn't mean crying and carrying on, you understand. It means—"

"Yes, I know what hysteria means," I cut him off, only to find that I had nothing to say. Poor little Ann, how really desperate she must be! I felt powerless to help her. How could this actually be happening? Dr. Crosby broke in on my thoughts.

"I had a long conversation with your husband this morning when we admitted her," he said. "I gather you have a long history of emotional disorder. Spent quite some time in a mental hospital, I think he said."

All my old fears came breaking in on me. So it was true, then. Just to have me for a mother was sufficient to disable my children. Hard as I'd tried to protect them, it had all been useless. If they stayed with me, they were doomed.

Dr. Crosby went on earnestly. "Tell me, Mrs. Morgan, do you use your child for company? Do you treat her as your child or as an equal?"

My head was spinning. What could I tell him? Suppose it was all true, really all my fault? That letter Dr. Williams had shown me . . . it all tied together. Here was this man waiting for me to tell him it was my fault. I knew what he wanted to hear, what he expected me to say, but what was the truthful answer to his question?

"I don't know," I said slowly. "Of course, in some ways she is my equal."

"Mrs. Morgan," he said quickly, "no child can stand that. Let me urge you to consider a course that can change your child's life. Will you seriously consider foster placement for her? Is there an aunt who could raise her, or a grandmother? Or perhaps the county could help you find a family more able to give her the normal childhood she needs."

"I don't want to do that to Ann," I said. "If we put her in a foster home, she'd surely think we didn't want her. And I love her so much." I was in tears.

Dr. Crosby raised his big, earnest eyes to mine. "Think of your daughter, Mrs. Morgan. Do you want her life to be what yours has been?"

He had asked me the question for which I had no reply. We simply stood there and stared at each other for a few moments, then I turned and walked away.

On the long walk home from the hospital, I tried to put my thoughts into some sort of order. A succession of psychiatrists at a well-thought-of mental health facility had thought I was seriously schizophrenic. I had spent time in a mental hospital. Everyone who met my husband found him able, intelligent, sane. Only I thought there was something the matter with him; no one else did. The therapists had all tried very hard to get me to see I was wrong. It still seemed to me that what I remembered happening had happened, but if I were crazy, of course that was how it *would* seem to me. The person whose view is distorted is the last to see the reality, if he's ever lucky enough to see it at all. I knew that if the sins of the fathers are not visited on their children, their emotional disorders undoubtedly are.

Numb and shaking, I tried to take stock. Peter's school problem. He just would not learn to write. He was extremely intelligent, the sisters at the school informed me, but he was not trying. Could I think of a reason, they had asked. I could think of one now. Sasha's bouts of hysterical crying and blaming herself for Becky's death. And Becky. If she had had a sane mother, an ordinary, careful, watchful mother, would she not still be alive? Now Ann, in emotional pain so great that she couldn't speak. And always, always returning to the doctor's question, "Do you want her life to be what yours has been?"

No.

Then what?

A foster home was unthinkable. Ann would never understand. The other kids would wonder when their turn would come to be gotten rid of. They'd never be able to understand that sending them away was better than making them live with me. No, uprooting them would be all wrong; I knew it in my bones. I would have to be the one to go, to vanish from their lives, leaving them free to salvage what they could after the start I had given them.

I would have to die. The sooner the better. Now, soon. But carefully. And none of the stock trappings of the near-suicide, the tearful farewells, the muffed attempts where you ended up saved after all. This would have to be done carefully, so that the children would never dream I had meant to die. God, I didn't want to live, but I didn't want to leave them. I thought of Benjy, banging on the high chair with his spoon, and pulled my mind away.

Now, carefully. It mustn't look like suicide. That ruled out an overdose of pills or gassing myself with the car exhaust. Neither of those could be made to look like a mistake. An accident would really be best, with the car, or my bike, maybe, but it was so hard to be sure I'd really be killed. And I'd be sorry to involve others in my exit, even if they themselves weren't hurt. (I thought of the driver of the car that hit Becky, a young family man, and all he had gone through as we waited for her to die.) Off the road into the Sound? That seemed the most likely possibility. If only there were some way to be sure it would be final.

I had reached home.

Armed with the beginnings of my plan, I prepared dinner for the children, installed the sitter, and went back to the hospital. Ann was sleepy. She'd been through a lot that day. We watched television, a rare treat for her, because there wasn't one at home. I tucked her in, kissed her goodnight, and left for home.

On my walks to and from the hospital my plans gradually took shape. It made me feel much better to know that there was something I could do to protect my kids. Of course, another death would be hard for them now, and the death of a mother, even one like me, must necessarily be a wrench for any child. Sometimes, in fact, I doubted whether it was the right thing to do, but I always came back to the doctor's question.

Okay then, when? It would have to be sometime in the course of my normal activities. That would be Tuesday afternoon. Okay, Tuesday afternoon. An accident with the car would be better than trying to use my bike, more certain. That stretch of road along the Sound, where so many cars miss the sharp turn and go over the edge. I could see it clearly in my mind. Now all I had to do until Tuesday afternoon was show no sign that anything was different. I held myself in tightly and began saying my silent goodbyes.

I saw Ann twice a day, at afternoon and evening visiting hours. There had been no change since her hospitalization. Her laryngitis continued. The neurologist gave her a set of neck exercises to do four times a day as a sort of placebo. They were of no medical use, of course; the medical staff had devised them in the hope they might get her to abandon her symptom. Ann did them faithfully, but she told me that she didn't believe in them. "I think they just made them up," she whispered.

Sunday night, while Ann and I were talking during evening visiting hours, her normal voice returned. Without any warning, the laryngitis left and she spoke in her own voice again. Weak with relief, I leaned over and hugged her and she grinned up at me. The nurse came in then to announce the end of visiting hours, so I kissed Ann goodnight and left. As soon as I was out of her sight, I began to cry uncontrollably. I was so blinded by my tears that I almost ran head-long into Dr. Beamer as I rounded the last bend in the corridor.

Dr. Beamer was one of the young doctors on the hospital staff. I knew him a little; he had seen the children several times in the clinic. I had always liked him. His appreciation of how the children felt about themselves had always seemed to me to be very acute, and he was always kind and open. Now he remembered me. "Hello, Mrs. Morgan," he said. "You're the mother of the little aphasic girl who's puzzled us all so much, aren't you? How is Ann doing?"

I tried to answer him, but I couldn't stop crying. Without any hesitation, Dr. Beamer beckoned me into one of the dark and empty offices that lined the corridor. He switched on the light, settled me into a chair, dug around in the desk for a box of tissues, shoved them across the desk to me, and then sat down and said nothing.

I cried and cried. I thought I'd never be able to stop. Every once in a while I'd try to say something, but the sobbing wouldn't stop and I couldn't get any words out. I've always envied women who can weep daintily and look charming in distress. When I cry, my face turns a blotchy red and white and my nose runs bucketfuls. I look awful and know that I do, and it never helps. I had made serious inroads on the box of tissues before I cried myself out. Still Dr. Beamer said nothing except to tell me a couple of times not to worry, to take my time.

When I was calmer, he said, "You were going to tell me how Ann is getting on."

"Her voice is just back, just tonight," I said.

"What happened exactly?"

"Nothing special. We were just talking, at the end of visiting hours, and all of a sudden she was talking normally again, just like that, without any warning."

"Want to tell me about all these tears?"

I suddenly found that I did. I hadn't had anyone to speak to since the blow had fallen. I didn't have to tell him about my plans, I thought. I can just leave that part out and talk a little about the children. I told him about Ann's illness and my talk with Dr. Crosby. "He feels that Ann should be sent to a foster home, that living with me will make her sick, destroy her."

"Why living with *you*, necessarily? It's true that she must be under a lot of pressure, but that's a big leap to a conclusion. Do you know Dr. Crosby well?"

"No, I've only seen him once. But when you think about it, you can see that it must be true. Everybody's been trying to make me see it for a long time, but I just wouldn't believe it. It took something like what happened to Ann to show me it must be true. It's been staring me in the face for a long time."

I told him about everything: being in the hospital, the times with Mal Rogers, the letter from City Mental Hygiene, what Dr. Williams had said to me. "You can see," I finished up, "if it took me so long to realize I'm sick, and it's gone on for so long, that I'm never going to get any better. You can see from what happened to Ann what's going to happen to my other kids. Dr. Crosby's right. I've got to leave them free from me." I blurted it out, then realized I'd said more than I had meant to.

Dr. Beamer was quiet for a while. "Well, I can see that you're serious about that," he said at last. Another pause. "I'd like to hear a little about the family."

I began to tell him how patient Scott had been through my long illness, how he'd taken care of the kids while I went to therapy, how he had tried to get shock treatments for me so that I'd get well faster, and so on.

"I'm getting a little of the picture," he said. "I'd like to hear what some of your feelings were while you were working with Mr. Rogers."

I launched into a description of how I'd felt when I left City Mental Hygiene. After I finished, there was another long silence.

"And now, since Ann got sick, you're finally convinced that you really *are* seriously psychotic? Is that how it's been?"

"That's it," I said.

"Mrs. Morgan," he said evenly, "if I had just one wish for you, it would be that you were a great deal more neurotic than you are."

"That makes no sense."

"Yes it does. Neurosis is meant to protect people from suffering too much pain in their reality situations. You are not at the moment crazy enough to protect yourself from the pain of what is happening in your family, and you're in agony. You need to defend yourself more and better. As far as what living with you is doing to your helpless children, you told me just now that Ann's voice returned to normal while she was talking to you. I don't know if that says anything to you, but it says worlds to me."

I thought it over. "You're saying that it means she's not afraid to talk to me."

"That's what I'm saying. And if you remove yourself from her life right now, if you remove yourself ever, you may be taking away the greatest—maybe the only—defense she's got going for her. Think that one over. Okay?"

"Okay," I said, getting up from my chair.

"And it may be useful," he said as he walked with me down to the hospital door, "it may be useful to think over why Dr. Crosby asked you that question. I would definitely think about that."

Ann was discharged from the hospital ten days after she was admitted. To all appearances she was again healthy, happy, and secure. At her posthospitalization checkup, the pediatrician made a plea for therapy for the whole family. The hospital, he said, had an excellent psychiatric outpatient unit that specialized in counseling the entire family. Ann was obviously deeply troubled; an incident like hers didn't exist in isolation. Underneath her quiet exterior, Ann must be in pain, perhaps in danger.

I reacted with my newfound anger. I was through with therapy, I said, especially family therapy. My husband had used it solely to back me into a corner. I definitely wasn't having any more of that. To which the pediatrician responded over and over, "And what about your daughter?"

That was a question I still couldn't answer. I saw quite well that Ann simply could not be abandoned to hunt as best she could for her own solution to the problem. She was only ten years old and obviously in very shaky shape. She *must* have help, and I knew from the times I had tried to get help for Peter that any therapy for Ann would demand my participation. On the other hand, I simply was not prepared, even for Ann's sake, to travel again the route we had taken through City Mental Hygiene. My faith in the future of my marriage had been reduced to rubble, although I still believed that marriage was an indissoluble contract. I was still prepared to live in the same house and participate in raising the children, but my capacity to believe in Scott's good faith seemed shattered for good, and without it, of what use was therapy?

But again, what about my daughter?

At last I allowed the intake appointment to be made. I did not, however, do so gracefully. Anybody on the hospital staff who broached the subject to me got an earful of my very best invective. I made it plain indeed that I was cooperating under protest and only because I could think of nothing else to do. The policy of using invective, of making my resentment crystal clear, was one I was to follow for over a year. I realize now that I was very tough to handle and that occasionally I gave some innocent bystanders a very rough time indeed. But looking back, I think that altogether my actively verbalized anger served me very well. It greatly increased my odds of survival during that difficult time, and I'm definitely not sorry I chose that way to handle the situation.

Scott and I went to the intake appointment. The plan for therapy seemed to me to be ingenious and fairly realistic. Scott would work with a male therapist, I would work with a female therapist, and the four of us would have conjoint sessions. (It was obviously no use involving the children until Scott and I had squared away our major problems.) I was very reluctant, but my first appointment was scheduled anyhow.

The whole project almost collapsed at my first meeting with Jean Dalton. I outlined my feelings to her in great detail, going over my experiences at City Mental Hygiene and with Dr. Williams.

"Now look," I said, "the official version of what has been going on is very plausible. If I were a paranoid schiz and my husband were okay, we would both be behaving just like this: He would be calm and rational, and I would be ranting accusations. If, however, my version of what's happening is correct, isn't it possible that we still would be behaving *just like this?*

"A smart schiz, assuming that's what my husband is, would have the sense to look calm and rational. And if he is doing what I say he is—leading the therapist on and saying I'm the one who's crazy but admitting to the whole thing at home—wouldn't you expect me to be furiously angry, as angry as you can see I am right now?

"I'm not asking you to agree with me right off the bat. Both versions can't be true, and you'll eventually have to decide on one of them. But what I am asking you to do is to suspend your judgment for the time being. Simply keep in mind that both interpretations explain the facts equally well, and withhold judgment until you have more facts on which to make a judgment. I don't think that's too much for me to ask. Can I count on you to do that?"

Miss Dalton was silent for a while. At last she replied, "I'm sorry, Mrs. Morgan, but I find I can't. Mal Rogers is a more than competent therapist. He worked with you for a long time. And I've been over this with your husband. I'm afraid I can't accept your version of the story."

"Then perhaps you would like to explain to me how you plan to function as my therapist?" I asked. "I'm going to have weekly counseling sessions with you, and you're going to be my therapist in our four-way meetings, right? And I'm to review with you all the circumstances of my daily life, and you're going to help me see them in perspective, right? Except that you've already told me in advance that you're not going to believe anything I say. Fine, I can see already that that's going to be a lot of help. It's really made me feel a lot of faith in you and confidence in your judgment, and I feel better already. Thanks an awful lot, lady, but no thanks. I've already had more than enough of that kind of therapy.

"I'll come to the four-way counseling sessions. I've promised to do that for the sake of the children. But as for working with you, not on your life! I'm shaky enough as it is. I don't have to assist you sweetly as you dump my remaining sanity right down the drain. Even for Ann, that's just too much to ask."

I stayed with that decision. I went only to the conjoint therapy sessions and refused to see Miss Dalton separately. The pressure on me to participate in "my own" therapy was very heavy. I countered with vitriolic sarcasm, thanked the therapists for all their help and support, and ironically drew attention to all the benefits they were providing to the marriage and the family. And there we remained for a while. They endeavored to persuade me with all the force of rational reason. I refused with every ounce of anger I could muster. It looked as though the net result of the counseling was going to be a standoff—three against one. The anger just surged out of me. It was marvelous, exhilarating, after all those years of passive acceptance that whatever was, was right. But it also required an enormous investment of energy. I was not sure how long I could keep the anger running without having it turn once more to depression and rebound against me. It seemed time for me to make some positive move, but I couldn't figure out what it should be.

Therapy to save the marriage now appeared hopeless. Scott seemed heavily committed to a course of action that was plainly destructive to me. He no longer bothered to justify it as a joke or a test of the therapists. Communication between us from that time on was at an end. It became more and more bitterly apparent that one of us was going to "win" and the other to "lose." It seemed possible that the loser might pay with his sanity if not with his life. Battle lines were drawn. We spoke to each other almost solely in the therapy sessions.

The pressure on me was heavy indeed. I was in no way tempted to give in, give up, or plead guilty to insanity to validate Scott and the therapists' view. What I wanted was an advocate, a helper, someone who would work for me, stand up for me. But any attempt to get therapy for myself alone seemed doomed to failure. Every therapist as a matter of course wants a statement from your former therapists before beginning with you as a new patient. And I knew only too well what my former therapists were likely to say. Any statement from them could only land me right back where I had started. Still, there must be something I could do. But what?

Then I remembered something important that turned out to be a brilliant idea. Two of my close friends were seeing a social worker, Margaret Goodwin, for counseling. They both thought she was wonderful and spoke of all the help she'd given them. I myself could see how much better they were doing. It wouldn't hurt to talk to Miss Goodwin, especially when I recalled what one of my friends who was seeing her had told me. Miss Goodwin had heard that I had gone to a party my first evening home from the hospital (though I was still feeling pretty rocky and stayed only for a little while). My friend quoted her as saying, "You mean to tell me it was her first day out of the hospital and she was at a *party?* There's a woman whose courage I admire! If she ever needs help, tell her to come see Meg." I was about to take her at her word.

Now I must stop and describe Meg Goodwin; I'll try, but I know that anything I say will fall far short of the reality. Meg has a master's degree in social work, with long and solid experience in social casework. (This was before the term "therapy" was in general use by social workers.) For years Meg had been head of the Family Service Bureau in a nearby town. When I first met her, she had been retired for several years and had a small private practice in her own home. I suppose she could technically be described as elderly, but I can't think of a word more at variance with her person and manner. A small, energetic, warm, practical woman, intensely interested in everything and everyone around her, she radiated confidence and a sort of humorous acceptance of whatever the world might bring to her door. When I, in desperation, turned up on her doorstep, she took me in without a moment's hesitation.

Actually, I phoned her first to ask very diffidently if she would see me. Yes indeed, she knew of me from both my friends. I sounded like a person she'd really like to know. Could I come to tea tomorrow afternoon? We could talk about my problem then.

Seated at the tea table before the fire in Meg's comfortable library, I felt that the world suddenly seemed like a more manageable place. I told my story, detail by detail. "I know it sounds unbelievable," I finished lamely, "but I swear to you it's all true. And I'm afraid if I don't find somebody to help *me,* to believe in *me,* I just won't be able to go on."

Meg responded without hesitation. "No, it's not hard to believe you. I've seen this very thing happen any number of times. The husband says his wife is crazy and everyone believes him. No one believes her, but all the same he's really the one who's sick. I don't find it hard to believe at all. Do you want to work on it?"

"I do want to, very much," I answered, "but promise me two things. The first is that you'll work with me without getting the report from City Mental Hygiene. I'd never feel safe if you read that report. It was so convincing and so absolutely damning. The second is that if you ever find you don't believe something I say—I mean if you don't believe it literally happened the way I say it did—you'll promise to tell me so right there and then. Oh, and I don't know when I'll be able to pay you. I haven't any access to what little money there is, and my seeing you probably isn't going to be very popular with the man who handles the money."

"Don't worry about the money," Meg said. "I know you'll pay me when you can. Anyway, your main job for right now is to get better. Don't even think about the other two things. Let's see, I think we'd better work twice a week for the time being. How about Tuesdays and Fridays at three?"

So Meg and I began what proved to be my first serious work

in therapy. Several observations that Meg made in our early work together stick in my mind.

"It seems to me you have a serious *reality* problem. Why are you trying to treat it as if it were a psychological problem? The conflicts in your marriage and the problems your children are facing exist in the actual world. They're not just a function of your own psyche, and you can't solve them just by readjusting your attitude." I can't describe the enormous relief that simple statement brought me.

And again, "It sounds to me as though your marriage has never been a happy one. What we have to do is to see why you've stuck with it all these years." She made it sound so simple.

Meg also said, "It's possible you may be schizophrenic; I would say it's probable. That doesn't mean you have to be hopeless. I've seen many people recover completely from schizophrenia, and many others live happy and manageable lives even if they didn't get completely well. So there's no reason for you to give up hope. We'll have to work hard, of course." And we worked hard.

Meanwhile, at the clinic the lines were running as follows:
*Me (to Scott):* Lloyd brought me a bottle of wine when he came Sunday. He said it was not very good but was okay to get drunk on. Obviously he still believes what you told him—that I'm an alcoholic.
*Scott:* No, no, I'm sure he understands it was a joke.
*Therapists (together):* But, Mr. Morgan, you told us you'd never said anything like that at all.
*Me:* Would he lie to you? (Everyone remains silent.)

Meg also fed me, perhaps the most important element in my therapy with her. I don't mean she fed me symbolically; I mean she gave me real food. (I have a feeling that she knew real deprivation when she saw it.) My appointments were in midafternoon. I arrived each time to find the tea table set, a pot of tea steeping, a huge plate of cookies in place. Frequently I cleaned up the plate of cookies. There were plenty more in the kitchen. I put on some weight. I also learned that the good things I experienced didn't dissolve or go away, that there were predictable places of sustenance in the world. Nourishment didn't vanish the minute I set eyes on it. Good experiences are repeatable.

At the clinic:

*Me (to Scott):* I know you deny it, but I really feel that you're to blame for my accident.

*Therapist:* What happened?

*Me:* The brakes on the car failed, and I crashed into the back of the car ahead. It was lucky no one was hurt. I was slowing down for the toll gate, so I wasn't going very fast. The car was wrecked, though. The radiator was demolished and can't be repaired. We'll have to replace the car. The highway patrolman checked the brakes and said they went clear down to the floor about every other time he braked. *(To Scott)* And I told you twice last week that the brakes were failing. Why did you say they didn't need repair? You knew I had that long drive to make.

*Scott:* I thought it was just your imagination. They seemed okay to me.

*Therapist:* Thank God for the highway patrol!

And Meg said, "Don't you think you've suffered enough? Why don't you quit suffering?"

"Is it all right to do that?" I asked.

"You have my permission," she replied.

A not atypical transaction at the clinic:

*Me:* It's imperative to deal with our family problems because the kids are so upset.

*Therapist:* Can you give us an example of what you mean?

*Me:* Sure. The night before last Sasha had a hysterical tantrum and put her hand right through the glass pane in the porch door. She put it through with such force she hardly even cut herself. She kept saying it was her fault that Becky died. Then she lay on the floor and cried and cried, saying over and over that she wished she were dead.

*Therapist:* Is this the first time she's done something like this, Mrs. Morgan?

*Me:* No, it happens pretty often. She's really feeling desperate.

*Scott: She's* the one who keeps stirring them up! No wonder they're upset. She keeps talking about Becky to them and makes sure they're hysterical all the time. I've never seen Sasha do anything like that. The kids are fine when they're with me.

*Therapist:* So you've never seen them behave like this at all, Mr. Morgan?

*Scott:* No, never. Not only that, she never tells me when something like this has happened. She never tells me anything. She's cutting me off from the kids into the bargain.

*Therapist:* Is that true, Mrs. Morgan?

*Me:* It's true that I never tell him. He can't keep cool when anything goes wrong and it just makes everything ten times worse.

*Therapist:* One of the aims we've agreed on in working together here is to improve communication between you, which you've both admitted is very bad. Don't you think your husband, as the children's father, is entitled to be kept informed of what's happening with them?

*Other Therapist:* It's only fair for him to know. Don't you agree?

*Me:* I wonder if you realize what you're asking me to do to the kids.

*Therapists:* Why? What do you mean?

*Me:* The children are going to feel really betrayed.

*Scott:* God damn it, I'm their father! The betrayal is all in your own head.

*Therapist:* How about it, Mrs. Morgan? You'll have to take some chances that you don't want to take if you're going to get this marriage back together.

*Me:* Oh, all right. Next time something happens, I promise I'll tell him.

*Therapists (reinforcing patient's progress):* Good!

At the clinic, the next week:

*Me:* Well, I kept the promise I made you last week.

*Therapist:* What do you mean?

*Me:* Friday night Sasha had another crying fit. She said over and over that she wished she were dead. Nothing I could do would comfort her.

*Therapist:* And you told your husband, as you said you would?

*Me:* Yes. He said he'd handle it. He took her out for a drive with him on Saturday morning. When they came back, she was crying. As soon as he went into his room, Sasha came running to me and said, "Mommy, *please* don't tell Daddy the secrets I tell you. That was a secret I told you, and he got mad and grabbed me and said he'd hit me if he ever heard me say that again." *(By this time I'm crying.)* Can't you realize what you've made me put her through? She's only eight. She can't defend herself!

*Therapists:* Is that what happened, Mr. Morgan?

*Scott (shamefaced but still belligerent):* Well, yes. When I heard her say she wanted to die, I lost my temper. She shouldn't say things like that. *(The therapists are silent. I sit and glare at them.)*

And another transaction, later:

*Me (to Scott):* I don't see how you can deny there are psychotic manifestations in your life. Only night before last, you came into the kitchen asking if I had called you. You told me then that you were hearing a woman call your name, over and over. If that's not a hallucination, then please explain to me what it is.

(Scott is speechless with shock and horror. I had just deliberately broken our most basic and sacred contract. Never before had I told an outsider, in Scott's presence, about this kind of incident. It was very firmly understood between us that Scott could tell others my problems but that I would never, never blow the whistle on him, at least publicly.)

*Therapists:* Is this true, Mr. Morgan?

*Scott (giving me a dirty look):* I would never have believed she was capable of telling that kind of lie.

(Silence. I am wondering what will happen when we get home.)

And Meg said, "It was so nice to meet your daughters. I enjoyed talking to them. The curtains Ann made look so nice in the kitchen. I can see that your children, no matter what terrible things they've been through, have a lot of strength to work with. You've given them a great deal. When you see them as healthy, happy adults, able to give love to their own children, you'll have the reward for all your struggle."

I burst into tears. Hope can hurt, too.

Meanwhile, at the clinic:
*Me:* I suppose this may be dirty pool, but I'm going to say it anyway. A friend of mine who knows Jean Dalton told me that Jean is currently going through terrible problems in her own life. My friend said, "Seriously, I wouldn't want her as a marriage counselor right now. I'd ask for another therapist." I'm asking for another therapist.
*Therapist (to male therapist):* What do you think, Gary?
*Male Therapist:* We could talk it over at staff meeting.

Then, the next week:
*Male Therapist:* Most of the staff felt a new therapist at this advanced stage of therapy wouldn't be a good idea.
*Me:* This is advancement?

Meg said, "I have your friend's permission to tell you this. She told me how much it had helped her to talk to you about her troubles with her husband. You're a very strong and real person in your friends' lives. You count for a lot with the people who know you."

More tears. More hope.

At the clinic, talking of the time around Becky's death:

*Therapist:* Did you realize from the beginning that Becky's death was a certainty?

*Scott:* No, not for two days.

*Me (at the same moment):* Yes, the doctors told us right away. *(Therapists look surprised.)*

*Therapist:* Which was it?

*Scott:* We didn't know.

*Me:* Scott, the doctor told me and I told you. It's one of my most vivid memories. Father Michaelson was standing right there. I know he remembers it, too. How *can* you not remember it?

*Scott (shamefaced):* It's possible that I blocked it out.

*Me:* So *that's* why you were telling everyone I was crazy because I kept saying I knew she was going to die! You blocked it out!

*Therapist:* Mrs. Morgan, do you think it's possible that this has happened on other occasions as well?

*Me (confusion . . . clarity):* My God!*

Finally, at the clinic:

*Scott (archly):* You know, Martha, I've always wondered if the reason you were unable to work with Mal Rogers was that he was my personal therapist before the three of us began to work together.

*Me (open-mouthed with astonishment):* Scott, what do you mean? He was no such thing. You continued with him after I quit, but you had never seen him individually before that. In fact, it's the other way around. I saw him alone before I went into the hospital.

*Scott:* That's not so! That joint therapy at City Mental Hygiene was your first time there, but I was there before you.

*Both Therapists (jubilant):* At last! At last a disagreement between you that we can check out factually. Mrs. Morgan, what's your version of this?

*Me:* I started with Dorothy Jackson just before Becky was born. Then she went on jury duty. I was transferred to three guys in succession. I finally quit after about two years but went back after Becky died.

Before I went to Kirkpatrick I started with Mal Rogers. Then Scott and I saw him together till I quit. He went on alone for a couple of months, then he quit, too, last March or April. Scott, how can you not remember? You used to baby-sit every week while I went to my appointment.

*Therapists:* Mr. Morgan, what's your version of that time period?

*Scott (puzzled):* I don't remember any of that. As far as I can remember, I went there first and saw Mal Rogers alone before we saw him together. But if that's how Martha remembers it, she's probably right.

*Therapists:* If you both will sign this release, we'll send for the records.

(No further mention of this was ever made in subsequent therapy hours, though it seemed to me of primary importance. I waited to see if anyone would bring it up, but no one ever did. I never raised the question myself. By that time, I was solidly aware of what had in fact been going on between Scott and myself, and I really didn't give a damn whether the therapists ever caught on.)*

And Meg said, "Would you like some more cookies?"

And I said, "Yes, please, I would."

## esther comments

Martha is now giving a very clear picture of exactly what she was doing, which was to turn the table on Scott. Where previously it had been he who had won and she who had lost in therapy, the situation was now reversed. With the support she was getting from Meg Goodwin, it was Martha who was strong enough to put her points across and Scott who was discredited. Of course, any therapy—or any relationship—that operates on such a win-or-lose basis is at best something of a failure. At the time, however, Martha had to prove that she knew what she was talking about, and from that standpoint the therapy was a success. Whether she could incorporate it all into her continuing view of the matter, and whether she could get some sense of her own power into her image of herself, remained to be seen.

Martha's account of the four-way sessions seems a parody of family therapy rather than an example of it. Nothing went quite as one would expect from a process designed to promote communication. In any case, communication in itself is not the answer to every problem. I must say that I marvel at the restraint of the therapists as Martha slashed around in all directions, including at them. But again, neither the "rules" of therapy nor the self-discipline and good will of the therapists could make a dent in the problem. By this time, the only remaining question that might have been at all useful was probably: Is this marriage completely dead? And it was the family caseworker Martha found for herself who helped her to recognize and build her strength sufficiently so that she could afford to face and deal with that question.

Looking back, it may not be too far off the mark to describe Martha's entire story as an elaborate effort to avoid considering the question of divorce, an effort about as common among women who believe in divorce as among those who do not. Divorce, like marriage, does not in itself assure a happy ending, of course, although it may be a first step on the way to something better. From here on—and this was perhaps the most important consequence for her—Martha would be dealing primarily with her own problems, however severe they might be, rather than with the confused and complicated product of her problems and Scott's together, multiplied astronomically by the interaction between them.

## martha continues

One morning, after months of virtual silence between us, Scott walked into the kitchen and said, "Nothing on earth is worth this. Let's get a divorce."

"Yes, please, let's," I said. We made the agreement with almost no discussion at all.

From that time on, therapy at the clinic and with Meg was devoted to working out the practical details for a separation. We announced the separation as a joint decision to friends and, with much hesitation, to the children. The children were obviously upset by the news. It seemed to throw Peter especially into a very severe depression. He was already beset with serious, almost unmanageable, school problems. He began to refuse to go to school. When he did go, he would often leave after the first or second period and wander around town or hide at the houses of his friends. I would never know whether he was in school until the vice-principal would phone me to ask if he was home ill. Ill he might be, but he wasn't at home.

We proceeded with the practical arrangements. I would keep the house. The children would remain with me. Scott made a few token threats to take them away from me, but it was apparent that he had no real leverage, nor did he truly want the responsibility of raising them. Because I had no income of my own and had the house payments to meet as well as the five of us to feed, he would have to make some sort of financial arrangement. How the money from an assembly-line job that had never been enough to support one household was going to support two was something of a problem. (Eventually, we sold the house and I took my share of the money to set up a new home for me and the children in a sunnier, and I hoped happier, location, but that idea came to me later.) Several times during this period Scott said to me with considerable satisfaction, "You'll be on the psychiatric ward again two weeks after we separate."

At last we completed arrangements as well as we could. Scott moved his things to a small apartment about half a mile away (across the street from an apartment we had lived in for six years). I was very apprehensive at first. I had read many times that when a couple separates, each partner invariably discovers that most of the problems believed to be caused by the other remain just as before, that all the marital difficulties ultimately come home to roost with the individual. I was prepared to find out that all the trouble between us had been my fault after all; instead, a feeling of peace and security settled on me. I was beset by all kinds of practical problems, financial worries, upset children, and Peter's ever-worsening school trouble, but the sense of calm and security was growing in me all the same. From the day that Scott left, I did not ever regret the separation, and I never looked back.

I remember one last incident at the Family Guidance Clinic. We were winding up our work there in what we all agreed were our last few appointments. Because Scott had the car and I had none, he picked me up each week for our appointment. One day he did not appear. Time passed; the appointment hour came and went; still he didn't show up. At last I phoned him and asked why he hadn't come. He snarled that he didn't want to keep the stupid appointment and I couldn't make him. I was furious. "Since it's you that's breaking the appointment, will you at least phone them and tell them we aren't coming?"

"They can go fuck themselves," he said. "I'm not phoning anybody."

In tears of fury I called the clinic and told Scott's therapist what had happened. His response surprised me. He set up a four-way telephone conference hookup with himself and Jean Dalton at the clinic, and me at home and then dialed Scott's number. When Scott answered, his therapist asked if he was coming to the appointment. Scott excused himself courteously. He was sorry but he was ill this morning and couldn't come.

I broke in angrily. "That's not what you said to me. What you said to me was 'I don't want to go and you can't make me.' "

"Is that what you, in fact, said, Mr. Morgan?" asked Jean Dalton.

A long silence. Then Scott's resistance suddenly broke. "Yes," he said, "it's true. That's what I said."

"And you're not, in fact, ill?"

"No. I just didn't want to come."

The therapists thanked him and hung up. I thanked them and hung up. As I put the phone down I felt somehow definitively: I am free!

OO    BEGINNING TOGETHER

## esther's narrative

# 1
# The First
# Round

knew nothing of Martha's story, of course, when she first came to the Family Service Bureau, where I work. She had called for an appointment a week or so before and had filled out a simple application form in our waiting room. She followed me upstairs to my office and sat down across the desk from me. I saw an attractive woman in her mid-thirties, becomingly but not fashionably dressed, hair in a natural, simple style, and wearing no makeup. From her appearance and speech and manner, she might have been a teacher—or a social worker. I noticed that she held her head high, sat straight in her chair, and seemed very much in command of her voice, her thoughts, and her body. It was not my practice to call clients by their first names, at least until we knew each other so well that it was natural to do so, and there was nothing about Mrs. Morgan in that first hour that would have encouraged any but the most brash to call her Martha.

She mentioned having had some therapy before coming to this city from the Northwest some time ago, therapy that had culminated in her obtaining a divorce. Although she didn't feel she needed a great deal of further help now, she knew she needed some. Emotional pressures had been mounting, and her economic circumstances were grim. She was trying to avoid going on welfare, earning what she could by baby-sitting and thesis-typing in her home. She said her ex-husband had followed her to this area and was perpetuating some of his old hold on her through child support, paying or not paying it according to his own convenience. Since the support had been ordered by an out-of-state court, Martha had little leverage beyond what she herself could exert, which forced her into more contact with Scott than she could afford, emotionally speaking.

Recently an old college friend, Arlene, financially well off but seriously alcoholic, had reappeared in Martha's life. She demanded much time and attention from Martha during periodic bouts with her demon and occasionally rewarded Martha with considerable gifts of

126

money. What with the emotional drain on Martha from her contacts with Scott and Arlene, the burden of providing day care for three children as well as meeting the everyday needs of her own four, the exacting requirements of her typing assignments, and the constant uncertainties of her financial state, she felt pushed to the wall. Fearing a recurrence of the symptoms that had originally brought her into therapy, Martha had turned to the family service agency for help. She chose the family agency instead of a clinic because she wanted to be sure she would be seen by the kind of therapist who had been the most helpful to her in the past: a social worker.

Martha told me immediately that she had been diagnosed three times as schizophrenic, giving as the source of this diagnosis a psychiatrist in private practice, a clinic, and a mental hospital, all known—even at this distance—to have good reputations. She added that her social worker had also accepted this diagnosis and had based her treatment of Martha on it (though she had said that from Martha's description of Scott, he was also schizophrenic). Martha asked that I not obtain reports from any of these sources. I felt that she was testing me, but I was already hearing the quality of what Martha had to say and seeing the quality of her appearance and manner, and I did not mind being tested. It seemed to me more than likely that the diagnosis, if it had ever been really appropriate, was irrelevant to the present circumstances.

I had long since acquired sufficiently independent status at the agency so that I was free to make my own decision in such matters. By then, too, I had seen enough instances of reaction to severe marital conflict not to be surprised by any of the manifestations of the struggle for survival by one partner against the onslaughts of the other, especially when each feels his own mental life to be at stake. I was reinforced by knowledge from my own personal experience that, at a time of extreme pressure, more "normal" defenses against psychological stress can fail, and the mind will grasp at any means, even "psychotic" ones, that will save it from being overwhelmed by uncontrollable emotion. Within that context, there was no way that I could fail to pass Martha's test. It was obviously more important to get on with the problems at hand than to delve into their past vicissitudes.

This is not to say that I entirely ignored the past. On the contrary, in the hours that followed I was careful to get from Martha enough of a picture of her family of origin and her experience within it to account for her having made a bad marriage, and to get enough of a picture of that marriage to have a pretty good idea why Martha had had to leave it in order to survive. I did so in order to be able to anticipate some of the pitfalls that might lie ahead and the strength that Martha might be able to bring to bear upon them. Martha was not asking "How did I get this way?" but "How can I hold on to what I have made of myself?" and "Where can I go from here?" The first question is intrinsically as important as the others, but it was not the question that Martha was asking, and she seemed to know very well what she needed.

I was concerned, both immediately and throughout this period of contact, with the extent to which Martha remained dependent on child support from Scott or counted on monetary gifts from Arlene to get by, because she would be in some measure vulnerable to both of them as a result. I am not prepared to state that financial power always bestows emotional power on the possessor or that there are not also many other ways by which one human being can exert emotional control over another. However, I will testify to the fact, professionally and personally, that the role of money in human relationships is certainly of as much consequence as that of any of the psychological factors so well described and so carefully documented in the literature.*

In any case, Martha was operating on a precarious economic base, with insufficient material or emotional return for all the hours she was putting in. Although neither she nor I immediately raised the question of finding more rewarding employment, it was in the offing from the start. Meanwhile, Martha explored and dealt with a number of problems about the way she saw herself and the way she related to other people, all matters that had some bearing on her past and some significance for her future.

For my account of our sessions at that time, I have turned to the summary I wrote for her case file at the end of our year or so of work together. I have long felt that a case record, if there be one at all, should be so written that one can comfortably let a client read it. I had never tested this out with anyone, but when we began writing, I offered Martha the opportunity to read her record. She finally summoned up enough courage to do so, having by then progressed far enough in therapy to risk it with no ill effects. Because the record tended to ramble, I have summarized it here; thus our discussions, so far removed from the original give-and-take, will inevitably seem more academic than they actually were.

Like many other women, Martha had had trouble handling her intelligence. As a child, she had not been aware of her own intelligence, had simply experienced herself as somehow different and rejected. When she began to be aware that she was indeed very intelligent, she did not know how to handle this recognition about herself. If she hid it or played it down, she was denying her own identity, yet if she displayed it, she would offend or alienate others. She had never experienced her intelligence as something that inspired confidence or won admiration and recognition. For Martha, intelligence was a handicap rather than an asset.

She did not have enough self-esteem to risk herself in competitive situations and did not develop the kind of aggressiveness required to achieve success in competition with others. She felt that she must never compete, for it was as dangerous to win as it was painful to lose. Without ever having tried herself out in reality, Martha had no means by which to place herself accurately in relation to others. She would veer from the frightening thought that she was far superior to everyone else to the sickening thought that she was no good at all. To escape this dizzying swing, Martha had turned to the substitute that is not only permitted but actively encouraged if you are a woman: the love relationship in which a woman makes herself so indispensable to a man, and later to her children, that she need not compete or achieve in the world outside her home.

Unfortunately, when such a pattern contains within it the

conviction of being unlovable, as it did with Martha, it may demand that a woman give absolute, unqualified service to others; that she must try to meet the other person's needs at whatever cost to herself in emotional deprivation, anger, and anxiety; and that she put herself through agonies of guilt at any real or fancied failure to do so. In return, of course, Martha expected absolute and unqualified love from others. When they fell short, she would experience tremendous rage, which could turn into depression of suicidal proportions. (Aggressiveness that is not constructively used on one's own behalf is always available to be turned against oneself.)

Martha's problem was increased by her reluctance to practice the pretenses and prevarications of ordinary, polite social behavior, and she had not developed much ability to speak her "truth" without threatening or offending others. Because she did not have a sufficiently strong and consistent sense of her own value, she was unable to protect herself against the rejection she encountered. It was as though she constantly put her value as a human being "on the line" and thus was always in a position either of shattering others or of being shattered herself. Martha had fought back by confronting people with her awareness of their deceptions and self-deceptions, thereby further bringing their wrath down upon her head. She did not paint a pretty picture of her actual behavior despite her dedication to being "good," and I was inclined to believe that it was a fairly accurate picture, although a somewhat intellectualized one.

These were all Martha's own insights. I am quoting her almost verbatim, although of course in abbreviated form, because her conclusions were the product of over a year of therapy hours. Although I had raised questions of my own and questioned some of hers, as time went on I found myself in substantial agreement with the interpretations she had made, and I participated in the conclusions she had drawn from them. What I had been doing, basically, was to go along with Martha's exploration of her problems in using her intelligence and handling her aggression. I was accepting for myself as well as for Martha that a woman might have trouble with these aspects of her personality and might resort to other than effective or even rational ways of dealing with them. I had had my own problems with these things and had by no means learned to handle them all that well myself, so that Martha often put into words some of the questions I was raising for myself and some of the ideas I was still in the process of formulating. I already knew quite definitely, however, that I had parted forever with the notion that femininity demanded I be always good, kind, loving, and giving—and never, never angry or demanding or vengeful.

The circumstances of my childhood within my family and my immediate environment had caused me to develop characteristics of dependence and submissiveness, which had their usefulness in a society that values women for their "femininity." I had derived considerable approval from my docility and my ability to avoid anger, my own and that of others. It was difficult to see any connection between such feminine virtues and such psychoneurotic symptoms as anxiety and depression. I had finally come to the conclusion that the role for which I was getting approval was not getting me much of anything else that I wanted.

My efforts to affirm rather than to efface myself were by no means welcomed by people who had valued me for my "niceness" or who were threatened by the aggressive and demanding behavior I was suddenly exhibiting. I was badly handicapped, too, by a simple lack of assertive experience over the years, so that I really was very ignorant about ways and means of making room for myself in anything but the little corners already allotted to me. As I met with resistance and rejection instead of approval, I found myself quick to express anger, which seemed not at all an attractive trait. I had the feeling that I was sacrificing my femininity in a very dubious cause, but I had to admit that my symptoms were dwindling. I saw a resemblance between my problems and those of many other women, both clients and friends, though I was not yet able to put the clues together.

Because for some time I had been sifting my own experience and that of others for clues, I naturally found Martha's efforts at self-understanding of great interest. From the standpoint of her own questions, it seemed to me that she was making some real progress in therapy. She was beginning to recognize how destructive and self-destructive some of her patterns had been. She was also coming to the point where she could begin to talk about limiting her expectations of herself; thus she eventually could be expected to develop a more authentic acceptance and tolerance of others. I continued to be concerned, however, with the financial dependency that made it impossible for Martha to assert herself effectively and encouraged a perpetuation of her old ways of relating to people. She agreed that financial independence was essential to further progress, but she seemed no closer to taking steps toward achieving it.

We had settled into something of a comfortable though interesting and rather academic rut when one day, without any warning, Martha suddenly turned on me and repudiated everything she had ever said to me: All her "great insights" were just fake; she had, in essence, conned me, had persuaded me that she was always the "good" one taken advantage of by others, when all along she had been just as she had been diagnosed to be, schizophrenic. For this I had no preparation, personal or professional, and I felt the ground being washed out from under me. My heart was pounding, my head reeling. I was feeling the full tide of her conviction of "wrongness," of unworthiness, and I was myself implicated in it, terribly wrong in having gone along with her and having believed in her, and so I was obviously incompetent, unworthy of being a therapist at all.

But then I became angry and the thought came to me, "She can't do this to me!" I was not going to let her pull me under with her—I, who was her bulwark against these feelings—I was not going to be swept away by this annihilating tide. What did she think she was doing anyway? So anger came to my rescue and to hers. I recognized that this was, in a way, a second run—this time the real run—of the original test. Martha was once again inviting me to buy the evaluation of previous therapists, the evaluation I had rejected in our first hour. I was not now going to reverse myself. There was no way, after having known Martha for a year, that I could throw away the evidence of all my senses. I knew with the utmost conviction that

Martha was actually what she had seemed to me to be: an intelligent woman asking her own questions, evaluating her own answers, and doing all of this as openly and honestly as she was at that time able to do; a woman with serious problems, of course, but trying her best to look at them and to come to grips with them. I knew this, whether she knew it or not. I was not going to let her throw herself down the drain—and I certainly was not going to let her take me with her!

It occurred to me that Martha had probably gone through this many times before, in one version or another, and that she might very well have convinced a good many people of her "wrongness." If this was how she turned against herself and invited others to do so, she was endangering herself far more than anyone else could—except, of course, at her invitation. I by no means understood the mechanism that was at work, although I was sure there was anger in it somewhere. Until then, although Martha and I had discussed anger quite a bit, neither of us had expressed nor had even seemed to feel any real anger toward each other, on either a reality or a transference basis.

Anger is always important in anyone's therapy and especially so with women, who are not encouraged by our society to express anger directly and openly. I do not hold with those who believe that "bringing out the hostility" is the major purpose or method of therapy. However, because anger is so often expressed indirectly in psychological symptoms, or in unconsciously destructive or self-destructive behavior, it is always one of the tasks of therapy to bring anger to conscious awareness so that it can be expressed in more useful ways or directed into healthier channels.

On the level that Martha and I had been working, I could see no way of reaching deep enough, or far back enough, to identify the underground source of the anger and make it available for some constructive use. It seemed enough at the time to identify very clearly what had happened. Martha had suddenly turned against the positive view of herself that I had accepted and was helping her to accept and had switched to a negative self-image: an exaggerated one of weakness, wrongdoing, and craziness built up over past years in which she had been criticized or belittled or found wanting in some respect. Because I had gathered that much of Martha's previous therapy had reinforced the negative image (although I did not know just how it had come about), I had tried to avoid anything that she might see as a repetition. I knew that Martha's view of the marriage and of Scott had been in question at that time. I did not see such a question as likely to be useful now, and I did not go into it with her. From her standpoint, I suppose, I had "bought" her story.*

Because it is impossible for anyone to do complete justice to another person's point of view, especially when the two are in mortal combat with each other, I certainly would not expect Martha to make a case for Scott. I had no reason not to proceed with her on the basis of her own story, as with any other client coming for individual help. It weighed heavily with me to hear about Scott's prediction to Martha at the time of the divorce that she would land in a mental hospital within weeks—and to know that she had not, in fact, done so. I was impressed as much by Martha's ability to survive Scott's remark as I was by the psychologically ingenious malice of it. Although I did not assume that I thereby knew the whole story of the marriage, I did feel I had at least some hint of its flavor—enough for the kind of work we were doing together at that time.

It seemed possible to me that Martha's recognition that a job was the next step, with the very real difficulties it would entail (four children depending on her and no one on whom she could depend) and the anxieties and angers that were inevitable, may have produced considerable ambivalence toward me for having helped her arrive at this point. But I did not feel ready, for Martha or for me, to get into the negatives in our relationship, and Martha showed no inclination to do so either.

What had for a moment been a mortal threat to our work together ended in a pragmatic conclusion that might provide a more solid foundation for Martha's future: Martha decided that she could never be sure of being 100 percent "right" in anything, and if she found herself wrong in even some small way, she could judge herself 100 percent "wrong"—if she wanted to. But by and large, she felt experience had shown her that her view of things was usually correct enough to be an adequate base of operation, and there was no reason why she should continue to perpetuate a view of herself that she should have abandoned long ago. Whatever the true explanation for it may have been, the danger subsided almost as quickly as it had arisen, and we pursued it no further.

Our contact then moved rapidly to a close, with Martha devoting more and more time and thought in her hours with me to the kind of job she could hope to get and making active efforts in that direction. Without a college degree, the possibilities were quite limited. The most desirable opportunity required the taking of a highly competitive examination. Martha took it, scored high, and was hired immediately. Martha now saw herself as beginning the next phase of her life and felt ready to terminate appointments with me.

I suppose one might look at this entire contact as having promoted a "flight into health"—to which I would reply, "And more power to it!" It was understood that Martha could call me in the future if she wished to do so, but she called only once to say all was well, and I did not hear from her again for more than four years.

## martha's view

At last, with great trepidation and reluctance, I made the decision to pull up stakes and move to a new area. Hoping for a fresh start, I sold the house and, with my share of the proceeds, packed up and moved south to California. The children and I stayed with a friend while we looked around for a house to rent.

Gradually things fell into place. We found a house, somewhat rundown, it is true, but it seemed to us warm and sheltering. We settled into our new surroundings; the children put down roots in the new community. I began supporting the family with thesis-typing and taking care of small children, both jobs that a woman with no training can do at home. With Peter's school problem still simmering, it seemed very important that I should always be available to cope with any crisis that might surface.

Actually, things were going rather smoothly. Peter himself found a continuation school in a nearby school district that was running an experimental project for potential high school dropouts. He talked the school into including him in the program and voluntarily began to attend regularly and work for credits toward graduation. Ann and Sasha seemed happy in their new schools. Ann found a new piano teacher who was willing to exchange weekly lessons for baby-sitting. Sasha began to study the flute, something she had always wanted to do, and made tremendous progress. Benjy was a little jealous of my baby-sitting charges but seemed happy and secure in our new community.

Soon after our arrival, Scott also moved south "to be near the children." He visited frequently, much more frequently than I liked. He was apt to show up at almost any hour of the day or night, and I saw a great deal more of him than I wanted to. After all those years of enforced propinquity, I valued my privacy and independence very highly indeed.

Economically, things were uncertain in the extreme. I was very dependent, despite my earnings from day care and typing, upon Scott's child-support payments. From the time he arrived in California, these were irregular and I had no money to hire a lawyer to straighten things out. I was afraid to tackle Scott on the subject of his unannounced and unwelcome visits to the household for fear he would discontinue support payments altogether and leave me with no choice but to apply for relief, a solution that, in my newfound independence, I really dreaded.

Once settled in my day-to-day routine, I began to think of continuing in therapy. In our last work together Meg Goodwin had said, "Martha, with so many years of illness behind you, you'll probably always have a continuing vulnerability. Your life may run smoothly for long periods of time, but it would really be a good idea to make contact with a therapist in your new community. That way, if you hit a rough spot or things begin to come to pieces, you'll have someone you can trust to turn to."

A friend was in a women's group at the Family Service Bureau and enthusiastically praised the therapist who led her group. I was also influenced by the fact that Meg had been, for years before her retirement, head of a family service agency. I called the Family Service Bureau and asked for an appointment.

I arrived for my intake appointment a minute or two early. The agency had a welcoming atmosphere. I was greeted warmly by the receptionist and given a short factual questionnaire to complete: age, family composition, religion, education, income, and so on. I then followed Esther, the social worker who greeted me, upstairs to her office and seated myself across the desk from her. I saw an alert and attractive woman some years older than myself, fashionably but simply dressed. Her greeting was warm and direct but not patronizing. She did not invoke a first-name familiarity that neither of us as yet could feel. I did not feel belittled in coming to ask for help.

I thought at once: Here is a woman with solid and real experience of the world who accepts me unquestionably as her equal. I liked her, and as we began to speak of the life circumstances that had led me to seek therapy at her agency, I felt that I could trust her. Each of us, looking back, remembers that intake hour as unique. I felt immediately that we could work together. Esther was clearly much more interested in my strengths than in my weaknesses and respectful of what I had already learned. She made no effort to deny or disguise her own intelligence and thus made no tacit demand that I do either with my own.

I wanted very much to impress her with the progress I had already made in therapy and with my acceptance of those problems I couldn't do anything about. I told her that I knew I was schizophrenic and that I understood I would always have to live with it, but I asked her nevertheless not to get reports from previous therapists. The last thing I needed was for that City Mental Hygiene report to follow me here. Also, I needed very much to know immediately how much trust Esther was willing to put in me and in her own direct evaluation of the situation. I knew that I was testing her and that she understood and accepted my need to make the test. She readily agreed not to request reports of previous work, and I felt that preliminary testing, which usually goes on for weeks, was disposed of in a matter of five minutes.

We went on to discuss my day-to-day problems. I told her briefly of my marriage and divorce and of the aftermath—Scott's continuing visits and the problems in collecting my much-needed child-support payments.

Toward the end of the hour, we had a short discussion of my financial circumstances. Family Service Bureau charges its fees on a sliding scale based on the family's ability to pay, and we set a fee for my ongoing therapy hours. As the hour ended, we both agreed that we could work well together and set a time for the next appointment. I left feeling that I had been very lucky to find a dependable new friend and co-worker on my first try.

Our second hour together inadvertently provided another testing situation. What happened was this: Together we had set the time of the next appointment. Esther had written it in her appointment book and had also written out an appointment card for me: "Your next visit is at 2 P.M. on Thursday the 16th." But when I arrived at the agreed-upon time, the receptionist was dumbfounded. "This *can't* be your appointment time," she said. "Mrs. Fibush has a regular 2 P.M. appointment on Thursdays, has had it for months. Let me double check."

Sure enough, the appointment book gave my hour as 3 P.M. I was alarmed. Had I unconsciously mistaken the appointment time? I was fairly sure that I had not. But was this an agency where everyone assumed that if a misunderstanding occurred, it was automatically a mistake upon the client's part? That because you came here asking for help, you were understood to be sick, irrational, the cause of any misunderstanding?

I was immensely relieved to find that wasn't the assumption at all. Both Esther and the receptionist accepted it as an open possibility that they might equally have been mistaken, that I wasn't assumed to be automatically in the wrong because I was in the disadvantaged position of being the one who asked for help. (And when I dug the appointment card out of the bottom of my purse, it did indeed say 2 P.M.) With testing quickly and satisfactorily out of the way, Esther and I settled down to our work together.

Esther has written about the commitment that a professional therapist must bring to his work. It seems to me useful to speak of the commitment that the patient, or client, must make in order for therapy to be fruitful.

First of all, there must be a choice for health—a determination to make, whenever choice is possible, the most constructive choice. Honesty is of prime importance in a therapeutic venture. It is always essential to be willing to examine the whole of one's life circumstances, with as few reservations as one can bear. Also, there should be some willingness to examine, profit by, and use any disasters and mistakes, both in one's life situation and in the therapy itself. And finally—perhaps most important of all—there should be willingness to assume responsibility for one's own life, to see oneself not as a helpless victim (nor, of course, as the total manufacturer of one's life circumstances), but as an active and able participant in the shaping of one's daily life.

The work that Esther and I did together in that first contact was almost entirely oriented to the ongoing exigencies of my day-to-day life—on my economic and occupational problems, my difficulties in raising by myself a large brood of intelligent and sensitive children, and, above all, my need to carve out some sort of personal life of my own in the face of all the manifold pressures and demands on my limited time and energy.

Several milestones stand out in my memory. One very fruitful area we discussed was the part played by *luck* in the circumstances that determine one's life. My heavily Freudian background had encouraged me to believe that I alone was somehow responsible for the shape of my affairs, that I must have been very warped indeed to bring my daily life to such a pass! Esther would have none of a viewpoint so extreme. Luck, she said, has a large part to play in how well or how badly things turn out.* We discussed that in detail, and as I slowly came to see that this is so, a large load of guilt rolled off my shoulders.

Another area we discussed was my need to try to place myself somehow, somewhere, in relationship to the abilities of others. My feelings about my own abilities swang wildly from the feeling that I must be the most stupid and contemptible woman alive to the notion that everyone was hopelessly retarded but me. Why, Esther wanted to know, was it so overwhelmingly necessary to ask that particular question? Why did I have so little idea where I fit in? How was this lack of information handicapping me in my daily life? And why wasn't it enough just to be what I was, to live my life on my own terms and let the rest of the world take care of itself?

But from all that first period of work, one morning in particular stands out in my memory as a landmark in my ongoing struggle to value myself. I came to my appointment that morning after a week of really severe depression. Scott was on my back; I was in a financial hole and could see no way ever to dig myself out of it. Between my own children's needs and the needs of the day-care children, I felt drained of any ability to make an emotional response at all, let alone to construct a personal life of any sort. If this was all there was going to be, of what use was the continuing backbreaking battle to make it from day to day? I struggled to put it into words that would make my feelings intelligible.

"What's the use?" I burst out. "I realize I'm doing as well as could be expected under the circumstances. Sure, for a hopeless schiz I'm doing well, I guess, but what good is that? As well as could be expected isn't enough for me. I don't want to do well for a hopeless schiz. I want a real life in my own right! I want to be a real person, not just okay considering how very little I've got to work with."

Esther looked at me with astonishment. "But, Mrs. Morgan," she exclaimed, "you *are* a capable person in your own right. I've *never* thought of you as barely making it, as substandard. Anyone would be proud of your accomplishments. You're one of the most real and substantial people I've ever known!"

It wasn't only the substance of the words, it was the conviction with which they were spoken that in one moment restored me to the human race. That was the moment I took myself off the "crazy" list and began to consider myself simply as another human being. I suddenly saw myself through Esther's eyes as existing in my own right, not just by the sufferance of others but truly as the simple equal of all my human brothers and sisters, equally real, equally deserving. It's hard even now for me to put into words all the meaning that moment had for me. I continue to draw strength from it each day of my life.

Ironically, I barely remember the incident that Esther refers to as the second—the real—testing. I have had that experience so many times: the sudden drop through space, the total disappearance of my self-esteem. It had literally never occurred to me until I read what Esther had written for this book that that collapse, which contains my most total neurotic reaction, could have any meaning within my relationship to another person. Typically, when I'm in that state, my sense of all relationships is severed. I feel so worthless that it seems impossible to me that I could have any emotional connection with another person or any personal significance in their lives. While my crisis is going on, I see all warm relationships as illusory, artificial, a dream I construct out of my own need to keep going but with no basis in reality, no meaning in the lives of others. I've learned how to live through those episodes, but that they cause pain and difficulty to the people around me, and that this is so precisely because they do love me, is information I'm still assimilating, part of my ongoing "work in progress."

Esther and I had been working together about a year when, without warning, Scott was laid off his job. Paychecks came to an end, and therefore child support for the time being also ended. I applied for assistance, for Aid to Families with Dependent Children. In our first interview, the intake worker told me that she was not a social worker but an eligibility technician. The job category required no specialized training or academic background, only a high school diploma and passing a civil service exam. She recommended that I make an application for the job: "I bet you'd do well at it," she said. I was not so confident, but I made the job application and presented myself for the exam. It was held one Saturday morning in the county hospital auditorium. To my dismay, the room was jampacked. More than a thousand people took the test that morning, as I later learned. I knew from the conversations around me that many of my competitors were already county employees, which automatically entitled them to a five-point bonus on the test score. I didn't think I stood a chance. Nevertheless, I plowed through the exam.

To my astonishment, two weeks later I received a card saying that I had passed the test. I was given an appointment for an oral exam at the Civil Service Commission. I presented myself on the assigned afternoon, nearly beside myself with fright. I was interviewed by a panel of three Civil Service examiners who went over with me, in very routine fashion, my qualifications for the job.

Three weeks later my test score came in the mail. I was number sixteen on the hiring list. Would I accept the position, effective immediately?

Would I! A chance to work with people, to use my own experience of poverty and illness in the defense of others. A job with some semblance of professional status. Above all, a chance to earn my living and support my own family at a real and substantial job. I accepted the position and began my month's training the next week.

Esther and I agreed that our goals for the therapy had been met. We discontinued our hours together, with the understanding that I could always call her if things went wrong and I felt I needed her help.

And so I graduated from therapy and began a new phase of my life.

## 2
# Return
# Engagement

## esther's narrative

Almost five years later, I heard from Martha again. She telephoned, saying she felt under a great deal of pressure—mostly reality problems, she thought—and would like to come in and talk to me. It might be just a matter of a few appointments, Martha said, to sort out what was going wrong and to decide what she might do.

Though she looked her usual well-put-together self when she came in, Martha told me she had "just folded up" at work one day and had gone home in a panic. A thorough physical examination had revealed nothing wrong, though she had been having a continuing recurrence of migraine headaches. Her job was frustrating in many ways, but this was nothing new or different and did not seem enough to account for her symptoms.

Martha expressed concern about the children. As we explored this, it seemed that Ann and Sasha were doing well despite some vehement sibling rivalry, and Peter, after a rocky start, was showing signs of being able to make it on his own. Although Martha had for a time been in a running battle with the school over Benjy's learning problem, the school guidance consultant had come to the rescue with a referral to the Special Learning Center, which Benjy now attended twice a week. Scott had rather generously offered to pay part of the cost without any apparent emotional strings attached, and Martha was genuinely grateful. Martha was obviously concerned about the children, but she seemed to be coping with their problems without imminent psychological hazard either to herself or to them. I was therefore surprised and curious when she ended the hour with the suggestion that perhaps some family therapy was needed.

So we had a second appointment, and a third. Gradually, we began to turn up a number of things Martha was angry about, outside the family. Although she had been discharging some of her anger at appropriate targets, the result seemed not to be relief but a further building up of inner rage to an almost uncontrollable intensity. Martha finally burst out with the complaint that everyone else is so

143

vulnerable she does not feel entitled to say what she thinks, to tell the truth as she sees it; yet it seems to occur to no one to spare her any unpleasant or hostile words that might come to mind. That seemed possible to me, for Martha was describing a very common pattern: Some people feel quite justified in saying anything they please, regardless of other people's feelings. I knew from Martha's own past reports to me that she had ways of taking care of herself in her more desperate moments with some pretty deadly verbal weapons of her own, so I was puzzled by her feeling of utter helplessness.

It was only at the end of the third hour that I thought we might have a clue. The children had been asking questions about the past. Why didn't you do this or that when we were little? Why did things go the way they did? Why is our family so weird? And of course they had been comparing their family with the storybook version. No wonder Martha was feeling helpless. You don't lay your children low for asking perfectly natural questions, but what do you say when they begin to ask you to explain things you yourself do not fully understand, things weird enough to suggest that someone had to be crazy? You don't just nonchalantly say, "Daddy was crazy," or "I was crazy," or "We were both crazy."

It had therefore occurred to Martha that family therapy might provide a protective framework within which to talk with the children not only about what had happened in their family in the past but also about things troubling them now. I did not dismiss this suggestion lightly, for I knew how valuable family sessions could be. Still, I was not convinced at this point that the problem was primarily one of communication or that it would require the children to become directly involved. If Martha herself could arrive at a sufficient understanding of what was the matter, I had no doubt she could convey to them whatever was necessary or appropriate in relation to the questions they were raising and the troubles they were having. It seemed to me that Martha was asking for the opportunity to explore for herself the significance of what had happened in the marriage and also to find some new and better way of dealing with the anger she was feeling now.

What convinced me of this was the fact that Martha was beginning to think about relationships with men and to wonder why for so many years she had steered entirely clear of them. She said she was determined "never again to get on anyone's merry-go-round" and allow herself to be used or devaluated or in any way victimized. A relationship bought at such a price was a kind of slavery. But how was she to get into a relationship with a man on new and different terms, terms she could accept? With all the anger that was erupting now, it was hard enough to maintain a friendship with a woman, where the additional hazard of sex was not involved, let alone enter into a possible love relationship with a man.

So Martha's question was not so much "What shall I say to my children?" as "What do I myself think about what happened to my marriage, and how do I now guard against repeating such an experience?" By the end of the fourth hour, after we had arrived at this view of the question, we decided to go on working together toward a more useful perspective on past and present events, events that we knew were heavily loaded with the potential for anger.

By the eighth hour, Martha was feeling desperate about her anger, for it seemed constantly to be getting in the way of her relationships with people and continually endangering her image of herself. She talked as though she were fighting with everyone, as though she were actually looking for excuses to get angry. This sounded very familiar to me because I went through a similar stage after I had decided it didn't pay to go around always being "good." No doubt anger was often the appropriate behavior, the only way that some circumstances could ever be changed. Anger must be at one's disposal when necessary, not something always and forever taboo, but we agreed that it hardly served Martha's present purposes to go around constantly chopping people's heads off, as though she were the Queen of Hearts in Alice's Wonderland.

To some extent, as so often happens in therapy, we were reopening old questions and our work would consist of deeper and more intensive exploration of territory we had covered before. Some of Martha's reality had not actually changed very much for the better. The matter of giving and getting, obviously so out of balance for Martha in our earlier contact, had still not shifted very much in her favor. She was in the position of so many divorced women—not exactly out of the frying pan into the fire, but certainly not into any promised land either. Though her job had given her an opportunity for independence and autonomy, and thus some solid ground on which to stand, it did not pay well enough to make her life easier or more rewarding in material ways. It also had some very serious built-in frustrations of its own, so that she was not reaping the emotional and psychological rewards she needed. Martha had no personal relationship in which she could, as she put it, "rest herself," for too often she was still putting herself at the beck and call of others in order to earn acceptance and approval—love being too much to hope for. But how to get out from under this situation? And how to avoid, in her anger, cutting herself off from everyone? Martha had proved to herself that she was strong enough to stand alone, yet it was perfectly clear that so much aloneness was hardly what she really wanted.

Surely it should be possible to find some middle way, some alternative to the hitherto seemingly inexorable choice of going along with others at any cost or, as she put it (I think with considerable satisfaction), "telling them to shove it." For both of us, the latter represented a masculine solution as well as a masculine expression; giving—above all, giving in—represented the feminine solution. As we began to talk about our notions of masculinity and femininity, an intellectual enough topic in itself, I began to be aware of considerable stepping-up of the emotional charge, as though a catalyst were at work. In joining with Martha to question traditionally assigned masculine and feminine roles, I seemed to be giving her permission to reopen some closed doors and to be assuring her that it was safe to do so. In psychological terms, I had reopened with her the whole question of identity, thus moving the level of therapy, at least potentially, into deeper territory.

In our previous contact, Martha's "good" image of herself had proved to be precariously established, still too entangled with the old, impossible-to-achieve standards, easily shaken by even some of the quite ordinary pushes and pulls of daily living, and dangerously prone to give way to the older, more strongly established "bad" image without warning. Inspecting herself now for what there might be of solid identity to build on, Martha could define herself with any certainty only as "one who can survive." From my standpoint, such a definition was a vast improvement over her old roles of "Mother" and "Saint," which had automatically placed her in bondage to almost anyone who might choose to ask something of her. But I realized that, for Martha, guilt and self-blame could still surge up in cataclysmic proportions when she recognized how far she sometimes fell short of her old ideals.* I knew it would not be exactly easy for her to look at the past and present with more open eyes.

The inducement for taking a new and seemingly dangerous look at things was, ironically enough, her hope that it might not be entirely impossible once again to have a relationship with a man— but without falling into the trap, as Martha put it, of "trying to get a man to love you." Yet if a woman no longer plays that game, what does she do? Presumably, she finds a man who will neither be turned off nor threatened by the real person she is—if such there be and if by some miracle he happens to be available. And, given all that, she does not drive him away by dumping everything on him, by demanding that all her needs be met, and overnight! From these remarks it seemed to me that Martha was quite realistically considering how to get "from here to there." She clinched it by saying that she would first have to deal with the leftover emotions of her marriage.

So we went to work on it. We started, quite fortunately as it happened, in the middle of the spring flu season. Each of three clients had reported to me during one week that she and her whole family had been sick, but the one who had had to get up and get the children fed, changed, medicated, or whatever in each instance was my client, the wife and mother. Because there was reason to think that she was at least as sick as her husband, each woman asked why she should also have had to wait on her husband, cooking for him and serving him in bed. Surely the man, who is supposed to be the strong one, should be able to take care of himself under these circumstances, shouldn't he? Why should she wait on him when she was sick, too? All three brought the question to me; none had said a word about it to her husband.

From Martha, I heard a similar story, but one out of the past —the story of the train of events that had led her to call for help from Father Michaelson. As she told it to me now in therapy, her family had all been ill at the same time. She had been sicker than Scott but had gotten up without question to take care of the children and then had started back to bed. Scott had thereupon said that he wanted breakfast, too. Martha had asked what he wanted. An egg, he told her, and she had been cooking it when Scott began to threaten suicide. She was sure it was in retaliation for the note of hostility in her voice, and she did not deny that the hostility had been there.

I was struck at the time with the fact that Martha's reaction had been the same as that of my three other clients: unspoken but undoubtedly observable hostility. In each instance, there had been a conflict of needs, with the man feeling entitled to have his needs met and the wife feeling obliged to meet them. I suspect that the other husbands were quite aware of their wives' hostility but let it go. After all, their needs were being met, no matter how ungraciously, and why look a gift horse in the mouth? But in Martha's case the conflict of needs was escalated immediately to what seems like bizarre proportions. In view of the incident that was the precipitating factor, Scott's suicide threats would seem excessive, to put it mildly, and almost designed to arouse in turn the maximum possible emotional reaction from Martha. She probably felt guilty about the hostility she had allowed to show and might therefore have feared she actually was in some way responsible, but it would also be natural for her to be very angry at the injustice of it all. Her call for help from priest and police at the end of a day of listening to suicide threats was a very human last-straw reaction, whatever the emotions that entered into it and whatever its effect on the marital situation. That it was the culmination of many such episodes over a long period of time I had not yet learned, though certainly I assumed that the circumstances and events of that one day were not an isolated phenomenon.

In any case, it is in the nature of marital conflict to escalate, but that between Martha and Scott clearly had already escalated so far beyond the common everyday variety as to be well into the "Russian roulette" category. Except for the extent of the escalation, however, Martha's situation had been much the same as that of my other clients. While talking of the common elements in the problem, I made the comment that led to the writing of this book. I think the recognition that she could identify with other women struggling with similar problems was very strengthening for Martha and helped to pry her loose from the "Saint Woman" of her ideals. The episode, stripped of its excessive escalation, was clearly typical of many marriages. An examination of it might be useful not only to Martha but to other clients, too, and it was of interest to me as a woman as well as to me as a therapist.

At this point in Martha's return to therapy, I did not, of course, have the advantage of the background material that has since come out, both in Martha's writing and in our later therapy hours together. I had only the sketchy story of her childhood and marriage that I had gotten from her in our first contact for the sake of a cautious, reality-based, here-and-now kind of therapy. My limited knowledge of her history had proved sufficient for that purpose —though it did not explain the episode toward the end of the contact in which Martha had shifted gears so unexpectedly and so nearly disastrously. Although that event strongly suggested there was much more of significance and perhaps of danger in Martha's background than I knew, I did not feel it ruled out our working together on a deeper level toward Martha's present goals. On the contrary, I felt that Martha had confirmed my estimate of her potential by her conduct of her life in the years between our first and second contacts. Also, my still vivid memory of the dramatic near-reversal of my original evaluation simply whetted my curiosity and stimulated my interest in working with her. (I suspect something of the same curiosity operated here that goes into my taste for murder mysteries.)

The one possible obstacle to our present purposes was that Martha still seemed to be hooked on the dangerous and terrifying notion that if she couldn't prove Scott was crazy, then she would herself be eligible for the "crazy" label—and all the things Scott had ever said about her or other people had thought about her might be true. If Martha had any therapists in the past who were *not* caught on that hook (and it seems to me from her account that she had), they had not been able to convey to her that the question "Who is crazy?" although certainly of some significance, was not as crucial a question as it had come to be for both her and Scott. I was convinced that somewhere along the line in Martha's current therapy with me, we were going to have to shift from what I considered a less useful question to some more useful ones.

Martha had originally told me little more than that Meg Goodwin, her social worker, had decided from Martha's description that Scott was a paranoid schizophrenic. I neither accepted nor rejected Miss Goodwin's assumption that Martha, too, was schizophrenic; I simply felt the label had little meaning in any case and was certainly not an essential consideration in the work I was undertaking with Martha at that time. If I were now to go along with the game of "Who is crazy?" I felt that I would have great difficulty in arriving at much real understanding of what had gone on between these two people and of what Martha could do to alleviate or remedy the aftereffects for herself and the children.

I felt that I needed some understanding of Scott as a human being, with the facets of personality and the variety of behavior so often obscured by the dehumanizing label of schizophrenic. Unless Martha could now begin to provide more of the information I needed, I would have to resort to a great deal of speculation. In any case, it was essential to Martha's further growth at this point that she be able to confirm for herself that she saw what she saw, heard what she heard, and knew what she knew. I would now very actively encourage her to provide the factual material I had not previously sought.

I needed to know what Martha had been exposed to and the effects that the exposure had had on her. Whatever a husband's symptoms may be, whether they are neurotic, psychotic, or simply eccentric, they are bound to have some impact on his wife. If a woman is dependent on him in some important way, a man's psychological state, his attitudes and ideas, and his patterns of behavior are likely to operate as "givens." They are the framework within which the woman is expected to find a solution to her own problems. A woman must deal in some fashion with what is dealt out to her, though what she does in return may have a good deal of bearing on the relationship, too. I felt there was much more to Martha's experience than could be understood simply in terms of the story of a marriage to a madman. To the extent that the matter of "Who is crazy?" would throw light on that experience, we would have to explore it; but to the extent that it would obscure other, perhaps more meaningful facts, we needed to put it to rest.

If one must be hung up on the horns of a dilemma, I would prefer it to be an unavoidable one, common to many human beings, and, at least as of now, one of interest to me as a woman. The problem of who is to get up and do the cooking when the whole family is sick —the question that set all this off—though not exactly impressive at first glance, seemed to me to fall into the proper category. Reduced to its essentials, it can be seen as a typical conflict of needs, a situation basic to most problems in marriage. When needs conflict, whose need is to be met? The woman's answer is likely to be: first of all, the children's, and traditionally she will feel that she as the mother will meet them. Traditionally, too, it would be she who would cook her husband's egg, though my clients now dared to question this. (I note with interest that none suggested her husband get up and cook an egg for her.) Here is a subject far from trivial, for it relates to the most fundamental of all human needs—the need to be fed, cared for, nurtured, a need common to all human infants, female as well as male.

In examining each of the instances reported to me by clients, the man seems to have felt entitled to have his need for nurturing met by the woman, but it didn't even occur to the woman that her same need might be met by the man. Except in power situations, where might makes right, it usually happens in a relationship that the person who most strongly feels entitled to get his way is the one who does so. There is something about the strength of expectation rather than the matter of sex as such that seems to make the difference, hence those situations in which the woman is clearly dominant. But the nurturing situation is one in which the feeling of entitlement belongs almost exclusively to the man and the feeling of obligation just as exclusively to the woman.

This difference in expectations arises out of an inescapable historical necessity: the girl child has had to shift her expectations of fulfillment from the mother, who clearly does the nurturing in traditional families, to the father, whose role in fulfilling such primary needs is a good deal more obscure, if it exists at all. The boy child has had to make no such shift; he continues into adulthood looking to the woman for nurturing and need not become a nurturing person himself. So the husband might well be affronted if the wife were to ask for mothering from him, though she is expected—and expects herself —to be willing to mother him.

But women need nurturing, too. They do not come into marriage with their needs for sustaining emotional experience already met once and for all, thereby having a limitless fund of energy, patience, and ingenuity with which to meet every kind of demand for sustenance made on them. Any woman who expects herself to function as such a paragon is embarked on a collision course, a collision with the facts of life, of reality, of what is possible, and with her own basic needs and desires as well. Yet that paragon is exactly what has been portrayed, more often than not, as the ideal woman, the model whom all women must strive to emulate.

Anyone who marries young—or without sufficient experience in the world and with other human beings to have come to terms with the yearning to be cared for left over from the prolonged experience of infancy and childhood—expects from the partner many things that cannot be given, or can be given only at great cost or much sacrifice. The history of the marriage then becomes the history of how these two people are able (or not able) to grow and to change, sometimes to accommodate to and sometimes to give up on this or that need or desire or longing on the part of one or the other, and finally, with great good luck and considerable effort, to make a mutually satisfying life together. Or with almost as much luck and effort, they may come to an amicable parting of the ways before too much damage is done.

I do not believe, as some "experts" do, that people find partners by some infallible radar system of the unconscious, exactly at the same level of maturity and mental health as their own, or that one partner's neurosis or psychosis is thus exactly matched by the other's. Such identicalness is in any case impossible, for maturity and mental health are not monolithic entities but exist in different measure in different areas of a person's mental and emotional life. Neurotic and psychotic manifestations are often quite privately handled by the people who suffer them. Even where similarities are great, there are still some differences. It is the existence of the differences, the greater ability of one or the other to give or to understand, to grow and to change, or to take action of one kind or another, that determines the outcome of a marriage.

Where needs are not so intensely held as to be nonnegotiable, they can be talked about and some kind of agreement can be effected. But suicide threats are not exactly in the category of give-and-take communication. It was not the request for nurture as such that Martha was revolting against, no more so than my other clients, but the bind she was put in by Scott's suicide threat, a bind that was related to far more than the matter of food. Martha seems to have accepted as a condition of her marriage that she find within herself a sufficient supply of emotional resources to meet an infinite demand for emotional nurture. According to such a contract, she must not just cook Scott's egg but must do so *cheerfully*, must cheerfully give up her own need to be taken care of (or, at least, to take care of herself) in order to provide the care that he needs. Martha had finally reached the end of her rope. She could cook Scott's egg but she was not willing to take responsibility for his entire existence, for whether, in fact, he would continue to live at all.

My first reaction—and this was how I originally wrote it—was to see Martha's experience as set apart from the others primarily by reason of the tremendous escalation it exhibited. Looking back on it now with far more information to go on, I still think this is true; but I think the real significance of the incident lay in the fact that Martha was finally taking some action. From the standpoint of what had been going on in the relationship from the beginning, the question was not why she acted as she then did, but why she had not acted earlier. Even at that point, however, Martha was acting out of sheer desperation. She was without any firm conviction that she could deal with the consequences, whatever they were: Scott's anger, of course, but also the possibility of blowing up the marriage completely and forever, leaving her with no one but herself to take charge of her life.

As it happened, her action did not blow up the marriage. Instead, it set into motion a series of events that made it possible for her, much later, to be ready for the end of her marriage when it came. But the initial act of revolt was essential to the final act; without the former, the latter might never have taken place. Two people might have continued in a miserable existence together in which the crucial question might eventually have become, irrevocably, whose suicide would end it. So Martha's action, which she thought of at the time as necessary to Scott's survival, was actually the first step in assuring her own.

Eventually, the incident led to the writing of this book. I do not think that the decision to write was a mere happenstance. I think it may very well have been the result of Martha's unconscious recognition that she needed some inducement to shift the course of therapy into more productive channels. At the time we made the decision, however, I had no idea how or when or even if that shift would take place. It would seem I was taking a gamble, a gamble that Martha's therapy would proceed at a rate that would make it possible to write the kind of book we had in mind.

OOO    BOTH SIDES OF THE DESK

# 3
# Remarks
# by Esther

I note with some misgiving that the end of the last chapter suggests we already had in mind the kind of book we would write. We did in a way, but only in a vague, general way. There were some things we definitely hoped to accomplish. We wanted to demonstrate something about the nature of casework therapy through Martha's therapy and in the process to look at some of the general problems of women and of man-woman relationships. Exactly what we would cover and what results we would come out with in the end, we could not predict.

This combination of a few fairly well-defined purposes without any specific formula for achieving them and with no claim whatsoever to producing precise, predictable results is typical of therapy, at least as I practice it.* In general, I expect some growth and change on the part of the client, but the exact kind and amount of growth and change will necessarily be affected by many factors so entirely outside the range of therapy that it would be foolish to predict specific results. Nor would I want the therapeutic experience hamstrung by being measured and measuring itself by some artificially imposed "objective" standards. Still, we were writing a book, and a book demands a plan of some sort, or at least a specific theme around which to organize material.

Early in our work together, Martha and I had sketchily outlined the kind of book we hoped to write. We did not attempt to spell out in detail exactly what we would cover. To do so would have placed us in the position of predicting the course that therapy would take and, more likely than not, would have tempted us to follow that course for the sake of the book, an untherapeutic if not disastrous procedure. There were, however, two safeguards against this danger: Martha and I. I, because I am constitutionally incapable of putting restrictions on freedom of thought or forcing the mind into unnatural channels; Martha, because she is constitutionally incapable of accepting anything that does not make sense to her from the standpoint of where she is in her thinking at the time. So it was not likely that we would either start out or end up with a book alien to us and our real purposes. We were destined, instead, to write a book that would grow and change in the course of the therapeutic experience, much as we would.

Martha began writing with the material she felt most able, and most motivated, to put on paper. According to our outline, she was to begin with her earlier years—if not all of them, at least those that led to her marriage—and her experiences prior to therapy. Almost immediately, however, we saw that Martha had to start with an account of her previous therapy and her reactions to it. She had to get that off her chest before she could go on to the more difficult subject of the beginnings of her marriage and the earlier history of her family of origin. Even now, she has written and spoken of her childhood only peripherally, though very significantly. If she eventually were to go into that material in any detail, we might have quite another kind of book. But a book, like therapy, has its limits, and we would have to discover together what these might be.

I, too, had had my trouble getting started. I had originally planned to plunge right into some autobiographical material, but I found that I could not do so. It was as though I had to establish my professional identity before I dared to risk something of my personal identity. So I began by writing a position statement (see Appendix). And then, when I did begin writing more personal material, I did so in response to Martha's story, taking my cues from her. Here again the writing process and the therapy process seemed to be of the same nature, a responsive and developmental nature, not a superimposed order of events.

Just as Martha and I had respected one another's autonomy in the course of therapy, so had we agreed to do in our writing—by keeping out of each other's material as much as possible. Although we would give each other copies of what we had written and would welcome each other's comments, neither of us would in any way write the other's story. Martha would be responsible for the final draft of her material, as I would be for mine. This sounds like a simple rule, but it didn't turn out to be that simple. Apart from the conscious influence we deliberately exerted through our suggestions to each other, we soon became aware of the working of unconscious influences. I would occasionally find myself plagiarizing a remark Martha had made, or I would recognize in her manuscript some idea I had expressed. The unconscious is, of course, constantly operating; it underlies whatever conscious agreements and conclusions we arrived at. I use this example of two-way borrowing in our writing to illustrate the process of unconscious identification that takes place on the therapist's as well as the client's side of the desk. It also illustrates the working of the positive transference and countertransference by which we each viewed the other in the light of any happy and constructive experiences we may have had with significant people in the past. This helped us to find and to identify with things we liked in one another.

There is much more to the interaction than such sweetness and light, however. There are inevitably a great many differences between therapist and client. Some of these are simply the ordinary run of differences in personality, which may coincidentally help or hinder the course of treatment. There are also those differences inherent in the simple fact that no life is exactly the same as any other. Since only the client has lived his own life, the therapist can never know exactly what that life has been. I could not actually experience Martha's story, no matter how accurately and movingly Martha might tell it. I could understand it only in the limited fashion possible to me, with the help of my identification with her and whatever enlightening experiences, personal and professional, I could bring to the matter.

To begin with, we really didn't know each other very well. Our previous contact had been confined mostly to a somewhat intellectual understanding of Martha's immediate real-life circumstances. Now we gradually became acquainted with one another in a different way. It should be remembered we began this part of our work together without having covered the material that now comprises the first two parts of this book. We had just started to do this writing when we began to tape our interviews. The reader is thus approaching the transcriptions of our therapy hours with a far greater acquaintance with Martha and me than either of us had of the other at the time.

We also ran into problems with negative transference and countertransference. The client is entitled to, and often (for the successful outcome of his treatment) absolutely must, transfer to the therapist whatever angry, distrustful, destructive, or otherwise unpleasant and unhappy reactions may be left over and unresolved from traumatic experiences with significant people in the past. It is up to the therapist to recognize any equivalent negative feelings that may be aroused within himself in the process and to handle them in some way that will not be damaging to the client or detrimental to the course of therapy.

In this regard, it became clear fairly soon that the interaction between Martha and me was going to be far more affected by the writing of the book than we had originally expected. The negative transference became much more intense and complicated than is usual even, I think, with equally difficult therapeutic tasks (though, of course, no two therapeutic problems are exactly comparable). The most obvious complication was the fact that Martha and I were dealing with one another not only in therapeutic hours but also in what we were writing. We both had very real thoughts and feelings about this very real project and reacted constantly to one another in this entirely real-life situation. Our reactions, of course, were a mixture, sometimes an alternation, of actual and transference elements. Both kinds of reactions were discussed in therapy hours. The process of sorting out which response partook of which factor, to what extent and in what combination with other factors, was a most difficult and complicated affair. The fact that negative transference and countertransference were immensely stepped up in the process of writing made the whole matter of "the book" fraught with tremendous emotional implications for both of us.

Since we survived, I am inclined—and I think Martha is also —to look at the extra hazards and the additional pain as having contributed much to the emotional effectiveness of the intellectual work being done and as having produced a far greater depth of understanding than we would otherwise have achieved. But I have some of the same feeling that I had about the intensity with which I experienced my disturbance in the course of my own therapy: There ought to be some easier way! By and large, of course, there is an easier way. When therapy is not impinged upon by some difficult reality situation affecting both client and therapist, its course usually runs more smoothly. It seems possible that Martha needed a therapeutic experience of the special sort that arose out of our writing project and unconsciously chose this way for herself. I suspect that clients often find ways of seeing to it that they get the kind of therapy they need, whatever that may be.

Fortunately, collaboration on the book demanded a personal relationship that would not otherwise have developed and that proved to be an advantage rather than a disadvantage. When the negative transference and countertransference developed, Martha and I could compare our feelings about each other as we experienced them in therapy hours with our experience of each other on ordinary, everyday occasions, and we could take some comfort in the contrast between the "real life" and the transference feelings. That Martha was able to make such comparisons was, of course, a tribute to her strength of mind as well as an attribute of the benign setting of home, friends, and so on within which the personal contacts took place. Still, I would guess that every possible positive factor had to be thrown into the scale at the height of the crisis in order to outweigh the increase in negative factors produced by the problems of our literary collaboration.

We had, of course, not anticipated sufficiently the extent of the ramifications and repercussions we would encounter, but we did at least anticipate correctly the strength of the working relationship we had built in our previous experience as therapist and client. That relationship managed to withstand the fact that our writing project (and most especially my written comments) brought about an unexpected shift in emphasis in our work together, from "supportive" therapy to "insight" therapy. The switch is essentially from a process that focuses on a recognition of strengths and ability to cope to a

process that obliges the client to look at troubled areas, inner conflicts, and deeper levels of personality. As it turned out (and again
perhaps as unconsciously "planned"), Martha was ready for such a
shift—but I think just barely—and there were some extremely anxious and painful moments for both of us.

The matter of timing is tremendously important. Some questions can be safely explored right away; others must wait until sufficient strength has been attained and enough other insights incorporated to permit their being looked at in greater depth. To the extent
that we could time our writing to accommodate the needs of therapy,
we did so, but we were by no means aware of all the ways in which
it might impinge upon the process of therapy. Occasionally, I could
be quite certain that I was holding to safe limits in what I was writing,
but often I was not that sure of my judgment. Sometimes I seemed
to be proceeding as though I believed that when in doubt, take a
chance. Such a procedure was not at all my style; my sins are far more
often those of omission than of commission. I assume that my unconscious was willing to take risks my conscious mind usually will not.
I can only account for this behavior on the part of my unconscious
as a manifestation of what proved to be a justified faith in our ability
—Martha's and mine—to deal with what developed.*

A number of factors finally coincided to produce a crisis in
our work together. I had been writing my account of our second
contact, "Return Engagement," but had found myself unable to get
beyond the point at which we decided to work together on a book.
I didn't know what was holding me back, I just knew I was blocked.
By the time I realized that I could not bring myself to write something I was afraid Martha might not be ready to read, she had in some
way let me know—I can't say just how—that she was ready. I finished
the writing with some anxiety, however, and made sure that not too
much time would elapse between Martha's reading of it and our next
therapy hour. I just wasn't all that sure!

By coincidence—or unconscious timing—we had reached a
point in the book where it became necessary to discuss the matter
of disguise in more than just the very general terms in which we had

originally considered the matter. Martha was writing under a nom de plume, so a great deal of disguise would not be necessary for her, but I was writing under my real name and would have to stand behind whatever we ended up doing about disguise. I suppose I assumed that since I would have to take the entire responsibility, I should have the final say. Actually, I had not thought much about it, and it was not until Martha disagreed with me over some of the specifics of the disguise that I became fully aware of the matter. Only then could I see that this was, after all, Martha's story, whatever my professional responsibility in it, and that she also had rights in regard to the form of disguise we used.

Quite apart from this area of disagreement, we discovered that Martha and I differ in a great many respects, and not necessarily neurotic ones. We have all kinds of ordinary differences of opinion, style, taste, and so on. Martha, for instance, would be apt to call a spade a big, black dirty instrument for digging graves, while I would be more likely to speak of its sterling contribution to the beauty of a garden. So whatever suggestions I would make about Martha's writing would naturally be in the direction of softening her blows, of looking at the positive things in other people and in herself. Martha, on the other hand, would tend to see in my writing every trace of criticism or hostility toward her it might contain. When two such contradictory tendencies collide, especially in a situation in which some very important dynamics are operating on an unconscious level, there is likely to be some kind of explosion. And eventually there was!

The verbal interaction in our work together will be presented from transcribed tape recordings, beginning with the slow-moving preparatory work that culminated in a lengthy recording made a month or so before the crisis in our relationship—and in the therapy itself—erupted. In this "marathon" session Martha spoke of events she had at most just touched upon before. She gave supporting details that enabled me to begin to understand her story, emotionally and intellectually, in a way I could not possibly have done earlier. (Empathy and intuition, essential as they are, must be firmly grounded in facts if therapist and client are not to take off on speculative flights of mutual fantasy.)

In the hours preceding this session, important work was done, the kind of preliminary work that must take place before material deeply felt and high in anxiety content can be usefully dealt with. Martha moved gradually toward incorporation of some crucial insights, a necessary process before there could be any basic shift in her feelings and attitudes. In our marathon session, we experienced the outcome of those many long, patient hours, and together we recognized how those insights might produce a different way of looking at oneself and one's problems.

We would not recommend marathon sessions as therapy, especially those that deliberately promote discomfort and fatigue.* Our own venture beyond the "fifty-minute hour" arose out of our wish to get on with the book as rapidly as we felt it safe to do so, and it was made possible by a weekend that combined relaxation and recreation with recording. We have no reason to assume that the length of the session was in itself particularly valuable; even though interrupted by lunch, it was extremely exhausting. When we finished, we felt as though we needed a few hours in a psychological decompression chamber before venturing back into the ordinary rhythms of living.

In no way did we try to use tape recording as a treatment method either. We did not play the tapes back for purposes of elucidation or confrontation; for me, such a procedure would have disrupted the network of emotional and intellectual rapport on which our relationship rested. We simply used the tapes as a method of recording our work together without, we hoped, affecting it adversely. The advantages seemed to offset the difficulties, especially after we lost our self-consciousness about the recorder there on the desk between us. Martha recognized the potential usefulness of this method for our project before I did, and I am indebted to her for persisting with the idea despite my reluctance. Not only does a concrete record independent of our own statements now exist to confirm what our work together has been, but also it seems to me that only by this means could we really have demonstrated the interaction between us.

Our guiding principle in editing the tapes has been to retain enough of the transcriptions in their original form so that our work together would be seen as clearly as possible from the actual communication between us without the need for a great deal of technical or analytical explanation.* This principle inevitably meant that we would be demonstrating some of the slowness of pace and seemingly endless repetition by which progress takes place. Important themes surface slowly, are examined gradually, and are looked at first from one angle and then from another. After a good deal of going around and around emotionally and intellectually—each time in a somewhat different way—it is possible to come to grips with some of these matters.

The crisis in our relationship proved to be a useful crisis in the course of therapy, for it gave us the opportunity to deal with problems on a deeper level than we had originally anticipated. There followed a slow working-through process in which issues were resolved and shifts in attitude and behavior took place. Such a process is typical of any therapy where problems are deeply rooted and have existed over many years. It is not, of course, typical of situations amenable to brief treatment. We are presenting excerpts from nine months of therapy; for the kind of problems we were dealing with, this was quick work!

The transcriptions, of course, cover only the verbal part of our interaction and only the work that took place during therapy hours. It is through our notebooks, in which each of us reflected on what was going on in our lives as well as in therapy, that we hope to reveal some of the interaction not recorded on tape. I hope, too, that the notebooks can serve to balance somewhat the fact that Martha refrained from rewriting her story (from personal inclination as well as in the interest of historical truth) while I revised and rewrote all the way through. Incorporating much of Martha's insight as well as my own, I must seem a far wiser and more rational person than I actually was at any one point. Martha's notebook provides some familiarity with the part of her personality that dealt creatively throughout this period with emotional and intellectual matters not necessarily tied in with her actual therapy hours. We have placed her notebook after the "working-through" phase with the expectation that its random sampling of Martha's feelings and thoughts during the course of therapy will answer some questions and close some gaps.

Much of my notebook, especially the earlier part, is based on interview notes I made as we went along. I shall use this material to bridge the gap between our transcriptions and to provide some connecting themes. But I found that, as time went on, I was writing more and more out of my own experience. In doing so, I was falling into a kind of free association in which thoughts and feelings stimulated by the professional purpose made connection with events and reminiscences from my personal life, which could, in turn, be brought back to bear on the professional task. If I have not spelled out exactly what these connections are in each instance or in any great detail, so be it. Free association is valuable to therapy in part because of its ambiguity, leaving each person free to make of it what he wishes.

from esther's notebook

# 4
# Opening
# Phase

This was our first therapy hour since we started writing, and I think we were both anxious. Last week we met at lunch to share what we had written thus far. It was just a beginning, but I thought we were both relieved to find we could at least get something down on paper. It seemed to me that our hope of writing something together was not unrealistic.

Apparently that feeling of cautious optimism was my own, and I had projected it onto Martha. Today she reported that she was experiencing an old familiar feeling that what she is producing is in some way substandard, that she really doesn't know what she is doing, and that it is presumptuous of her to be trying to do anything at all. She tied this in with her childhood, when she was so much younger than her two sisters that she constantly felt herself the one child, isolated and alone, in a grown-up world.

Martha had called her parents before she began to write (in reaction, I gather, to something I had said about my parents), and she said her call had confirmed what she had already known: She could not now, any more than she could as a child, establish satisfying communication with them. (Was she envying what she imagined my relationship with my parents to be?)

Martha then immediately went on to talk of her feelings about the Brahms *A German Requiem,* now being rehearsed by the choral group of which she is a member. Martha said she invariably goes to pieces not on the death theme but on the theme of joy, the resurrection, the affirmation of hope. Once, she added, she had thought that if she could only rule out the possibility of happiness, she could manage to live life; that what the Greeks had meant by the story of Pandora's box was that hope is the last, the worst, cruelty of all!

Martha went on to speak of her wish to try once again to find love and her hesitation about mentioning this wish to me. She felt I had settled for something less than what she was seeking and thought

I would be threatened by her search for love. In her marriage she had paid an exorbitant price for the semblance of love, not knowing that love was something that might actually exist.

It seemed to me Martha was saying that she did believe love could exist and that if other people had it perhaps she could, too, but she would need my permission to believe in it and to seek it. What must I ask myself in response to Martha's questions? Do I believe in love? Of course, but there are so many kinds of love. What kind was she talking about? Martha had implied that she recognized there had not been and now could not be the love between father and daughter she must have longed for as a child. And she recognized the possibility of religious love; she could sing about it in the *Requiem*, though tears coursed down her cheeks as she did so. But if she were to believe in adult sexual love between a man and a woman, what then? What might be the danger for her? She would not want to repeat what had happened in her marriage.

I wondered if Martha hoped that I would say something about my own experience, and I decided that she should have some kind of personal response. Any psychoanalytically oriented interpretation, however correct, about the forbidden incestuous love for father and the attempted sublimation through religion would seem irrelevant if not fantastically absurd. Nor was this the occasion for an intellectual consideration of the subject of love in general. Yet the facts of my own life could have no possible therapeutic value, it seemed to me, at this point. So I simply said that my feeling and thoughts about love would necessarily be different from hers, if for no other reason than that I was considerably older than she and had had to struggle with my own questions in my own way at earlier times of my life; and if I should need to do so once again, that was all right with me, too.

We ended up agreeing that Martha was doing now what she needed to do at this stage of her life. At seventeen and at thirty, she had been, as she said, in no condition really to struggle with the question of love at all. It had been all she could do to survive. Now, entering her forties, she was asking my permission to hope—not just for love but that life could somehow be different and better than it had been, and that she was as much entitled to that hope as anyone else.

*April*

During the past three sessions, Martha and I had experimented with ways of combining therapy with writing a book and floundered around quite a bit in the process. We tried the tape recorder, feeling very awkward and self-conscious about it. Then I discovered we had gone through a whole hour with the machine plugged in only half way because I had failed to check it properly, and the entire session, of course, went unrecorded. I immediately made some notes from memory but had the feeling that terribly important observations had been lost forever. Since I had been very dubious about the value of tape recording for our project, my failure to see that the machine was plugged in properly was an amusing instance of unconscious resistance. But now I was suddenly a complete convert: Deprived of our mechanical aid, I imagined the loss to be far greater than the actual value of anything we had managed to capture in our recording thus far.

Martha was trying to explore her childhood and growing-up experiences, but, as she herself acknowledged, her recollections added up to mere intellectualization without any emotional impact. Though she would begin to talk about her parents, she would invariably slide away from this material. The only truly experienced fact for her seemed to be "they didn't want me"; everything else was an emotional blank. Martha was convinced that no one in her family had wanted her. But then she talked of her sister Annette, seven or eight years older than she, who had introduced her to music and poetry and thus had "saved" her; she had even told Martha where babies come from, since her mother was too embarrassed to do so. (Martha didn't say so, but could this have helped to save her, too?) Martha also remembered that there were times with her mother that were good —reading, and feeding the birds and the squirrels. She thought perhaps her mother did want her once she was born, though not before.

Martha finally said, "It's a frozen lump, not empty space, and maybe now not frozen all the way through."

Martha saw what she called a "parallel" hazard to our writing project from this earlier time. She had been a poor student while her sisters had been brilliant ones. Everyone was careful not to downgrade Martha by comparison, but because she would get approval for just ordinary achievement, Martha felt it as condescending, false, not reflecting any actual merit at all. In the end Martha became confused about the value of anything she did, unable to differentiate between praise that was truly meant and praise that was just "people trying to be nice." When I asked Martha how she was handling my recognition of her ability now, she said, "By an act of faith!"

Martha was also trying to get at the facts about her marriage, but she would touch a single point and then drift off into generalities. I knew she must be feeling tremendous anxiety, more than would ordinarily be expected. She would say such things as "People who are closest put their ego trips on one another," wondering whether she had done this to Scott, as she felt he had done to her, but she would never actually explore the question. Martha was aware of the theory that marriage partners often choose each other for unconscious and sometimes very sick reasons and wondered to what extent this might have been true for her. I injected the observation from my own experience and from the literature of marriage counseling that marriages are often out of balance because one partner is considerably less mature or more neurotic than the other. I added my own conviction that the more open-minded partner can often be maneuvered by the other into feeling guilty and responsible for all the problems between them. Because Martha had originally been in some way willing to accept the blame—and because of her own uncertainty as to what her problem in the marriage actually had been—even now she felt in danger that "the whole thing will reverse itself" and somehow Scott would prove to have been "right" and she "wrong."

Then Martha told me something that indicated to me she must have known exactly what the truth *for her* had been. During her brief period of hospitalization, one of her visits to the outside world had been to the home of a Jewish friend for a seder. This ritual reenactment of the travail of the Jewish people on their long journey from slavery to freedom had had a tremendous impact on Martha— as though it were not just a religious tale but her own personal story. To go from slavery to freedom was to come back to life from a kind of psychological death, and Martha could not have identified so strongly with that journey of an alien people had she not been emotionally traveling the same path. I was convinced that though on an intellectual level she was not quite sure what she had been doing in the marriage, on the emotional level she was deeply aware that she had been engaged in a desperate battle for her own survival.

Attacks by one partner on the other are often so indirect and so unconsciously motivated that it is very difficult to detect what is happening. Even though Scott at times acknowledged exactly what he was doing, Martha still could not be sure exactly what it was doing to her; she had no way of gauging to what extent Scott's problems were contributing to her own. Someone like Martha, who had tried all her life to be "good," finds it difficult to believe that others do not operate in the same way and, as a matter of fact, is likely to be quite naïve about other people's motives. Outrageous behavior, openly admitted, may then seem either literally unbelievable or horribly fascinating; if one continues in such a situation, there comes to be some acceptance of the behavior. I began to suspect that Martha's anxiety was related less to whose "fault" it was that the marriage was a disaster than to the question of her inability to maintain for herself a clear and unequivocal position toward Scott's behavior by her own criteria.

No two people's definitions of reality coincide exactly, but such differences in point of view, although often constituting the content of quarrels between marital partners, only rarely become so great as to jeopardize the mental stability of one or the other. Yet there seems to have been just such a threat, certainly to Martha and perhaps to Scott, too, so that at times it became a question of whose version of reality was in actual fact the "correct" one, with the sanity of each possibly hinging on the outcome. Martha had ultimately answered this question by an affirmation of her own view but apparently with little outside validation, since it seemed to her there was considerable acceptance of Scott's point of view. If she now risked her own interpretation to the evaluative process of therapy—and in a book as well—she was indeed risking a great deal.

My concern at this point was to neutralize as much as possible Martha's fear of losing her right to affirm her own view of both past and present events, and I cast about for a way of doing so. It was then that I recalled a chapter in *The Intimate Enemy* by Bach and Wyden, which had gone into considerable detail about what they called "sick" or "dirty" fighters and the "satanic" tactics that could literally drive vulnerable spouses mad. This was strong fare— stronger, in fact, than I would have ventured at this point on my own (I knew so little, as yet, of Martha's story)—but it testified to the existence of the sort of marital conflict Martha seemed to have been caught in, so I suggested she read it. She did, two or three times. It helped, at least enough so that she could begin to tell me a little more specifically about some of the things that had gone on in her marriage. It also helped her to begin writing of a time in her life when she had been so uncertain and confused about herself as a person and her role as a woman that she was, for all practical purposes, her own "intimate enemy."

The combination of the intellectual and the emotional is a powerful therapeutic dynamic with a built-in flexibility, for one can shift usefully from the more intellectual to the more emotional and back again—profiting from whatever may turn up at any point on the scale. Martha and I had built our original relationship and had done our previous work on what seemed primarily an intellectual level, but as we became more interested in "women's lib," we became increasingly involved on an emotional level. Now, as we began recording our work together, it seemed to me that we were still very much at the intellectual end of the scale and would have to find some access to emotional matters.

Sometimes such access comes through memories, often those

of early childhood and the growing-up years. Exploration of a life history may be far more than just a fact-finding operation, may indeed be a very emotional experience. Such an approach may fail, however, if emotions are so well covered over that they are not accessible to memory or, conversely, if emotions are not covered over well enough so that the whole matter is too fraught with psychological danger even to be attempted.

There is no way of predicting what will unlock the important doors—one must simply keep one's ears and eyes open and pick up on whatever clues come along. Sometimes clues come the other way around. Not memory but the here-and-now provides the access to crucial emotions from the past, emotions that must be reexperienced and reexamined in order to understand the present and to learn to deal effectively with it. Always, there needs to be a flexibility whereby one can go back and forth, from current events to past history and vice versa. The task for therapy in this opening phase was to operate as flexibly and comfortably as we could, Martha and I together, along whatever line of thought gave promise of furthering our quest.

The components of a life are not like the pieces of a jigsaw puzzle, to be put together in only one way, once and forever. A number of different pictures can be assembled from the same pieces, depending on how they are viewed, from what angle, in what context. The goal of therapy is for a new and more effective pattern, a different Gestalt, to take shape out of what has been there all along. I do not know exactly when or how it is to emerge, or what form it is to take, and I have no bag of tricks to bring it about. For me, there must be a spontaneous rising to the occasion with whatever I can bring to it. Out of a whole battery of possible responses I hope to hit upon some kind of special, quite individual, and partly unconscious adaptation to what my client brings. Sometimes, my best and only approach is simply to listen as intently as I can, not only to what my client is saying but also to anything I can "hear" at the back of my mind—or in my gut.

I don't like the word "technique" applied to therapy. It

makes what should be a shared experience sound like something imposed, no matter how altruistically and skillfully, by one person on another. But the combination of the emotional and intellectual as it guides and informs the therapeutic process is very dear to my heart. I remember from my undergraduate years what the Gestalt psychologists called the "Aha!" point, the moment of insight when the ape put two sticks together to reach the otherwise unattainable banana. I made immediate, wholehearted identification with that simian breakthrough, as I could never make with the correct running of a maze by even the brightest of rats. And in my years of self-exploration, a true insight would literally turn me on like the sudden lighting up of an electric globe—exactly as pictured in the comic strips!

*May 18*

After my optimistic entry in April, we seemed to be stuck. Despite my efforts at reassurance and my very active encouragement, Martha blocked each time she tried to come to grips with material from the past. She could not even produce amplifying or clarifying memories that we might examine together for clues. But while Martha was blocking at emotionally significant material from the remote past of her childhood and the more recent past of her marriage, she was having no such trouble with current happenings. Last week her house had been burglarized—"ripped off," as they say now, a phrase that more nearly conveys the emotion Martha expressed at coming home to find her stereo and Sasha's camera, among other things, stolen and her house violated by this ugly intrusion. In addition, the insurance company, resting on its fine-print clauses, seemed disinclined to make any reimbursement at all.

Today, Martha told of a situation at work that loosed a flood tide of emotion and of words. She was able to spell out in minute detail exactly what had happened, who had said and done what, when, and where, under what circumstances, and her own reaction to each facet of the situation. Not only that, but she came up with possible reasons why it had happened and with ideas about its deeper meaning in regard to her life experience as a whole, past and present. In fact, she provided so much substantiating detail in this hour that we had to edit much of it out of the transcribed interview in order to keep the entry within reasonable limits!

## therapy hour, may 18

**MARTHA:** They shifted me into another unit at work with no warning whatsoever. I walked into work one day and was told, "You're moving today." Okay, there's no use taking it personally. Another woman was shifted at the same time, and two more were shifted the next day. But it's revolting not to have more warning or more say. They shifted me to a unit that is set up on a radically different system from the one I was in. Anyhow, I walked up on Friday morning and said, "Hello, I'm Martha Morgan. I'm your new worker; I'm moving my stuff up now. Can you tell me which desk?" So they pointed out the desk. They weren't terribly cordial. I took the drawers out of that desk and put them on a rolling chair and took them on the elevator and moved all my own stuff (which is extremely heavy and someone is supposed to move it for you, but of course they don't) and I organized the drawers. I took out the stuff I didn't need and put my own things in. They briefed me very quickly on how their system works. I said, "Fine, I know I'm going to like it here. . . ."

**ESTHER:** You liked their system and you said so.

**MARTHA:** I liked their system and I let them know it. What I'm trying to say is I didn't do anything obnoxious that I am aware of.

**ESTHER** *(laughs):* Hm-m-m.

**MARTHA:** I guess you can see what's coming. Okay. I got an absolutely cold treatment from everybody. Just utter silence. They wouldn't include me in their conversations. Okay. When you first move into a unit, the supervisor takes you into his office and tells you how the unit works and what he's particular about and what he isn't particular about. He gives you a general rundown. And as he was doing this, he said, "You will find this unit is extremely outspoken." It had a resonance to it, and it vibrated in the air for a minute. I said, "That's fine. I am, too. I can live with that very happily." But I cannot be dreaming I am getting "the treatment," I really cannot.

These things are too far out, honestly they are. I had a push-button phone on my desk, and somebody moved it off and replaced it with a regular phone that does not work. When I dial for an outside line, I get the "You have dialed the wrong number" recording. I can't get outside on that line. I have to get up and walk to another desk to make a phone call or to answer the phone. I've never figured out how my phone, which has no buttons, ties in. I thought it was an extension of the phone on the other desk, but when I treated it as that, I was cutting people off. It's tied in to this system in a way that no one has explained to me and I can't figure out for myself, so I don't use it. I can't get an outside line on it and I can't talk on it without cutting somebody off. So I get up and move.

And I'm clerking for myself, too. Normally the clerk would keep my cards on her desk and clerk from there, and that's what I expected. When I asked, the second day, whether a certain case card of mine was there, she said, "I couldn't possibly tell you." And when I asked why not, she said, "I put your cards in a stack on top of your file. If you want to know, go look." So I went and looked. Okay. I have to do my own clerking for now, but she didn't tell me that. Nobody told me. This group has been together for two years and they work very efficiently together. But they're leaving me out. And my first feeling about them was: a high school sorority.

**ESTHER:** So you don't belong.

**MARTHA:** No. I never worked before with a group of women who behave like women are accused of behaving. You know: "Did you see what Laura had on today? She really hasn't got the figure for it, but I'm not surprised, I've seen her wear lots of stuff like that. Boy, she sure looks crappy!" And so on. Laura is really a great person. It was a dumb dress she had on, but I really like her a lot. She's also an extremely competent worker, so they couldn't get at her that way. She's somebody who works downstairs, somebody in another department who is none of their business. This unit is supposed to be extremely outspoken. I think "outspoken" means outspoken behind your back.

They pride themselves on being excellent workers. They know every single rule in the whole book. And the treatment I'm getting is based on the fact that I'm supposed to be an incompetent worker and will not hold my end up. It's as good as been said to me that I'm going to make a lot of work for them and not do anything. The second day I was there, the person who was on waiting-room duty had to go to a meeting and she asked, "Who's going to cover while I'm gone?" and I said I would. You know, I don't have any assignment until my cases are integrated into the unit. So I've been getting all the crappy cases the last worker hadn't worked on cleaned up and moved out. I'm about three-quarters through that now. So I said, "I don't have an assignment. I'll cover it." And the girl at the front desk said, "Did you hear that, everybody? The new girl said she'll cover it." I'm not making it up; I'm not paranoid. I swear that is what happened.

I've been thinking all week that I was paranoid, when it finally hit me that they were not going to talk to me. They won't tell me where the supplies are. I have to ask for each thing I want to know. Of course I can't hold my end up if they don't tell me what holding up my end *is*. I'm no good—it's a self-fulfilling prophecy: They won't give me the wherewithal to work, so I can't work. And I'm aware of the situation, but it isn't cricket to drag the supervisor in. He wouldn't do anything anyway. He doesn't want grit in his operation, but he's not going to exercise authority because that isn't what he does.

ESTHER: How do you know that?

MARTHA: Just by general observation. . . . Okay, I really blew my cool.

ESTHER: What did you do?

MARTHA: I started bitching at them and simply ignoring them and bypassing them with everything I did. But I was on the verge of tears most of the day. I had to go away and cry quite often.

ESTHER: Mmmm . . . Let's see what you were doing. They were giving you the silent treatment so you were giving them the silent treatment back, except you were on the verge of tears. You were doing it back to them in desperation, not knowing anything else you could do about it. You felt you couldn't go to the supervisor.

MARTHA: No. It's not the way to handle it anyway. It isn't cricket—it isn't the way it's done—to take that kind of thing to the supervisor. In effect, what I'd be saying if I do that is: Can you make them like me or behave as though they do? I don't care if they like me. What a bunch of bloody bitches! You know, I'll not play ball with any of the things they're doing. But on the other hand, I'm motivated and want to learn more. It's clear I'm not going to get any help from them and I'm going to be kicked in the face every time I ask a question, but I'll just pull through that. It isn't going to take me long to learn . . . I know the basic principles enough so that . . .

ESTHER: So that you actually feel you can operate in this situation and find out what you need to know on your own, and finally get to the point where you are as efficient as they are, even though they don't clue you in or cooperate with you in any way?

MARTHA: Right.

ESTHER: That's probably an okay thing to do if you can do it.

MARTHA: That's my feeling. But my problem is whether I can keep my head together enough to do it. At this point I think I can. The burglary was immensely cathartic and put my head in shape in very fine fashion.

ESTHER: How do you mean?

MARTHA: I don't know exactly. It was the last straw.

ESTHER: It made you just mad enough so . . .

MARTHA: It made me just mad enough so I could say, "Oh, fuck them!" It's like a high school sorority. I don't want to join the sorority, but if the first sentence anybody says when you're introduced is, "You can't join our sorority!" Okay. Now we have only five minutes for the most important thing. What this aroused in me was my most rock-bottom reaction. . . . I got down to the core of my vulnerability, and I know what it is. I know why I stayed with Scott all those years. My reaction to this is that there's something grossly wrong with me, something that's just grotesquely obvious. Nobody has ever liked me. It has been grotesquely obvious to every person I have met. I never made it in school—in elementary or high school. In college I only just made it, more or less. I never had a circle of friends. There's always been latent hostility toward me in all the units I've worked in, there always has been despite the fact that I've worked well with them. I felt quite positive. But I didn't conceal my intelligence. Maybe people are affronted by that. And you know what I said to myself about three-quarters through? I said, "I can't tell Esther about this."

ESTHER: Oh? Why?

MARTHA: Because I only see you for an hour a week. So I've managed to present to you a front of capability and being put together that has no basis in fact. It's a fantasy that I can only manage for one hour a week. I have just blown everything in the typical fashion that I've always blown it. I've always blown it—in grade school, in junior high, in high school. I've blown it in every work situation I've ever been in. I just had a fight with Hazel and I blew it there. I had a fight with Arlene and blew it there. I'll go on blowing it. This is a lifelong pattern. Esther is the only person who really believes in me, and she only believes in me because I have her fooled. I can't bear to have her see —even though it's what I'm there for—I can't bear to have her see the pattern because I need to have her fooled; I need to have somebody who believes in me. I was absolutely serious.

ESTHER: Martha, I don't know whether you're aware of it, but you've sprung this one on me before in a slightly different version.

MARTHA: I'm quite aware of it. But I wasn't aware of it when I was thinking what I've been telling you.

ESTHER: As a matter of fact, it's what I have just written up for the book and was going to give you to read.

MARTHA: Don't give me anything to read for six weeks.

ESTHER *(laughing):* Okay. So you've come up with this: your need to keep me fooled, as you put it. Now, what do you want to do with that?

MARTHA: What do you mean?

ESTHER: Well, you said you weren't going to tell me because you had to keep me fooled, and then you come in and you tell me the whole thing. So . . .

MARTHA: Well, I'm in therapy. And this is pure gold. I stayed with Scott because I thought there was something grotesquely, obviously wrong with me. And as much as he charged me for the service, he kept the world off my back, kept it from falling on my head the minute I walked out the front door if he were not there.

ESTHER: Oh, it was Scott who protected you from what the world would do to you for being so terrible?

MARTHA: Yes.

ESTHER: Beautiful.

MARTHA: That's one sentence about sixteen years of marriage, but that's what was in play—far more than masochism, though it was a classical sadomasochistic situation.

ESTHER: Oh, yes, from the "diagnostic" point of view, but each such situation is different. The only thing that is classic is that all these situations have something in common: The pattern is alike, but the reasons for it are different in each case.

MARTHA: Right. One thing I want to say about that sadomasochistic thing. The thing about masochism, at least in me, isn't that I like being hurt. It's that I feel I'm going to be hurt no matter what I do, and I prefer familiar pain to unfamiliar pain. I prefer being rejected in the way that is familiar. I prefer being rejected "Daddy's way" to all the manifold kinds of rejections that I feel I would get.

ESTHER: At least the familiar is the familiar, you might as well stick with it?

MARTHA: Exactly right. But I've got to go.

ESTHER: Are you really afraid to read what I wrote?

MARTHA: Right now I am, because I'm still in it.

## from esther's notebook

A door had been opened, a very important one, and Martha recognized this immediately: From the standpoint of therapy, what had happened had been "pure gold." I wondered (to myself) whether she would be able to pursue the matter further in her next hour, or whether she would have to back off. It is clear that Martha still feels very vulnerable.

## therapy hour, may 25

(Again we start in the here and now, and again we have cut the transcription drastically, for there was far more detail than we need.)

**MARTHA:** Financially I'm in an ongoing crisis. Inflation is just beating me. This week was particularly bad because it's the last week of the month. The cat got sick and had to be taken to the vet. It's Sasha's cat. I thought Sasha had enough money and she thought I had enough, and of course neither of us had enough. When they said the bill was $22.50, knowing we couldn't have enough even between us, I smiled sweetly and wrote a rubber check. Then I went home and scraped up all the money in the house, including the food money for next week, and put it in the bank to cover the check, but it leaves no money for next week. You know, everybody's being very good. We did exactly what we had to do, but when you're down to taking pop bottles back to the store to get your bus fare. . . . It's a constant struggle, and also . . . people who are my friends are so much better off financially that there's an enormous disparity. Ann and I were talking about it. She said, "I used to hate to bring friends home when I was little, the way the house looked." And this made me feel very bad because that's purely a function of money, or almost purely. When it wasn't a function of my health, then it was of money. If you don't have a vacuum cleaner, it's almost impossible to compete with somebody who does have one. And if you can't replace worn-out furniture, you can make it look clean and tidy, but . . .

ESTHER: Even that's hard to do.

MARTHA: It's hard to do with worn-out things. They don't come clean or if they do, they still don't look good . . . and after a while, you just . . . well, you give up the struggle. And my yard is a total shambles. That's been a function partly of my health, and no relief in sight unless I get some money. I'd have the yard landscaped in something that doesn't require work, something that doesn't have to be mowed once a week, have the weeds dug out, God knows what, but something. You know, it's beyond me, and it's not an advantage to have developed good—which always means expensive —taste.

ESTHER: This is a thing a lot of people are caught in.

MARTHA: A lot of *women* are caught in . . . I got up with migraine today, which is trouble, and I should have stayed home, but I didn't. I took two codeine, because there's too much that has to get done. I wanted to come here and I've got stuff to do at work. It's Benjy's Special Learning Center day, and I have to pick him up at lunch hour and take him back to school. This is all draining. And you know, just to go into a store and see groceries priced so that I can hardly afford to get a decent number of grams of protein into my family, that's draining, too. Ann is just a mastermind at getting delicious meals out of practically nothing, so for the money we've got, we do miraculously well. But it's a struggle, a lot of energy goes there.

ESTHER: These are the realities psychotherapy can't cure.

MARTHA: I can't do anything about living in a high-crime area either. It's very invading and depressing to have your home burglarized. You can't believe how much that stereo meant to me —you know, buying one component a year with my income tax refund and going without every month to put money aside. Sasha has located a second-hand camera. I'll give her a part of the insurance money if there is any, and she'll pay off the rest baby-sitting.

ESTHER: You know, your girls sound really great at this point.

MARTHA: They're marvelous kids, just incredible, all of them. They're all so realistic and human and so stable, I just can't believe it. You know, all the work I've put in is more than justified, when that was my only goal, the only thing that kept me alive, to pull them out of it somehow, and somehow I succeeded.

I've had some conversations with Ann and Sasha in the past few months. Ann said to me the other night, "You used to say you were schizophrenic. Why?" I told her I'd been diagnosed by people whose judgment I had no reason to doubt, and I knew so little about how other people were inside their own heads that I fell for it. Ann said, "But all a psychiatrist does is tell back to you what you tell him. What did you say to him?" I said, "Well, for one thing, they asked me if I had voices in my head; and you know I do all my thinking in words." She said, "Oh, gosh, you didn't tell them 'Yes,' did you?" I said, "Yes, because when I think, I say this to myself and that to myself." Ann said, "That isn't what voices in the head means." I said, "I didn't know that because I'd always been told I was so weird that I was afraid to compare what was in my head with other people. You don't go around saying, 'I think like this. How do you think?' At the times when you might do that, if you think you're crazy, you don't do it because you're afraid other people will catch on." But anyway, the point of what I'm saying is that Ann is perfectly well tuned in to what had been going on.

Ann and I and Sasha and I sit and talk for an hour or so quite often now, about general things, not mother-daughter things, comparing what we think of this or that. Ann said to me the other day, "You're having a lot of trouble with your friends. You're parting with a lot of people." I said, "I used not to know when people were attacking me, and I used to let them attack me."

Esther, did I ever tell you about the time Arnie Wilson said to me, "Every time I see you, I want to spit in your eye?" The Wilsons were people we knew when we lived in the Northwest. I said, "How come?" And Arnie said, "Because they are so little and piggy and close together." I had no idea why he said that.

ESTHER: *What* did he say?

MARTHA: That they were little and piggy and close together. Now I had no idea what was on Arnie's mind and all I said was "Oh," but I thought he had told me something important about myself. I was quite grateful.

ESTHER: *Grateful?*

MARTHA: Yes. I thought the reason I don't fit in with people is that I'm physically repellent. I was always looking for the reason why I don't fit, like when I go into the unit at work, I don't fit in. Why don't I fit in? There must be a reason. And if I'm physically repellent, that would explain a lot, so I was grateful to him. . . . That isn't something someone would normally tell you, especially if it was true. I assumed he was explaining something to me. Really, really, really, this is true. But now when someone says something to me, like Joe, when he says to me, "Are you still working for the county?" I know that he means I'm such a helpless creature, helpless and idealistic, that I will go off on some tangent and take a stand on principle and they will fire me. He asks me every time he sees me, "Are you still working?" I don't need friends like that, you know. As the saying goes, with friends like that, who needs enemies?

ESTHER: Well, . . . yeah . . . but, you know, I'm stuck back there with the idea you had that you were physically repellent.

MARTHA: Well, Scott reacted to me as if he had to make love to me, not as if he wanted to.

ESTHER: Okay, but we'll have to go back further than that for it to be so strong within you, this notion that you. . . .

MARTHA: Well, it wasn't a notion that I was physically repulsive, exactly, but that other people must feel that I am a repellent person in some way because they don't take to me. And so whenever Scott said a really dirty thing to me about myself, I thought he was just explaining to me what was wrong with me. It's one of the reasons I stayed with Scott so long. I figured he was telling me what was wrong, and I really wanted to know, needed to know. I'd really like to get on with people a lot better than I do.

ESTHER: Where did that really wanting to know what was wrong with you come from?

MARTHA: It's so strong, it's so deep, it can only have come from my childhood. It was so well established . . . I was odd man out by the time I was six or seven.

ESTHER: I think I have some idea what you're talking about. I have a vague memory of some kid, some little girl, in my childhood who for no reason that I could understand was considered repellent in some way. For no reason that I could understand whatsoever. You know, the other little girls would be making fun of her behind her back, and I couldn't see why.

MARTHA: Exactly, that's precisely the thing. I don't know what it's about. Where did it come from? It must have come because the little girl allowed it or encouraged it. Did I ever tell you that when I was seven or eight I had almost a total breakdown? I don't know if we've been through this before.

ESTHER: I don't seem to remember. It's not the kind of thing I would forget.

MARTHA: This is very, very important! And I have no idea what triggered it, none at all. School pressure maybe, to some extent.

ESTHER: What kind of school pressure?

MARTHA: I couldn't do arithmetic. And I had bad astigmatism that wasn't corrected until between second and third grades, when I got glasses. And that surely had something to do with it. I had violent suicidal impulses. I spoke of wanting to kill myself to the children at school, but it was not particularly as a dramatic thing. Even if it were only an attention-getter, it would be an unusual attention-getter. In an eight-year-old. But I was quite sincere, I really wanted to die. It was the same kind and intensity as the suicidal push I felt around the time Becky was born, when I was so suicidal for all those years.

ESTHER: What happened at seven or eight?

MARTHA: After about a year and a half, it went away, slacked off. But it never really did go away.

ESTHER: But what were people doing? I mean, you know, certainly people knew about this.

MARTHA: Well, I said it to a girl who told her mother, who told my mother, who told me not to say things like that. So I didn't say things like that. She said, "You mustn't say things like that, it frightens your friends." So I never said it again until I got into therapy. That was the next time I spoke to anybody about it except in the confessional, and I went through it with Father Michaelson. Well, but when I was a kid, I was really beside myself for about a year and a half. And it had very few outward manifestations because I controlled it, because I had damn well been told to. But really, in that year my head just exploded. I had the sense of being odd man out and just not able to handle things, not able to handle schoolwork, because I was doing so badly at arithmetic. I think I had something like Benjy's EH problem [educationally handicapped, often because of neurological dysfunction]. It was trying to learn cursive writing and it just eluded me. I can remember the teacher making fun of my capital S's because they looked like capital G's, and she held them up to show the class.

ESTHER: You know, there could have been an EH problem, a neurological block. . . .

MARTHA: The blocking was here. (Pointing to her forehead.) It was the dissociation between the eyes and the hand. I eventually learned to do it; I can write cursive. I can do arithmetic, too. I thought I'd never learn to do multiplication, but now I do it in my head. It wasn't lack of aptitude. I don't know what it was. It must have been purely a psychological problem.

ESTHER: Well, I'm not so sure of that. There does seem to have been some kind of eye-hand problem that we now associate, even if very minor, with neurological dysfunction.

MARTHA: But that doesn't make most children want to kill themselves. Or perhaps it does.

ESTHER: Well, I think it would depend on the child. Here you were, obviously a terribly bright child, yet failing.

MARTHA: I *wasn't* obviously a terribly bright child. No one thought of me as a bright child.

ESTHER: All right, then let's see how to visualize what this must have meant. . . . You know, some very minor neurological problems can bring about very severe psychopathology. EH kids are often scapegoated by other kids, even now when the neurological problem is recognized. And when you were a kid, it wasn't recognized. Teachers didn't know about it. And kids are always ready to scapegoat when they get a chance. This whole scapegoating thing could be terribly important. I think we should take the time to do a whole hour on it sometime. I think we might come up with something.

## from esther's notebook

Reading Martha's story as she writes it and hearing the new material Martha is bringing to therapy hours, I'm beginning to get a glimmer of understanding about something that has puzzled me a great deal: the fact that her present stance is not at all what she described at the beginning of her story. Martha, who once felt reassured to think that she knew all the "bad" things there were to know about herself, is not willing to admit any of them now, even to me—or perhaps especially not to me. It's as though she's afraid that anything she says will be used against her. Is this what her previous therapy did to her? Is it what her marriage did? Or did they simply reinforce something that had already happened, long before?

It is difficult for me to visualize Martha as ever having been anyone's willing victim, but victim she certainly was as a child, willing or not, and victim she continued to be for a long time. It occurs to me that Martha may once have been the kind of person who uses her capacity for insight against herself, so that everything that happens is understood in terms of "something wrong with me" and never "something wrong outside of me." Insight can then become very dangerous, and Martha may have experienced that kind of danger in its most extreme form.

Some kinds of masochism have adaptive value, but a mind turned relentlessly against itself for whatever reason can become an irreversible malignancy. When I have a client who uses her capacity for insight against herself, I work very hard to turn her attention outward instead of inward, to help her use her evaluative ability to understand her world, the people around her, and the impact of outside forces upon her.* Understanding one's own contribution to one's fate is essential to therapy, but to do so without considering the realities—both the actual, concrete matters and the interpersonal climate within which one operates—is to court disaster.

If the masochistic use of insight goes unrecognized in therapy, the client is likely to be praised for her insight into her problems, with the result that her already far too great willingness to look within herself becomes further exaggerated. It is this very willingness that is the problem, at least initially, and if this trend is not counteracted the client may remain trapped forever in a kind of psychological martyrdom, aided and abetted by an interminable "therapy." Or anger will inevitably mount, consciously and unconsciously, to the point of constituting a serious suicidal risk.

Even before the development of a specific theory of family psychopathology I was aware that some wives, if their husbands refused to take any responsibility for the marital problems, were not only unable to defend themselves against their husbands' projections but would accept them as "insights" about themselves. I have seen a number of variations of this pattern, including the psychosis-generating one in which a woman is led to doubt the evidence of her senses by a husband usually defending himself against discovery of infidelity or of some other transgression he wishes to conceal from his wife. The label sadomasochistic, which I feel is often too freely applied to marital conflict in general, is an understatement when applied to this particular kind.

I am arriving at the realization that I now see in Martha what might be called a "reformed masochist," someone who has run the gamut of masochistic dangers and has come out of it determined never again to repeat the experience. There are disadvantages to her present therapy in this position, but not nearly so much disadvantage as there was danger in her previous pattern. Martha has learned her lesson well, and now that I begin to see what has been going on, I am glad that she learned it before coming to me. I am thus spared the long, difficult struggle to reverse the masochistic use of insight.

But how did this all come about in the first place? I think that the matter of scapegoating may be the clue, the one that will open other doors for us, so that eventually we shall be able to make a fairly good guess about what has been holding Martha back and what may free her to move ahead. Martha's feeling of being different from everyone else comes in here. Of course, most people have some occasion to feel "different," but Martha's experience seems far more intense, indeed overriding other experiences for her, and seems almost to have been definitive not only of her self-image but of her very identity.

I am interested in the way Martha has been comparing notes with her daughters lately, as though she had never before done so with anyone. If she had not, she would have had no means of discovering ways in which she was not so different from others after all, or ways in which the "difference" might have been seen in a favorable rather than unfavorable light—or at least discovering some better way of handling the difference for herself.

An important shift in Martha's experience of her difference must have come with the famous therapist's visit to the psychiatric ward. I was surprised at his encouraging Martha to continue the dialogue with him to the exclusion of the others, and I marveled at his pointing out in so public a fashion the level of her intelligence. Perhaps he felt it safe to assume that patients on a psychiatric ward would be more generous-spirited than people in the more ordinary walks of life. If so, what a commentary on sanity in our competitive society! The group, with only one exception, accepted Martha's being singled out as different in a favorable sense, without apparent resentment or retaliation. The only person who attacked Martha did so quite ineptly and, far from inspiring the others to enter into a scapegoating operation, ended up herself as a minority of one. Scape-goating doesn't work when the majority refuses to enter into it. Nor does it work, apparently, when the leader of the group gives clear and unequivocal backing to the different one.

When Martha described the reception she received in the

new unit at work, I was struck by the fact that here she encountered a reaction with all the elements of the scapegoating that often goes on among children at school. The scapegoated child knows very well that the teacher is unable to do anything about it; even the most well-disposed teacher would be hard put to find some way of making other children *like* the child they have chosen to scapegoat. Martha saw the supervisor much as the scapegoated child sees the teacher, and she knew that she was once again repeating an old and painful experience. A situation that represents a deeply suffered and unresolved past trauma is likely to be repeated over and over again until it is mastered in some new and effective way. So of course I wanted to pursue it with Martha in the hope that this time she could master it.

I was also interested in the subject of scapegoating for my own reasons. I have worked with children who were scapegoated, and I know how difficult and often impossible it is for them to extricate themselves once the pattern is established. What is a scapegoated child to do? The child doesn't understand why he is being scapegoated, yet he has to try to make sense out of what is happening. He is likely to see "the treatment" either as persecution, dooming him to a deep distrust of his fellows perhaps forever, or as something that he for some reason deserves, dooming him to self-contempt and self-rejection, again perhaps forever. The choice would seem to be between becoming paranoid and becoming suicidal. In either case, the scapegoated child is likely to feel that he has been ruled out of the human race entirely.

It is understandable that a teacher may turn against the scapegoated child out of anger and guilt at his own inability to control the other children in the interest of justice. Since he cannot right the wrong, the teacher must perforce hope that the victim himself can find some way of preventing or bypassing or undoing the wrong —and the teacher may eventually blame him if he does not do so.

A child needs, of course, to learn how to avoid being scapegoated, but his need should be the occasion for special help. He should not be left to his own devices whereby he will inevitably develop patterns that make matters worse for him, and he will then be blamed further for the predicament he is in. Without help, such a child is likely to continue in some kind of scapegoat role throughout life and then be further condemned for being a "loser," a provoker of others' cruel or criminal behavior, or, perhaps more commonly, the willing victim of a lover or spouse.

I have watched with appalled astonishment what seems to have become a fashionable trend in recent years: to blame the victim rather than the perpetrator of a crime. This is a trend that encourages adult bystanders who are aware of adult injustices and adult forms of scapegoating either to remain aloof to the problem because they feel it is no business of theirs or, worse yet, to assume that the victims themselves are responsible for their own exploitation or victimization. It is true that some people unconsciously invite such treatment, but those who do so are in as much need of special psychological help as the scapegoated child. To assume that all who fall victim to the ruthlessness of others are responsible for the injustices committed against them is not only adding insult to injury, it is utterly and tragically absurd. Such an assumption is in the same category as blaming the Jews for their mistreatment at the hands of the Nazis.

I have scanned many recent books on children's problems and see very little attention given to scapegoating behavior—perhaps naturally enough because the books focus on how to produce a "well-adjusted" child. Such a child would no doubt never be enough of an outsider, never sufficiently different to occasion the scapegoating impulse in others; or if he did, he would have sufficient self-esteem and appropriate social techniques to handle it. It was only in one of the older, psychoanalytically oriented sources that I found the word "scapegoating" in the index, and the matter was discussed in the text as a problem arising out of such things as sibling rivalry, competitiveness, and so on. I suspect that the psychoanalytic view, with its willingness to believe in the power of the destructive drives within human beings and its customary focus on the negative side of every coin, has its usefulness.

I think the truth of the matter is we all want a scapegoat at one time or another (no doubt more so as our own lives go awry) for the very basic reason that we want someone upon whom we can wreak vengeance for the wrongs done to us. Even as adults we are often helpless and without power in the face of injustice. This experience of helplessness, of powerlessness, pervaded my childhood, and I believe that it is the common position of the child in relation to almost any adult. When I was twelve or thirteen, young enough still to be in that position but old enough to see the prospect of its eventually coming to an end, I swore a solemn vow to myself: I would never, when I became an adult, forget what it was like to be in the position of a child. I had no trouble keeping my vow. Throughout many of my adult years I found that I remained in the position of a child in many situations and relationships—sometimes for my own neurotic reasons but more often because those situations and relationships were designed to keep me powerless. So there was little danger that I would forget what it felt like to be a child!

I suppose my vow could be called a choice for masochism over sadism, for the traditional "feminine" solution, but though I reject the invidious implications, I embrace quite wholeheartedly the ethical principle involved. I no longer feel that this choice requires me to abjure the expression of anger or self-assertion or constructively aggressive behavior, however, but only that it obliges me not to abuse any advantage in power I may on occasion have.

## therapy hour, june 16

(We have been back for a while to a discussion of Martha's immediate problems. Martha had had a cold but continued to go to work. Finally she went to the doctor and learned she had bronchitis; she should have been staying home all along. She came in for her hour today because she gets depressed when she is sick and felt that the value of coming for therapy outweighed the value of staying home to rest.)

MARTHA: You know, if I am lying in bed, I think of all the time being wasted. I know better, but I . . .

ESTHER: That's right, you know better.

MARTHA: But I get so depressed. I feel so sick and think I should be at work. You know, this is no way to endear yourself to your fellow workers—to take off sick so soon after you start in a new unit. But that's silly, too, because there is a back-up person for anybody who is out sick, a floater who takes that job.

ESTHER: So you add to the reality problem with unrealistic guilt.

MARTHA: Yes . . . I'm my father's compulsive daughter. You know, my father, who won't come down from painting the ceiling to eat his breakfast and then complains that he doesn't feel good. Oh shit, and then I know I'm doing that, and then I feel guilty about doing it. It's just a never-ending spiral.

ESTHER: Yes, you really get yourself caught.

(There follows a rather lengthy dialogue regarding physical illness and the difficulty of sorting out which feelings are due to being sick and which may be contributing to making one sick. The dialogue ends as follows:)

ESTHER: We've confused ourselves so much by recognizing that there are psychological and emotional components in physical symptoms, but it's a truth we need to deal with even though it's a very confusing truth.

MARTHA: Well, there's enough truth in it to keep me completely confused. All the time that I've been in such misery with bronchitis I haven't had a single migraine.

ESTHER: Well, okay, all we can do is make a note of that kind of thing and maybe at some point we can understand it.

MARTHA: But I shouldn't try to deal with it when I'm sick.

ESTHER: I wouldn't think you could, very well.

MARTHA: No, because I know my head isn't on straight when I'm sick. I know I'm just horribly irrational. Why I should feel so hideously guilty?

ESTHER: Mmmm . . . I remember something that helped me on this. There was a supervisor at a social agency—when I was a stenographer, before I went to graduate school—and I thought she was a person of tremendous common sense along with intuition and education and so on. I remember her saying it's just too bad that we can't even allow ourselves a common cold anymore without feeling guilty. She said it in such a heartfelt way that it did something for me.

**MARTHA:** Well, I need to hear it repeated over and over.

**ESTHER:** You know, when I think about her. . . . She had a bastard of a husband. She did divorce him eventually. He was a genius, a brilliant man in his field, and somehow this brilliance was supposed to excuse everything—all his meanness to people—because he was a genius and had to be himself.

**MARTHA:** Now, that's very familiar. I mean that's the basis on which I bore with Scott for so many years—that the ordinary rules didn't apply to him.

**ESTHER:** I'm beginning to get a glimmer. . . . I'm reading a biography of Whistler, and I'm beginning to get a glimmer of what that kind of person is really like. It's always been very difficult for me to understand people like that. And the thought came to me: I bet this book is going to help me understand Scott. I also got that feeling when I read a biography of Picasso by one of his women friends—that he was an impossible person but people loved him in spite of it. Very *few* people loved Whistler in spite of it, yet he was obviously a charming, witty person who could always draw people to him. Anyway, it's interesting to me because I've been trying to make a guess as to what Scott might be like.* It's very difficult for me to make any kind of an educated guess, but I'm beginning to get a little of the education I need. And, of course, the Fitzgeralds, Zelda and F. Scott; I suspect there was that kind of rivalry in some fashion in your marriage.

**MARTHA:** I never saw it. It wasn't any contest. We were long divorced before that could occur to me, but . . . you know, I think it's true.

**ESTHER:** I would imagine that when you are able to look back on this it will fall into place in many ways.

**MARTHA:** The thing . . . I think the reason that I keep slipping off when I try to work on my relationship with Scott or that I run off into generalities immediately when we start to talk about him . . . it seems to me the reason has to be an extreme thing, like: Unless I can prove that he has no redeeming qualities whatsoever and that he set out deliberately to threaten me, then he is right and I am wrong.

**ESTHER:** Oh, Martha, that's it! I think you're saying it just the way it's been: You had to prove that he had no redeeming qualities whatsoever, or you would be all wrong and he all right. And that's impossible.

**MARTHA:** I'm by nature an extremist anyway. It has to be, you know, total, complete, whatever.

And unless I can prove . . . I feel as if unless I can prove that he set out deliberately to get me and engineered everything singlemindedly, with only that in mind, then whatever he said is true, then whatever he said about me is true.

ESTHER: Oh, great!

MARTHA: It has to be one way or the other . . . and we're going to decide by writing this book who's right and . . . you know, I just don't have it in me to prove he has no redeeming qualities. On the other hand, if he actually has no redeeming qualities, then I'm the world's most absolutely perverse maniac to have stayed with him so long. So I lose whichever . . .

ESTHER: Well, all right, now, what are you going to do about that?

MARTHA: I'm starting to do what I have to do . . . which is to see that in normal human situations, it's *not like that* . . . that he may have been extremely destructive to me quite unconsciously. And though he may have had many redeeming features, the threat to me was so extreme it would not have been sane for me to stay with him. He may have been part consciously and part unconsciously destructive. But destructive he was, whether he meant to be or not. And it does not make any sense for me to have stayed with him.

ESTHER: Well, having seen how confused women get when they are up against destructive qualities in their husbands, conscious or unconscious, I can understand what a state of confusion you must have been in. I have seen other women in confusion that amounted to temporary psychosis, and perhaps for less reason than you had. This kind of thing is almost fatal, so that I can understand your confusion just on the basis of that alone. Now, when I put your confusion together with a childhood and growing-up situation that really didn't help you to understand other people at all . . . you didn't do comparing of notes with other people very much . . .

MARTHA: I didn't do any of it.

ESTHER: . . . the things that help us to know why other people act the way they do. I think we learn a lot of that in childhood. I have the impression that you were fighting for your life so desperately that you couldn't figure out what other people were doing. It wouldn't have occurred to you, you were so busy just fighting for your life. And that's where your anger came in. It may have saved your life in a way, but when you're that angry, you can't learn anything about what's going on.

MARTHA: But why was I fighting for my life, even in childhood? Why?

ESTHER: That's a very interesting question. . . .

MARTHA: To me . . . it's a good thing I came in today . . . to me it just proves that I was defective from the start.

ESTHER: You know, I have a feeling that the mystery lies in this whole question of scapegoating, that if we could understand it. . . . Were you scapegoated almost immediately on going to school? Or was there a period in which you were liked?

MARTHA: There was a period in which I felt completely isolated. . . . Well, I had several friends whom my mother sort of promoted for me, two little girls I used to play with. Neither of them lived nearby. There were no children in the neighborhood at all, so that it had to be sort of arranged that I have somebody to play with. And after I went to kindergarten I used to play with Connie and Maurine. I'd go to their house after school or they'd come to my house . . . not neighborhood children, kids who were in my class in school. I felt that I was not made of the same material they were.

ESTHER: Okay, can we go back a little before that? Weren't there any neighborhood kids at all?

MARTHA: None at all.

ESTHER: Why did you live in a neighborhood where there weren't any kids?

MARTHA: Oh, it was a sort of a physical fact. Right to the west of us was a big sand pit, huge acres of it, and right behind us was a very, very steep hill. You could barely scramble up it. There just happened not to be many houses around.

ESTHER: Was it on the outskirts of town?

MARTHA: Well, no, there was just a lot of empty space. There were only four houses on the street. One was occupied by my grandparents, one was occupied by us, one was occupied by friends of my grandparents, the same age they were, and one was a duplex that was rented out. From time to time there were kids in that, but they weren't kids my age.

ESTHER: If that house didn't have children for you, none of the others was going to.

MARTHA: It was just luck, so far as I'm concerned.

ESTHER: I have the feeling it was very bad luck, because as I look back on my early years, I realize that I began to get a picture of the real world through other children. It didn't come from adults teaching me or guiding me or . . . I think it came a lot by way of scraping edges with other kids.

MARTHA: I had hardly any of that. The years before I went to school I spent almost totally in my mother's company. She was almost my only contact with other people.

ESTHER: And if she had been a good person to introduce you to what the world was like, that might have been fine.

MARTHA: But she wasn't. She wasn't, partly because she elected to see no evil and partly because she had then and still has a mania for deciding that whatever she believes, *is*. She wanted a child with naturally curly hair and she never got one. She put my hair up in curlers every night of my young life and swore that I had naturally curly hair. And I never could convey . . . I tried a number of times . . . I tried to tell her how miserable I was in school.

ESTHER: That was later. . . .

MARTHA: That was later, when I was in the third or fourth grade. I'd make maybe one try a year for a couple of years, and she was just not tuned into it. She'd say, well, sometimes when they tease you, it means they like you. Which confused me even more, because that wasn't what it meant.

ESTHER: No. Sometimes it does, but that's more often when it comes from boys than from girls. When a girl teases a girl, I doubt if it ever means she likes you.

MARTHA: Well, I think she said it in the context of boys, but it definitely wasn't true. The boys scapegoated me as well as the girls. And I couldn't convey the nature of the situation to her.

ESTHER: Well, it would have been such a difficult thing to understand, and in a way I can see what your mother was trying to do there.

MARTHA: I can too, but it just . . .

ESTHER: But that wasn't what the facts happened to be, that was all.

MARTHA: It wasn't totally her fault that she misread it.

ESTHER: Yes, I can see that. And so it comes back to that scapegoating.

MARTHA: Yes, it really does.

ESTHER: I've puzzled over it quite a lot as I began to realize that that was an important part. . . . And, of course, I've puzzled over scapegoating a lot anyway, because I've worked with kids here at the agency who have been scapegoated.

MARTHA: Well, the thing that most explains what happened to me is what happened when I went into the new unit at work. And that was that I couldn't keep from showing how upset I was, that I reacted. And I reacted, you see, with a reaction that was: If you won't have me, I certainly won't have you.

ESTHER: A retaliatory reaction, which I have a hunch is one of the worst.

MARTHA: It doesn't work very well, but it works. And it would have worked even better if I could have kept from showing how upset I was.

ESTHER: That's right. Maybe if you just plain retaliate, it works, but if . . .

MARTHA: But if you show pain and retaliate, it doesn't really work at all. And that's been the most revealing thing to me. Going through, in a way, a parallel experience to the one I had at school. Esther, there is no reason why they should land on me. And that's what really . . .

ESTHER: Yes, I think that's why that was such an extremely important experience. It's that you went through it *now,* with a whole lot more understanding to bring to it.

MARTHA: Exactly. Now, what I did when I was a child, by the time . . . I kept that sort of relationship with the two little girls my mother had set up for me through grade school. When I got to junior high—there was only one junior high in the city, so it meant all of us were thrown into a much bigger pool of people—they deserted me instantly. Connie said to me one day—we used to walk to school together when we first started to junior high; it was about a mile and a half away, a long walk—she said to me one day, "I don't want to walk with you anymore 'cause you walk too fast and people will think I'm funny. People think you're funny and they will think I'm funny if I walk with you, so I'm not going to walk with you anymore."

ESTHER: Okay, I have the feeling that all these items you are producing are explanatory, piled one on top of another.

MARTHA: And I literally did not know how to talk; it's literally true that Father Michaelson taught me how to talk.

ESTHER: All right now, I think this has been an extremely important subject.

MARTHA *(coughing):* I'm drowning in my own cough, I've got to go home and go to bed. You know, I'm so compulsive about keeping on the move. I have so much to do and I can't let myself off any of it. I was going to go down and buy Benjy his shoes yesterday. And Sasha said, "You're going to dig yourself right into your grave if you don't stay in bed." So she took Benjy down and got his shoes. But I was prepared to do it. I said to Sasha, "Maybe I'll get pneumonia and they'll have to put me in the hospital. Hallelujah!" She said, "I really think you like being sick." And I said, "It's the only way I get any rest," which is simply true.

ESTHER: Yes, it could be serving that purpose.

MARTHA: And the only thing to do is to get rid of the compulsion. You know, I can let the house go, but then I feel terrible about it. I can let it go physically, but that doesn't help.

ESTHER: No, you have to let it go in your mind.

MARTHA: And I just can't do that.

ESTHER: Well, I guess you can, a little bit. You probably can't as much as you need to. But if you do it even a little, I think it would help. I know a lot of people who share this awful compulsion and I can't remember any of them going to the opposite extreme and becoming completely relaxed. But it does seem to me they've learned to ease up a little. Maybe that isn't enough, but it's a whole lot better than it was.

**MARTHA:** Think about what they do that works.

**ESTHER:** All right.

**MARTHA:** I'm going to go home and put me to bed.

## from esther's notebook

I have finally gotten around to my notes on the beginning of our second contact [written for the book as "Return Engagement"], and there were a few surprises in them. I had remembered that Martha had initially requested family therapy, but I had forgotten that the purpose would be "to give the children a diluted version" of what had happened in the marriage. I don't recall asking Martha what she meant by that, and I cannot now, of course, speak for her as to what she really had meant. I suspect it had to do with diluting her own felt need to blame Scott, which suggests to me that she wanted to cut down on her anger and bitterness.

But I must remind myself that I am always coloring my thoughts about Martha's experiences with my own colors. And so often mine are so pallid, so inadequate to the true picture. I have simply not experienced, perhaps haven't allowed myself to experience, many things in what may be their actual colors.

I am trying to understand a situation—Martha and Scott's—in which suicidal feelings and suicidal threats were almost the common coin of everyday transactions. From my own experience, and from what I find significant in the theory underlying family therapy, I am convinced that suicidal feelings arise when one cannot make room for oneself in some vitally important situation—the family, marriage, social group, job, or whatever. As a child, there were so many things I could not do for myself that I could not afford to alienate the adults upon whom I depended, and so I could not allow myself to say or do anything that would make these people angry at me. How could I have made room for myself under those circumstances? I walked a constant tightrope, effacing whatever aspects of myself might upset the careful balance I was maintaining, hardly daring to breathe at crucial moments. (It is no wonder that my first overt psychoneurotic symptoms came in the form of breathing difficulties.)

Somewhere along the line, a child must find room to be himself, or he will become nothing, or literally die. I must have succeeded in making some room for myself, or I would not have survived at all. And little by little in my adult years, I learned that I could say some of the things I really thought on some occasions and to some people. But too often I have repeated the situation of my childhood; too often I could not find a way of meeting my own needs that was acceptable to others; too often my efforts to meet my own needs seemed to threaten others in the course of their efforts to meet theirs. I have had a very hard time finding room for myself among other people. (What makes me think my experience has been so different from Martha's, just because I wasn't actually scapegoated?)

I have thought at times that my own problem came about because I have always in some way been dependent upon others. Do I have to do everything for myself before I can really breathe freely? How does one manage to live without ever becoming beholden to anyone for anything? I must still not alienate anyone upon whom I am in any way dependent, so I smooth things over here and bend a little there in order for the fabric of my life not to fall apart. But I never succeed entirely, and I can always look back and think: I should have said this, I should not have done that, I should have anticipated and forestalled the other. This is hardly being a liberated woman. (I sometimes think it is a slave's existence—even now.)

I had known since early childhood what it meant to grow up

within the shadow of a family neurosis. Although I could not have used that term until well along in the course of my professional career because it had not yet been invented, I had been using an equivalent idea in my own mind from the time that I could formulate any considered thought at all. My earliest memories include a recognition of trouble within my family, trouble—whatever it was—that seemed to me to have always been there, as though it had started before I was born. I knew that my mother and father and sister were all involved in the trouble because they would so often be angry at one another; none of them seemed ever to be really happy.

I suppose I was outside of this family trouble by the mere fact of its being a triangular matter, the triangle having been formed with the birth of my sister. There was no role in a triangle for a fourth member, for me, when I came along. By early adolescence I was very clear in my own mind that although each of these three people separately was a most decent human being of excellent intelligence and interesting personality, together they were destroying one another—no doubt, in order to survive. The child who sits on the sidelines of such a situation suffers distortions and deprivations in the course of assuring his own psychological survival, but he does survive, and he may learn something in the process.

During my earliest years, I had the notion that it was not only within my power to avoid contributing to the trouble but also within my power to "cure" the trouble, whatever it might be. I recall vividly the recurring fantasy that I would fall gravely ill and that out of their concern for my life, my parents would become kind and loving to one another and my mother and sister would no longer clash. A few years later when I developed mastoiditis and my life did indeed hang in the balance, no such happy resolution of conflict took place. If anything, matters became worse, since each of my parents could find something for which to blame the other, and my sister could only be envious of the time and attention accorded me at her expense. I nevertheless continued to harbor a fantasy of family harmony for many years. It did not so much disappear as become gradually translated into romantic dreams of love. Having given up the hope of being the child of parents who were happy together, of living in a family in which everyone loved one another, I would bring about such a situation in my own marriage and my own home. Dreams do not die; they live on in some other form to plague us!

When Martha suggested family therapy, my first thought was that if this was now the treatment of choice, it would best be done by someone other than me. Martha's relationship with me was of no small consequence to her and was surely known to the children as something that in a special way "belonged" to their mother. I might try to form a relationship with them that would be something special for them, too, but I did not feel I had that much to give, at least not under these circumstances.

In considering a transfer to another therapist for purposes of family therapy, I had to take into account some of Martha's very unfortunate experiences with previous therapists. Because I was not at all certain I so completely understood the various imponderables involved, I could not assure Martha (or myself) that some other therapist would not inadvertently face her once again with hazards to her individual welfare; nor would I want to control another therapist's approach, even if I could do so.

Also, I have an aversion to trying a new approach until I am convinced that the old one will not do. I had been one of the first to welcome the theory that family interaction was a major cause in a variety of emotional and mental problems, and that it was often responsible for keeping a person locked into the very kind of situation that produced the problems in the first place. But I had been, and I remained, doubtful that it necessarily followed that one always had to work with the whole family together in order to remedy or alleviate those problems. I felt the important thing was to take the family patterns into account. So long as the work was done within the framework of an adequate knowledge of the family interaction, working on an individual basis with the person most willing and able to examine his problems was often enough to accomplish its purpose. It was when this approach would clearly not do the job that I would switch to whatever combination of family members, including the family as a whole, seemed most likely to be able to work together to useful purpose.

Still, I cannot deny that I see total family-group therapy as something of a last resort, both despite and because of my profound respect for the power of family dynamics over the fate of the individual member. I view it as a potent remedy, one with its own dangers, to be used only when specifically indicated and then with the utmost sensitivity and caution. Thus, I must face the possibility that my reluctance to follow Martha's suggestion was due to my own anxieties. But as I review my notes, I see that there was no threat to Martha's—or anyone's—survival, psychological or physical, in the family situation at that time. Conflict there was, and plenty of it, as each sibling asserted rights, needs, and desires; probably none was entirely content with the results of the battle for *Lebensraum*. Yet room for each to live and breathe was being underwritten by Martha herself, and without sacrificing her own space to *be*. It was clear to me that Martha's problem, this time around, would have to be confronted in some other arena.

## therapy hour, june 27

(I was now increasingly convinced that the original scapegoating experience and the reasons for it would provide clues to an eventual understanding not only of later episodes of that kind but also to something important about what led to the scapegoating in the first place. We started as usual with current realities, good and bad, and finally returned to the subject of scapegoating from the standpoint of Martha's recent experience with it in the new unit at work.)

MARTHA: They have laid off considerably, with the understanding that I am not interested in friendship. You know, there was a point . . . I don't know what was in their heads . . . there was a point when they would have accepted me. I am not even faintly interested in being friendly with them. We cooperate very easily now on the work, convey to each other as much information as we need.

**ESTHER:** You cooperate? It sounds like you've done something to handle this and to handle it rather well.

**MARTHA:** Well, I don't know. I'm in a typical position. I have no contact with them at all, as people. I don't *want* any contact at all with them as people. I could have done better than that, but I didn't want to. As far as the people who work at this agency go, I would put them at a pretty low level. They are by far the most—I don't know how to put it—*un*knowledgeable in the world.

**ESTHER:** Martha, do you have any idea how *they* feel?

**MARTHA:** No, no! I can't! Nothing, nothing would make me behave the way they behave. There's no button or trigger or hook that would cause me to behave that way. I can't find anything in myself. . . . You know, they resent my attitude. I've been resented for it many times before.

**ESTHER:** I'm trying to figure out how you can make a bridge between youself and people like these in some other way, because obviously the bridge of intelligence or knowledgeability or compatibility or whatever won't be it. But it seems to me there is some way of identifying with people.

**MARTHA:** Oh, I know how to do it, I've done it before. You do it with sympathy, a sort of empathy, you know, with the experiences that are common to you. That's the only bridge I know to that kind of person, and they cut that bridge the first ten minutes I was there, they cut it. You know, I just stood about three days of doing that kind of thing, and they just froze me out. Everytime I said something like "I've got four kids. How many have you got?" or "How old is this little girl who called you on the phone today?" they just froze! So fuck them!

**ESTHER:** It occurs to me, you see, that you have been involved with people like these and in situations like this all your life and will continue to be.

**MARTHA:** I sure have. And I'm sure tired of it.

**ESTHER:** There just has to be some way of living in such a situation with less emotional stress. You see, I'm trying to see where the problem lies. There are a lot of people to whom you can make a bridge who are not so knowledgeable or sophisticated as you. It's not that, really, that is the problem. There's something else involved.

**MARTHA:** We're seeing an identical replica of my school situation.

**ESTHER:** Okay. And I think it's something we have to think about.

MARTHA: Well, I think I understand why I was scapegoated. It's that I can't hide the intensity of my reaction to it, just no way. The first week I was in this unit I was on the verge of tears all the time.

ESTHER: I think what I'm getting is the vulnerability. . . . You describe it as the reaction you can't hide, but I have some feeling that the problem is a step back of that, that the vulnerability itself is causing the problem in the first place.

MARTHA: I want to tell you what I think happens. I don't think it is a clear or accurate perception of what does happen, but my telling you what I think happens will tell you where I am. I know I'm not perceiving the situation quite accurately, you know, or that it's off to the side in some way.

ESTHER: That may be.

MARTHA: My reaction when somebody puts me to a test like that is: If you are the kind of person who puts me to such a test, you are a person I don't give a shit for. I don't care whether these people accept me or not. The basis of the original pressure from them is: She's got to come around if she is going to work here. She'll see that we can make her life hell if she doesn't come around. And my reaction is: You can't make my life hell—who are you? But I'm going to work here!

ESTHER: You know, what I'm interested in is that you arrive at that conclusion immediately: "If you're that kind of person, I don't care if you like me or not."

MARTHA: Yes, it's like instant hate for that person.

ESTHER: You have an instantaneous reaction.

MARTHA: Well, not entirely, because I go through this with people whom I have known for a long time, too, known well and liked. My fight with Hazel was on this order. After knowing her for ten years, I could say, "Well, if that's the way you are, I don't ever care again if you like me or not." And mean it. And that was the permanent end of the relationship. I work on some kind of "critical mass" model, the straw-that-broke-the-camel's-back model. Beyond a certain point, there's no return. Beyond a certain point, it's exploded . . . I don't care. And you can reach that with me in five minutes. Three days is more likely. Which these ladies did. Or you can reach it over a period of ten years, as Hazel did. But it's an irreversible reaction.

ESTHER: Hmmm . . . You see, all this sounds so familiar to me. The only thing is, it's so stepped up in you. It's the same as anybody's reaction, but in you it comes faster, it's more intense, it's more complete, and it's irreversible.

MARTHA: It's irreversible! In my mind that's the main flaw. It ought not to be irreversible.

ESTHER: Now, how could I have put down in my notes here "It's reversible"? Ha!

**MARTHA:** Oops! Well, both of us know that's not true.

**ESTHER:** I guess I think it's not really irreversible, it only seems that way to you. Because I must have written it down unconsciously, which suggests to me it's what unconsciously I really think.

**MARTHA:** Yes. You know, with this group of people it's reversible, even now. But it's not reversible in me.

**ESTHER:** Why should you care so much? I think . . . what I'm trying to get at here is . . . why are you so vulnerable to this? As though it really mattered, as though in some way these people could really hurt you, as though you have to defend yourself this way because they could really destroy you.

**MARTHA:** They can destroy me . . . because of that other image of myself that Scott polished up so shiny, that image the school kids and my parents and my sisters and my psychiatrists were at such pains to build—of a substandard, crazy person.

**ESTHER:** The negative image.

**MARTHA:** The negative image is still there. I have learned not to buy it.

**ESTHER:** But you have to do that deliberately, consciously . . .

**MARTHA:** I have to consciously, constantly, *not* buy it. And I am still vulnerable to the line of thought: They have no reason to think badly of me, therefore they are assessing my true value, because they have no need for prejudices about me—which is nonsense. I am so threatening to them, you cannot believe.

**ESTHER:** Oh yeah, I can believe it.

**MARTHA:** I'm not going to say "I'm just folks." The way they think, I'm not.

**ESTHER:** No, you couldn't say it because they wouldn't believe it anyway. It wouldn't be true in their sense. But the problem is that negative self-image, which can be aroused at the slightest touch.

**MARTHA:** I bought that negative image again for almost a whole week.

**ESTHER:** You certainly did.

**MARTHA:** They caused me to say, "My God, I was wrong! It's all true, everything I was taught about myself, everything I spent so many years trying not to believe; it was all true. And they can see it when I walk in, and they've never even seen me before."

**ESTHER:** Well, I got the full force of *that* in that first dramatic reversal in the original contact between us. It was as though suddenly you had made me think for a moment that maybe you *were* this "bad" person. For a moment you had almost convinced me, and it was very frightening, terribly frightening. . . .

MARTHA: And it wiped away . . . it wiped away all your conscious thoughts.

ESTHER: It wiped *you* away—and at the same time it almost wiped *me* away.

MARTHA: Right, because your judgment was involved in mine, and if you wipe the *good* me away, you also wipe away your whole evaluating procedure.

ESTHER: That's right; it would wipe my whole . . .

MARTHA: Your judgment, and experience.

ESTHER: The whole bit.

MARTHA: Everything.

ESTHER: What gets wiped out is what the Freudians call the ego, which I think is a very useful term—the judging, perceiving, evaluating, reality-oriented . . .

MARTHA: In transactional analysis, the Adult.

ESTHER: That's right.

MARTHA: It gets wiped out. And that's what happens, that's what those people can do to me. That's the danger they are to me. Individually, they are no danger.

ESTHER: No. You see, if your image of yourself were what it should be—an accurate, solid image—these things they do you would find so inconsequential that you would have all kinds of casual means of handling them on an unconscious level. It would become so easy.

MARTHA: It would never come to consciousness. Right! But I've got to go now. Time is running out.

ESTHER: Okay, but this is very exciting because this . . . this is the root.

MARTHA: Right. We are hitting the very central problem.

## from esther's notebook

How *do* you handle the problem of being "different"? Especially if you are a woman and if the way in which you are different happens to be your very good intelligence? Martha must somehow find a way of being what she really is without letting it threaten others. There is no self-esteem to be had in pretending, no matter how successfully, to be something that one is not, for then whatever comes one's way in acceptance or recognition is not truly one's own. And how isolated a person then feels from all other human beings!

How does a woman handle intelligence? It sounds stupid or insane to suggest that intelligence can be a problem. But it is—for women. It always has been for most women, and to some extent it still is. If there is one main thing that women's liberation is about, it is about the intelligence of women and the need to set that intelligence free not only in the eyes of the world but also in their own eyes; to free women from their discomforts and inhibitions and prejudices about their own intelligence so that they can begin to use it more constructively for whatever purposes they choose. To put it simply and incredibly, women are far too often afraid of their own intelligence, so afraid that they sometimes don't even recognize that they have it—even so afraid that they might just as well not have it at all, for all the good it does them.

I doubt that men are very often afraid of their intelligence. I think they would be more likely to claim superior intelligence than to disclaim it, for any superiority a man may have is at least of potential value to him. He is in no danger of being condemned for recognizing it, or for being aggressive in using it. I doubt that men are very often put down for their intelligence by other men, though they may be feared for the power it gives them or disliked for the way they use that power. But women often put other women down for their intelligence. It is as though women who let their intelligence show have broken some unwritten law, some covenant, some bond of sisterhood.

I feel that the "cult" of the I.Q., to which our society has become addicted, is most unfortunate. It has fostered the illusion that "intelligence tests" do in fact measure true intelligence, whatever that may be, and encourages people in the notion that there is something intrinsically objective and scientific about classifying individuals by numbers indicating their place on some scale or other. I think that such procedures contribute to the already unfortunate consequences of pecking-order mechanisms, which are unattractive and destructive even among chickens. I am nevertheless convinced that it is far more useful to one's view of oneself and the world to think of oneself as intelligent rather than otherwise. In fact, some of the most damaged people I have known are those who are highly intelligent but who have gone unrecognized as such by themselves and by others.

The real problem with regard to intelligence is, first, to recognize it as an asset that is as much a matter of good fortune as anything else, and second, to find ways of using it comfortably for the benefit of oneself and others. Martha has solved the first part but must still deal with the rest of it. That part was hard for me, too. I used to have the feeling that every time I let my intelligence show —which meant just about every time I let my real self show—no matter how tentatively or diffidently, I was struck down, often by someone who had some kind of power over me, even if only the power to hurt me. I suspect that this has been the experience of many women.

If your special gift happens to be intelligence, then in order to be yourself you must talk in ways that reveal your intelligence; otherwise you are not being you. But if you are a woman and you do this, there are people who think you are trying to flaunt your superiority and feel threatened or resentful—and many of these, of course, are men. As a matter both of culture and of individual psychology, men are expected and expect themselves to be more intelligent than women. They are unlikely to choose, either for dates or as their brides, women who are obviously more intelligent than they; so, if the woman is not actually the less intelligent one, she feels she must pretend to be. A common solution among women—and one Martha seems to have attempted, perhaps unconsciously—is to try to find men who are indeed their superiors in intelligence so that it will not be necessary for them to dissemble in order to play the appropriate feminine role.

Yet intelligence is by no means synonymous with strength, or wisdom, or sanity, or even just plain adequacy. When a woman discovers that it is she, after all, who is the "superior" one in the partnership, despite all her efforts to be the "inferior" one as prescribed by custom, the shock can be a very great one indeed. I have not found it commonly mentioned, however, in the usual textbooks and handbooks on marital matters. I am indebted to an article called "The Paradox of the Happy Marriage," by Jessie Bernard, for an illuminating formulation of this subject as well as for the equally illuminating report, backed by statistical studies, that men are a good deal more often happily married than their wives! Here I had confirmation for matters I had been observing professionally and personally for many years; only then did I become completely free to use the fruits of these observations for the full benefit of clients.

I think that Martha has had trouble "forgiving" people their lesser intelligence because they would not forgive her for her superior intelligence. But who should forgive whom? Who has the advantage? In a group situation, the others have the advantage of numbers, and that is a considerable advantage.

In a one-to-one situation, things can go wrong, too. But I didn't react to Martha the way she fears—and expects—people to react. I didn't react with the "Who do you think you are?" bit, which is preliminary to the "You must be crazy" bit. By the same token, I am not at all inclined to pursue the arid question of madness with Martha. Instead, I want to pursue further those questions we have turned up that hold promise of being explanatory and liberating for both of us. (I must watch myself on this, for I must not distort Martha's therapy in order to pursue my own interests.)

**5**
Development

# from therapy hours in june and july

**ESTHER:** It seems to me that in going into the new unit at work you were going into a peer-group situation. If one of the group decided to scapegoat you then, because it was an ingroup, the others would have to follow the leader, as it were—even though there might have been a few who were not really that kind of person, individually speaking.

**MARTHA:** That was true, and I was aware of it at the time. There were two or three people in the unit of eight . . . there were two who would not go along with it at all, and they are slightly apart from the group. They absolutely . . . they remained friendly. They went out of their way to maintain conversation.

**ESTHER:** That's what I would count on in the average group situation, that there are always a few who won't go along with it.

**MARTHA:** There were a couple of others who didn't want to go along with it. They would smile at me, and when we had to discuss a case, they would unbend and try to make me somewhat welcome. And then there were two ringleaders and two, three just absolutely blind followers.

**MARTHA:** About my recollections of being scapegoated in childhood and this thing that happened when I came into the new unit: I had done nothing, nothing they could complain about, if you see what I mean. I hadn't done anything to them, or refused to do my work so that they had to do it, or set them up for something. It wasn't on a reality basis.

**MARTHA:** I think the trouble is that I care, I obviously care about my clients. And when I'm talking to the clients, I don't put on a suit of armor and behave in a certain way. I talk the same way that I always do. Most of the workers in that unit use a very stilted vocabulary when they talk to the clients. I talk to clients the same way I would to you. My manner toward clients is, I consider, part of my respect for them. My manner conveys that we could easily be in a reversed situation—they could be the worker and I could be the client.

**ESTHER:** In other words, you're saying you are not handling the job quite the same way the others are handling it.

**MARTHA:** They use a defense on the job that I don't have and I don't need.

ESTHER: So you're saying the people in the unit who resented you did so because you were doing something in a way different from theirs.

MARTHA: I'm also saying that the way in which I dealt with the clients revealed a kind of vulnerability. The clients could have turned on me and cut me in pieces because I wasn't keeping up a defensive armor against them. I don't do that. I show my vulnerability, and it's part of my pride to stay that way.

ESTHER: Even though if you are vulnerable and show it, you know that some people are going to take advantage?

MARTHA: Oh, yes.

ESTHER: Well, I should think it would be possible to operate the way you do—even have some people resent it—and yet not let it get to you, to upset you. In other words . . .

MARTHA: I don't have to give up what's good in order to get a defense?

ESTHER: That's my feeling, that it's a matter of finding a way of defending yourself without changing yourself.

MARTHA: Right! I think it can be done. But I'm hair trigger; I have a hair-trigger response. I walk around with a sign saying "I'm vulnerable," I really do. I'm an obvious victim and that's why it's happened to me so often. As a matter of fact, I could not contain . . . during that week when I was being actively scapegoated, I could not contain my reactions. I was publicly on the point of tears most of the time.

ESTHER: I think someone who encounters this kind of scapegoating over and over again without knowing why it happens is bound to be naïve about people. Until you know what is happening and why it's happening, you have no guideposts to go by.

MARTHA: Right. It takes enormous naïveté to be a scapegoat. I think it's an unrealistic way of thinking about people that goes into the makeup of the victim-type personality. It's what the victim personality is made of.

ESTHER: But what is it you need to know about people to learn to protect yourself?

MARTHA: That they are not operating on the same set of criteria that I am.

ESTHER: Well, what are they operating on then?

MARTHA: Self-interest. They're taking care of themselves. I don't have the personal security to deal with it.

MARTHA: I have a large body of negative pictures of myself set up and ready to go.

ESTHER: What's that negative picture all about, actually?

MARTHA: Well, it's the same one I tried to feed you in our big blowup in the first contact. It's that I'm visibly sick, that anybody can see I'm visibly sick. I walk into a group of strangers and they can all tell just by looking at me that I'm sick.

ESTHER: That there's something wrong with you?

MARTHA: That there's something the matter with me. Of course, when I am with extremely kind people, they won't call me on it. And this has been the case in my other work situations. But now I'm with a group of honest people and they are going to call me on it because they are not extremely kind. In other words, I just exist on the kindness of other people. I can't make it on my own at all.

ESTHER: Okay, how do you think that started when you were a kid? Everybody had to be kind to you or you would be shattered? That's how it started?

MARTHA: That's how it started.

ESTHER: Everybody had to, in a sense, accept you and like you.

MARTHA: No. There was never any possibility of being accepted and liked.

ESTHER: Well, I think that was your *reaction* to what happened. But I think that originally you must have gone into a situation at school or in the neighborhood expecting, or at least hoping, that the kids would accept you and like you.

MARTHA: I don't think I ever . . .

ESTHER: You can't remember that far back.

MARTHA: No. I don't think I ever did. I think this was set before I ran into other people. I didn't play with other kids until I was almost five years old, until I got to kindergarten. I didn't know how to adjust to other children. Also, my sisters were almost seven and eight years older than I, and they constituted a unit themselves, operating on their own level. I can see this in my own family. Benjy is seven years younger than his next older sibling. We're all talking away on a semiadult level, and here's Benjy, who doesn't understand a word we're saying. He keeps breaking in and getting it all wrong, and we say, "Oh, Benjy, you're distracting us."

ESTHER: And he's made to feel like a nuisance.

MARTHA: Right. "You're distracting us from what we're talking about. Go away." You know, I think this is a "normal" reaction.

ESTHER: Maybe. But if it's the *only* reaction you ever got—*that* isn't normal.

MARTHA: Superunderlined in my family by the fact that my first sister was conceived out of wedlock and not too enthusiastically greeted for that reason. My mother got pregnant again a few months after that birth, when my parents were really down, and there couldn't have been much enthusiasm about that either. My father had to quit school and take a factory job, which he hoped would be temporary so that he could get back to school. And then bang! my mother got pregnant with the second baby. She was born just a little more than a year after the first. And finally, "Thank God, we're not going to have to do that again! Now maybe we can settle in and do something." Then six years of going forward and along comes the depression to put everybody's life out of whack, psychologically and financially. My father was damn lucky to have a job, and they were just barely making it through. Wages went way down. The workers couldn't get a union going, and the company cut wages several times. You had the option of taking a wage cut or quitting. There were no other jobs to get, so you had to stay there. And right in the middle of the depression, there was I—after my parents thought their family was complete. They weren't too glad to see me. Here was this close-knit little family of four people, with me dragging along afterward. They did their best not to make me feel it, but . . .

ESTHER: But you couldn't help feeling from the beginning that you weren't wanted.

MARTHA: I felt from the beginning that I wasn't wanted.

ESTHER: So that any place you went after that, you expected not to be wanted.

MARTHA: I didn't know what else to expect.

ESTHER: When I was a kid, I was always trying to conform as much as I could to what other kids seemed to think was the way to be. I guess it was partly because I had always had to try to conform to the way my parents thought I should be.

MARTHA: It never occurred to me that I *could* conform to the way anybody thought I should be. I took their word for it that I was *very* odd.

ESTHER: There was no way you could come through and be the way they expected you to be, so there was no use trying.

MARTHA: No way, no way, just no way. The promise that "we'll make you one of us" or the threat that "we'll read you out of the human race if you don't conform"—neither one packed any wallop with me. Because it was never a possibility. I couldn't imagine being accepted, so the promise of acceptance or the threat of nonacceptance carried very little weight.

ESTHER: I think I finally realized that I would never be allowed to become part of that happy inner circle, and I know I stopped trying. But I could put on a show that wouldn't look too bad and that would satisfy me in some way, too.

**MARTHA:** I knew that I was always going to look bad. I still know that I am always going to look bad. And I fight and fight and fight to look good in another sense—to develop my own alternative.

**ESTHER:** What does it take to look good?

**MARTHA:** You have to *be* what the others are, you can't fake it. You have to be what they are, and I can't be anything but me. They're different in some way. They know what to do or they have this sense of how to operate in terms of other people.

**ESTHER:** Well, I always had a feeling that other people somehow knew how to be—some way that I didn't know how to be . . .

**MARTHA:** That's exactly what I'm talking about.

**ESTHER:** . . . that somehow other people knew about something that made it possible for them to operate in a different way than I could. It was as though they had a secret and I didn't have that secret.

**MARTHA:** You're right on the beam with what I'm talking about.

**ESTHER:** And because I didn't have that secret, there was no way I could ever become part of any group.

**MARTHA:** Right. There's no bridge from here to there.

**ESTHER:** But I managed, you know, okay. I made do with one or two people. Of course, they also were always outsiders of a sort, but that was all right. Still, I kept having the feeling that there was something missing, something wrong.

**MARTHA:** I see something, something important. I married an outsider who was absolutely convinced he was a one-of-a-kind genius. My reaction to being scapegoated in childhood, my sense that there was no bridge between here and there, no way were they ever going to accept me, no way could I be a person they could accept . . . my reply to all that was to develop a strong alternative: I'm a different kind of person. I will create an alternative way of being, out of nothing. What I did when I married was to marry a sterling representative of the alternative convention. I married to confirm, to reaffirm, the convention of the brilliant outsider. And that's why I bought Scott's brilliant outsider story for so long.

**ESTHER:** Why did he marry you? Why did he want to marry you?

**MARTHA:** Because I'm a victim.

**ESTHER:** Because he could take advantage of you? Because he could scapegoat you?

MARTHA: Yes. He could scapegoat me.

ESTHER: In a way you're saying, then, that Scott was your defense. Here was this brilliant outsider who proved it could be done, proved there were people who were so special, so different. He proved it.

MARTHA: Exactly. Scott was to be my success, he had to be my success. I never felt that I could make a success on my own.

MARTHA: (Back to the scapegoating theme again.) The basic thing—the basis on which other people can take advantage of you—is if you weren't sensitive that way, they couldn't do it. I think it's on a physical, a constitutional base first. But then, I agree the adults put it on you next . . . and then the kids just pick up on it because you've already learned to exhibit the symptoms.

ESTHER: Well, it seems to me that what you are trying to do now is to find some way of no longer being so vulnerable to other people as you have been.

MARTHA: Yes. I've always looked at it in my typical all-or-nothing fashion: Either I must go on being as vulnerable as I am now, or else I must give up what I consider my integrity. Either/or.

ESTHER: Ah! I see why you're so stuck.

MARTHA: My integrity requires involvement with other people with a minimum of defenses on my part, with a maximum of exposure of my human frailties in order to comfort them about their own human frailties, and so on and on and on: This has been a point of honor.

ESTHER: Well, that's how I do therapy. But I don't think I have to do that in real life, and that's the saving grace. It's what I do in therapy.

MARTHA: Save it for where it's useful, in other words, and don't try to do it where is isn't feasible, or even to your advantage.

ESTHER: Yes, I think it really boils down to whether it's practical or not.

MARTHA: My point about virtue is that you must not analyze.

ESTHER: You must always just be virtuous.

MARTHA: You must always just be virtuous.

ESTHER: You must not decide whether this is a situation that requires it of you . . .

MARTHA: Virtue that's by convenience is not virtue. Therefore if you are going to be good, you must not consider your own convenience. If you do, you're not being good, you're merely being expedient.

ESTHER: Well, I think there is a strong element of expediency in this, but I do not see it as becoming unvirtuous. I just see this as becoming maybe nonvirtuous or avirtuous—that is, virtue doesn't apply in this way in certain situations. I wouldn't go to the opposite extreme ever. But there are times when you simply do not expose your human frailties, and virtue just doesn't enter into it. You have to take care of yourself. With some people, you just don't operate on that basis. Even with my best friend, I will occasionally hold back a little something for fear of hurting her if I say it completely at that point.

MARTHA: But if you hold back for fear of hurting her, it falls into a different category for me. If you would hold back for fear of hurting yourself . . .

ESTHER: Well, I don't think those fears can be separated.

MARTHA: Now, that's very interesting.

ESTHER: You see, because if I hurt her, it would also hurt me in some way.

MARTHA: It would damage the friendship between you, which you need.

ESTHER: It would damage the friendship, that's right.

MARTHA: I'm so naïve about how other people operate—you know, what the scale of operation on virtue is.

ESTHER: I think it finally dawned on me somewhere along the line that you don't have an operating scale that is really working for you. You don't have a range to go by. It's always either/or. I don't know what scheme is set up in the back of my mind, but I've got one that takes care of my feeling of virtue insofar as I need to take care of it. And it's fairly flexible; it's a scale, a range.

## from esther's notebook

I must write something about the problem of "being good"—Martha calls it "playing the Saint"—one of the roles identified by Eric Berne in his cast of neurotic characters. Women are assigned this role by our society, which equates womanliness with goodness. (A man, unless he is a member of the clergy, cannot take on this role without jeopardizing his claim to manliness.) There have, of course, been Jezebels, "fallen women," witches, and bitches throughout history. Although some of them were reputed to have awesome powers of seduction, none is considered exactly the epitome of femininity. And all forfeit entirely woman's claim to the rewards of virtue—whatever these rewards may be.

The rest of us, huddled for safety and comfort within the virtuous bounds of our assigned role, may find those rewards rather equivocal. The truth of the matter is that goodness becomes synonymous with dullness; it has none of the appeal of the siren's song. If it is not seen as phony, as the hypocritical cover for a multitude of sins, if it is only too clearly genuine and thoroughgoing, then goodness is likely to be resented as self-righteousness. Men may expect—even demand—that their women practice the socially prescribed womanly virtues, but they may then proceed to hate the women for those very virtues. The more virtuous the wife, the more the husband is open to reproach (or to self-reproach) for his shortcomings. O'Neill's Hickey in *The Iceman Cometh* is more than just a figment of the dramatist's imagination. Hickey's story has the awful ring of human truth: if the female of the species takes on the full burden of goodness, the male is thereby saddled with the full burden of guilt, a neat little psychological arrangement with almost infinitely expandable ranges of misery for all. Such may be the rewards of feminine virtue!

Social work has suffered from the image of the female "do-gooder," with all its guilt-making propensities. Social workers are seen as dull and stodgy, hypocritical or self-righteous, nosy, officious, and obnoxious—and usually stupid. It is rare to find them portrayed in literature as attractive and interesting human beings, trying to help people find better ways of dealing with their circumstances, with themselves, and with one another. No doubt some social workers deserve to be criticized on personal or professional grounds or both, but to saddle the entire profession with such a stereotype is to indulge in a vicious kind of scapegoating. (No wonder I have such intense feelings on that subject!)

The scapegoating theme has taken us in several different directions, all of which are helping me to understand Martha better. I am beginning to see that Martha was not able to help me understand more quickly because she herself had not really assimilated the meaning of the experiences she had been through. And this has been partly because she had no adequate frame of reference within which to do her assimilating.

Sometimes when I was talking about myself, I have had the feeling that I was actually talking about both of us—telling myself who Martha was out of similar emotional experiences of my own, and filling in parts of my life from the outline Martha was sketching of hers. There was no other way I could have comprehended her story, made sense of it for myself, identified with her. I am reminded of the child who says to the parent, "Tell me the story of my life." (Was I that child? I remember feeling so strongly in my own therapy the wish that someone, some father person, would take me on his lap and tell me the story of my life in a way I could accept, all the while comforting me with the assurance, "It's all right, it's all right.")

It seems to me the matter of identity is the crux of the problem for Martha. Somehow there was a failure of identification, a two-way failure, in her childhood: She could not identify enough with her mother, nor her mother with her. No doubt, the same could be said for the other family members—except, for a while, one sister. And Martha had little opportunity for identification with neighborhood children. She had not developed enough of an identification mechanism by the time she started school to make it possible for her to identify with the other children, or they with her.

Such failures in identification underlie and reinforce the failure to develop a satisfactory pattern of communication. Martha acquired no really adequate way of understanding others or of obtaining understanding from them. It seems to me it would be extremely difficult, perhaps impossible, to come to a sufficient understanding of oneself under such circumstances. To some extent, Martha and I are going through the whole process over again together—the identifying and differentiating process human beings must go through in order to understand themselves and others. Identification and differentiation: One is as important as the other. Out of the antithesis of identification and differentiation comes the synthesis *identity*. (A client of mine who had gone through experiences in therapy similar to Martha's had said, early in her contact with me, that she had had enough analysis; what she wanted now was some synthesis. And she was right!)

Identification and differentiation and synthesis: In childhood, if all goes well, one goes through such a process unconsciously; in adolescence one goes through it much more consciously. In adolescence, the synthesis is often called into question, examined and reexamined, modified and manipulated according to notions of present and future usefulness, sometimes discarded temporarily if not entirely, and occasionally lost—as it may be by adults also at a time of great stress. In childhood, one made certain choices out of love, or a need for love, and other choices out of anger toward, or conflict with, one's parents. Thus, the groundwork for adolescent consciousness of self and for later adult identity was laid long since, on the unconscious level.

I think that early marriage often represents an attempt to flee from the individuation process back into an earlier mother-child relationship, but one in which the nurture obtained in this way may have to be paid for by psychological death as an independent individual. Martha had saved herself, had saved the core of her personality, and she had fashioned from it the idea and ideal of an alternative to the never-to-be-achieved acceptance. Long before the counterculture movement, Martha had her own version. If one is to be ostracized, to be crucified, for being different, then being different in whatever way one must be becomes a value in itself—and a higher value by far than any unthinking conformity. Well and good! But such a course demands the strength to be independent. Martha, underestimating herself and overestimating Scott, fell into a typical "feminine" solution, however "differently" she may have arrived at it: She would achieve her fulfillment through identification with her man, remaining dependent upon him and looking to him for some kind of nurture. (And so, of course, had I and most of the women of my generation; and how many women still do?)

When Martha talks about her clients, she sounds like me, not because of identification with me but because of identification with the same principles: the dignity of the human being, the right of the individual to self-determination, the built-in equality of people as people, the respect for our fellows implicit in our common humanity. There are many ways of arriving at these truths and of endeavoring to live by them—philosophy, religion, democracy, whatever shape or form one chooses. They also happen to be the principles on which social work was founded, and they are the basis of the psychosocial therapy that I practice.

Martha's work is not granted the title of social work, nor are its practitioners encouraged to dedicate themselves to social work principles. Indeed, the principles themselves are often subject to ridicule and scorn even when not actually accused of producing the evils they have attempted to alleviate, evils that, of course, only massive social, economic, and political change can begin to "cure." Martha and her fellow workers are called eligibility workers or technicians. They are expected to carry out their assignments in a strictly businesslike manner, without the saving grace of even a modicum of human involvement with clients. Yet someone like Martha cannot avoid operating on social work principles, for they are part of her very being. It was women like Martha who laid the foundations on which the profession of social work was built. She is a direct descendant in spirit, though not in name.

I have a habit to which I am happily addicted, a very fruitful one from the standpoint of therapy. Whenever I read the biography or autobiography of a writer in whom I am interested, I also try to read or reread that person's literary productions. I think I have learned at least as much about the nature of human beings in this way, in terms of usable understanding for my own practice, as I have gotten from professional sources. I find that the technical material supplements the literary, and vice versa, so that when I happen upon a special problem in therapy, one I need to know more about, I turn to literary as well as professional material.

While reading Martha's story, I found my thoughts somewhere along the way turning to F. Scott and Zelda Fitzgerald, especially, of course, in relation to the marital problem. Later, when my attention shifted to women's problems in general, I found myself thinking of Sylvia Plath. Neither of these associations is unusual; Plath and the Fitzgeralds are likely to be mentioned whenever any literary allusions are made in connection with the women's liberation movement. I had been reading everything published by or about these authors since I had first heard of them, and I was not surprised to find that they were drawing considerable notice from that quarter.

There actually seems little resemblance between Martha's Scott and F. Scott, but the competitive situation in the Fitzgerald marriage caused me to speculate a good deal about the possibility of an equally life-and-death competitiveness between Martha and Scott, a competition that might be similarly based, though expressed in a quite different fashion. (The fact that we had given Martha's ex-husband the name of Scott was an odd sort of happenstance. Neither Martha nor I picked the name. My husband, a teacher of mathematics with no interest in literature and no familiarity at all with F. Scott, happened to be tutoring a student named Scott and suggested the name to us when we were discussing pseudonyms. It just happened that Martha and I both thought the name combined well with Morgan, or so it seemed at the time.)

So far as understanding Martha's Scott is concerned, I found more fruitful substance for speculation in some of the biographies of artists, Whistler (whose portrait of his mother served an aesthetic and not a sentimental purpose) being the most evocative for me. I therefore noted with interest that when Martha wrote of Scott's penchant for telling tall stories, one of the examples, that of "a Japanese painter [who] will paint nothing but black furniture in dark rooms," might have been a story told of Whistler.

Sylvia Plath was of Martha's generation, not mine, but her

career—except, of course, for her suicide and her suffering—seemed to epitomize what I would have chosen for myself had I had the talent and the drive and the courage to be aggressive. When I recently began reevaluating that earlier period of my own life, I found myself in some kind of identification with Plath. I felt I had retreated from competition into the self-effacing role that was the prevailing notion of womanliness in my day, when what I really would have wanted was to win that competition, as it seemed to me Sylvia Plath had done.

It was partly on the strength of this borrowed identity that I was able to identify with Martha. Sylvia Plath had become a writer and poet, a winner of academic prizes, and (perhaps most important in those days of typical middle-class values) a *Mademoiselle* guest editor. I know that some of Martha's fellow students have matched or more than matched the achievements of Plath. They were the contemporaries against whom Martha was measuring herself and finding herself lacking; whereupon she retreated rather quickly to the recourse favored by my generation, the traditional woman's role. But Martha did this with somewhat greater sexual daring than was usual in my generation, in that respect anticipating something of the counterculture of today—in that respect, also, resembling somewhat the character Esther in *The Bell Jar*. But Martha, without Plath's (or the fictitious Esther's) advantages in the circumstances of her life and with a far more limited range of alternatives available to her at the time, moved unconsciously in the direction of survival, no matter how restricted and painful, rather than self-destruction.

I was struck by the term bell jar, Plath's metaphor of a glass enclosure symbolizing the impenetrable barrier around the closed-away person, within which a human being can be utterly and helplessly alone. Because of Father Michaelson, who got through to Martha with his love as much as with his help in communication, Martha forever escaped the bell jar, the harbinger of doom that continued to hang over Plath's Esther as well as over Sylvia Plath herself.

Plath's famous poem "Daddy" provides something closer to a shared, perhaps universal, female experience. Despite the fact that very few fathers could conceivably deserve the degree of hatred expressed by daughter toward father in this poem, "Daddy" has a tremendous appeal for most women. It does for me, and I had a father whom I loved very much. Where does all this free-floating hatred come from, hatred so ready to attach itself to such a song of hatred triumphant, hatred guiltless and without shame, hatred so extravagant as to approach psychosis? And in so many women? And in me?

I suspect that, at least for me, there is a case of split transference at work, with my conscious feelings toward my father—and most men—embodying the positive transference. This phenomenon of splitting the transference is thought to be at work symbolically in folk tales about wicked stepmothers. On their shoulders can be unloaded all the unacceptable feelings of hatred toward the real mother for any rejecting, depriving, punishing, or controlling behavior that arouses anger in the daughter, thus permitting a more positive relationship to prevail. The girl child must, of course, eventually turn elsewhere for the sexual relationship she cannot have with her mother, and the phenomenon of the split transference would then come to be a natural enough device for dealing with angry feelings in relationships with men. Positive though a woman's relationships may be with the men in her personal life, she would still have need for a symbolic male figure upon whom to bestow the hatred built up inevitably in a society heavily dominated by men and heedlessly exploitative of women. What a powerful residue of anger there must be floating around in a woman's unconscious! No wonder we women need a Sylvia Plath to provide us with a "Daddy" through which our feelings are expressed for us.*

# reflections on an interview in july

We had to abandon the tape recorder today, as I couldn't get the tape to work properly and I had brought no spare along. I was angry at myself for this, but I had also the curious experience of feeling the same kind of self-consciousness now at *not* recording that I had originally felt *about* recording. I didn't feel quite myself throughout the hour. I decided, on finding that my schedule showed a cancelled appointment the next hour, to write up my notes immediately in the hope of feeling better. (It worked.)

Martha rarely mentions dreams, but she had one so meaningful last night that it constituted for her an unconscious validation of her interpretation of what Scott's feelings had been toward her, regardless of what he said or did. I said that was fine, that the important thing for her was to be clear about her own interpretation, to know what was happening within herself—ignoring what the outside reality had been. I think I was so concerned with how we were going to present Scott's problems (about which I could have no independent source of information) in the book that I probably sounded to Martha very much like some of her previous therapists. Martha caught this immediately and said something that made it possible to talk a little about it. This gave me the opportunity to clarify my position somewhat, but I don't think I did so fully enough; hence my discomfort and my need to write up the hour immediately, with the benefit of hindsight.

In Martha's previous therapy, if the focus was constantly on her inner experience, the reality of Scott's problems (what Martha was up against in actuality) was not being taken into consideration. Martha's fear of being found "crazy" was thus reinforced, making it impossible for her to arrive at an accurate evaluation of the total situation at all. The therapists' hurry to get in there with some interpretation of Martha's own problems defeated the very purpose they no doubt had in mind, which was for Martha to be able to arrive at a balanced, judicious view of the total, overall marital situation based on her own dynamics as well as on Scott's. Had I not been concerned with the book, I doubt that I would have fallen into this error. But had I not made the error, I doubt that I could have seen so clearly (and felt so definitely) what went wrong between Martha and some of her other therapists.

We nevertheless were able to examine Martha's feelings that her parents were "so peculiar" and that this was why she was, too. Yet she said they seemed "so normal and middle class." I remarked on how little I felt I understood what her parents were really like, that although she had told me things that were perhaps somewhat "different," nothing seemed so terribly peculiar about them. I then mentioned my parents' immigrant background and my feelings of embarrassment, even shame sometimes, because of their "difference" on that score. But Martha pointed out, quite correctly, that my parents didn't sound as though *they* thought of themselves as odd, whereas her parents did. She thought that, since her parents themselves had made so great a distinction between themselves and other people, there must really have been something terribly wrong. Though we never did define just what was "so peculiar," Martha did in this way establish for me that the idea of being peculiar was part of her fear of (and her willingness to accept) the label of "crazy"— and also why she had been so slow to question her life with Scott.

## from esther's notebook

In writing my comments on Martha's story, I was aware that I was leaving a gap in my own story: the period between the flare-up of psychoneurotic symptoms, when I went to work so that my husband could get his teaching credential, and my own return to the university for the graduate work that would qualify me as a psychiatric social worker. This was a period of about ten years, a period during which a very real physical problem was added to my already very real psychological problems. I suspect that the physical problem had forerunners that I had managed to suppress and repress, for I remember having an occasional moment of worry about my hearing during my undergraduate years. But the crude hearing tests of those days showed no hearing loss, and I was happy to be assured that I had none. I was aware that the hearing in my left ear was not quite as good as that in my right, but I knew that such a difference was not unusual and that it could easily be accounted for by the ear infections I had suffered as a child and the mastoidectomy I finally had.

It was not until my early thirties, when I suddenly experienced a noticeable loss of hearing, first in my left ear and then in my right, all within the space of a week or so, that I became alarmed. I experienced the loss originally as an interference with my hearing due to head noises. (I later learned these noises are technically termed "tinnitus," defined as the sound of roaring and ringing in the ear caused by no external stimulus.) When the sounds persisted, I went to an otologist, for I knew that my father had begun suffering a hearing loss in his forties and I was determined to avoid his fate, let alone be subjected to it at an even younger age. I must say that my father felt only very slightly handicapped until his sixties, did not try a hearing aid until his seventies, and did not actually wear one until he was eighty—by which time his hearing was so poor that even he could no longer ignore the problem. I did not inherit his capacity for denial and repression, but I did, as it turned out, inherit the genetic factor that produces the condition known as otosclerosis.

My loss of hearing took place before the development of the surgical techniques that sometimes alleviate the problem. There was little the doctors could do at the time, although they tried a number of somewhat painful and entirely futile procedures. I went to several different otologists, for I was not at all ready to accept my fate. This was before the days of small at-the-ear hearing aids, or even of relatively adequate ones (no hearing aid produces normal hearing), and all the doctors advised against trying a hearing aid while my loss was still minor. When I finally did begin to use one, I understood what they meant. The constant distraction of background noise and the shock of sudden loud sounds battering one's defective auditory system are physically and emotionally exhausting. The advantage of amplification in volume is more than offset by these disadvantages until one's hearing level has fallen low enough to make one willing to endure the side effects.

I finally resorted to a hearing aid, but only after the newly developed surgical technique of fenestration proved to have come too late to be of any substantial value to me. Technically, the surgery was successful, although somewhat in the sense of "the operation was successful but the patient died." My nerve loss had by then progressed so far that eliminating the conductive loss through surgery could not restore me to a level of hearing sufficient for my purposes. Since I had already tried everything, including the study of lip reading (at which I was spectacularly bad), I had to give up on everything except an extremely skeptical hope for a miracle.

Meanwhile, I settled for a hearing aid. In those days, it was of a size and appearance, including its cord, to suggest that if "men seldom make passes at girls who wear glasses," a woman in her thirties wearing a hearing aid was so beyond the pale as to be unmentionable. That comment may sound facetious, but I am reporting exactly how I felt at that time, and there was nothing the least bit funny about it. (I do not, incidentally, find jokes about hard-of-hearing people any more acceptable than jokes about any other minority group; and the hard-of-hearing certainly constitute a disadvantaged minority, often economically as well as psychologically, and always socially.)

My feeling about wearing a hearing aid—and it was very great indeed—was nevertheless far less than my feeling about the head noises. There was nothing the doctors could do about them. One otologist said to me, "You can drive yourself crazy listening to them, or you can turn on the radio and drown them out." Later, when I began wearing a hearing aid, I found that its amplification of background noise had a fringe benefit. It did at least drown out the head noises. But I had to face the fact that I would never hear silence again. I think that I always knew how precious silence is, how much peace and quiet meant to me. When I mourned my hearing loss, I knew I was above all mourning the loss of silence. Solitude is an absolutely essential compensation when I can get it, but it is no substitute for silence.

There was nothing the doctors could do about either the hearing loss or the tinnitus. What they could have done was something that apparently never occurred to them: to encourage me to talk about how I felt and what I might try to do about it. Except for one doctor who made noises about "people feeling sorry for themselves," I did not feel they were lacking in sympathy, but I had the distinct impression that they were extremely uncomfortable about the whole subject. I soon discovered that no one seemed comfortable with it. There was literally no one to whom I could talk. If there were mental health clinics or social service agencies to which I could have gone, no one told me about them. I found myself fantasizing that some day in every medical building there would be a room with a listener to whom one could go and pour out one's feelings and cry as much as one felt like without being told not to feel sorry for oneself.

After the first impact was over and I had talked with no one about it, I found that I not only did not want to do so but for a long time was even more uncomfortable than everyone else about the whole thing. It was not until I had had some contact with social workers and with social work philosophy that I realized my fantasy about an understanding listener bore a distinct resemblance to some well-known social work theories and goals. From that time onward, though I had no idea how I was going to get the money for graduate training, there was no doubt in my mind about what I wanted to do with the rest of my life.

It seems a little ironic that I should have come to the mental health field because of a physical condition, since I could just as easily have come because of neurotic symptoms. Of course, the reality circumstances and the emotional dynamics are never entirely separable; with hearing loss, as with other somatic disabilities, emotional and physical factors contribute to one another. In the course of investigating the matter for my master's thesis, I came across the theory that hearing loss may sometimes be a substitute for a schizophrenic break. At the time, I found this theory more comforting than alarming. If it were true, I could look upon my body as having at least saved my mind, and I must have valued the latter somewhat more highly than the former.

But the schizophrenic label is not so readily disposed of on an unconscious level. The suggestion of it came back to haunt me during my period of disturbance in the early part of my psychotherapy. I was convinced then that I was schizophrenic, though my psychiatrist obviously viewed me as hysterical. I literally prayed that he was right and I was wrong, not only because I could no longer take the schizophrenic label so lightly but also because if I were sufficiently hysterical, my hearing loss might prove to be psychological in origin and therefore reversible. I suppose this was my way of hoping for a miracle. I continued to work on my master's thesis, for it was the one thing I felt sure that I could do. It represented the culmination of all the thinking and reading and growing I had done, and it held out the possibility that I could make some contribution of my own toward understanding the problem that had brought me to this point.

The social work school had recently begun to favor group research over the individual thesis for the master's degree, and I needed special permission to get my degree under the old plan instead of the new. I had done all the research in advance and was ready to do the writing by the time of my appointment with my faculty advisor. When she heard what I was proposing to do, her first question was whether I had been psychoanalyzed. When I said no, but I was in therapy, she shook her head impatiently: that was not the same thing at all. I was doing a very dangerous thing in writing about a problem of my own without first having been psychoanalyzed; I might very well be schizophrenic—many people with hearing loss were. She urged me to go to a psychoanalyst before it was too late. I said that although I had not specifically discussed the matter with my psychiatrist, he was aware of what I was doing and had never raised any question about it, which was enough reassurance for me. Again she shook her head, and this time she said that I would, of course, never be able to work in a psychiatric clinic if I were not psychoanalyzed. At this point I came to the conclusion that one of us might be crazy, but it was certainly not I.

I was also angry enough to muster some support from other faculty people and from the university clinic for my thesis proposal, and my adviser did finally give her permission. She was necessarily the formal chairman of my thesis committee, but she chose to have nothing whatsoever to do with the project. Though I felt it necessary to say something respectful about her in my introduction, I felt beholden to her only for allowing me to proceed on my own, with neither her blessing nor her interference. There was a fringe benefit, too. From that time on, I no longer feared the schizophrenic label.

I had not thought of this episode for years, though it had been very strengthening at the time and I had often looked back on it as a landmark in my development. I knew that it belonged somewhere in the book, for in one way or another it was essential to an understanding of my work with Martha.

Everyone must find some way to make a life with some comfort and contentment for oneself, despite the pushes and pulls of other people bent on the same ends. There is a Freudian formulation that has always seemed to me to be to the point: The task of the ego (the perceiving, thinking, evaluating "executive" part of the human being) is to manage the instinctual drives (the id) and the repressive forces (superego) within the individual in such a way as to provide as much satisfaction of one's own needs as possible, considering outer circumstances and the needs of others. Eric Berne called these aspects of the human personality, respectively, the Adult, the Child, and the Parent. The ego's task, the Adult's task, is easier said than done in a world where everyone is pushing and shoving everyone else in an effort to perform the same task, a world that bestows advantages and disadvantages quite unequally among its inhabitants, who were not born exactly equal in every respect either.

In the course of Martha's wanderings in such a world, for which she had not been at all prepared, I imagine that she could find very little space readily alloted to her, and she knew very little about how to make room for herself. As she put it, she was *strange*—and the stranger is the outsider against whom the herd closes ranks. Still, everyone is different from everyone else, so it is not the mere fact of being different that creates the problem. In recent years, Martha has undertaken the task of the ego once again—to make a life for herself, to find space for herself, in some new way.

At this point in her therapy, Martha seemed ready to put some things together about the past in a way that would enable her to move on into the future instead of having to go through the same trauma over and over again. As we began marshaling our material for a book, she had let me know there were matters so painful, so psychologically dangerous to her at one time, that even now she could not simply sit down and write about them. These were, I gathered, some of the details about her marriage and her earlier life that had been missing from her story, both in the writing of it and the telling of it to me. I expected that many of my unanswered—and unasked—questions would be cleared up in the process. So we planned a weekend for this purpose.

# 6
# Exposition

Therapy as I practice it is a collaborative effort in which the client and I look at as many pieces of the puzzle as possible, adding new ones as it becomes safe to do so, arranging them in different ways, trying them here and there for size and fit, and eventually putting them together again in a somewhat different and more satisfactory way.

By now, the major themes of the work Martha and I were doing had emerged and been identified. Together, we had seen that Martha had had a great deal of leftover anxiety from her marriage and that we were transacting some unfinished business on that score. We had begun dealing with the question of Martha's anger and why she was having so much trouble handling it. An examination of her current work situation led us to the theme of scapegoating and to the masochistic pattern arising out of it. In looking at Martha's earlier experience with scapegoating, we saw her inability to find any common ground with her peers, and we speculated on what her fatal "difference" might have been. We wondered about the emotional vulnerability Martha had brought to the situation, seemingly from the cradle if not from her very genes. We could see that she had defended herself with automatic rage and with irreconcilable hostility toward those who had aroused it. She seemed to have been buying her psychological survival by means of withdrawal and isolation, but she was perpetuating a negative self-image that could overturn her shaky sense of self-esteem and her hard-won sense of identity at any time.

The major exposition took place in the course of one long session instead of being spread over a number of hours, as would ordinarily have been the case, because we wished to cover background material on tape for purposes of the book. Martha had felt unable to write this part of her "story" as we had originally planned. I knew she wanted some emotional support from me in order to be able, even now, to talk about it. The amplification of factual matters in this session brought understanding that had not been possible before for either one of us. And explanations began to evolve quite naturally and spontaneously as we went along.

233

## special session, august weekend

(This transcription, lengthy though it is, has been cut down considerably.)

**MARTHA:** I think the fact that Scott was the third-generation child of immigrants played an enormous part in his life, also the fact that his father was a policeman. His family had what I take to be rather routine gangster connections. His grandfather died on the kitchen table with his wife digging for the bullet . . . his mother saw her father die on the kitchen table after being shot by a gang rival. And the family joke is that Scott and his mother have a family resemblance because his father broke both their noses, which is true. He broke Scott's nose in a fist fight they had when Scott was thirteen. His father was corrupt as well as brutal; he had funny stories to tell about black marketing during the war, for example. He kept his loaded police gun at home and waved it about during family arguments. He did, on one occasion, kill a burglar in the course of arresting him and felt rather bad about it afterward; he had qualms about having killed someone in the line of duty. I think it's very pertinent, the sense of the family being outside the mainstream of respectable middle-class immigrants.

**ESTHER:** Where did Scott grow up?

**MARTHA:** In a very tough town in Indiana that was in the heart of Chicago gangland territory. Prohibition had originally set things up, and the underworld was still in the saddle.

**ESTHER:** Weren't there any softening influences in the family?

**MARTHA:** Not really. The women in the family were just as tough as the men, as witness the grandmother digging for the bullet. His mother was not in the corner screaming, she was right in there.

**ESTHER:** How did a boy from that background get to the University of Chicago, among a bunch of intellectuals?

**MARTHA:** By brains. He is the most intelligent person I have ever met, or one of the most intelligent, and that covers a great deal of territory. He went into the Army from high school, partly because he didn't know what to do with himself and partly because he wanted G.I. Bill benefits. It was the only way he was ever going to get to college.

**ESTHER:** That sounds intelligent, purposeful, normal.

**MARTHA:** It was intelligent, it was very purposeful . . . it's a very common and constructive thing to do. But then some of his weirder stories have to do with the time that he was in the

Army, in Japan during the occupation.

**ESTHER:** That's interesting. What do you mean by weirder stories?

**MARTHA:** He said, for example, that he was walking along a sea wall one night and saw an old man, an old ragpicker, going along the shore. Scott said he went back to the post, got his gun, went back to the sea wall, and shot the man dead. He told this to me as a factual story when we were first together. In later years, when he tried to discover whether it had actually happened or not, he was unable to remember. I believed the story at the time, and I think it's important that I did believe it because it says something about my gut-level feeling about Scott's psychological makeup. It wasn't a story about getting into a fight with somebody in a bar and shooting him, or arguing over a woman, that kind of thing. It was a story about seeing a man and something going click in his head. He never spoke to the man, he simply shot him dead—a psychological kind of thing, not something arising out of actual facts of life.

**ESTHER:** Well, okay. I think at this point we need to know how you ever put yourself in the hands of such a man. I mean . . . I don't mean for you to defend your personality *(laughing)*, but explain how you could be so mixed up that you landed in this marriage.

**MARTHA:** I grew up in my family believing that there was something weird about all of us. I was never able—I still am not able—to put that into any context, but it made me not hesitate to put myself in a weird position because I believed I was already in a weird position. All of us knew we were weird.

**ESTHER:** Could there be at all some feeling of "We are so different and it's a superior thing to be"?

**MARTHA:** Yes. There was a great deal of that feeling. It was very much underscored with Scott because he obviously was superior. To me—I was seventeen, he was twenty-two—he seemed extremely sophisticated. He *was* extremely sophisticated, extremely witty, extremely intelligent, extremely talented, extremely able—and quite handsome. I had heard through friends . . . I heard that he was very odd, and it was just more sauce for the pudding, so to speak. It made him more interesting. At seventeen, I had no notion of what the real components of insanity are, and for a long time he didn't treat me badly.

**ESTHER:** Can you help me see you as a seventeen-year-old; can you tell me something of who you thought you were and what you hoped maybe your life would turn out to be like?

**MARTHA:** I had no hopes . . . I had no vision of my life in the future. I didn't have any vocational goal. I didn't have a marriage goal either. I didn't think I'd meet some nice man who would love me and then I would settle down.

ESTHER: Why did you bother to go to the University of Chicago if you didn't have any goals or any idea of who you were and where you wanted to get?

MARTHA: From the time I was in junior high, the teachers said I was brilliantly intelligent, and I knew that Chicago was the place for "brilliantly intelligent" students. I needed to get away from home; I needed desperately to get out of there. I was enormously, hideously unhappy at home, you know. I have no words to describe the degree of allergy I felt toward my parents. I just could not tolerate them.

ESTHER: So it was a way of getting away from home, like some girls get married to get away from home, or run away to—where was it in those days?—Hollywood, or New York.

MARTHA: Exactly. I ran away to the University of Chicago, and I was able to do so because I won a full scholarship. The University was willing to pay me.

ESTHER: Well, okay. It was a running away from home, but in some way was it not also at least a vote of confidence in you as an intelligent, capable scholar?

MARTHA: Yes, but that got knocked out of me in the first week after I got to Chicago. I came from a small-town high school in Iowa, where we read *Ivanhoe* in senior English. We also read *Macbeth*, but the teacher with whom we read it had no inkling what was there. The first assignment I got in Chicago was to read *Swann's Way*. I had never heard of Proust, I had never heard of Joyce, literally never heard of them, never heard their names. And here I was, surrounded by people who had gone to fashionable private schools, who were sophisticated in the extreme. They had been reading this kind of thing since they were thirteen. They knew what it was about. I didn't know how to dress, I didn't know any of the intellectual jargon—all those things are so important at that age. I had "lower-middle-class" table manners, which everybody thought were rather funny. I was terribly tense all the time. It was the first time on my own, the first time I was ever allowed to stay up as late as I wanted to without being yakked at. I didn't know what the teachers were talking about; I didn't know what the students were talking about . . .

ESTHER: So whatever idea you had come with about your own intelligence must have been blown to the winds . . .

MARTHA: It was blown to the winds within a week.

ESTHER: Which must have been very tough, with nothing else to fall back on.

MARTHA: Yes. People made fun of my Iowa accent—

ESTHER: —and you had nothing to fall back on in terms of considering yourself pretty or popular or . . .

MARTHA: In high school I was as popular as a leper. I didn't have a single date in all my years of high school.

ESTHER: Okay. So, there you were . . .

MARTHA: And Scott was able to swim in that stream very nicely.

ESTHER: He was in that intellectual crowd?

MARTHA: It wasn't that he was intellectually brilliant in a scholastic way. It was that he could fake it brilliantly. It took me years to realize that he was faking it, though he had a much broader background than I did. He had read Nietzsche. . . .

ESTHER: And he was holding his own, or better than holding his own. He looked pretty good.

MARTHA: He looked fine. He had the reputation of being weird, as I say, but it was never quite specified. That just made him more intriguing to me.

ESTHER: That didn't stop him from having friends and being in the crowd?

MARTHA: No. He was quite popular. I had heard him mentioned, you know . . . five or six times his name had come up in conversations, always in the context of being intriguing because he was so weird. There was no class attendance requirement; you just had to pass the finals at the end, that was all. So I didn't go to a lot of classes. They made me feel embarrassed, for one thing, because I couldn't tell what was going on. I had never written a paper in my life; I didn't know what a paper was. We hadn't been required to write papers in high school.

ESTHER: Okay. You were in a situation in which you couldn't possibly compete with any success.

MARTHA: Esther, I could have if I had been *made* to do it. If somebody had said . . . When I finally did write a paper in the spring . . . I finally wrote it because that teacher said it was required. And I got a B-plus on it. I had thought I was flunking.

ESTHER: So maybe your background wasn't as inadequate as it seemed to you. You were overawed by the other students, by their flashier . . .

MARTHA: Right. A lot of it was faking. Looking back, I realize these were just eighteen- and nineteen-year-old kids, and they were faking a lot of it. And if I had known how to fake, I would have, too. But I assumed they were the genuine article. Well, I finally learned to keep my mouth shut until I found out what it was about, and to present myself as slightly ahead of where I was, in order not to . . . I still get into social situations occasionally where people say things like "Well, of course, if you don't know anything about good wine, you're really nobody."

**ESTHER:** Well, okay, but if you are vulnerable to this even now . . . what you must have been at that point . . .

**MARTHA:** At that point, I was just totally wiped out . . . I didn't flunk out. I passed all my exams, but my scholarship wasn't renewed. If I had been forced to get in there and compete, I think I would have pulled up my socks and . . .

**ESTHER:** If there had been somebody who had cared enough to push you.

**MARTHA:** Right. Or if the rules had been just a little more stringent.

**ESTHER:** I see. That was one of those instances where there wasn't enough . . . and you didn't have the self-discipline . . .

**MARTHA:** I didn't know what the discipline was needed for. Not writing the papers was for me a way of avoiding one more poisonous competition when I already was in so many. . . . You know, I was catching it in the dining hall and in the dormitory, and I didn't see why I had to catch it in school, too.

**ESTHER:** It didn't occur to you that maybe on writing papers, you would be ahead of the field, even though you were behind on all these other things?

**MARTHA:** No, and it wouldn't have been true then either.

**ESTHER:** But you did get a B-plus when you finally wrote a paper.

**MARTHA:** That was the only paper I ever wrote.

**ESTHER:** Well, all right, but I still feel that you sold yourself short. Your strongest asset at that time was your intelligence, but okay, so that's how it was, and that's why Scott must have looked pretty good. You were a failure and he was at least a partial success.

**MARTHA:** Well, he was a roaring success because if he was failing, he really didn't care . . . and he really didn't. Anyhow, I met him at the end of the year, in spring semester. A friend arranged a blind date for me for a party, my roommate arranged the date with a boy who was visiting from New York, a folk singer. She did it by telling him that I had asked for a date with him and by telling me that he had asked for a date with me. Each of us assumed the other was more eager than either of us was, which was a very bad basis for a . . .

**ESTHER:** That already tells me something about the environment, about the kind of situation you were in—in which people did this kind of thing.

**MARTHA:** Yes, they did, they certainly did. There was a lot of wheeling and dealing and manipulating. You know, the place was full of bright, neurotic kids. . . .

ESTHER: Everyone was operating on a pretty sophisticated level around you, and you probably saw it happening but you figured that's the way it goes.

MARTHA: One of the girls—she's famous now, a writer—she was there, at fifteen, already well-known as bisexual. Well, she was a very sophisticated fifteen-year-old, let me tell you, and she put me down like you wouldn't believe.

ESTHER (laughing): Well, in that league you had to be pretty good even to get put down—you know, to qualify for that honor.

MARTHA (laughing): I wasn't sensible of the honor on the occasions when it occurred. So, I went to the party and it was a total dud. I had been dying to sing with the folk singer, and instead he had thought I was dying for a date with him. And I had thought he was dying for a date with me, which turned out not to be true. About five o'clock in the morning, he simply fell asleep. And there I was, just sitting around, still drinking at five in the morning. I was—everybody was—really sloshed. Scott was at the party, but I had been unaware of his being there. At about six in the morning, when I was just drifting around by myself because my date had gone to sleep, Scott took me out to breakfast. You know, I don't remember too much, just that we were talking over the eggs and bacon. He said afterward that he had had a very profound feeling at the time that we were going to get together at some point. That was how he phrased it. Not that he would like for us to get together, but just as a matter of fact. It was already laid out. Our fates were to be with each other.

ESTHER: How did you feel over the eggs and bacon?

MARTHA: I was grateful that somebody was taking notice of me. I was glad that it was Scott. He seemed very sophisticated and I was impressed by him. I was very shy. I didn't know exactly what to say. I still was always afraid of putting my foot in it, so I didn't say very much. I mostly listened to him. We went back to the party, which went on to maybe ten in the morning. Then I went home.

ESTHER: Did he take you home?

MARTHA: No. The other guy didn't take me home either. I went home by myself.

ESTHER: How does this compare with other experiences you had around that time?

MARTHA: I went out with anybody who asked me because I thought that was what you did. I didn't really differentiate among the boys I dated because I thought going out was just something you did. When I got to Chicago, I began to be asked out quite a bit, but it really didn't mean anything to me except that it was important to be asked out because I never had been before.

ESTHER: But the idea of finding somebody you would really like and could have a real relationship with didn't occur to you?

MARTHA: Well, Esther, I had never had a close relationship with anybody.

ESTHER: And you hadn't picked up the idea from books or magazines or movies that girls did sometimes go away to college and meet men they might love?

MARTHA: It occurred to me, but not as something that could happen to me. No, that isn't true. Because I tried to make what happened between Scott and me mean that. But I had no notion of what it would feel like from the inside. The need that would be satisfied didn't exist as an identified need for me. The sense of closeness with friend or lover or parent or . . . I had no idea what it was like to be that close to someone.

ESTHER: But you must have read about the idea in books and so on.

MARTHA: Oh, yes, of the love affair and lovers who are close, but I didn't know what it would mean, so I couldn't identify or not identify it. I couldn't try out the relationship with Scott and say, "This isn't what I'm looking for."

ESTHER: Okay, we need to go back to what happened after that breakfast together. How, then, did you get together later?

MARTHA: Well, that was a piece of rather bizarre action on my part. The school year had ended, but I stayed in Chicago. I moved out of the dorm and into an apartment with a friend, only she was never there because she was having an affair with a married man downstate. I got a job as a waitress. It was my first real job, not just baby-sitting.

ESTHER: So that had some meaning to you. In some way it was an achievement—there was something real in that for you.

MARTHA: Right. My roommate was gone. Everybody was out of town for the summer, guys who had dated me. Here I was, living alone in a Chicago apartment and working among people I didn't know. I was enormously isolated . . . very isolated, and I had hardly anybody to talk to. I really got kind of weird that summer.

ESTHER: Yes, I think a seventeen-year-old living that much alone and to herself—even with a happier background—might get a little weird.

MARTHA: And I had been through a lot of really hard knocks that year. I tried to make them look as though they were nothing, including the bad grades—I think a B and two C's. I didn't get my scholarship renewed, so I didn't know what I was going to do. My parents could not really afford to send me to a school as expensive as the University of Chicago. They thought I ought to come back home, but I said no. I knew where Scott was living and I made several trips there to find him. I think I found him home on the third trip.

ESTHER: Now why did you choose Scott?

MARTHA: Well, most of the men I knew were out of town.

ESTHER: Would there have been someone else you would have . . .

MARTHA: I think what I had in mind was getting rid of my virginity.

ESTHER: Well now, that's a remarkable statement. What do you really think you had in mind?

MARTHA: I think that's what I really had in mind. Because I had no experience with relationships. I just went through the motions.

ESTHER: All right. But when you talk about losing your virginity, it seems to me that what you really must be saying is that you were going to try and see if sex would give you . . . if sexual experience would give you a feeling of closeness and belonging with another person.

MARTHA: No. It wasn't that at all.

ESTHER: It wasn't that at all?

MARTHA: It never occurred to me . . . the closeness I now know you can have with another person . . . I did not in my wildest dreams imagine it at all. It isn't that I didn't have any friends and was looking for some. I didn't know that friendship existed.

ESTHER: And you didn't think, as so many young people do, that sex would open the door to something closer or more exciting or more satisfying or more . . . ?

MARTHA: No. It was something you were supposed to do.

ESTHER: It was something you were supposed to do. Now why did you get the idea that you were supposed to do it?

MARTHA: Because everybody I knew had just done it.

ESTHER: And you weren't in touch at all with your own inner, deeper feelings? You were operating on the notion that this is the way other people act, so you should, too?

MARTHA: I had been . . . just . . . you know . . . I don't know how to explain this . . .

ESTHER: All right, except that I keep thinking you may have been hoping for more than you knew you were. But that might depend on the kind of father you had, whether or not you would hope for something from men.

MARTHA: What would you hope for?

ESTHER: Okay, I see the difference; I'm going on my own experience. With the kind of father I had . . .

MARTHA: Well, I had no inkling of anything. It was the thing to do.

ESTHER: On the other hand, it does seem likely that on a deeper level, with which you were not in touch, you were trying in some way for what you really needed. And you did have the cultural idea that a girl should have a boyfriend and a young woman should be looking around for a man to marry, so that on some level there was more going on than you were aware of at the time.

MARTHA: It seems to me there was. I think that's true.

ESTHER: The way you describe yourself—incidentally, I have a hunch this is how those therapists got the idea of labeling you schizophrenic: because you are describing yourself as without normal affect.

MARTHA: Yes.

ESTHER: And I don't believe it because I know you. . . . But I can see how you could convince others.

MARTHA: You see, because up to that point, I had never had it. You know, my relationship with Father Michaelson occurred in the middle of it . . . in the middle of my therapy at City Mental Hygiene and later. . . . I had already built up this picture of myself, and yes, it is the picture of someone without affect. There was no way in which normal affect had been in my life. And where would it have?

ESTHER: Okay, I see what I'm doing. I'm not seeing normal affect where it didn't exist, but I *am* seeing it operate beneath the conscious level . . .

MARTHA: It was there.

ESTHER: It was there, you know. Otherwise, there are all kinds of things you could have done, but what you did do was something that a seventeen-year-old girl with normal affect often does.

MARTHA: Right. And that was what I did. I went and rang Scott's doorbell one evening. He answered it and I said, "Hello, you bought me breakfast once. Come on." Almost in those words. He said okay and got his jacket, and we went back to my apartment and went to bed. Just like that.

ESTHER: He got your message and without trying to explore what it meant any more than you were trying to convey . . .

MARTHA: Exactly.

ESTHER: So on both sides it was up here on that surface level "without appropriate affect," as the psychiatrists say.

MARTHA: Yes. But the affect just was not in evidence, it was there.

ESTHER: Well, you were not in touch with it. Whatever it was, it was operating at a level you were not in touch with at that time.

MARTHA: I didn't know that level existed.

ESTHER: I'm kind of curious. There you were, already a person for whom poetry had been a saving grace, so I know there was plenty of affect operating at that level though you were not in touch with it.

MARTHA: I had to have Beethoven transfusions at least twice a week or I couldn't make it.

ESTHER: Okay, it was just that you hadn't made the connection that would have made you aware . . . the connection wasn't there.

MARTHA: One of the reasons was that I didn't know anyone else, literally. There was no one who could have made the connection for me because there was no one who was in touch with that at all . . . only my sister, but she was married, living her own life. My parents did not. And when I got to Chicago, this kind of thing was an intellectual game. You didn't speak of your feelings or your reactions . . .

ESTHER: You played all these games with them . . .

MARTHA: You played all these games with them. If I had, you know, walked into a room and heard someone say, "Beethoven makes me feel . . ." this way or that, or "the Shakespeare sonnets make me feel, . . ." I would have known. But I thought no one else had that level, the feeling level, and I had better keep my mouth shut about it.

ESTHER: You thought *what?*

MARTHA: That level—I thought I was alone in the world in enjoying, in experiencing things at that level . . .

ESTHER: Yes, but Shakespeare wrote the sonnets, Beethoven wrote the music. So there were at least two other people who lived at some time in the world who . . .

MARTHA: Right. But they weren't within my reach. For all I knew, there were only ten of us in the human race for all time.

ESTHER: But other people listen to Beethoven and . . .

MARTHA: Yes, but the things they say about him! You know, they talk about the echoes in the Vienna Concert Hall . . .

ESTHER: What has that to do with it? Oh, you mean the acoustics?

MARTHA: Yes. One girl was talking to me about the Beethoven Third, and she told me where her recording of it had been made. It turned out to be the Vienna Philharmonic. She had gone to concerts in that auditorium when she was a child, and she identified the echo. That impressed me so much.

ESTHER: Now let's see what this is about. It's as though it had something to do with superiority, a hierarchy of superiority, and as though that was the only scale by which you measured yourself in those days. Somehow you had to hold on to the highest level you could reach on that scale or you were nothing and nobody. *(Martha is agreeing all through this.)* So these people were much more able to put others down and themselves up, and with such a high level of sophistication, they had it all over you. You were fighting for your life in that company.

MARTHA: Every minute, yes.

ESTHER: And on the wrong scale completely, really. But all right, that was where you had to be. There was no other place for you to be at that point. You had never had anything else. It's very frightening, your measuring yourself on only one scale. That's very frightening.

MARTHA: Isn't it? You know, I could have gone under at any point. I did try to kill myself during that year, that spring. I drank a lot and took a very large dose of pills. I threw them up, but I was still out cold for maybe twelve hours. I was very surprised to wake up in the morning. I could have gone under at any point at that time.

ESTHER: That you could! Well, all right. You were hanging on one thread, and, of course, on that thread Scott was. . . . He was high up on your scale, so not quite knowing yourself what you were doing, you nevertheless did something that I think you felt was going to save you, or help you in some way.

MARTHA: Well, what I envisioned was Scott moving in with me for a week, two or three days or a week.

ESTHER: And why did you visualize that?

MARTHA: Well, I couldn't see what would keep us together. I wasn't aiming at anything other than that. I had no idea of a permanent or long-lasting relationship.

ESTHER: You know, I suspect that on an unconscious level you were doing a whole lot of rather constructive, basically constructive things. You picked the wrong person, but it was in all the movies in those days, in movies and stories, the girl who rescued herself by finding the right man.

MARTHA: Oh, yeah, the happy ending.

ESTHER: Sure. So, unbeknown to you, you were probably engaged in a rescue operation. . . . But because your view of things was so narrow and you were measuring everything by this one scale, you couldn't help picking somebody who probably wasn't going to do you much good.

**MARTHA:** I think that's the least you could say.

**ESTHER:** Though he looked good. Your unconscious was probably thinking, "He's so bright and knows so much, and he was so nice to me; he took me out to breakfast."

**MARTHA:** He continued to be quite nice to me during that period.

**ESTHER:** But we don't know what his expectations were, though I suspect. . . . How do we know? What do we know?

**MARTHA:** Well, only that he had had the idea we would end up together in some way.

**ESTHER:** Just that you would get together, which probably meant sexually.

**MARTHA:** Yes, but that wasn't the main idea. I think establishing some point of contact was the thing, maybe living together.

**ESTHER:** He already foresaw that much, somehow, in his own way.

**MARTHA:** Yes. I didn't tell him I was a virgin. I knew it sometimes scared men off. So I didn't tell him until years later that he was the first man. He certainly knew I was not very experienced, but for a number of years he had no idea that he was the first. Anyway, things went rather well at the beginning. He moved in with me. . . . The initial feedback was that he was very pleasantly surprised. I was living on music at this point. This was the first time I had a really full-time job and I bought a lot of records and played them all the time. We got up from making love one day and I put on a record and he said, "That's astounding! That's just what I feel like. How did you know?"

**ESTHER:** That sounds like closeness.

**MARTHA:** I didn't experience it as closeness. I knew it was a compliment, a good thing to have done, but what he was talking about was, you know, miles from my comprehension because I didn't know it existed. There is a possibility that if I had known then and had gotten in there and fought for it right there, it might have worked out all right. Scott and I might have been, you know, kind of a possible combination. But I didn't know what he was talking about. I couldn't establish the relationship on that level because I just simply did not know what he was talking about.

**ESTHER:** That was beyond you, miles beyond you. If anybody could have done it at that point, perhaps he could, but then maybe he just said that without its meaning very much.

**MARTHA:** I don't know . . . though all through the marriage he was appreciative of my ability to come close to where he was. He leaned on it extremely heavily all through the relationship and experienced the death of it as the true death of the marriage, at the very end of the time we were working with the therapists at the hospital psychiatric clinic. I washed my hands of the marriage long before he did.

ESTHER: So by saying that the record you played was just what he wanted, he was, in whatever way he could, expressing his need of someone to come up with what he was wanting.

MARTHA: Right, and he counted on me for that in an almost absolute sense all the time we were together. It started immediately . . .

ESTHER: But you didn't know . . . you sort of . . . it just happened.

MARTHA: I was supplying it without having the least idea I was doing anything.

ESTHER: All right, but later on you got the idea, I'm sure, what you were doing. But okay, we're in that early period, so let's . . .

MARTHA: As far as that period goes, yes, I was providing real closeness for him, but I didn't . . . it's complicated. I had no idea that it existed, but also I had no idea that there was less than that to do. Do you see what I mean? I couldn't be in a room with somebody without doing everything I could. I still can't. I can't even sit down beside someone on the bus . . . if some little old lady on the bus turns to me, I can't say, "Shut up, lady." I feel I have to meet her need. I do it all the time. I do it on my job.

ESTHER: Well, yes, I do it, too. I'm paid for it.

MARTHA: It doesn't occur to me not to do it.

ESTHER: It occurs to me all the time not to do it. As a matter of fact, I think one of the reasons I became a professional social worker was so that I would no longer feel guilty about not meeting the need of anyone who asked it of me, because that's what was happening. People were turning to me and I was feeling obliged to meet their needs, and I began to see that I was being drained, constantly drained.

MARTHA: Well, people turn to me in great numbers and I hardly feel I'm living a human life, much less a creative or constructive life, unless I answer all the needs of everyone who asks.

ESTHER (laughing): Oh, I feel that you are not leading a creative and constructive life when you *are* filling all these needs.

MARTHA: I wish this were what they paid me to do on my job. I've learned to turn off what I can't bear.

ESTHER: Well, that's good. You've learned some protective devices, though not very many. But this was what, then, at the very beginning Scott found in you: somebody who would rise to his needs, would fill his needs as best you could.

MARTHA: Esther, I was thirty-five before I learned, first, not everybody can do this and, second, people who can do it sometimes don't. I was literally thirty-five before I learned those two pieces of factual information about the world. How I managed to stay alive until I was thirty-five, I have no idea.

ESTHER: Well, you must have been going around constantly drained, constantly depressed, and angry without knowing what you were angry about, constantly guilty for not quite coming up to what they expected of you anyway, because nobody can.

MARTHA: You better believe it!

ESTHER: Yes, I can see it. All right. But until you met Scott—because I don't think you had that much opportunity to do it, you did it when the occasion arose—but until you met Scott, you weren't in a situation in which it was being asked of you all the time, the way you are if you are a wife and mother.

MARTHA: Yes, indeed!

ESTHER: Okay, so you got yourself into it with Scott, and that was what he came to expect of you because you automatically, spontaneously, and without complaint or resentment did it.

MARTHA: Yes. It never occurred to me not to. I didn't know that everybody didn't do it, for one thing. I knew that nobody met my needs, but . . .

ESTHER:  . . . but that was just coincidental.

MARTHA: It was because I wasn't worthy of having my needs met, or I was asking for it the wrong way. If I had learned to do what I was supposed to do the right way, people would have met my needs.

ESTHER: The misinformation that you got in the earlier years of your life is phenomenal. All right. So, given that you didn't know any better . . .

MARTHA: Right. What baffles me is that I survived, and it baffles me that I was able to learn later, at least to an extent. . . .

ESTHER: Well, what baffles me is that you didn't learn sooner, because it seems to me that if you had had even half a chance, one little opportunity, you would have caught on. And there was just never that one little opportunity, or that half a chance, or whatever? There wasn't one person that you could really compare notes with? I think this is the thing I come back to over and over again

—the fact that from the very beginning, there was nobody you could rub elbows with, compare notes with, share questions and quandaries with.

**MARTHA:** As far as I knew, I was the only person in the whole world who had any of the feelings I had. As a child, when I tried to share them with my mother, she got them all wrong, just completely wrong.

**ESTHER:** Yes, well it seems to me that is where your miseducation started, your misinformation. Miseducation started with a mother who did not understand, did not identify with, was unable—perhaps because she herself had no idea what it was all about—was unable to convey to you what it was all about.

**MARTHA:** Yes. The other thing was that my parents never admitted making mistakes. I never heard either one admit to doing less than a superlative job.

**ESTHER:** Well, that, you see, proves they didn't know what it was all about. So how could they convey to you what people in the world were like and what life was like if they couldn't admit to themselves the most essential thing, which is that people make mistakes, make damn fools of themselves, and that as a matter of fact, we all operate on far less than perfection.

**MARTHA:** Well, I had no idea.

**ESTHER:** Okay. You came into this with Scott, and it felt good because you were meeting a need of his. You were meeting his needs, so he was appreciative.

**MARTHA:** Yes. The other thing was that I rejected any move on his part to "repay." My feeling was that he had done me a favor by coming with me, coming to stay with me. Since this wasn't how it's usually done—I mean, usually the guy likes you a lot and asks you if he can—but since I had required it of him, I had written off his obligation to do anything for me. So . . .

**ESTHER:** He had already done it—for you—just by coming.

**MARTHA:** He had already done it just by coming. So he didn't have to repay me with kindness or pay his half of the food bill, or, you know, anything. Essentially I said to him, "You don't have to pretend anything. Just stick around, that's all, stick around for a little while and you will have done everything I expect you to do." And I think he was a little baffled by that. I think it may have registered as a rejection, though consciously I had no notion that I was rejecting him. I just wasn't making him be hypocritical by pretending to more than he felt or by making him pretend to want to do more for me than he in fact did.

**ESTHER:** You see this as in some way rejecting him, though you didn't intend to reject him.

**MARTHA:** No, I think it . . . I just view it as a rejection.

ESTHER: Can you go into that a little more?

MARTHA: Well, he wasn't working then or doing anything in particular. I was working; I was a full-time waitress. And he said, "I'll come and meet you at your job and walk you back." I had to walk quite a way to the El to get back to where I lived. One of the men in the kitchen had told another guy that he and his friends were going to rape me some night, and the kitchen guy I knew told me I had better be careful. I told this to Scott and he said, "I'll come and meet you and walk you to the El, and then you'll be safe." I said, "You don't have to do that. You know, I don't put any kind of price on your being here." It was a bar and restaurant on the Near North Side of Chicago, and I had to walk through a pretty tough district. At night.

ESTHER: Did he come anyway?

MARTHA: He came anyway.

ESTHER: He had better sense than you did.

MARTHA: I had no sense at all.

ESTHER: I think part of the trouble between you was that when you started out together, he did have better sense than you did.

MARTHA: I think that was a good deal of the trouble.

ESTHER: Whatever his problems were, he was at least a little more aware of what goes on in the world, what people are like.

MARTHA: Yes. I thought everybody was like me. I hadn't a sufficient idea of how alike people were, and I hadn't a sufficient idea of how different people were. I thought I was weirder than everyone else when in fact I wasn't. Everybody I know is at least that weird. And I thought everyone was as well-intentioned as I was.

ESTHER: Some rather bad notions to have.

MARTHA: Rather dangerous notions to have.

ESTHER: So . . .

MARTHA: We got together, let me think, near the end of the summer. I was going home to visit my family before the school year started. I was just going to make a quick trip home. My summer job was over.

ESTHER: Were you planning to start another school year?

MARTHA: Yes.

ESTHER: Did you have enough money to see you through the school year?

MARTHA: No.

ESTHER: But you had this vague notion you were going to do it?

MARTHA: I had this vague notion I was going to do it anyway. But as a matter of fact, I didn't get very far.

ESTHER: Okay, you were going to visit home before . . .

MARTHA: Yes. And I just assumed that Scott would clear off. And that would be the last I saw of him. But he wanted us to stay together. It was he who proposed that we stay together through the coming school year.

ESTHER: Did he offer to help you go to school or anything like that?

MARTHA: Not to pay my expenses, but to pay his half of the living expenses. He had G.I. Bill money. I was quite surprised that he wanted us to stay together. He had been maintaining his apartment, but while I was away, he moved all his things over. I couldn't imagine what was in it for him.

ESTHER: Why not? What was wrong with your sex life?

MARTHA: Nothing. I certainly wasn't very experienced, but he seemed . . . you know . . . I had nothing to compare it with. I didn't enjoy it very much, but I didn't know you could. But he did, apparently.

ESTHER: So he was satisfied even though you weren't responding particularly. He wasn't one of the men who feels bad when the woman doesn't.

MARTHA: Well, I was faking a lot.

ESTHER: You knew enough to fake?

MARTHA: I knew enough to fake. Right.

ESTHER: Well, okay. You probably had the feeling he was getting something there.

MARTHA: Yes. But he could have had it anywhere he wanted it, was my feeling. He would have had no trouble picking up somebody else. Just no trouble at all. A lot of girls were after him, as a matter of fact, because he was very good looking.

ESTHER: But he chose to live with you, and you did recognize that as a choice on his part.

MARTHA: Yes. I was always quite clear about that.

ESTHER: Were you glad that he made this choice? Did you feel good that he had?

MARTHA: I felt good that he chose me. I just couldn't understand why. He was definitely a social asset.

ESTHER: Okay. I can see your self-esteem went up here, somewhat—quite a bit, as a matter of fact. Your status in whatever group you were in also went up.

MARTHA: Right. Here I was, sleeping with such a complex and fascinating man. It made me complex and fascinating, it really turned people's heads. "Boy, you really do get around! You know, you don't look like that kind of person at all."

ESTHER: I see. It gave you a notch up. For a while there, you had been only on one ladder, the intellectual one, and now you were on the status ladder.

MARTHA: Yes, it got me on the status ladder, positioned me on the status ladder not too badly.

ESTHER: So, while Scott was getting something very, very satisfying, that is, his needs met by someone who just automatically and spontaneously felt that was the way it should be, now you were getting something out of it, too.

MARTHA: Oh, yes, now I was getting something. And it was considered. . . . You have to remember that this was back when it was quite daring to live with a man without being married.

ESTHER: That's right. That was somewhat before the liberated period.

MARTHA: Right. I was liberated ahead of my time.

ESTHER: And that was what put you up on the status ladder in the University of Chicago group. You weren't doing badly for yourself, that way.

MARTHA: And, of course, I was picking up quickly on what one said and what one did. I began to dress better; I changed my midwestern accent. I killed it on purpose; I adopted a totally artificial accent that isn't the accent of anywhere—I still have traces of it—to kill my midwestern accent.

ESTHER: So you were learning how to go through the motions in a liberal intellectual group.

MARTHA: Right. I was learning all the time, and I was learning from Scott. He told me a lot about what not to say and do.

ESTHER: Like?

MARTHA: Well, things like expressions not to use, or . . .

ESTHER: I see. He was sort of educating you that way, and you picked it up very rapidly. But this again was still on the surface level. It wasn't connecting with those deeper feelings about music and poetry. It was still . . .

MARTHA: Father Michaelson was my first love experience.

ESTHER: So while you were doing better for yourself, it was still not on solid ground in the sense of being connected with your deeper feelings. . . . But still, all these things are not to be sneered at; they add to one's strength. The ability to go through the motions well, even on that basis, is something.

MARTHA: Yes, it is. Because I can compare with a time when I couldn't even go through the motions, so when I could, it was far better than nothing.

ESTHER: Well, all right. . . . Did this situation just go on sort of indefinitely? No talk of marriage?

MARTHA: No. There was no reason to marry. Not in my mind nor his. It was very like what people are doing today. I am certainly a spiritual member of this generation. I did all those things people are doing now, but before them.

ESTHER: Okay. Now, how long did that go on?

MARTHA: Well, after I came back from the visit with my family . . .

ESTHER: I'm curious about that visit with your family. Just briefly, how did that go and what did that mean?

MARTHA: Nothing very much. I didn't tell them anything about Scott, of course. I think I had a miscarriage while I was there, probably at about six weeks, so I couldn't be sure.

ESTHER: But you hadn't been terribly worried and then terribly relieved?

MARTHA: Well, I was somewhat worried about what I would do, but I was operating on such a tiny—

ESTHER: —margin of reality?

MARTHA: Of reality, exactly. . . . I was so lost in so many ways that one more thing would not have made a great deal of difference. But I don't know what I would have said to my family. Scott asked me after we had been to bed once or twice if I was using anything, and I said, "Gee, no. I suppose I should, shouldn't I?" He said, "Well, if I got you pregnant, I would marry you."

ESTHER: Well, all right. That was some reassurance.

MARTHA: I did then go instantly and get fitted with a diaphragm.

ESTHER: Could that be another kind of unconscious rejection? If you were to get pregnant, he would marry you, so you weren't going to get pregnant?

MARTHA: No, I don't think so. I wouldn't rule out the possibility, but it doesn't come to me as that flavor . . .

ESTHER: Well, I couldn't help but snap that one up because it came so close on top of . . . but, okay, it doesn't click.

MARTHA: Right. The visit with my family was extremely superficial, and I was looking forward to getting back because I had this new social status.

ESTHER: So you went back under this kind of new arrangement with Scott. And then what?

MARTHA: Well, there began to be strains in the relationship. He was seeing another girl. I would come home and find them sitting there talking. I'm sure now that he was sleeping with her, but I asked him and he said he wasn't. I was upset about it. He would accuse me sometimes of seeing some of my old boyfriends, which I definitely was not, had no thought of whatsoever. Once in a great while, he would grill me: So and so has been here, hasn't he, and you've been to bed?

ESTHER: Completely out of the blue, without any . . . ?

MARTHA: Completely out of the blue. Like the only way he knew about so and so was that we greeted each other on the street when Scott was with me; we said, "Hi!" Scott would say, "Who's that?" And I would say, "A guy I used to go out with." But, you know, there was nothing I was doing. It was far out. It upset me. And we had some rather grim fights.

ESTHER: Okay, I'd like to know something about those fights. I've had the feeling that your anger, even though it was often self-destructive, was also often what saved you, so I'm curious.*

MARTHA: It wasn't that. The fights—the only fights I ever had with Scott from the first day we lived together to the last day we separated—were over whether I was meeting his needs properly.

ESTHER: Over what?

MARTHA: Over whether I was meeting his needs properly or not.

ESTHER: That's what the fights were over?

MARTHA: That's what the fights were over.

ESTHER: Well, how did they go? How does that kind of fight go?

MARTHA: I can't remember. I seem to have blocked it out.

ESTHER: What I'm trying to figure out is, what were you doing? You claimed you were meeting his needs and he said, no, you were not?

MARTHA: Yes, that's how it went.

ESTHER: Which is not what a fight is supposed to be about!

MARTHA: I didn't know that. I had no experience—no more experience in fighting than I had in any of those other areas.

ESTHER: I gather, then, what would happen was that Scott would complain you weren't doing this or that, something he needed or wanted, and you would say, "I am, too! I did thus and so . . ."

MARTHA: There's something a little odd that I had put out of my mind. When I went to visit my parents, I asked my ex-roommate from the dormitory to come over and cook for Scott. Which is an odd thing to have done. I was in effect telling him it was all right to have other women, so long as he stayed with me. Well, when I got back, they continued seeing each other. Anyway, when I saw her afterwards, she said something like "Scott and I had a lot of laughs about you while you were gone." She said they had listened to my records and laughed at my taste. And another thing she said that upset me very much was they'd both agreed I was not the "black-lace-panties" type.

ESTHER: Why did that upset you?

MARTHA: Because I thought Scott was saying that I wasn't any good in bed, not exciting enough. I never discussed that conversation with him. And the girl was bitchy in the extreme to tell me. I feel sure that it was true, however, that the conversation she referred to took place.

ESTHER: So, you set it up against yourself and that's what you got.

MARTHA: That's what I got. I think in a way I was giving him a test to pass.

ESTHER: In what way?

MARTHA: I thought maybe when I got back, she would say, "Gee, he really likes you a lot," or "He didn't show any interest in me at all."

ESTHER: So all this bohemian stuff was not so important really as the dream that a man could love you and prefer you?

MARTHA: I think that was the real aim.

ESTHER: The real feeling within you was the wish to be loved and preferred.

MARTHA: Yes. I didn't really expect it. It wasn't that I expected it. It was that I wished for it. I don't think I even hoped for it. I think I only wished for it.

ESTHER: Well, this is interesting because Scott had indicated to you that he wanted to continue the arrangement, which then put it on his initiative rather than yours. And instead of just accepting that and building little beginnings of some kind of hope or faith or dream of love, you had to invite another girl in, presumably to take care of his needs in your absence. You had to set it up in such a way as to defeat the beginning of something that might have been good.

MARTHA: I don't know why I did that.

ESTHER: And yet, had your little test worked the way you wanted it to work, it would have meant to you, "Yes, maybe he does really love me."

MARTHA: Double or nothing.

ESTHER: Yes. All right, very interesting.

MARTHA: It's interesting to me. I don't like it particularly, but it's interesting.

ESTHER: Oh, well, I don't know whether we have to like it or not like it. It was very human in a way.

MARTHA: That's not allowed, though.

ESTHER: Human foolishness?

MARTHA: Right. It was stupid. . .

ESTHER: But it was in the realm of what human beings do, and they're often foolish.

MARTHA: Oh, it didn't strike me like that. It strikes me as superhumanly foolish.

ESTHER: Well, all right. But I wouldn't . . . you put a more extreme evaluation on it—and probably on many things—than I would. But, all right, let's go on from there.

MARTHA: In any case, we stayed together. I went home for Christmas—and had an enormous fight with my family.

ESTHER: What was that about?

MARTHA: Pure guilt, as far as I can tell. The occasion for it seemed to be a remark by my sister Annette that I was draining my parents of money, that I had no right to go to an expensive school when they were paying for it. They were paying a good deal of my expenses. Fall quarter ended at Christmas, and I went home. I had done very badly, and Annette took me to task about spending their money. She had gone to a state university and had lived at home, and I could damn well do the same. I was feeling very guilty about living with Scott instead of just going to school. And I parlayed it into an enormous family fight and walked out the day after Christmas. I said, "You are never going to see me again!"

ESTHER: You were feeling guilty because not only had you not gotten all A's, but unbeknown to them you had been living with a man, of which they would not have approved.

MARTHA: No. Definitely. They would have hauled me home if they'd known.

ESTHER: And they would have considered you a fallen woman?

MARTHA: They would have considered me a dumb kid. A stupid fool. Not sense enough to be wicked. So I told them I was never going to see them again, not to try and find me, I'm going— and I went. I took the bus back to Chicago. Scott was in Indiana, and I called him there and said I had a fight with my family and broke all my ties, would he take responsibility? For living with me? And he said, "Yes, I'll be back as soon as I can."

ESTHER: At that point you called him about a need of yours, which was for somebody to take responsibility, and he said he would be back as soon as he could. So he came through.

MARTHA: He came through. Okay. When he got back, it was clear that I wasn't going to take any more money from my family, which was a correct decision on my part. We decided we would both look for jobs. I eventually found one with the telephone company. The personnel woman who hired me was a graduate of the University of Chicago, and she took me on against her better judgment. She said, "You're not going to stay. This is dull work. You won't like it. You'll be gone in three months." I said that I might not like it but I've got to eat: "Give me a break." She did and they took me on. Then Scott and I lived together more or less indefinitely. . . .

**ESTHER:** Did Scott find a job, too?

**MARTHA:** Yes. He got one with the post office. We both dropped out of school.

**ESTHER:** You know, it's ironic—two terribly bright people and this is what they settled for—but okay, it happened.

**MARTHA:** It's too bad. But I was what—eighteen? I was seventeen when I started to live with Scott. I turned eighteen during the month we began living together. He was twenty-two. So we worked and saved our money and lived together, it seems to me more or less without incident . . . I can't remember. . . . You know, I think Scott was sleeping with other women. We were working eccentric schedules. I was on a night job. But we continued to live together in a more and more householdy way. And the next August, I threw away the diaphragm and got pregnant, more or less with his permission. It wasn't "Now we'll have a baby," but we began to talk about having a baby . . . yet in a way, he left it open enough so that he was technically trapped, if you see what I mean.

**ESTHER:** It sounds a little as though that might have been something along the line of game-playing, or double-binding.

**MARTHA:** I think there was a very big element of that. He never accused me of getting pregnant in spite of him, but he left it open for his friends . . . oh, that's another thing—he would put me down to his friends very badly.

**ESTHER:** During this period when things were in some ways going all right?

**MARTHA:** There were things that went wrong. One was that he put me down very badly to his friends.

**ESTHER:** How would he do the put-down?

**MARTHA:** I was just a dumb young thing.

**ESTHER:** He would show you up, or tell stories that showed you up as dumb?

**MARTHA:** Oh, "If anybody comes to the door and asks if I'm married, I'll say no, I'm her father" was one of his lines, indicating he was so much older and wiser than I was.

**ESTHER:** Was this necessarily all put-down?

**MARTHA:** I took it as pure put-down and I rather think from the fact that it continued in later years it was pure put-down. Scott never really budged from his original view of me, which was justified when he first met me but not much longer because I'm a good learner and I learned fast.

ESTHER: Well, what I'm trying to do now, I guess, is to see whether there were, if not strengths or positives in this relationship, at least not all negatives—such as when you called him and asked would he take responsibility. . . . And though he sounds like the kind of person who needs to feel superior to those around him, he could also have had some of the more ordinary male willingness to provide for . . .

MARTHA: No, very little element of that . . . well, I could be wrong about that. I'll leave it open.

ESTHER: Yes, I think there are some things that we will probably have to leave open and that we will never know about because they were not developed, because things went in another direction. But I think it's a possibility.

MARTHA: Another of the things about Scott was that he was enormously secretive about his own things. He had a locked footlocker in which he kept voluminous notebooks. He told me at the time that he was a writer and he kept these notebooks. But he kept them locked up in the footlocker to which there was only one key, which he kept on his person at all times.

ESTHER: Did he ever talk with you about what he would like to write or was trying to write, or the kind of writing he admired?

MARTHA: He talked a lot about the kind of writing he admired in others, but very little about what he was trying to write—simply that he kept a notebook in which everything went down. On the other hand, I would find he had read letters of mine, old letters from boyfriends, that were in the bottom drawer behind some clothes. He had gone through my stuff with a fine-tooth comb. . . . When I spoke to him about a letter he found in the back of my bottom drawer and said it really didn't seem to me he had any business reading it, he said, "If you saved it, you must have meant me to read it. If you didn't want me to read it, you wouldn't have kept it."

ESTHER: Were you trying to hang on to some personal life of your own, separate from Scott? You weren't married; you had a right to.

MARTHA: Well, I did, a little. I would go to visit my friends by myself—I would go back to the dorm and visit the old gang because Scott didn't like them particularly.

ESTHER: But you weren't trying to hold on to some relationships with other men? Why did you hang on to this letter?

MARTHA: No . . . it was a feather in my cap that a guy who wasn't there would think of me when he was away and write to me.

ESTHER: So you kept it to reassure yourself that you were interesting and valuable to somebody.

MARTHA: Right. But it wasn't an emotional letter. It wasn't a love letter. It meant nothing.

ESTHER: It was just something you kept . . .

MARTHA: It was a notch on my gun, essentially.

ESTHER: Well, okay. I notice you use a rather derogatory term for what you were doing.

MARTHA: It's because this thing . . . because it wasn't . . . because the relationship represented by the letter was not anything.

ESTHER: You don't see it as the need for reassurance on the part of a girl who had never had what she needed? You don't see in it your need for some kind of acceptance? You see it only as "a notch"?

MARTHA: I don't . . . you know, it seems human and understandable to me, just barely, not in a real sense, not in the sense really . . .

ESTHER: See, what is coming through to me is that you give the most harsh and unaccepting explanation of your own conduct and your own feelings. It's as though you have no warm and accepting impulse toward yourself and your feelings and behavior.

MARTHA: I don't.

ESTHER: This is what's coming through to me as odd: how you could be so rejecting of yourself, how you never found a kind explanation for yourself, how the only explanations you find are these nasty put-down explanations. So now, when I see tears come into your eyes, it's as though . . . as though . . . this is what you needed all along—to know it was all right to be the way . . .

MARTHA: That is what I needed, but I learned to make this negative kind of judgment from Scott. That's exactly . . . what you're saying now . . . is exactly . . .

ESTHER: You see, I have the feeling that this is—was—true all along, that you never gave yourself the benefit of the doubt.

MARTHA: Oh, right. I never did.

ESTHER: You never saw yourself as a justified person, a lovable person, an acceptable person. So of course, if Scott didn't accept you and give you justification, that was only what you expected.

MARTHA: Absolutely. He just walked right in. You know, the whole thing . . .

ESTHER: So that you saw yourself that way first.

MARTHA: The whole thing was ready-made, it was already there. And in the long run, I'm sure, that's where his neurosis or psychosis hitched onto my neurosis or psychosis—right in there.

ESTHER: You offered it to him. You gave it to him. You handed it to him on a silver platter: Here am I; I'm no good. Do with me what you will, because I'm no good. I don't deserve anything . . .

MARTHA: Absolutely. And you know, he might have been reluctant to take that up originally, but he got to like it quite well.

ESTHER: Well, of course. Well—I don't mean of course.

MARTHA: No, there are people who wouldn't have come to that conclusion.

ESTHER: That's right. There are people who would have said to you at that time, as I did now. . . .

MARTHA: Right. They would have said, "Why are you doing that to yourself?"

ESTHER: Martha, why shouldn't you—given how little you had in self-esteem, in validation of yourself as a person of some worth—why shouldn't you have hung onto a letter like that, to say to yourself, "At least this person thought I was worth thinking about when he was away from me." You know, it wrings my heart that you had to do that.

MARTHA: Well, it does mine a bit, too, but that's the way it was. I was so deprived, you cannot imagine . . . you really cannot. . . .

ESTHER: I'm beginning to, a little bit.

MARTHA: As long as you have known me and as much work as we have done together, you can't really imagine how deprived I was. Father Michaelson was the first break in that deprivation. Other people offered. You know, when I was in Chicago, when I was dating, there was at least one guy and probably two who really took me seriously, who would have done anything for me, who I think were in love with me—and it affected me not at all. I couldn't take it seriously.

ESTHER: They had to be crazy or something?

MARTHA: I can't tell you how I reacted because in a sense I didn't react at all. It was as if that were outside myself, a piece of foreign information.

ESTHER: You know, at this point I'm thinking about Sylvia Plath. What did she call it—*The Glass Jar?*

MARTHA: *The Bell Jar.*

ESTHER: *The Bell Jar*—the glass hood over you so that nothing came through to you.

MARTHA: Nothing. And you see, that's why I accepted the diagnosis of schizophrenia, because when I look back at those years, that's a schizophrenic experience. That's what the schizophrenic's experience is.

ESTHER: Well, the words get in the way. But okay, you can call it a schizophrenic experience if you want to, and maybe that's a perfectly correct way of using the word. But why bother? Why do it? It doesn't get you anywhere.

MARTHA: It doesn't mean anything. Right. It doesn't really mean anything. But what schizophrenic meant to me was that I'd never be able to do anything else because I had that illness. I was condemned to the glass jar.

ESTHER: Well, it's as though for reasons of terrible emotional deprivation you were unable to allow yourself to feel your feelings.

MARTHA: Think what my feelings must have been. Can you imagine how angry I must have been?

ESTHER: Well . . .

MARTHA: I mean just try a little, don't try very hard. What if I really had to experience the full force of those feelings? No way could I have survived it! I would have killed someone or killed myself. As a matter of fact, I came quite near killing myself.

ESTHER: Well, okay, but because you couldn't allow yourself your angry feelings, you couldn't allow yourself your warm feelings either.

MARTHA: I couldn't allow myself any feelings, right. Any entry into that world was to open the whole can of worms with which I could not possibly have dealt.

ESTHER: Yes, I guess that's it. I guess it's the force of those angry feelings—so great and so frightening and so dangerous that you have to block out the other feelings, too. You can't afford any at all. You can't. So that you can't be kind to yourself, you can't be good to yourself, you can't give yourself appreciation because you've got all that bad angry feeling in you.

MARTHA: Esther, I just saw this: If I accepted the diagnosis of schizophrenia, it protected me from the feelings in the past. If I'm schizophrenic, that just happened because I was sick; it didn't happen because I had all those feelings to deal with, so I never have to go back and deal with those feelings. It's just that there's something wrong with me. I never have to take into account the mechanism of what really happened.

ESTHER: Okay, "I plead guilty to the charge of schizophrenia in order to escape the more difficult problem of looking at all the feelings I actually did have."

MARTHA: Exactly. That seems true to me. I would have preferred to have been schizophrenic.

ESTHER: It seemed to me all along that you bought that diagnosis rather eagerly, you know, and I tried to figure out why you would do that.

MARTHA: Yes, yes. Well, when I fed it to you, I also was trying to impress you with my courage in facing reality.

ESTHER: Oh, that's what you thought you were doing?

MARTHA: That's what I thought I was doing. Right.

ESTHER: There was a point at which I thought you might have bought that diagnosis in the past in order to throw it in people's teeth. You know—"Okay, you called me schizophrenic, so I'll just be schizophrenic." That kind of thing.

MARTHA: No.

ESTHER: I suppose that's more what I would do than what you would do. All right. But that was . . . because I tried so hard to figure out why you bought it.

MARTHA: Well, I think I was avoiding all my feelings. That's my answer.

ESTHER: Obviously it had to have some value, some usefulness to you.

MARTHA: Yes. It protected me from the alternative of having to face a lot of very, very powerful feelings.

ESTHER: Okay. You didn't really have to look at any of this if you were willing to accept the diagnosis. Why is it so hard to look at these very natural human feelings?

MARTHA: They are so overwhelming. That deprived child is still alive. You know, we can look back and ask to whom was I the most important person then? To whom—outside my children, who are outgrowing and growing away from me—to whom am I the most important person now?

ESTHER: And you're not yet able to say: to yourself?

MARTHA: Yes, I am, but it's not enough. It has to be validated from outside myself in certain ways.

ESTHER: Well, I guess it does, in certain ways. It hasn't been before? It has to be validated somewhere along the line in order for you to be able to say: I am important to me, and that's good.

MARTHA: It has to be . . . it has to come from elsewhere, too. Now, my mother's father did some of that for me.

ESTHER: Tell me about that.

MARTHA: This is a terribly important feeling . . .

ESTHER: You know, I want to say something about you. You come through in some way that is so right. It's as though . . . I don't know . . . I can't say it.

MARTHA: I hear you. I hear what you're saying. You know, I'm not the only woman in the world who is in this situation.

ESTHER: No.

MARTHA: If all this can get out and be made available to other people in this situation so they can see that they don't have to give up, that would be a good thing to do. Now, where were we?

ESTHER: Well, okay. What was this you were going to say about your mother's father?

MARTHA: He was absolutely pleased just to be with me without my ever having to earn it. I didn't have to do something to be of value to him. Like when I visited him . . . we would go to the butcher's to buy meat for the cat and along the way he would introduce me to people he knew.

ESTHER: He saved your life.

MARTHA: He really did. If I hadn't had him, I couldn't have hung in there.

ESTHER: How long . . . you had him all through your childhood?

MARTHA: Yes. My grandparents lived in Des Moines.

ESTHER: They weren't the grandparents who lived in the same neighborhood?

MARTHA: No. That would have made a lot of difference. I didn't see my grandfather very often. We would have those excursions once every few months or something like that. But I saw enough of him to do the trick. He was a very simple man.

ESTHER: You knew, you knew. And that knowledge stayed with you between visits. You knew that for him you were fine just the way you were. Your very existence was a joy to him. A satisfaction to him.

MARTHA: Yes. I was a satisfaction just by being me. And it was absolutely taken for granted. He never made any kind of fuss over me that I can remember. I didn't have to do anything. I didn't have to be anything. I just *was* and . . . you know, that's why I can operate in the world at all. My grandfather was very tall, and I think it's funny but very tall men still catch my eye. I'll still turn my head around with the assumption that a very good-looking man is there. It's the first thing I notice in a man—how tall and skinny he is.

ESTHER: Was he still alive through the period you were writing about?

MARTHA: I'm trying to remember. I think he died before Becky died. I know it was before the divorce, sometime in there somewhere.

ESTHER: I'm thinking how terribly important it was to know that somewhere in the world was somebody who truly loved you.

MARTHA: I don't know. It didn't stick in my mind as that.

ESTHER: No. You couldn't know it then, but I know it. So though it couldn't have meant what it might have on a conscious level, on an unconscious level it did.

MARTHA: My grandmother remained alive, and I got some of the same feeling from her, and from my grandfather's sister.

ESTHER: On your mother's side. I keep wondering how your mother could have been so distant from her own real feelings, so somehow in a bell jar, with parents who could be the way they were with you. And then it occurs to me . . . you know, sometimes that kind of love can happen between the grandparent and grandchild when it cannot happen between the parent and child.

MARTHA: I think my mother's glass jar was serving the same function for her that it did for me. Here is a girl whose boyfriend got her pregnant before she graduated from high school, who went to live next door to a fearsome—a truly fearsome—mother-in-law and was dominated by her, whose husband was without enough backbone really to establish her in a life of their own, and who proceeded to have three unplanned babies and a lot of financial problems. All that would have made me very angry. And if I didn't want to think about being angry, the price that I paid might be to live under a bell jar, pretending that everything was just fine. And everything *is* "just fine." My parents are still together.

ESTHER: Instead of taking to drink or dope, your mother took to the bell jar.

MARTHA: Yes, I think so. "Everything is for the best. Things are not what they seem; they are much better than what they seem. Everything is the way I say it is."

ESTHER: Somehow she had to get through her life, and that was the way to do it.

MARTHA: I think so.

ESTHER: Your mother sounds as though she might have had something to give, at least potentially, but with your father you didn't feel there was even the potential?

MARTHA: One reason I have such bad luck with men is that I start with the feeling there is nothing much to be hoped for from that direction.

ESTHER: Well, okay. We thought we weren't going to get into your childhood, but we did this way, and I suspect that this may be the way we will do it, insofar as we do go into it.

MARTHA: Right. So where were we with Scott and me? Let's see, I got pregnant and we moved to the Northwest.

ESTHER: You became pregnant, sort of with the unspoken or . . . there was some kind of collusion between you and Scott—

MARTHA: That's it—that's extremely well put.

ESTHER: —that you would get pregnant, though nothing exactly was said to plan it.

MARTHA: Well, it just about was said. And he never protested the pregnancy. We moved to Washington at the end of September and got married at the end of November.

ESTHER: Well, now, why did you go to Washington?

MARTHA: We didn't want to raise a child in Chicago, and Scott had some idea he would go to the University of Washington.

ESTHER: Again, that sounds a little like . . . well, normal folks.

MARTHA: Yes. We knew people there to whom we could send our stuff.

ESTHER: Now tell me why you didn't want to raise a child in Chicago.

MARTHA: The climate's nasty and it's no place for kids.

ESTHER: Those sound like perfectly normal reasons. And it was both of you feeling this way, something the two of you had together, saw together—everyday, reasonable kind of thinking. But Scott would have had to pay out-of-state tuition.

MARTHA: Well, that realistic we never were.

ESTHER: That realistic you weren't. It was this rather vague idea and the fact that you had friends there . . .

MARTHA: Right, to whom we could ship our cat and our household goods, which we needed to send on ahead of us.

ESTHER: Now, how did you happen to have such good friends?

MARTHA: They weren't good friends. I used to baby-sit for them. We admired them partly because they were an interracial couple and partly because they were the only married couple we knew. They were just enough older than we were so that they could be sort of like surrogate parents.

ESTHER: And you kept in touch with them after they moved to Washington?

MARTHA: I didn't keep in touch with them, but I knew what their address was. I was working for the telephone company, so one night I just put through a call and said, "Hey, if we decide to come to Washington, can we send our stuff to you?" Arnie said, "Sure, sure," and went back to sleep. Later he said he couldn't remember whether my call was a dream or it really happened—until our stuff arrived. Then he knew it had really happened.

ESTHER: Well, you have to know people pretty well to make that kind of call and do that kind of thing.

MARTHA: You don't, really.

ESTHER: You don't? Who doesn't?

MARTHA: I don't. We were . . . we were hippies before there were hippies. We just . . . we lived that way. You could move in on anybody with no prior notice if you had to. It was bohemia . . . we were the prebeatniks . . . the natural children of the Greenwich Village era, that was us. And we absolutely imposed on each other all the time. Everybody did it. We were moving in an agreed-upon value system. The community we moved in, in Chicago, and the community we moved into when we came to Washington operated on the same system. At that time, people didn't maintain crash pads exactly, but that's how it was . . . the world view by which we were living. And this is a value system I still validate to a large extent. If people say to me they haven't got a place to stay, and if I know them well enough to know they are safe to have in my house—or if they know somebody I know and somebody I know will verify it—I'll let them use my house as a crash pad for a day or two.

ESTHER: But you would set some limits on that?

MARTHA: I would set limits now. I would not have set any limits at all on it then.

ESTHER: I think I'd be concerned if you hadn't learned to set limits on it. But okay, that's where you were and where they were, so you moved to Washington.

MARTHA: I told the telephone company I was getting married and moving to the Northwest, and they transferred me under my new name.

ESTHER: That was when you first took Scott's name?

MARTHA: No, we'd been living . . . we had rented our apartment under his name. By the time we decided to leave, you could say we were living together as a married couple; we just hadn't bothered to get married yet. We did get married out there. I was about four and a half months pregnant. I think Scott was always really ambivalent about the whole marriage business. On the one hand, he clung to it and used me more and more to interpret the world for him, to tell him what was real and what was not, and to fill his emotional needs. On the other hand, he made a show —and I feel more than a show—of being sorry he ever married. He'd advise people in my presence not to get married. "Don't tie yourself down. Your life will be misery from the day you marry and have children," and so on and so on. That ambivalence was always with us.

ESTHER: Okay, let's take it back to your coming to Washington.

MARTHA: I was working there before Scott got a job. Then before Peter was born, I don't remember exactly at what point, he went to work at an aircraft plant on the assembly line.

ESTHER: He never did actually make an effort to get back to school?

MARTHA: He talked of it but never did anything solid or factual toward getting back. We lived far out in the other direction at first. The only couple we knew were the Wilsons, the people we had known in Chicago, whom we stayed with when we first moved. We met another couple, Bob and Ellen Jones, through them. We had no other friends, knew no one else, and when the Wilsons left the area, Bob and Ellen were the only social connections we had. We met people at their house but didn't take up friendships with them. We were living a rather isolated life. We didn't have a car. Neither of us could drive at that time. We both learned after Becky's death.

ESTHER: Not driving is so unusual, at least for a man. I don't understand.

MARTHA: Scott's father tried to teach him by beating him when he did something wrong. That was when Scott was in his teens, and it definitely put him off. That's more or less the way his father tried to teach him to swim and to play the piano. It's no wonder Scott was where he was.

ESTHER: I would think that would have been hard on his self-esteem, not driving, I mean . . . in Washington, anyway, not Chicago maybe.

MARTHA: I think it was, but I think there were other things so much harder on his self-esteem that not driving was a negligible blow.

ESTHER: Okay, what else?

MARTHA: His inability to find work at his intellectual capacity, though he never really tried. He's always worked at menial jobs.

ESTHER: Well, of course, what can a guy do who is terribly bright but doesn't have a degree or any kind of training?

MARTHA: Right. I would have supported him to get a degree. I would also have supported him if he decided to do something else—take a chance, quit his job, write. He continued to write, but he wouldn't learn proper grammar. He would use me for things like correcting his grammar and then get mad at me for correcting him. I was in a constant double bind because he used me to interpret reality for him, and then he denied what I said. Even when he acted on it, he would give me a lot of acrimonious backchat. . . .

ESTHER: By reality, you mean things like "This spelling is wrong"?

MARTHA: Yes, but also I'd tell him things like "You really can't expect to tell someone to fuck himself and then be friends with him the next minute. It's not a reasonable expectation to have." He continued through those years to use me, to bounce things off me. The other thing about that period after we settled in the Northwest, all through those years of the marriage, almost up until the end—until we got to the point where we weren't speaking to each other anymore—he would flood me constantly with the contents of his unconscious. Just absolutely. And this was a reality-testing also.

Very early on, when I first knew him, he told me he thought he might have had intercourse with his mother. I think he determined later on that this was not true, but he told me about it as if it were true. He told me a lot of other things. Some of them were the kind of stories—just bullshit stories—that men tell women, but he would also tell me these other things. I was disturbed by them initially, but I felt it was wrong of me to be disturbed. He's just very honest, I thought, and very sophisticated. But his material got more and more extreme. One of these stories had a catalytic effect on me, had a lot to do with my going into therapy. By that time we had three children and I was expecting the fourth. He told me one day, "You know, when we were living in Chicago, I had a plan to have some of my friends kidnap you and gang-rape you." He spun it out in great detail, and it struck me as absolutely true.

**ESTHER:** Whether it was or whether it wasn't, it's bizarre.

**MARTHA:** It was a shocker. He also said he wanted to shoot me with heroin and get me addicted. And he spun this out in great detail, too. It was plausible enough so that it frightened me extremely, and for this reason: I had always thought I could recognize which things Scott might act on and which things he would not, but with this he was sitting on the borderline where he could have acted on it. I had been confident that I would be able to read him well enough to get out, to take the children and get out, if he went over the line. I realized then that he could be over the line and I might not know it, that the children and I might be in danger. Now, it was years later when I realized this. But looking back, it was perfectly plausible; he knew people perfectly capable of doing the kind of thing he was talking about.

**ESTHER:** You know, it strikes me that perhaps when you first began to live with Scott, though, he may not have been as far out as he became later, even if he had these fantasies . . . and at that time, in that earlier time, at least he didn't tell them to you, which suggests that in those days he had the good sense not to.

**MARTHA:** Right. The material with which he began to flood me kept getting more and more bizarre.

**ESTHER:** I would think that would have been terrifying.

**MARTHA:** It was. It was terrifying, and that upset me. That was the catalytic factor in my going into therapy.

**ESTHER:** That was when you first tried to get him to go and when he wouldn't go, you did?

**MARTHA:** No, that was when I went. I had tried to get him to go along before that . . . well, I've jumped four years ahead. Scott was working at the aircraft plant. I had Peter. Let's see, Peter was born in April. In about October of the year that Peter was born, Scott broke down completely. He had an acute, extreme attack of . . . I realize laymen are not supposed to say it, but if I ever saw a textbook paranoid schizophrenic reaction, I saw it then.

**ESTHER:** Okay, describe it.

**MARTHA:** He hallucinated constantly. He heard voices calling his name and he could not distinguish them from reality. He would come into the room, genuinely questioning whether I had called him, because it was a woman's voice he heard. He felt hands touching him constantly, although he looked at himself and could see that no hand was touching him—this was very frequent, many times a day. He believed that the post office was holding up his mail and opening it, that he had checks and money coming in the mail but the post office was withholding them. He believed he could influence the score of a baseball game by listening to it and going through calculations. He had an attack . . .

ESTHER: All right, you've given me enough evidence. Do you have any idea if there was some precipitating factor that threw him over into an acute psychotic episode?

MARTHA: No, I don't know of any. . . . He had gone downhill ever since the marriage, and I think Peter's birth . . . well, when I was expecting Peter, he said to me one day, "If this baby is a girl, I'm going to wait until she is thirteen and then I'm going to rape her." Also, we had been having a lot of trouble with the landlord. Scott said to me one day as we were just sitting there and I was big and pregnant, "If there were any way that I could prove that this is his baby and so disgrace him, I would do it." Both those things terrified me, but I thought he was just being sophisticated and honest.

ESTHER: Or funny?

MARTHA: No, not funny.

ESTHER: Well, how could you put the label sophisticated on it?

MARTHA: Everyone has these feelings, but not everyone knows he has them . . . a person willing to examine himself and face them in himself. . . . The people we associated with were psychologically very sophisticated . . . also, Scott had an attack of hysterical paralysis. There were several weeks when he could not walk, though nothing had occurred, nothing was visible.

ESTHER: Surely he must have been aware that these were signs of some kind of mental or emotional illness. Did he ever get any help, make a stab at getting help for himself?

MARTHA: No. He never . . . he rejected the idea of help when I brought it up.

ESTHER: Then somewhere along the line you finally did bring it up. How did you happen to do this?

MARTHA: I can't remember. It was in the nature of: I can see that you are desperate, please won't you do something? I could see that he was suffering. He was not willing to do anything about it. As far as lay diagnosis goes, that's the rule, not the exception. You only go to the therapist or the psychiatric clinic on your own or when your family drags you. If you won't go, then your family drags you, like sending for the police—which I eventually tried to do when I thought Scott was going to kill himself—and the family must have made the diagnosis before they call the cops. When the chips are down, it's the family that has to make the diagnosis.

ESTHER: Well, yes, but you didn't call the police at a time when you had good reason to.

MARTHA: No, I didn't want to. Idealistically I did not believe in taking anyone's freedom away. And I didn't think they were going to do a damn bit of good at the hospital. I truly believe even now that it was a correct decision. That was before tranquilizers. The hospital had nothing to offer but electric shock and custodial care. I don't think either one would have done a bean's worth of good.

ESTHER: But you did try to get him into therapy.

MARTHA: The public health nurse had been coming around ever since Peter was born. She got to know me and she would come partly as a social call. And she became aware, because I made her aware, that Scott was going downhill. I asked her what I could do, and she said to call City Mental Hygiene. That was when I called and tried to get Scott to go. I also . . . well, of course, he stopped working when he collapsed, so there was no money. He said, "I'm never going to work again. I'll see you starve first." We came very close . . . did we come close to starving? I don't know. I kept us alive on oatmeal and powdered milk and horse meat from the dog-food store. We must have eaten at least a horse a piece during that time.

ESTHER: What on earth were you thinking about your life, your fate, your destiny?

MARTHA: I wasn't thinking of it at all. My job was to protect my husband and my kid. My job was to keep Scott going. He used to take off his clothes at night and go and lie in the crawl space, in the dirt under the house. He had a dozen rituals like that, bizarre and frightening. One day he broke the glass in the glass door and walked back and forth barefoot in the broken glass all day long. You know, it isn't a problematical diagnosis . . .

ESTHER: Oh, I don't think anyone would question your diagnosis!

MARTHA: He would sneak around the house trying to catch me poisoning him. I was the focus of the paranoia—the post office and I were the focus—the expression on his face when he was . . .

ESTHER: Did you ever talk to a doctor or anybody during that time about what was going on?

MARTHA: Well, I talked to the public health nurse. And I broke down at the Well Baby Clinic one day. I was just newly pregnant, had just gotten pregnant again, and my milk was running out because I had almost nothing to eat. Finally they questioned me one day because Peter hadn't gained as much weight as he should. I said there is nothing to eat and I broke down crying. I told the whole story to the doctor, everything. She was a very nice woman pediatrician, a very good woman. And that afternoon a doctor and a nurse came out with a couple of cases of baby food. The doctor's story was that he was there to help carry the baby food up the stairs, but he was actually there to see if, you know, if commitment was in order. But Scott was having a rational day, and they stayed and talked for twenty minutes or so and left. We ate the baby food. All of us. I had to stave off the landlord. I had to stave off the utilities people. There was no source of money; I had borrowed everything I could. I don't know how we stayed alive.

ESTHER: You know, I'm sitting here thinking . . . Martha, you've apologized to me and the world for making a diagnosis. It seems to me this is an example of your almost apologizing for living.

MARTHA: Well, yes. But I get it in the teeth, not uncommonly, when I say to a professional person, "Look, my husband was a paranoid schizophrenic." What I get in return is, "You're not competent to make that diagnosis."

ESTHER: Nobody ever said to you, "Give me some examples of what he was doing"?

MARTHA: People who ask that . . . anybody who says "Give me some examples of what he was doing" doesn't say "You're not competent" to me.

ESTHER: You know, this is the thing . . . what the professional does in a situation like that . . . it's as though, you know, you pushed the button that—

MARTHA: —that just preempted his occupation. The professional loses his mind. He does, indeed. He loses his mind.

ESTHER: Well, all right. I realize that in a way you have been trained to apologize for this particular part of you, but you know, you've apologized for being you all of your life.

MARTHA: I certainly have, because I've caught it in the teeth for being alive all my life. When I went into that new unit at work recently, all I did was be me. That's all . . .

ESTHER: Of course, by now you are so traumatized that I don't think you can possibly go into a situation . . . I don't know how to explain it . . .

MARTHA: Well, I know what you mean. No, I can't, because I have caught it in the teeth repeatedly.

ESTHER: Okay, but let's get back. You made your stab at getting help for Scott. A doctor came out and found him to be rational at that point, which must have been a little as though somebody comes to rescue you, only to find that what you said doesn't seem to be the case.

MARTHA: No, I don't think they doubted me. I really don't think they doubted me. But he was not committable against his will.

ESTHER: You really told them the whole thing—you said exactly what was happening?

MARTHA: But you can't commit someone who doesn't want to be committed if he is still able to talk all right. That's the bitter truth. No matter how nutty he is, if he's sane enough to protect his own interest, you can't commit him.

ESTHER: Okay. Was Scott aware that you had brought them there? In a sense to look him over? *(Martha nods.)* Okay. So at least you didn't get into trouble, but it must have been a disappointment to you.

MARTHA: No. I still don't think it would have done any good if they had committed him. I don't think it would have improved . . .

ESTHER: Well, I guess you would have had very mixed feelings. It occurred to me that just being out from under the . . .

MARTHA: I would have felt so guilty.

ESTHER: All right. I had the feeling that if you just could have not been in contact with him for a while, it would have been such a relief that you would never have wanted him back again.

MARTHA: No, no, I was absolutely committed to saving him.

ESTHER: Saving yourself by saving him, I would imagine.

MARTHA: Yes, that's relevant. The breakdown went on in its acute form for, I'd say, about four months, where it was constant, day to day. The expression on his face as he tried to catch me poisoning him, you know, is with me to this day. I was twenty years old. We didn't have any money, literally. We were not maybe really close to starving, but when I became pregnant, I weighed 106 pounds and I was as tall as I am now.

ESTHER: Well, you were definitely malnourished.

MARTHA: Yes. I lost the baby I was pregnant with, at four and half months. I was trying to nurse Peter. You know, we had no car. I had to take Peter—I didn't dare leave Peter alone in the house with Scott—I had to take Peter with me anyplace I went and carry him.

ESTHER: Well, what on earth were you doing for money?

MARTHA: I don't know. I can't remember. I had had a little in the bank. I borrowed . . .

ESTHER: Didn't Scott have some unemployment insurance, or disability, or something?

MARTHA: No, he hadn't been covered, hadn't worked long enough in covered employment. We weren't eligible for welfare either. I tried all those things. We'd been in the state about a year, I think, but not long enough in the county. They would have sent us back to Chicago, that was all welfare would do for us, I know, because I had applied. I was just up against it, every day. And up against out-and-out delusion, active delusional behavior. Bob and Ellen knew what was going on with Scott, the crazy stuff, but no one else knew. And we just hung there.

Eventually, Scott pulled himself back together a little bit, got another job. I don't remember exactly, I think in a factory. But he never pulled himself totally back together from that breakdown. It was always a patch-up job or . . . at least, I was never able to believe that he pulled himself together, and I think, in reality, he never did. He would have some delusional episodes, afterward, but he would take sick leave, he didn't stop working. And I covered for him. I told him what he could and could not expect to get away with. He continued to work, but with very poor attendance, and we never did have enough money even then. We would have moved to a cheaper place, but we didn't have any money for a deposit, or moving, or anything. But okay, I covered for him, I believed that was what a wife should do. I tried repeatedly to get him to go to therapy, repeatedly, repeatedly, repeatedly.

ESTHER: What kind of things would he say when you would try to get him to go into therapy?

MARTHA: Between episodes he would say, "I feel fine now." During an acute episode he would say, "I'm too sick to go now." I told him that he was like the man who won't mend his roof when it's not raining and can't get out there to mend it when it is raining, and he agreed that this was true. But he never went. He wouldn't do anything. He was afraid of therapy, in fact.

ESTHER: What was going on between the two of you in this period, just as people?

MARTHA: I don't even know what that means. I kept him afloat. That's all there was. He was grateful. . . .

ESTHER: Did you go on vacations? Go on picnics?

MARTHA: Oh, no. There was no money.

ESTHER: Well, he went back to work eventually. Did you visit friends?

MARTHA: We went to visit Bob and Ellen. Scott would go out to the movies sometimes, alone, or sometimes to the race track, but he never took me out.

ESTHER: You went on having sexual intercourse?

MARTHA: Yes, but less. He was impotent the whole time that he was sick. That got better. He could do it again, but it . . . there was no satisfaction. Esther, he was so crazy that it was frightening to get close to him. It isn't something that you would want to do.

ESTHER: But you didn't consider leaving him?

MARTHA: What would I have done? I kept having baby after baby, for one thing. I would have the baby and nurse the baby for a year, and then get pregnant at the end of the year.

ESTHER: What was going on in your mind? You weren't a Catholic then.

MARTHA: No, I became one during this time.

ESTHER: Now, how did that come about?

MARTHA: I had always been very much drawn to the Church, even as quite a small child. Then I was reading a great deal about Zen Buddhism, and the mystical element in Catholicism drew me. I began to go to Mass during that time.

ESTHER: Did Scott participate in this with you?

MARTHA: No. He was born a Catholic but had never practiced his religion. He made his First Communion and quit. His family wasn't serious . . .

ESTHER: You did it all on your own, without talking to anybody?

MARTHA: Bob Jones was interested in the Church. I talked to him about it some. I talked to other people very little. I literally didn't know how to talk then. If someone else brought a subject up, I would talk about it, but I . . .

ESTHER: So that you were going over this in your own mind, alone, thinking this was something you wanted to do. Do you remember the emotional components, or was it simply an intellectual decision?

MARTHA: No, it had emotional components and one of the chief ones was that it gave me . . . I had previously taken Scott's value system. When Scott broke down completely, it was obvious I couldn't do that any more. I couldn't make up a value system of my own. I had no firm ground to stand on, and I moved on to the Catholic value system in order to have something.

ESTHER: Yes, I can see that. I believe that a lack of value system was operating all the way along with you, too. Along with all the other deprivations, you were somehow deprived of an adequate value system. Now, why was that? I don't understand that. Your parents weren't able? . . .

MARTHA: My parents didn't think. I mean they literally didn't think about anything. It's good to go to bed at eight o'clock at night and get up at six in the morning, not because it's good for you to get a certain number of hours of sleep, but because those are good hours to sleep and to rise. If you go to sleep at two in the morning and get up an equivalent number of hours later, even if your job demands it or your pleasure is served, that is a bad hour to go to bed and a bad hour to get up. It was just as unreflecting as that, and they believe it to this day.

ESTHER: You mean a superficial, sort of unmeaningful, set of rules rather than a true value system?

MARTHA: Right. They were conventional in their values and conventional in the way they defended their values, and I couldn't buy it.

ESTHER: It occurs to me that once again you were in a sense miseducated and couldn't buy this false education, so you were without education.

MARTHA: Yes, I think that states it well. I had been hassling it since high school. I did a lot of religious exploration when I was in high school—went to church, synagogues, with all my friends —you know, went everywhere and tried everything, and . . .

ESTHER: Now, by friends I take it you mean a kind of superficial friendship . . .

MARTHA: Yes, it was a superficial thing. And the values that they espoused were, as a matter of fact, what I consider superficially held, though nobody holds values as I hold them. But I also think I felt that religious experience is a common feeling, it's an experience that many people share, and if I could share this experience, I would be sure of sharing the same experience as other people. This turns out not to be true.

ESTHER: But I think it is one of the many things that bring people into religion. And often they feel they are sharing the same experience when they are not. They do have the illusion of it.

MARTHA: Well, I had the illusion of it. It turned out not to be true, and that's when I left the Church. But I had the illusion of sharing the same experience.

ESTHER: Now, it was obviously an emotional as well as an intellectual and philosophical need. Were you aware of how great the emotional need to have something to hang onto must have been?

MARTHA: I think so, yes. Yes, my conversion was an enormous experience for me. It was the first time I let emotion break through, and it really broke through in a big way.

ESTHER: Tell me about that.

MARTHA: I don't know anything more to say. I fell into mystical prayer, which I still believe to be valid. I don't think something else was happening to me that I thought at the time was mystical prayer. I think I did in fact experience what is considered to be—

ESTHER: —the kind of thing that William James wrote about.

MARTHA: I haven't read William James. The kind of experience in which the sensation of time and space disappear.

ESTHER: It sounds beautiful.

MARTHA: It was beautiful. I think it was real. I still believe that I . . . that what I took to be direct contact with God was in fact direct contact with God. What I should do about it now remains a serious question for me. In a sense, I left the Church to work out problems, not because of disillusionment with the tenets of the faith. I still believe essentially what I have always believed. I have to work out many problems with those beliefs, but I don't feel that I have really left. I bought it for many of the wrong reasons. I'm straightening out now what my wrong reasons were.

ESTHER: But did you buy it for wrong reasons? I don't know. You say that very glibly, but I'm not going to buy it that quickly.

MARTHA: Well, you can't take . . . it isn't religiously sound to buy somebody else's value system even if it's a communal value system.

ESTHER: I would believe that, but I don't know that you would have to.

MARTHA: I think you have to. At least, I have to. In other words, if you buy those values, it has to be because you experience them directly for yourself. Otherwise you have to reject them. And my religious value system made things even more difficult for me with Scott. I really couldn't defend myself against him.

ESTHER: Shall we go back further on that? Have you covered as much as you wanted to?

MARTHA: Just about. One of the important things is that I feel either Scott never regained his health or I was so damaged by what was about a year of minute-by-minute exposure to incredible mental illness that I was never able to trust him again. And he continued to flood me with that kind of thing. I remember he showed me a picture of a boxer in the newspaper one day and said, "You would really like to be raped by him, wouldn't you?" I said, "No," but I didn't know what was expected. I mean if you're a really good woman in bed, should you say yes? Did saying no mean I wasn't any good in bed?

ESTHER: Those examples are very useful. Any others?

MARTHA: I can't think of any right offhand, but—oh yes, he would say he had had a dream about "unnatural sexual activity with a man" and go into, you know, fifteen minutes of description. It never occurred to me to say, "Keep your garbage to yourself. I've got all the garbage I can manage myself." It never occurred to me that he shouldn't. I knew it wasn't good for me. But that wasn't a criterion I could go by.

ESTHER: You couldn't, seeing that this was bad for you, you couldn't for your own sake—

MARTHA: Oh, I knew it was bad for me.

ESTHER: —protect yourself? Didn't you see that you had the right to protect yourself by saying, "I can't listen to this. It's making me sick!"

MARTHA: No, it didn't seem to me I had any rights at all. And that's where that perversion of Freudianism comes in: Women crave to be possessed. Women crave this. If . . . I would have been an unnatural woman if I had said anything like what you're suggesting.

ESTHER: Well, I guess it's true that there have been some terribly crazy applications of Freudian doctrine. Especially by Helene Deutsch. I think she wrote about women enjoying, in fantasy I guess, being raped. I can't quote her exactly and I may be exaggerating slightly, but yes, there are some extremely crazy . . .

MARTHA: Well, there's a little component of truth in that, you know. I might enjoy rough sex once in a while.

ESTHER: That's the danger in this kind of theory, of course, that there is a component of truth in it. But to make it out as the whole thing or the basic thing is crazy.

MARTHA: Right. But you're scared to say it's crazy because you think you are the only exception, the only person who feels the way you do.

ESTHER: Well, I must tell you about the Helene Deutsch bit. When we were in graduate school, my friends and I, we would all warn each other not to read Helene Deutsch. "Don't read her, for heaven's sake, don't read her! It'll traumatize you!" And we all, of course, tried reading her and were really terrified. You know, we were terrified both ways—we couldn't win. On the one hand, we were terrified that we were those masochistic women who enjoyed being beaten and mistreated; and on the other hand, we were terribly afraid that we were not, that we were masculine women who wouldn't react properly.

MARTHA: Right. Exactly. You're not feminine if you don't want to be raped.

ESTHER: Yes, it was awful. But okay. In a way it seems what happened was that you got a lot of misleading or distorted psychological material without ever having had any solid point of view on the matter. It seems to me that if you come to this with at least a relatively solid sense of things, you can read Deutsch without being terribly damaged or even terribly upset by it. I'll have to admit I was terribly upset, but I don't think I was terribly damaged by it. But if you come to it, as you did, without any real way of looking at the world and people and life . . .

MARTHA: Yes, I had no cohesive world to draw on.

ESTHER: It was as though you didn't have . . . you weren't on solid ground when you exposed yourself to this approach—or were exposed to it—so that you wouldn't know what to do with it. You didn't know when to say something was just plain crazy, to protect yourself that way.

**MARTHA:** Right. Nothing was obviously crazy to me. The other thing is that you have to see this from the level on which my day-to-day reality was lived: Not only were there constant money problems and constant coping with Scott's unconscious material that in one form or another was being dumped on me constantly, but we had . . . we lived on the top of a very tall hill. I had baby after baby. We lived on the top of that tall hill until I had three children within two years and I was pregnant with the fourth. I had lost one in between, so I was on the fifth pregnancy.

**ESTHER:** So in this way you were just terribly isolated. It was the "barefoot and pregnant" thing.

**MARTHA:** Not only that, we had no washing machine, for example. I had two babies in diapers and was expecting a third before we got a washing machine. We had no refrigerator. And of course we didn't have a car. We were dependent on bus transportation and the bus was four blocks away at the bottom of the hill. After you got off the bus, you picked up all three children and carried whichever ones had to be carried—usually all three of them—most of the way up the hill, including the one you were pregnant with. You know, no refrigerator, so we had to go for groceries every day. The physical circumstances of life, like washing diapers for two kids and not enough food, to say nothing of no recreation . . . I didn't go to a movie, or out to dinner, or to friends, or whatever. Not to say that Scott wouldn't suddenly decide at seven o'clock in the evening that he was tired of seeing me, and would I go to bed, please. It did not occur to me to say, "No, but I'm going to a movie," because I had no money for a movie and no way to get there, and I couldn't leave him alone with the children in the house; it wouldn't have been safe. So my day-to-day physical circumstances were based on economic ones, which in turn were based on psychological ones, were such that they would have driven anybody into a hole.

**ESTHER:** What were you doing with your anger?

**MARTHA:** Nothing.

**ESTHER:** Were you occasionally blowing up at Scott?

**MARTHA:** No.

**ESTHER:** In these days, there were not those fights over your not meeting his needs, or whatever?

**MARTHA:** Well, I would defend myself when he said I was no good . . .

**ESTHER:** But you weren't actually . . . you weren't getting any of the anger out of your system?

**MARTHA:** No. Well, of course, I was religious so I had to adhere to my own value system. Scott was not religious so he had no value system he had to adhere to. He could wish me damned, but I couldn't wish him damned.

ESTHER: So that whatever you were getting from your religion, you were also being placed under an additional burden?

MARTHA: Right. I cried a lot.

ESTHER: Well, all right. Is this as much as we want to record?

MARTHA: That's as much . . . I think so. It takes me up to about the time I began to develop symptoms when I was expecting Becky and got myself into therapy. Do you see how dangerous it would be for me to get into a relationship with a man again? If somebody approaches me now, I'll end up just where I was before. Barefoot and pregnant . . . but, you know, I could never be put in that position again. I would defend myself now.

ESTHER: See, that's the point. I think you were speaking from last year or even last month, not from now.

MARTHA: But the deprived child is still alive in me because my need for love has never been met directly. It's been met in a lot of indirect ways. I get a lot of emotional support from my children, from close friends, from you, from incidental walk-on people in my life. The day I cracked up at work because of the medication I was taking a young doctor at the medical center put my head against his shoulder and encouraged me to cry. You know, I could have screamed rape; he trusted me not to. His supervisor could have come in and screamed rape, and he trusted him not to. I owe that doctor an enormous amount, but it's not the same as having had a husband, as having had a lover, as having had parents. I still would like to find somebody to be important to. I would like to be somebody's woman. I don't know if I will ever do it, if I'm too traumatized by what's gone before. I might . . . if anybody really headed toward me, I might be too terrified even to stand my ground and find out what would happen.

ESTHER: It seems to me that's because you're seeing it somewhat as . . . in terms of the deprived child, with the man then in the powerful position of the giving or withholding parent, which is what makes it frightening. . . .

MARTHA: Yes.

ESTHER: But you see, even though, as you say, the deprived child is still there within you, that's only one piece of you. You are no longer really that deprived child.

MARTHA: That's true.

ESTHER: And that man, whoever he is, who will seek you out is certainly not going to be a parent to you. He may be a parent to his children or your children, but he's not your father. He hasn't got that kind of power to give or withhold what you desperately need.

MARTHA: That's my only model of love. I . . .

ESTHER: That's where . . . there's something here that you still have to work on. It's what so many of the women I see as clients are working on—to get out from under the problems created by the child-parent idea.

MARTHA: Okay. This is my version of Sylvia Plath's poem: You've got to get rid of Daddy, not because he once did fill that gap in your life, but because he didn't ever fill that gap in your life.

ESTHER: Oh, yes. I think if Daddy really did fill that gap, you're not stuck at all. . . .

MARTHA: If Daddy really did. But if you are still waiting for Daddy to fill it, forget it.

ESTHER: Yes, that's when you're stuck.

MARTHA: And if Sylvia Plath had really gotten rid of Daddy, she would have gotten rid of the bell jar, too.

ESTHER: Oh, yes. And she would be alive. Her way of killing Daddy, I'm afraid, was killing Sylvia. Well, all right. Now, where are you?

MARTHA: I feel I'm where we all are, except that I've got some exceptional liabilities in the form of scars and wounds . . .

ESTHER: Oh, yes, and maybe some open wounds . . . sure.

MARTHA: I at least have sense enough not to put any more salt in them. You know, I can defend myself now. The question is whether I can do anything *but* defend myself.

ESTHER: And whether you are going to run scared the rest of your life. If it's that imaginary relationship you're visualizing, then you have to run scared because it would be an extremely dangerous situation to get into again.

MARTHA: Well, we'll see, because that's all we can do.

ESTHER: All right. I don't know where we go from here, but getting here was very important.

MARTHA: Yes, I think that's true.

# from esther's notebook

Martha and I seem to have been analyzing for the sake of synthesis. We have been looking at experiences and feelings in order to fit them into a frame of reference that will work better for Martha than the frame of reference she has been using.

As a child, Martha seems to have been handed a not very realistic frame of reference, one totally inadequate as an interpretation of the world for a child like her. The rulers and judges of "what is" and "what is not" were the adults—first of all parents, then older siblings and relatives, then no doubt outsiders such as neighbors, teachers, and policemen. The ruling and judging were conducted in a one-sided way: by the adults always, never by the child. None of the judgments originated with the child; all were imposed from outside, but the child was expected to incorporate them as her own and to perpetuate them within herself as a function of her own mind and personality.

Martha was a very bright child, a very strong one in terms of mental and emotional energy, who at an early age would have had the capacity to evaluate what was going on if she had been free to do so. But she must not ever, according to this frame of reference, judge according to her own thinking and feeling; she must always go by those of the adults. And she herself must never under any circumstances presume to judge the adults.

It seems to me that this is the most basic, the most total kind of double bind there could possibly be: the child caught between the irresistible driving force of her own developing intelligence and the absolutely unrelenting, immovable object of the adults' frame of reference. Where was there any room for this child to grow? There was almost no room for her even to survive as a person in her own right. Great intelligence needs great growing room. And powerful mental and emotional forces would press tremendously hard against the iron walls of an implacable, forbidding, reality-denying frame of reference. Of what use to her was her intelligence if everything had to be understood in terms of such a frame of reference?

This child must have had to go out into the world inadequately equipped to evaluate what came at her, but with a core of integrity and a mind that refused to bend or give way, whatever the crippling constraints upon her. Martha could not afford to be in very good touch with that core because it was the core itself that placed her in the intolerable bind. So she wandered around in the world, going through the motions that she saw other people going through but not quite knowing why. When she rejected her parents' framework, which, of course, she had to do, she didn't have another to put in its place; she did not dare to get in touch with her own core long enough to fashion a frame of reference for herself from her own choices. (She must not now take on my frame of reference either. Martha must finally be set free to make her own.)

Human beings seem to have a compelling need to make sense of themselves and the world around them. One has to make sense of oneself, first of all, and then, if possible, to make some sense of the world, too. The two things really go together. I believe this is why it is so hard for people to change: Having made sense to oneself within a certain frame of reference, the prospect of any change at all may threaten the entire foundation of one's personality and of one's world. I find it difficult to imagine anyone deliberately choosing to change unless he has to, unless his survival, psychologically speaking—and perhaps physically, too—depends on his changing.

The old framework may already be toppling, the known self already riven with gaps, and even then one doesn't really want change; it simply begins to happen. The change and growth in therapy take place because change was already in process and the choice has been made that it be in the direction of growth. Change can be progression, advancement, development; or it can be retrogression in the direction of retreat, deterioration. Martha's fear of unraveling if Scott had been proved to be "right" and she "wrong" was very real, very true. Unraveling isn't something imaginary. Unraveling happens. People have every reason to fear it.

Although one doesn't necessarily have to have some comprehensive *Weltanschauung,* some organized way of looking at life and the world as a whole, one does need something, some guideposts, some groove—if only a rut—whereby one's steps can be distinguished as moving forward, backward, left or right, up or down—as in motion or at rest. It is thus that one orients oneself in space, and perhaps in time also; it is thus that one orients oneself mentally and emotionally to one's own self and the world of other human beings. To lose such orientation would surely be to lose oneself. This seems to me the abyss over which one hangs suspended, the brink over which one is in danger of falling, the verge, the naked edge, the downward spiral into nothingness. The abyss is agonizingly apprehended by the one who clings to some sustaining strands, to whatever saving thread is left when all else fails. That thread, I suppose, is different for different people, but it must be there.

What is spoken of so glibly by psychologists as decompensation and by ordinary people as a breakdown is the unraveling of this thread. It is an awesome thing to contemplate, let alone to undergo, for once the unraveling starts, who knows where it may end? Who knows which broken strand may set the whole process in motion? Blithely to set out on such a process of unraveling would be foolhardy, no matter how great one's confidence in the essential strength of character with which one is endowed. Is the sustaining thread constituted of love, or faith, or the power of intelligence? I think there must be many strands, interwoven, from what has been given to one from whatever sources: the people one has known, the events one has experienced, and, with luck, a naturally strong constitution.

I suppose the fear of unraveling, of a break in some vital strand, is the reason why questions are so often considered dangerous and why the open, questioning person is often avoided or even hated. Who wants to come unraveled? One goes through life tying this knot and that knot until one is tied up in many such knots—as many as seem needed for protection against losing oneself and one's world, against dangling over the abyss of time and space with only a thin thread to which to cling. (I, who once hung so, do not contemplate this state of affairs lightly.*)

The need to make sense of oneself and the world accounts for the fascination of Piaget's work—no matter how difficult he is to read. He describes the way the child acquires his ability to move about within his world with some confidence that he knows what he is doing: If he behaves in such and such a way, this and that will happen. Thus does Piaget produce a delicate and complex and precise elaboration of how the child learns to operate in what Hartmann calls the "average expectable environment," which the child must have in order to be assured of a world that can be grasped and dealt with in a way useful to himself.

But what of a child like Martha, whose environment produces a faulty, erratic view of the world, the child whose view—like the neighborhood in which Martha grew up—is full of vacant lots, tremendous gaps in knowledge of the way people operate, of what she is actually dealing with in her daily life? The child whose way is unmarked by guideposts of any use to her or is marked by misleading ones? That child can only be heading for trouble as she ventures out from the world of her immediate family into a world populated with other, more accurately oriented individuals, all bent on surviving and on doing the best they can for themselves in the process. How does the child survive in such a world if she is given incorrect clues? And faulty measuring rods? And no method by which to adjust her sights?

I learned very young from a father who participated in family quarrels, but who hated the quarreling, that I could earn his favor by never being the instigator of such events. So I learned to avoid doing or saying anything that might lead to trouble. This was rather a sweeping interdiction, one that required me not only to sacrifice a great deal of my natural instincts but also to develop a kind of radar system so that I could get warning signals of possible trouble ahead. But how does one live and breathe that way?

Fortunately, there was one time quite early in my life when I had not been forbidden to express anger. I must have been two or three years old and I have no memory myself of the episode, but I heard the story a number of times in my childhood. My sister, eighteen months older than I, had systematically appropriated every toy given to me, and I had quietly acquiesced in each succeeding deprivation. This behavior had apparently gone on beyond the age that my parents thought it appropriate to intervene and restore my possessions to me; they did not have the notion, as some parents do, that children ought always to be willing to share with one another, and I assume that they felt I should begin to stand up for myself.

There came an occasion when my sister had consecutively taken my doll, my tea set, the play table, and one of the chairs, whereupon I quietly picked up the other chair and broke it over her head. I hope that the chair had already been about to fall apart so that I exerted little force, for I bear a burden of guilt toward my sister, who has been dead now for twelve years. I am beholden to her for the one early relationship in which I could give and take on an equalitarian basis, without having to pay the price of self-distortion that I paid in relationships with adults. Whether our relationship was equalitarian because of my early resort to force and violence, I do not know, but I am grateful, and guilty, nonetheless.

For many years, the only way I could assert myself at all was by following that pattern of my childhood: giving in and letting things go and getting along somehow until my rage reached an intolerable level, then lashing out with whatever was at hand, destructible furnishings or destructive words, justified as much by the long period of seemingly tolerant waiting as by the righteousness of my cause. To those who would dismiss this as a stupid or neurotic pattern, I can only say that it was the one way I could express any anger at all for a long, long time; to plagiarize a little, it might not have been very much but it was all I had, and I am thankful that I had it. It was my one absolutely rock-bottom hope of surviving as a person.

Most of the time, of course, I succeeded in avoiding anger. I had learned to be afraid of other people's anger, not because it was often directed at me (having been so successfully conditioned against arousing it) but because when the other members of my family were angry at each other, my own needs seemed to me to go unmet. When they fought, I would inwardly scream, "I hate you all! I hate you all!" My fear of other people's anger was thus in part a fear of my own anger, fear that someday I would let loose and say what I was really feeling—which would be the end of everything, of all the false security and love I had been buying for myself.

Afraid of other people's anger and proscribed from responding with anger of my own, I developed no adequate way of dealing with it. Eventually I must have lost much of my ability even to recognize anger, for I arrived at a point where I rarely felt myself to be angry at all. I also developed such tremendous skill in avoiding the doing or saying of anything that might bring someone's wrath down upon my head that I rarely had occasion to recognize the anger of others either. Of course, I had to restrict and constrict myself a good deal in the process, but I managed remarkably well. The success of my efforts could be measured (though I was, of course, quite unaware of the connection at the time) by the neurotic symptoms I developed. I used to pride myself on my "good adjustment," meaning, of course, what was considered a good adjustment for a woman. I once had a supervisor who described me in a written evaluation as self-effacing, and I took this as a compliment—official recognition, so to speak, of my femininity. But my psychiatrist stood up and cheered when I finally broke through in a screaming rage at him!

Some of my own questions are always reopened in the course of a client's therapy, and each time I must be prepared to begin anew: to reevaluate the defenses I am still perpetuating and the adjustments I have settled for; to consider the possibility that I have not, after all, done the best I could; and to contemplate alternatives, just as though I were truly free and young and able to do the whole thing over in some entirely different way! Each new client, each with a different course to run in therapy, forces me to reexperience and to reconsider my own therapy once again. And I was doing so now, in the course of Martha's therapy.

Conceivably, Martha and I could have terminated at this point. We had sorted out and filled in and summed up much of what we had been trying to deal with in our "return engagement." We had traced several major themes backward in Martha's history and forward into their implications for the future. Martha's questions and mine had brought forth some new understanding along with the new material, and an accompanying shift in our ways of looking at things.

It had become clear why Martha had been unable to experience meaningful communication with her parents and why she could not feel any closeness or warmth toward them. Unable to please them by conforming willingly to their demands, but equally unable to find much of anything to blame them for, Martha had been left with a great deal of confusion, guilt, and anger, all of which would contribute powerfully to a resurgence of the negative self-image at times of pressure and uncertainty. The child whose parents are well-intentioned but mistaken and who have had to repress and deny a great deal of negative feeling about themselves is sometimes more vulnerable than the child who is openly and obviously mistreated. At least the latter knows what is happening.

The difference between Martha's needs and her parents' ability to understand, accept, and meet them was a very great difference indeed. It was in part this difference or, more accurately, the results of this difference as incorporated by Martha into her view of herself that made her so unlike her fellows.* Then, with all her psychological vulnerability, Martha was subjected to the actual, unmistakable experience of rejection by other children in the form of scapegoating. The original "difference" was thus reinforced, making it impossible for Martha to communicate with her peers or to develop satisfying interpersonal relationships with them. And although her ostracism was clear to her, the reason for it was not, so that the original confusion was compounded. By the time it had been established that she did at least have the asset of superior intelligence, Martha was plunged into a highly artificial competitive situation in which she could not hold her own. It was not at all surprising that Martha then tried to "save" herself through a relationship with a man or that her judgment at that point was that of a child whose natural good sense had been dangerously distorted, first by the superficial wisdom of authoritarian adults, later by the false sophistication of adolescents on ego trips.

In this session, Martha finally made a convincing case for pinning the schizophrenic label on Scott and for her failure to do so earlier out of a well-founded fear of stepping on professional toes. But what proved to be interesting and productive for therapy was to look at the real meaning to Martha in terms of her struggle to survive and somehow to keep the family going against all odds, psychological and physical. The crux of the matter, whatever the symptom picture, seemed to be the common problem of a marriage that began with the woman as "child" and the man as "parent." But as time went by, a gradual reversal of these positions took place, and the marriage ended up with the woman eventually revolting against the "Mother/Saint" role she had taken on. When it became clear that as a matter of fact Martha had not been so different in this respect from other women, we could conclude that she was no longer in a state of alienation from the human race, if indeed she ever had been, and she need not be in any more—or less—danger from man-woman relationships than the rest of us.

So we were at a natural termination point, and there were several hours in which terminating seemed to be exactly what we were doing. There was some more writing to be done (all I had written thus far, of course, had been without benefit of the material brought to light in this session), and we had not finished reading each other's material. The only difficulty we seemed to be having was some difference of opinion about details of disguise for purposes of the book, and I think we both anticipated a fairly rapid and uneventful winding-up phase.

# 7
# Crisis

A few weeks later Martha called me to say that she was very angry about a couple of things I had written. (She was reading "Return Engagement.") I think I said, "Oh, that's very interesting," which is the kind of thing I'm likely to say when something comes at me and I don't know what to do with it. Then I remembered I had been worried about that chapter, mainly about my saying that the question of Scott's mental condition would not be so fruitful a subject for our purposes as some of the more general questions we had been raising about man-woman relationships.

I asked Martha which were the offending passages. To my surprise I learned that one dealt with her request for family therapy at the beginning of this return contact; the other dealt with her having called both the police and Father Michaelson when Scott had been so elaborately explicit about his suicidal intentions. Because Martha's reaction was not quite what I had expected, though she had indeed reacted very strongly, I had many genuine reasons for being interested now, and I said so. We talked a little about why these passages had bothered her so much, but I made no attempt to deal with the matter on the telephone because Martha felt able to wait for our next appointment a few days hence.

## therapy hour, september 21

MARTHA *(referring to what I had written):* Well, the first thing to say is that these passages registered as an accusation, which explains somewhat how the conflict between Scott and me escalated. Because when I'm told I'm behaving irrationally, I react as if it were a very serious accusation. I've been trying to figure out how certain things got equated with each other, how anger got equated with madness. For one thing, my parents would have experienced themselves as bad if they had reacted to my emotional responses. That's where bad and crazy and angry got confused, and I have to unscramble . . .

289

What is registering with me right now is this, and I realize you are not saying it but it's the theme of most of my previous therapy: "You were very angry, weren't you?" "Yes, I was very angry." "Let's talk about what happened with your husband." "Okay, this happened, and this happened, and this happened." Work, work, work, work, work. "So you see, you had no reason to be angry, did you?"

Now, I realize that probably the other therapists did not say this and you did not say it, but that is what I'm hearing. That's what unravels it all back to the beginning—at that point, the whole thing comes undone. I didn't make my point again. Because my point is that what happened to me really happened to me, and I had every right to be angry. I had as much right to be angry as anybody in the whole entire world has to be angry. I have got to defend my right to that.

You know, I've written up that therapy at the Family Guidance Clinic as if I were sure all along that I was right and they were wrong about the interaction, in their seeing me as the paranoiac. But I was not that sure. All the time, there was the danger that the whole thing would flop right over on me, and there I'd be, stuck with the negative image again. There's no middle ground, so to speak, it's either one extreme or the other. And when we come to this last sentence, "So you see, you had no reason to be angry, did you?" God damn! There *was* a reason to be angry, all the way!

**ESTHER:** But, you see, that's where the therapists were completely off base. It's hard for me to follow what they thought they were doing.

**MARTHA:** No, Esther, maybe they didn't really say that, and they may not even have thought it, but I thought they thought it. And there was a large enough component, certainly, when Jean Dalton came right out and said, "I can't believe you." There was an enormous component. . . . So what do you think it was? Angry, crazy, and bad equate with each other exactly with me. It must have started very early, I'm sure. But it got . . . for some reason, Scott had a diabolical chemistry; you know, he was the catalyst that made something happen, that made these feelings equate this way. I don't know why. I don't know how. But to tell me that I'm behaving irrationally is to threaten me with that whole sequence, that's why . . . I haven't defended myself, I haven't insisted that the marriage was crazy and that Scott was crazy for no reason at all. You know, there is something very, very necessary . . .

**ESTHER:** Oh, you had to . . . I mean, this shows you why I stayed off it; I just waited and waited and waited . . .

**MARTHA:** People don't have defenses of that strength for no reason.

**ESTHER:** That's right. You damn well needed it or you wouldn't have had it, and I was not going to fool around with it.

**MARTHA:** Okay, but Scott might have been reachable at some point.

**ESTHER:** But see, the trouble is then the man starts making an effort and everybody says, "Look at the man . . . It's the woman who . . ."

**MARTHA:** Yes. "Isn't it wonderful that he's trying so hard."

**ESTHER:** Yes, and look at her—she's just rejecting him, castrating him, the whole bit.

**MARTHA:** Okay, well, you've just taken a lot of guilt off me because I got the "look how hard this man is trying" bit—but that was, you know, after fifteen years.

**ESTHER:** Too little, too late—yes. Of course, the fact is that it really is too little so often. The woman continues to bear the same amount and the same intensity of resentment because even though the man is sincerely trying at that point, he is really unable to make these changes, so that the woman is being asked, in a way, to say to him, "Okay, you've made it," when he hasn't made it. It's as though just the fact that he's trying is enough, whether he's actually doing anything different or not, as though he should get credit for just being willing now to "try"—even if things go on the same as before. And that's likely to make a woman pretty mad.

**MARTHA:** Right. It really does. And the part in that passage from *The Intimate Enemy* that helped the most was they were aware such a person knows how to place his trying so that it looks like a great deal more than it is.

**ESTHER:** You know, I've been trying awfully hard to understand Scott. I've wanted so much to understand him because I felt that if I could understand him, I could understand you that much better. There had to be reasons why you stayed with him so long, other than self-destructive reasons. . . .

**MARTHA:** . . . But I had that other interchange—"So you had nothing to be angry about"—too many times. I got the same thing from my parents. They did the very best they knew how in raising me. They were assisted in destroying me by the then very "in" notions of child care. I just wasn't really . . .

**ESTHER:** Well, something just occurred to me on that. You were raised by that rule book I threw away because my son couldn't live by it.

**MARTHA:** But, you see, my parents were, one, strong and, two, intent on being good. With those two things that I have in my heritage . . . you know, that was what made them able to raise me the best they knew how, which was by that rule book, and which was just hideously destructive.

ESTHER: Yes, from your birthdate, I can see you would be a product of the heyday of that philosophy of handling babies so as not to "spoil" them.

MARTHA: It happened to accord rather well with the needs of my parents, which it played into. And what it played into would have been difficult to deal with even if that was all, but reinforced with a strong moral, social value—"I'm only doing what is good and right for you." You know, I had a lot to cope with, even without a crazy husband.

ESTHER: Well, what happens with us women who got involved early because we had to get into a "love relationship with a man" in order to save ourselves is that we went in essentially as though we were little children. It was almost as though we were still back there at age three or four, and everything that happened had the intensity and depth of significance to us that it would have had at that age. We were reinforcing everything that had gone wrong in the first place, so then it could go even more wrong . . . because we were immature, we put ourselves in bondage to a parent figure who would take care of us.

MARTHA: And then all of a sudden, fifteen years later, you wake up and say, "What's going on?"

ESTHER: I think from that standpoint an awful lot of women are in that boat.

MARTHA: Oh, I think you haven't been nearly strong enough in writing about how important the struggle of whose needs get met really is.

ESTHER: Well, I think we will get at that in many different ways. But I'll have to tell you how I felt when I wrote that passage. It was *that* passage I was nervous about. I was nervous in the first place for fear it was too soon to emphasize this idea with you. And I was also nervous for fear you would be insulted by my thinking it might be too soon. So I was nervous on two opposite scores. And about the wrong thing entirely, as it turns out.

MARTHA: Yes, I don't know what to do with all of this, my reaction. . . .

ESTHER: I have the feeling we ought to stay with it a little. You see, I would like to think we could lay this thing to rest once and for all. It's probably not possible.

MARTHA: Well, one doesn't lay that kind of thing to rest once and for all.

ESTHER: But if I could . . . it seems to me it should be so clear to you by now that I find you an accurate reporter of events.

MARTHA: That I'm sure of, but I'm not sure of the other thing.

ESTHER: That I don't find you bad? Crazy?

MARTHA: Yes.

**ESTHER:** If you're thinking that if you were irrational in any way, then I would feel you were all wrong, you're mistaken.

**MARTHA:** Right. Exactly.

**ESTHER:** Okay. That's what we've got to work on. You see, what I want to say is that everybody is irrational often. Everybody gets angry and makes more of something at times. . . .

**MARTHA:** I've got it—got it—got it! "Anger is irrational." But *my* anger is rational. It's related to what's happening. I don't for a minute think you believe anger is always irrational. My point is that anger got equated with irrationality for me. And God damn, the more rational I get, the more angry I get!

**ESTHER:** Yes, but that was my experience, too. I went through life not being angry, not knowing I was angry, not feeling any anger. Because I wasn't really looking at what was happening. The more I saw what was happening, the more angry I became.

**MARTHA:** Right. The minute you turn your attention—your clear rational attention—to what's happening, what's happening is lousy. And that's why I think you haven't made enough of a point of a woman's anger when she must meet the needs of everybody else but nobody meets hers. Because her anger in that case is very rational. And that's a concern for therapy, but not because she must readjust it, not because she must now make herself *un*angry, which is how therapy for women has been conducted from the beginning. No way. Her aim is not to overcome her anger. That's not the goal in therapy. It's not an appropriate goal.

**ESTHER:** The appropriate goal is to free her so that she can use her anger to change the situation so it will be more fair to her.

**MARTHA:** That's it—exactly! You know, that anger is equatable with irrationality. God damn, that just is not true!

**ESTHER:** Well, it was the greatest discovery of my life, I think, to discover that anger . . . that if you didn't have anger and didn't use anger effectively, you were nobody, you were nothing. You would be wiped out. That anger used constructively is . . . you know, it's creative. You absolutely have to have it. Without it, you can't do anything.

**MARTHA:** Sure. Right. But anger isn't irrational, not necessarily. Seventy-five percent of women's anger—I don't know anything about men's—is directed at things, injustices, that are factually happening . . . fundamental injustices, at the fundamental level of not being considered human or sufficiently human so that your needs are exactly 100 percent as big as anybody else's. What I have been threatened by in you is the feeling that you are trying to diminish my anger, which I refuse to have done. Every time you say, "I hope you saw it from this view of Scott," I think, "She's telling me not to be angry anymore." I can't protect myself. How will I protect myself in another relationship unless I get angry when that happens to me?

ESTHER: Yes, but you do need to figure out for yourself which of your interpretations were correct and which were not. I think you need to put things to rest by saying, "You know, that was something I couldn't tolerate—and yes, there I see he was trying and I just had gotten beyond the point of accepting it." You see, that's the kind of thing I mean.

MARTHA: There's one thing about which I have not been sure of you: your understanding that Scott might have been fine, might even have been succeeding, but by that time I was played out. No matter if he had grown a halo and sprouted wings and served me at every turn . . .

ESTHER: That's why there is such a thing as a dead marriage, and it needs to be recognized. It needs to be recognized as soon as possible because there is nothing that can be done to save a really dead marriage. It just leads to the kinds of things that were done to you.

MARTHA: But in any case, my anger has to be realized, has to be experienced as real anger.

ESTHER: And anger is not only often justified but very, very essential—and if you had not had that anger, you would have gone down the drain.

MARTHA: Oh, yes. That whole time at Family Guidance . . . you have no idea how I raged at those people.

ESTHER: Yes, that's coming through clearly in what you are writing now. You know, I've realized her anger is really getting in there now to save her.

MARTHA: You've never seen me . . . Esther, you've never seen me the slightest bit angry.

ESTHER: No, I probably haven't. No, I haven't really. Oh, I thought I saw a secondhand version when you've talked about people you were angry at, but . . .

MARTHA: You can't believe . . . you have no idea what it's like to be on the receiving end of my anger. To give those therapists credit, they sat there and took it for a year.

ESTHER: Of course, that's the other thing. I think you don't yet realize how devastating you are and how much . . .

MARTHA: You see, at the point where I'm that angry, I'm a three-year-old, and I experience myself as having no more power than a three-year-old, though factually I'm an adult woman.

ESTHER: Not only an adult woman, but one who is extremely intelligent, extremely articulate, who knows exactly the thing to say that can lay a person really low. And that's something people have every right to be scared of in you, and I would think there are a lot of people who are scared to death of you. You see, if you weren't as intelligent and as articulate as you are, if you didn't arouse the respect that you do . . . and I don't care how much they may hate you or plague you or anything else, they respect you. . . .

MARTHA: That's true, you know. I come across to everybody as much larger than life-size. Much, much larger than life-size.

ESTHER: Well, that's the way Scott came over to you, so it's rather interesting.

MARTHA: Well, I learned from him many things that I know how to do, that are not the nicest facets of my personality. I learned from an expert.

## therapy hour, september 28

MARTHA: I got a delayed reaction on last week's hour. It rose very slowly for two or three days, and then I was very angry. I thought: She had a different plot for the book from the beginning that she didn't tell me about, and she's maneuvered me into this position. I'm going to look like a perfect fool, and it's going to be apparent to anybody who reads the book that she had this plot in mind. I mean plot in sort of a double sense, not quite that you were plotting against me or that you were plotting for me, but that you were plotting, which is an unpleasant sensation. Nobody likes to be shaped into a preconceived pattern. So I was very angry and I thought, God damn! Before I'll look like that kind of a fool to the reading public, even though they don't know who I am, I won't publish the book! So my first response was of being helpless, and then of having no recourse in the helplessness but to cut off my nose to spite my face, and that's very important.

I raged for about twenty-four hours. Then, underneath began to rise reactions to what you had written, the two things I told you about on the phone. It sounded from the writing as if you didn't think I had any kind of family problem at all. And it comes out sounding like I just don't know what my problem is, that you have cleverly seen through the fact that this family problem is not a real problem at all. Well, the family problem is being resolved to the extent that I accept that one of my children will probably never speak to another one of my children again.

Also, I felt that in the section where Scott was threatening suicide, your response to my calling the police was that it was sort of an overblown thing to do, was escalating it. But I still feel that was a very reasonable thing to do. People like that public health nurse and the pediatrician had been telling me to get him into the hospital, and I had decided not to do it. But to preserve his life, I would have done it. And it isn't a matter of escalating. I would have had to write off the marriage completely if I had put him in the hospital. I had a choice between ending the marriage and seeing him end his life. And I chose to end the marriage. That was exactly where I thought I was. When the police didn't show . . . I finally made the decision after seven years of not making it, and then the police didn't show. Okay, so this welled up on top of the other thing and I thought, I'll go back and see what she really did write. And you know, I went back and read what you had written, and it was okay. There's nothing in there I can't accept. But I'm still very angry about these other things.

**ESTHER:** What was it you could accept, and what couldn't you?

**MARTHA:** It was the way it was written. The way it came out made me feel as if I had been maneuvered. But there wasn't anything in what you wrote that I couldn't accept. But I continued to be extremely angry. There was an implication that I felt indicated that my judgment was hysterically irrational. And I had a terrible fight with Ann.

**ESTHER:** Okay. A lot of the anger toward me must have gone into that.

**MARTHA:** Then it dissipated, more or less. It began to seem like something that needed to be straightened out but that could wait to be straightened out.

**ESTHER:** Well, part of the trouble seems to be that if I—or perhaps anyone, but maybe especially I—state the problem from a different angle, you come up with the idea that it means your judgment must be hysterically irrational. You know, that's a little bit excessive.

**MARTHA:** Right. One of the things that helped me dissipate the anger was to go back into details of things we'd been through before. I don't, for example, feel that you doubt my description of Scott's symptoms. And I don't feel that you devalue me personally, you know. Rather than the personal relationship between the two of us making the problem less solvable, it makes it more solvable.

**ESTHER:** So we can be very pleased with the fact that the personal relationship holds up enough and has validated you enough so that you can afford to look at this. You couldn't afford to look at this before. Now . . . but I want to ask you why you are still so fearful that your judgment about Scott was . . .

**MARTHA:** Esther, I was brought up, and so was Scott, in a context where everything is somebody's *fault*. And that's the basic burden I've been bearing all these years: If it wasn't his fault, then it was my fault. There is no accident, there is no luck, there is no unforeseen or mitigating circumstance—there is nothing but the raw fact of somebody's fault. And I can hear my parents to this day argue ad infinitum about whose fault it was that they took the wrong freeway exit. There is no circumstance of life so small but that if it turns out wrong, it was somebody's fault.

ESTHER: And you're telling me that you want to get rid of that. You don't want to inherit that point of view.

MARTHA: I have inherited it, and I have passed it on, and I am terribly sorry about having passed it on. But I would certainly like to get rid of it for me, and if possible, I would like to get rid of it for the people I have passed it on to. . . . You know, one of the big things in the first round of our therapy was your saying to me, "I think there is such a thing as bad luck." A very large weight fell off me. And remember, Scott grew up in this as well. My resistance went down in the marriage; I was unable to fight off the accusations that the trouble with the marriage was my fault. And that is what the hospitalization accomplished; it established for good and all that it was my fault.

ESTHER: The hospitalization seemed to you to establish that?

MARTHA: In other people's minds, not in mine.

ESTHER: So . . . even though you knew it was a sensible decision, thoughtfully arrived at, which actually accomplished some of the purposes that you hoped for and very intelligently knew you required at that time. *(Martha agrees throughout.)* Okay.

MARTHA: And I'm still getting the feedback from the world based on that period of time. Well, I'm exaggerating.

ESTHER: No, it seems to me there's something happening here. It's that either/or, absolutely this or absolutely that—as though the kind of thing like the hospital period has to be seen as either absolutely black or absolutely white.

MARTHA: There's no gray area. It's black or white. And I've got to prove myself absolutely faultless or everything is my fault.

ESTHER: Well, you get completely thrown by this either/or bit. You know, this is where the problem lies. It's as though in some way you get sucked into the same postion that your parents took.

MARTHA: Yes. There's no 90 percent, or no "nearly," or . . .

ESTHER: It's "I have to be absolutely right, right down the line, in order to have the right to live" . . . or something like that. Now obviously, nobody can live and breathe comfortably that way. You're just bound to be in utter agony an awful lot of the time; it's such an absolutely impossible position. So how do we . . . what do we? . . .

MARTHA: I don't know where we go from here. I don't know what . . .

ESTHER: Well, I think we probably stay with this recognition for a while: It's an extremely uncomfortable position to be in.

MARTHA: True. But seeing what the nature of this either/or bit is, if I react this way, which is an irrational and bad way to react, then I'm absolutely wrong, you know. It applies to itself as well.

ESTHER: Oh-h-h. You've got a trap within a trap. It's just as though you take off one layer and there's even a more difficult layer underneath.

MARTHA: Well, I think there are only the two layers—where angry and irrational and bad equate. But that's why I have never been able to deal with it, because every time I get close to it, I get put in that position about being in that position.

ESTHER: Well, it seems to me you've already taken it out of the absolute, somewhat, but you probably need to do some more of your own thinking and working on this, because you—like each person—have to arrive at this in the way . . . the most suitable way for you. And what is suited to me isn't necessarily suited to you. I think my hope would be that you would sort of struggle with it and eventually arrive at something for yourself.

MARTHA: Right. You know, I haven't any clarity on it at all, and I may not get any clarity on it this time around. I may not be able to do anything with it but just define the problem. But it's still enormous progress. You know, when I'm fighting the battle, I can't afford to define the problem. So if I can afford to define the problem, then I've come some way along.

ESTHER: This is the kind of thing that causes me to rewrite my material so much—because I want to preserve the literary purpose but at the same time tell it the way it really is. It's sort of a dual purpose, which is rather difficult to do.

MARTHA: But you see, I felt you had done something to disarm my defenses.

ESTHER: It suggests that you are extremely sensitive even now—and even to me—and extremely fearful, still traumatized by past experience. That means we have to do something to make you more comfortable and secure. That's going to take time. Perhaps a gradual, one-by-one sort of thing, with your getting some of my explanations and reasons when something like this happens. The other aspect is the inevitable advantage in my position, the advantage of the therapist over the client, and the way this feels somehow like a put-down of you. Some people find this just impossible to accept, just stay out of therapy forever because they will not ever put themselves in that position.

MARTHA: Right. The only reason I have been able to work with you is your philosophy of basic equality—that client and therapist are equals. And so they are. But in the book they're not. Because the book is about my dealing with my irrationality. So the whole of my irrationality has to show. Although I am aware that you are sometimes irrational, and I'm aware that you're aware that you are sometimes irrational, that's not the point of the book. So those parts of you that are irrational are going to show very little in the book compared to how much mine will show.

ESTHER: Okay. I started writing about that when I realized it was something that had to be said, and that's right at the beginning of the book. I have also written about the sacrifice you're making in allowing yourself to be presented as you were at earlier stages in your life. You are laying yourself open to the reader the way a client, in the strictest confidence, lays himself open to the therapist.

MARTHA: I wonder why I'm doing this.

ESTHER: Well, that's a good question. And I have my own need in this, too. In that sense, we're in the same boat. And in some respects we're dependent on one another to have certain of our needs met.

MARTHA: Right. And we'll have to work it out in the context of the book.

## from esther's notebook

I think we both realized that the lid was off and that before it could be put back on we would have to deal with whatever needed to be dealt with. No longer were we just talking about anger; we were experiencing it in the here and now. All anger is, in a sense, rational, for anger is a reaction built into the human animal to assure survival. Human beings, confronted with the far more powerful animals with which they shared the earth, would quickly have become extinct without the anger necessary to self-defense, but having survived by means of anger, the human race must learn to use it for constructive purposes or again risk extinction. As far as anger is concerned, Martha's problem is the problem of all human life. In any case, having taken the lid off, it was clear that Martha and I were in a crisis together, and together we would have to work our way through it.

## therapy hour, october 5

**MARTHA:** After we talked about it, it mostly went away. But I don't think it really went away. I think it mostly went back underground. It was too uncomfortable to live with for very long. I mean the whole anger phenomenon. But you know, I've been doing my work at the office. And canning tomatoes. The household is running normally and I'm running normally. I don't know where the anger went.

**ESTHER:** Well, okay. I thought I'd like to go back to your feeling about that first passage, the one in which I dismissed the idea of family group therapy. I may very well have made a mistake. I think mistakes are valuable if you understand and use them. I do have the feeling that my decision was probably not a mistake, at least at that time. But it may have been. And it may not only have been a mistake as a decision, but it may have been a mistake to write about it the way I did. When I read it later, after you brought it up, I didn't like the way I had worded it, and I could see why you would have reacted. Also, I do rewrite and rewrite and rewrite, and you know that when I give you something to read, I will probably rewrite it half a dozen times. (And now, of course, I will.) But I didn't say that, as I recall, with this particular material. Though I had been nervous about that whole chapter, I didn't make that kind of qualifying remark when I gave it to you. And I had to ask myself, Why not?

Then I thought maybe there's more in this than meets the eye! And I began to wonder. Could I have had some unconscious motives operating in there somewhere? Well, I knew I had been troubled and angry about our differences of opinion over how to disguise material for the book. Now, I have no business getting angry at you about this and certainly no business taking it out on you in an indirect fashion, but it could happen, it could happen. It could be one little piece in this.

**MARTHA:** The basis, the real basis, of my anger in this whole thing was that I was powerless, that you could get away with not admitting anything like you just did, if you want to. I believe you to be honest, you know, and willing to examine your own reactions or I wouldn't ever have been here at all; we certainly could never have arrived at this place. But I have no leverage to force you to deal with your own reactions if you do not volunteer to do it yourself. I am in a position of powerlessness. That was my childhood nemesis: having no leverage. That's when people drop the bomb, when they feel powerless. And I'm angry because if you don't choose to . . .

ESTHER: People drop the bomb when they feel powerless? Who is dropping the bomb, the powerless person?

MARTHA: The powerless person is dropping the bomb. He has no medium range of access. . . . He either can do nothing or he can do everything, but he can't do "something," if you see what I mean.

ESTHER: It's an all or none . . .

MARTHA: All or none! Because nothing else will shake the adult world except the maximum explosive. Which punishes the blower-up as well as the person who refused to budge.

ESTHER: Yes, I can certainly see that.

MARTHA: And I trust you. But the point I would like to make is the actuality of my powerlessness, not just the sense of it carried over from childhood. It was real enough then, too, but now in therapy and in the writing of the book, I would be without recourse if you didn't care to examine your own feelings. . . . The other thing is that I now understand very well why one pays one's therapist. I never could get angry at Meg Goodwin because I didn't feel in a position of equality with her. She literally fed me and she saw me without a fee. It put me so much in her debt that I could not get angry with her when I needed to. And that was a big, big . . .

ESTHER: So often that's the position children are in with their parents; they can't afford to get angry. But I really don't think that element is present between us, or if it is, it's in a minor way; the fifty-fifty position is so much stronger.

MARTHA: As is testified to by the fact that I did get mad at you. If I couldn't have, I wouldn't have. But I did, so I could.

ESTHER: You could afford to.

MARTHA: As it turned out, it's all right. As soon as I had called you that night, my enormous anxiety over my anger subsided. My anger didn't subside instantly, but my anxiety over it did. Because you were willing to deal with it.

ESTHER: Not only am I willing to deal with it, but also I feel this is our entry into whatever the core neurosis is.

MARTHA: Yes. It's been anger that screwed me up right along—my inability to deal with that anger except by pushing the button that explodes the whole situation. I've done that regularly throughout my life: either denied my anger, which I spent my whole marriage doing, or pushed the button that blew everything up.

ESTHER: You do realize, I'm sure theoretically at least, that it is not possible to deny and repress one's anger all that completely, that it leaks out through the cracks or . . .

MARTHA: Oh yes, here and there. It tends to fall on other than its reasonable victims. It tends to be let out on people who haven't done anything to you.

ESTHER: I should say here that I had as an incentive for recognizing my own anger about our difference of opinion over the disguise the hope of setting some kind of example. I could say, "Look, this anger is in me, but I'm not going to beat my breast and tear my hair and say I'm no damn good, as though this were the whole of me." I'm going to say, "This anger is in me, there is a thread of this in what I have done, it's an important thread and we have to look at it along with all the other threads, but it's not the biggest thread—or if it is, then we have to look at that, too."

MARTHA: We have to look at it, don't we?

ESTHER: Well, okay . . . I've written out my feelings about family therapy and my reasons for my decision about it in my notebook, so I won't go into it here.

MARTHA: Right. I've read it and think it's valid. And I think your saying that this was not the main problem for us to work on is perfectly true. It was more valid for us to have done at length what we did.

ESTHER: Well, I'm glad we did. I just feel that at that time it was probably the best answer I could arrive at under those circumstances.

MARTHA: I think it was a correct assumption. My reaction was really not to your decision as such, but to my sense of powerlessness—that you could write it up as you did and leave me with it.

ESTHER: It's your feeling of powerlessness that I'm interested in. I'm glad you've brought it up. I think you were so badly hooked on what Scott said about you because you felt he had all the power and you had none. But as I've gotten more and more of the story from you, I've begun to see that you had a lot of important and useful information at the time. Had you known how to use it, it would have carried a great deal of weight.

MARTHA: What do you mean?

ESTHER: Well, you had called the clinic and they had turned you down for an appointment for Scott. Then you went for yourself. But you could have presented the problem very clearly as it related to Scott. You could have said, "I have a husband who has had and still does have some very severe symptoms, and part of my problem is due to these symptoms; I think he is a paranoid schiz or I think he is psychotic, and I feel I have to tell you about him so you will know what I am up against." It seems to me, looking at it now, that you had a very powerful point to make about your situation—but you didn't know it.

**MARTHA:** I didn't feel like I had any case at all.

**ESTHER:** What came through to me was that you were so thrown by the contradictions in the situation, and no doubt in Scott himself (he was a manipulative, mystifying, confusing sort of person), that you didn't realize the power you potentially had. It begins to show up as you go on with your story. As you got a little support here and a little support there, it begins to be clear that potentially you had a great deal of power. It occurs to me that you may unconsciously have chosen not to use it because you would have had to face the whole question of how you could make it on your own.

**MARTHA:** That's maybe *the* most powerful reason why I did not. The most powerful reason that I did not commit Scott when he was in his most overt . . . when he was at his most committable . . . I could have called and had him hauled off to a hospital, but I didn't know how to make it on my own; I couldn't dream of doing that. I was too frightened of how I could survive by myself. The only way I knew how to survive was in his shadow, somehow.

**ESTHER:** Yes. I think this is true for so many women, and though the issue may not be . . .

**MARTHA:** It may not be overt insanity.

**ESTHER:** Yes, that's right. It may be alcoholism or—

**MARTHA:** —anything causing acute discomfort of some kind.

**ESTHER:** Yes. Anyway, as I got more of an understanding of what went on, I could see just how confusing and contradictory not only the situation but also the feelings within yourself were. They had to be, because you were being pulled in so many different directions. That's the standpoint you wrote from and I commented on.

**MARTHA:** From the standpoint of where I was rather than as I see it now. And it will make a far better book, a much more interesting book, because we won't be giving away the plot until I discover what it is!

**ESTHER:** The only trouble is that then you're in danger from what I write, from my interpretations of this material, my comments on your story, and all that.

**MARTHA:** Right. It puts me in extreme jeopardy because it puts me in a position that closely coincides with the core of my neurotic fears.

ESTHER: Oh, yes, this feeling of powerlessness is still with you.

MARTHA: The danger of doing it this way is that I might blow up again and bomb out of therapy —and the book. It's not a great danger, but it's a real danger.

ESTHER: Well . . . But . . . Let's see if we can get at that in some way because . . . See, what I feel is that you're in some kind of almost repetition compulsion. It's not a term I've ever liked to use, because it's been used so freely to explain everything that couldn't be understood any other way. Yet I have the feeling you have had to prove the very same point over and over and over again. And I found, when you told me the whole background, that you really, quite literally, had proved this way back at the beginning, yet here you were, still trying to prove it to me.

MARTHA: To prove it. Right. This is ridiculous. When I started to reexamine, the thing that kept me from blowing up and bombing out was to reexamine everything you had ever said about what I've told you. And you know, it sounds like you hear me all right, but I had to have concrete instances over and over again that you could hear me; otherwise I would have blown up. It's the sense of powerlessness that's at the root.

ESTHER: You have a sense of powerlessness in relation to me as well as to . . . where do you *not* have a sense of powerlessness?

MARTHA: With my children, by and large. Even so, they can back me up against the wall.

ESTHER: Yes, and yet I see you as a person who actually has an awful lot of power, not in the sense of status power or position power, but in the sense of the impact of your intelligence, of your verbal ability, of the strength of your personality—all except the kind of power bestowed upon one by virtue of being a man, or a father, or an administrator, or something.

MARTHA: Or a professional, or something. But I feel, for example, here I am trying to run a household, and the house is literally falling apart under me and falling into the creek. It's up to me to keep it up, and I just don't have the money. . . .

ESTHER: The powerlessness of not enough money is a tremendous powerlessness. It reinforces every other feeling of powerlessness. That was even more true then, when you went to the clinic, than now. The other thing that struck me as I started to think about your having all these facts to present: The clinic staff might have said, "Yes, we can certainly see that, but you're here and he isn't, and taking your report of the facts into account in working with you . . ."

MARTHA: Well, Esther, they may very well have said that and I was just unable to hear them because I was so bound up in my . . .

ESTHER: That's possible. There was another thing that struck me, the feeling you had that almost anything you said would be considered as castrating your husband. Now, I realize there have been some Freudian circles in which this might have been the case, that a woman could hardly open her mouth about a man without being considered a castrating bitch, but . . .

**MARTHA:** I didn't get that feeling from the clinic. I got it way before that. I brought it with me from Chicago.

**ESTHER:** It started way back in Chicago?

**MARTHA:** Yes, it started at age seventeen.

**ESTHER:** Now, what was going on there at age seventeen?

**MARTHA:** Well, we read a lot of Freud at the University of Chicago. Freud was a very big thing then.

**ESTHER:** Interpretations of Freud by seventeen-year-olds must have been just great.

**MARTHA:** They were just great; they helped a lot. And the corker was that if you said, "I don't see myself doing that at all," the response was, "That proves you're doing it."

**ESTHER:** True. There was that trend. This all speaks to the question of powerlessness, but the fact was that all along you had more power potentially than you realized. Probably the most real and concrete powerlessness you have suffered in adult years has been the economic one, which is a terrible, terrible kind of powerlessness. People can starve to death with that kind of powerlessness.

**MARTHA:** Right. I came close.

**ESTHER:** And we give that due consideration and plenty of weight. But then we go on from there to look at those places where you did potentially have more power than you had any notion you had, and to see if we can find out why you weren't able to recognize it, or if you did recognize it, why you were afraid to use it.

## from esther's notebook

During my own therapy, I remarked to a friend who had been psychoanalyzed (which at that time gave the analysand's opinion on anything psychological very great weight) that I did not accept all of my therapist's "interpretations" about me. She said, "Well, sooner or later you will. I felt that way for a while in my analysis, but I got over it. It's just that you're not ready yet. You're still resisting."

I didn't continue the discussion, perhaps because I feared I would be shaken out of my shaky enough conviction that I knew myself in some ways far better than my psychiatrist did. But I reported the conversation to him, adding that I couldn't see how my friend could end up agreeing with all her psychoanalyst's interpretations about her. My psychiatrist said, "It sounds as though your friend thought she was in analysis with God."

That remark was one of the most valuable made in my therapy, for it set me free—really free—to do my own thinking and come to my own conclusions. I knew that my psychiatrist had earlier granted me that right, too, but I had felt it then as something granted rather dubiously and somewhat unwillingly, as though it were a concession I had forced from him, not a free gift. This time, in contrast, he really joined with me in the matter, added his voice to my own, said it for himself as well as for me, and with a most significant and essential addition: He did not want in any way to play God with me. And so, in the end, I agreed with him about some things, disagreed with him about others, and always my view was of my own making—even when I agreed with him most thoroughly, for I had arrived at that agreement knowing I could have rejected his opinion completely had I found it necessary.

## from extra therapy hours: october

**MARTHA:** Of course, there's an immense amount of anger transferred that does not properly belong in this situation at all. In other words, I realize that we're dealing with a negative transference phenomenon. I understand that my anger is not at you; my anger is at hundreds of similar situations in which the person you represent in this encounter actually did impose or override or maneuver, so that my reaction is not irrelevant. And the negative aspects in the relationship between Scott and myself—not to see them in a paranoid fashion—were still very intense, very real, and very difficult for me to deal with. Frankly, I feel that scarcely anybody could have dealt with them. . . . But the situation in which we now have to deal with anger is the situation between the two of us. Although I realize it's transferred from other sources in my life, it's still real enough . . . the anger is still very close to the surface. I've had a lot of hostility dreams, and I experience it particularly when I wake up in the middle of the night.

ESTHER: So what are you going to do with your anger in the here and now, while we're sitting here?

MARTHA: Well, the second passage of what you wrote. . . . My anger hit the surface at your allegation—that's a telling word, but it's the word I want to use—allegation that it was irrational for me to call the police, for me to try to commit Scott when he was threatening to kill himself. It was not so much what you said but the tone of it, which seemed flip and superficial to what I had experienced, and which for me didn't come in on the same wavelength as the experience at all. It was as though you hadn't realized it was one of the three or four most horrible crises in my life.

ESTHER: As though it was just like anybody's little marital quarrel . . .

MARTHA: Right. I think you see my calling the police as getting even with Scott, which, of course, on one level it was, but a level so superficial that it hardly relates to what really happened at all.

ESTHER: But I think my idea is to get you to look at more than one level.

MARTHA: I see the other level, but it's almost irrelevant compared to the one I was looking at. And if I had the same situation today, if I were confronted with the same problem—even aware of how angry I was—I would still do the same thing. I think the most salutary thing I did that night was to act to convince Scott that I took him seriously.

ESTHER: That may very well be. In a sense, you were calling his bluff.

MARTHA: Right . . . saying, "Okay, let's take this into the realm of reality."

ESTHER: Yes, and that may be even a more important level to look at, your saying, in a sense, "You've threatened this over and over again; now I'm going to show you what it's like when I take you seriously."

MARTHA: Right. If I had to say the single most important thing that came out of that episode, I would say that's it, that I took a reality step based on the irrationality of his productions. I said okay, there are enough irrational productions floating around in the atmosphere, here is reality.

ESTHER: I really see that, I really see that now.

MARTHA: My feeling about what you wrote about this is that it's a superficial and negative view.

ESTHER: I think it is superficial, quite truly, and negative. It was superficial in that I really wasn't aware of all that went into it at the time, so it had to be superficial. It was negative in the sense that I brought out the negative aspects of it rather than the positive aspects. Now you've given me a very strong case for the positive aspects. And I want to be influenced by what you say. I don't want to be dictated to by you, but I need you to tell me how it really was for you.

MARTHA: You know and I know that I'm transferring anger to this that doesn't belong to the situation proper, but I must deal with it the way I feel it. I feel that you thought it was your job as therapist to make me see things your way. I'm putting things in the most loaded context that I possibly can; I'm expressing the middle-of-the-night extremities. The real problem is that I fear you may be right. That's an additional switch—it's a double switch. I object very strenuously to being maneuvered, but I feel that you know better than I do and that you're correct to maneuver me in such a fashion, however much I hate it and however destructive it is to me in the ongoing tenor of my life. I feel that you know better than I do what is right, and you're doing it, and I have no choice.

Well, I have a choice of saying I agree with you when in fact I do not, or of objecting. I feel if I stand up for myself and say, "No, God damn it! I won't let you do that to me!" I will be fighting against the forces of "good" and "right" in my life, will be exercising a destructive force in my own life by going my own way. Is that coming over? It's the child who knows in his bones that his parents are right, but who hates it nevertheless. The fight I'm fighting is with my parents, not you.

ESTHER: What can I do about it that will be at all helpful to you?

MARTHA: I don't see what you can do, except to be.... As we explore the situation more and more, I see more and more with my emotions as well as my logic that this is in fact not the case, that you're not manipulating me.

ESTHER: You know . . .

MARTHA: Well, the component is tiny, maybe 5 percent hostility or manipulation, instead of the 70 percent hostility and manipulation that I had felt.

ESTHER: I think maybe I should say here that for a while I had the feeling you were no longer letting us be equals.

MARTHA: I had the feeling that *you* were no longer letting us be equals!

ESTHER: It bothered us both.

**MARTHA:** It bothered us both.

**ESTHER:** And I was sitting here feeling: She's putting me in a superior position I don't want to be in, yet how can I get out of it?

**MARTHA:** You're not in it. My parents are in it. You just happen to be the mask on my parents' face.

**ESTHER:** You said something before that was very important. You said you could acknowledge there might be some need in me to be hostile, to manipulate, and yet you felt this isn't the truly operating thing with us.

**MARTHA:** No, it isn't. And I would not have been able to know it and to react that way with you if it had not been for my children. They're the first people I have fought with whom I have ever reconciled with. They're the only ones I can trust enough to keep the relationship going.

**ESTHER:** That's it. And so you had to cut people off because you didn't trust them. You had to do it because that was the only way you could protect yourself.

**MARTHA:** My original position is a position of isolation. That is my position of strength.

**MARTHA:** All this has something to do with the negative parental reaction toward me. This is terribly complicated to explain, but it's terribly important. My parents are reacting negatively to me. I feel, not I *think,* I *feel* that they are wrong. I had better think that they're right, because the thought that they are wrong—really believing that they are wrong—robs me of any world view at all. My parents' view of what the world is like—the view of the small child comes entirely from the parents' view—is the total, the only coherent view of the world that I have. If I say my parents are wrong, then I have no world view at all, I have nothing to go on; if my parents are wrong, I have nothing to put in its place. Whereas if I merely *feel* they're wrong but *think* they're right . . . Is this clear?

**ESTHER:** That makes you a bad little girl.

**MARTHA:** It makes me a bad little girl, but it preserves a solid world. So I *felt* Scott was wrong, but I *thought* he was right when he said, for instance, "Look what you've done to these children!" When he refused to father them at all and left me to do all the mothering and fathering and then said, "Look what you're doing," when things turned out badly—I *felt* this was wrong, but I *thought* he was right. Just as I feel that what you wrote was wrong but I think it may be right, because to think *and* feel that it's wrong puts me in the position of having to invent totally my own view of the world, and I'm not prepared to do that. I'm too tired.

ESTHER: Well, I do think one has to invent one's own view of the world, not entirely, but at times. I think that at times one has to decide: What part of the view around me can I accept and what part do I have to carve out for myself?

MARTHA: But that's the job of the Adult, and this frightened Child, which is what I'm reduced to when the circumstances around me beat on my defenses, the frightened Child is not able to take on the job of the Adult. And I lose the thread, I get reduced back to that Child state with no bridge to the Adult. The bridge gets knocked out some way, so I lose confidence in my ability to perform the Adult function, which is just simply that—to pick and choose. Am I making any sense?*

ESTHER: Yes, you're telling me something very important. I think you're giving me the answer to the puzzle in my mind: why you weren't able to establish your own definition of reality. You're telling me that you can't do it if you're coming to it like a little child, having to pay attention to what the grown people are saying. And they're saying things that don't make sense, so how can you expect to?

MARTHA: You can't—and the kicker in it is my fatal gift for detachment.

ESTHER: For taking, in a sense, a pseudo-objective point of view?*

MARTHA: Well, for striving for an objective point of view.

ESTHER: Where it can't be done and no one should try to do it?

MARTHA: Well, I feel almost always that my chief job is to know the truth—not to know what will make my survival possible but to know what is actually, truly going on.

ESTHER: That often coincides, but you don't arrive at it the way I think you've been trying to do it. It does seem to me that so often the more you can see of what's going on, the more you're likely to find a way of surviving in the face of it. You're not going to survive at all if you don't see what's going on.

MARTHA: I've been treating my survival in a situation as a piece of irrelevant information. I know it's not irrelevant; it's absolutely necessary to me, but I can't . . . you see what I'm saying?

ESTHER: There's something here that you don't seem to put together automatically and spontaneously, that you didn't learn to put together way back when and you still don't quite do it. Survival is the first thing almost, the basic thing. It doesn't negate the other things, but it has to be sort of taken for granted, doesn't it? That your first task is to survive? Of course.

MARTHA: But I don't take it for granted. It's the first thing I throw out.

ESTHER: But you can't really throw it out, because pretty soon there you are with your back to the wall. So after you've not used any of the defenses or whatever you could bring to bear that would be of any use to you, when you're completely stripped of any power in the situation, then you drop a bomb on everybody, or do whatever it takes to shake up the world.

MARTHA: Right. Self-defense comes sneaking in the back door in extremely irrational guises.

ESTHER: It does at least come. Okay. The fact that you found some way of surviving is a good thing. The way that you found wasn't very good.

MARTHA: It's not economical. It takes too much time and energy.

ESTHER: You're paying a terrible price for it. So how do you get yourself back in the picture and put the picture back together?

MARTHA: Well, I have to knock out the device of pseudodetachment.

ESTHER: But what does pseudodetachment mean? I think I used "pseudo" sort of intuitively, and now you've used it. I guess we both think it's useful, but we don't know just what we mean. I think you and I both admire the real kind of detachment, but neither one of us thinks that pseudodetachment is a useful thing.

MARTHA: Right. Except that I can't distinguish one from the other.

ESTHER: Well, I think you probably can if you just go ahead.

MARTHA: But I don't feel it's allowed for me to distinguish between them. It makes me "bad" to deal in this area at all, to question . . . to question the—

ESTHER: —the grown people's view of you, the outsider's view of you.

MARTHA: Right. I know in my bones they are more objective about me than I am. And what I care most about is what's really happening.

ESTHER: But what purpose does it serve to care more about "what's really happening"?

MARTHA: Because that's what the world is about. Well, let's take it back to my transferred anger at you. I can't say that what you wrote is negative and hostile and I don't have to buy it. I can't say that. What I have to say is, "Is this the way it really happened?" I can't knock it out by saying this is bad for me. I can knock it out only by saying it's wrong.

ESTHER: But this is not the way I do therapy. I don't believe the therapist produces interpretations, insights for the client. I believe that the client finds his own.

MARTHA: I know. You're not the one who's insisting you produce the world view; *I'm* the one who's insisting. And unbeknown to me, this is what I've done my whole life long. The only power

I have in this is to blow the whole thing up. That's why I keep blowing situations up, because I keep backing myself into the same corner.

ESTHER: Now, it's not that you're actually in a corner, it's that you get yourself into a position that feels to you as though you're painted into a corner.

MARTHA: It's not the reality of the situation but it's my experienced reality, and it's very profoundly experienced.

ESTHER: But it seems to me that it arises out of a failure to understand how the other person operates. You don't seem to have any notion that it might be possible for two people to think through their differences and maybe work out something that's mutually agreeable.

MARTHA: Well, if I didn't, you would simply never have heard from me again.

ESTHER: Or you could really blast me, just blow me to hell.

MARTHA: But I don't *think* I could. I don't see dropping bombs as dropping bombs at all. It seems to me I'm making little tiny taps.

ESTHER: Even though you know . . . you may be dropping on some people pretty hard? Dropping a bomb, a nuclear bomb, when maybe a flyswatter would do?

MARTHA: No, because when I drop the bomb is when I feel absolutely powerless. Also, it's when I feel so absolutely no good that I can't see that I ever had a beneficial or positive position in anyone's life—or that taking that position away or exploding it could be detrimental to them.

ESTHER: Losing you would be no loss to anybody?

MARTHA: There's nothing of any value that I can take away from the other person, because I have no value. This is the core neurosis right here.

ESTHER: Then what do you make of my reactions to you?

MARTHA: It's a matter of building up very slowly a set of alternative experiences. The therapy is not in anything you say. The therapy is in experiencing the fact that the same thing doesn't happen over and over—I work myself into a position where I feel I have to drop the bomb, but then something different happens. Then comes the information that something else can happen, but that's brand new information and it takes forever to assimilate it. I have to go through the new experience over and over again. And then, having gotten the clue from my relationship to you that something else can happen, I can begin to see it in other experiences and other relationships, too. But it takes forever to build up, and nothing, nothing, nothing whatever will do it except an alternative experience. Intelligence or rational insight has very little power.

**ESTHER:** I'm inclined to think you have to have a corrective experience to begin with, and then intelligence and rational insight and so on can come into play.

**MARTHA:** Well, I'm familiar with the concept. I'm just not able to exercise it in real life. When the chips are down, I get swept all away. My Adult knows all this stuff, but it's futile knowledge unless I can hook it up with what my Child experiences. The Child doesn't think anything; the Child is submerged in feelings. I have to create the link. What do you think creates the link?

**ESTHER:** I think there's something getting in the way of the link. It sounds as though the Child must never know better than the grown person, never . . . that's the greatest sin of all, for the Child to know more and better than the grown-ups.

**MARTHA:** Well, my propensity to tell it like it is when I get angry was one of the first things I had as a child—and when the Child in fact knows better than the grown people . . . you know how children are sometimes, opening their mouths and . . .

**ESTHER:** Oh, yes, the way children will say things and embarrass their parents. But, then, what do you do? You know darn well you're telling the truth, and yet you're using it . . . I don't know . . . you'll have to think about that some more.

**MARTHA:** Well, I've learned how to handle that situation. When I've got the Child and the Adult linked up, I handle that situation very well. I'm good with hostile clients.

**ESTHER:** Oh, yes, I imagine you're not so afraid of hostility as some people are because you've lived with it within yourself so long, and you don't think you do any damage anyway. . . . So you don't really expect anyone else's hostility to do you damage, either? I think you're awfully afraid to try it out in real life. . . .

Remember when I told you about a client who was worried whether I was going to be able to work with her or not? And I finally said to her, "Well, I think we're going to be able to fight this out with each other to some useful purpose for both of us." When I told you that, you said, "Be sure you remember that. Put it in the book. That belongs in our book." And I knew you were saying that it had something to do with us, though you didn't carry it any further. I'm sure it was the reason I entitled that first contact "The First Round," although I wasn't really aware of the reason on a conscious level at that point. I could sense that that was the first round of a useful battle, useful to both of us, and that "Return Engagement" was the second useful go-round, though I wasn't consciously thinking about our getting angry with each other and fighting out together something that could help both of us.

MARTHA: Well, I . . .

ESTHER: You're doing it with me, you see.

MARTHA: I'm afraid to try it out with me on the other end.

ESTHER: Why?

MARTHA: I don't know . . . I don't know what I mean by that, but I know it's true. I'm not afraid of hostility when I'm on the receiving end, but I'm afraid of hostility when I'm at the giving end.

ESTHER: You were afraid you were really going to destroy me with your hostility.

MARTHA: Probably.

ESTHER: And on some level you recognize how much weight you really carry.

MARTHA: I think so.

ESTHER: Because if you can destroy me with your hostility, it surely should be possible for you to destroy people who are not in my position of advantage.

MARTHA: It's the fear of the consequences of my own anger, I think, that's the root of all this. By "all this," I mean *really* all this.

ESTHER: You were afraid you might destroy me and blow up our whole project, the therapy and the book—the whole thing. But your Adult knows that at least with some people it should be possible to talk things through to a useful conclusion.

MARTHA: Yes. Except for the book, except for my having so much invested in it, I would not have been able to . . . if it had not been for the book, I could not have gotten to this point in therapy.

ESTHER: I think that's an example of the way some things that seem impossible to resolve get resolved.

MARTHA: Yes, I think that people are endlessly adept at constructing special circumstances that they need. Someone else might have done it differently, but this was the way I did it.

ESTHER: All right. Since you were able to do that, you should be able to do the other things you feel or want or need to do.

MARTHA: Oh, yes, I'm in the process of doing them. I'm already in the process of having the corrective experience.

ESTHER: Yes, and it's corrective for me, too. You know, I've had a great fear of other people's hostility. At first I didn't even recognize it. I could only begin to recognize it as I could afford to, as I built up some ability to deal with it. And I only let myself recognize it gradually because I only built up the ability to deal with it gradually. But I've had corrective experiences far beyond the opportunity, I'm sure, that you've ever had, because the people I've been associated with professionally have been people who have been committed to at least a theoretical willingness to look at themselves. Although that doesn't always operate the way it should, nevertheless there is a professional commitment on which I could usually count when the chips were down.

**MARTHA:** The corrective experience is the equality experience. That's exactly what it is.

**ESTHER:** That's right. It has to be a give-and-take kind of thing. That's just what we're doing, isn't it? And that gets scary, that gets feeling dangerous, that unleashes your anger and my anger, that risks dropping the bomb, bombing out of therapy, bombing out of the book. Why?

**MARTHA:** Because repeatedly in the past I have not been able to handle my hostility. And I'm having the corrective experience, but it's not a finished thing.

**ESTHER:** But we can talk about what we need to talk about, and that's a big part of my faith in the ability of human beings to work things out. I think when it is something that is worth it to both of them, people find ways of working things out. I think that is why some marriages can be worked out and some cannot.

**MARTHA:** My experience with human contact doesn't bear it out.

**ESTHER:** Somebody always had to triumph over somebody else?

**MARTHA:** Somebody always wins and the other person loses. That's why I have to retreat to isolation, that's the only secure position.

**ESTHER:** Because if you only partially win, there will be anger left in you.

**MARTHA:** That's the problem: the fact that you're left with residual anger. If you're left with residual anger, you're not an acceptable person. It destroys my ability to accept myself. Okay is not okay. Okay isn't good enough. I'm aware with my intelligence that okay is good enough, but in my feelings, unless I've come out perfect, I'm not acceptable—and that I did get from my parents. But if I didn't think we could work on it, I wouldn't have bothered to come this morning. The fact that we are working on it means I have some hope for us, for me.

**ESTHER:** Well, let's get back to that passage about escalating the conflict. I'm trying to see where our disagreement actually lies. We both agree that the conflict between you and Scott had been escalated out of all recognition, that is, as an ordinary marital quarrel.

**MARTHA:** But it was Scott who was doing the escalating.

**ESTHER:** At that point . . . but I think I felt you were implying that when the conflict was escalated, it was always Scott who escalated it.

**MARTHA:** Yes.

**ESTHER:** I see now what our point of difference is, because I can't quite accept that.

MARTHA: I know you can't, because I know it isn't true, but that's my "pit of the stomach" experience.

ESTHER: Though maybe nine times out of ten it was true, if I say I can't see how it could always be true, you're afraid we're going to reexamine all those times and find . . .

MARTHA: I'm sure I'm going to find that 90 percent of the time it was my fault.

ESTHER: That's why you can't reopen this, because you're so convinced that 90 percent . . .

MARTHA: Well, Scott told me it was 90 percent, and he had to be more objective because anybody is more objective than I am. "Not me" as a category is more objective than "me." It's an absolute. . . . Of course, that doesn't make any sense. I see that it doesn't make any sense. No, I don't think Scott's view is more objective than mine. I think my view is apt to be a little more objective than his because I was out of my head less of the time. And at Family Guidance, when the chips were down, he himself admitted that the way I remembered it was the way it really was. . . . But I just can't reconcile it with the fact that he was outside of me, and so could judge the situation, and was the objective one.

ESTHER: You were outside of him, so why doesn't that make you the objective one in judging the situation? You've got as much right, because you were outside of him, to judge his part in the situation as he has to judge yours.

MARTHA: But somehow I don't think so. I'm a child and the rest of the world are adults. It's one big, complex thing. I am powerless—that's part of this. I'm not objective. That's part of it, too. It's all one big ball of wax. And the sense of being too powerful, where my hostility can destroy, that's in it, too. The experience of being not objective because I'm inside, not outside, of me. It's all one experience. These things are always present together, always simultaneously, and they're all always parts of each other. And that's the core of my neurosis. That's where I got when I wasn't accepted by the unit at work, where I got thrown into that terrible panic. This is what it threw me into: I'm powerless to do anything because they're all ganged up against me (and they damn well were), and I'm so hostile and my hostility is such that I can destroy everybody if I want to. . . . And I damn well could, because I could have gone to the division chief with documented evidence of things they were doing wrong. But deep in my heart I know they are right. I have come into this kind of situation time and time again, where people don't accept me. I haven't done anything to them. So they are seeing something objectively, and it's the same thing other people have seen—independent witnesses agreeing about something in me. Everybody is an adult but me.

ESTHER: And you can't see how threatened they may be the minute you walk in the door, the minute you open your mouth?

MARTHA: I can't . . . I don't know . . . it doesn't make any sense.

ESTHER: But you know how bright you are, you know what kind of vocabulary you have, you know what kind of thinking you do, you know you got a scholarship to the University of Chicago, you know all your teachers from junior high on up . . .

MARTHA: Oh, I see what you're saying, Esther, but I'm the last person in the world to know anything. If I know it, then everybody else has known it for twenty years.

ESTHER: All right, how long is it going to take you to outgrow that notion?

MARTHA: Forever, it sometimes seems. I do know better and I try to operate with the knowledge, but when I get into a panic situation, I immediately fall back into my original feeling.

ESTHER: Well, there must be some way of getting at this. I have a feeling that if it could be done. . . .

## from esther's notebook

Following the last hour, I found it necessary to telephone Martha to share with her a discovery I had made, a way I had seen that unfinished business from my own therapy had come to the fore as I participated now in hers. I had suddenly discovered I was trying to do something with her that I had never tried to do with any other client: I was trying to "cure" her. I was quite aware that therapists are often driven by a tremendous need to succeed, and I have many ways of dealing with that need within myself. When it comes to evaluating with a client the net result of our work together, it doesn't occur to me to speculate about whether or not there has been a "cure." By that time, if therapy has gone at all well, such terminology has long since given way to the more useful language of growth and development. So why had I now fallen into the trap of trying to "cure" Martha?

But the question is really, Why not? What's so wrong with wanting to "cure" someone? As long as I am aware of it, that is, and don't let it get in the way of what we need to do together.

Very early in my field placement at the clinic, when I became so disturbed in the course of my own therapy there, my psychiatrist had said to me, "You will do social work, but you will never do therapy." At that time, social workers did not claim to do therapy; the very word was *verboten* in social work vocabulary. We called what we did "social casework," and we were very careful to speak of our relationship with clients in terms of "rapport," never in terms of "transference." The psychiatrist who was head of the clinic occasionally teased the social workers about this, implying that we were indeed doing therapy and were most certainly involved in transference phenomena with clients. Despite this invitation to speak "psychiatric language," I continued to remain true to social work vocabulary. Partly, I suppose, I was simply avoiding and denying any competitiveness in my approach to the situation; partly, too, I was just being my at-that-time timorous self. Mostly, however, because I had identified so much with old-line social work principles (which spoke so strongly to me for all kinds of reasons, ranging from very general social and economic considerations to the very personal concern with hearing loss), it would have seemed to me that I was abandoning an absolutely essential frame of reference.

I was therefore somewhat bewildered by my psychiatrist's pronouncement, because it seemed quite unnecessary and a complete misunderstanding of where I was in my thinking at that time. I also felt it as an attack on my essential self: forbidding me to be whatever it was that I might eventually have to be, setting artificial barriers to possibilities of growth and development that might be inherent in me, and denying my right to be "me," whatever in the future I might prove to be.* So, in the midst of all my transference disturbance, I had a very real grievance against my psychiatrist as well. (From where I am now, it occurs to me that this might not have been such a bad thing, for it gave me something real to hang onto in the midst of all my transference feelings.)

A week or two later my psychiatrist informed me that he had talked to my supervisor and had learned there was no question about my ability. He now modified his pronouncement to something that sounded more like a prediction: I would do therapy, but I would never do a "cure" in therapy. I decided this probably meant that although he was now satisfied about my ability, he had a question about my stability, and I worried about that, too. But mainly it added to my confusion. I thought of the word "cure" as something I hoped would be the outcome of my own psychiatric treatment, not something I would expect to achieve with clients, because social work goals were never expressed in such a term. What he said did not seem to be an attack on me, however; it was just a superfluous statement of a self-evident truth: Cures are effected by doctors, not by social workers.

A little later, when my psychiatrist seemed no longer concerned about my stability, he said that I wanted to be a psychiatrist. It felt to me as though he were accusing me of wanting to commit some dreadful sin or, worse yet, of already having committed it in some way. In those days, it didn't occur to me that such an aspiration, far from being a crime, might sometimes be a perfectly natural development. There are social workers, as a matter of fact, who have become psychiatrists, and no one seems to think the worse of them for it. But my psychiatrist might just as well have accused me of having delusions of grandeur—or of being unfeminine, or even a castrating bitch—for I felt all these things were implied in what he was saying.

Realistically speaking, I had no inclination at all to become a psychiatrist, because I was completely unwilling and probably also unable, at least from an emotional standpoint, to do the work required for an M.D. Also, I would in no case want to take responsibility for the treatment of patients as upset as I had been during my own brief bout with severe mental symptoms. The authenticity of that sentiment can be vouched for by the fact that I still use as the criterion of whether or not to refer to psychiatry—or at least to obtain psychiatric consultation and backing—a degree of disturbance equal to or exceeding mine at that time. And it serves the purpose very well!

A good deal later my psychiatrist remarked that he doubted whether the total change in basic personality sometimes claimed for psychoanalytic therapy ever takes place, though symptoms are alleviated or disappear under treatment and other changes and improvements may occur. Still later, he began first to imply and finally to say in so many words that I was doing exactly the same kind of therapy that psychiatrists do. I did not agree with him—not because I thought social workers did an *inferior* kind of therapy, but because I believed very strongly indeed that they did a *different* kind of therapy, a kind that is as much a treatment of choice for some people as psychiatry (or some other kind of therapy) is for others. I have no idea what his position would be on this matter now, but to this day I seem not to have budged an inch from my original position. I do not think that the difference between what psychiatrists and social workers do, however, relates so much to the question of "cure" as to the question of approach, of techniques, of frame of reference, and so on, where some real differences can be spelled out.

I eventually left therapy quite happy with what I had gained from it but with this disagreement still unresolved between us. My psychiatrist had long since admitted me to equality, had more than made up for any unfair attitude he might once have had toward me or toward social workers. I knew that what he had said and done in my therapy had been mostly for very good reasons, at a time and in a situation that must have had its traumatic aspects for him as well as for me. He himself had not been so long in his profession that he could view with perfect equanimity the sudden and spectacular blowing up of a case in so public a fashion! And certainly in the long run I had benefitted far more from having stood my ground, for the first time remaining my essential self all the way through—whatever the opinion of perhaps the most crucial parent figure of my adult life—than I had been hurt at the time.

I think it became very clear between us before I was through that the most important thing in my therapy had not been the interpretations my psychiatrist had made, many of which I disagreed with or reinterpreted in a somewhat different fashion of my own, but rather the relationship of trust that had developed. It was the first relationship I ever had with someone who began as an authority figure but who could allow me to differ with him, to dispute his judgment, to storm and rage, even to prove him wrong, without his retaliating, and so to become a peer. I remember upbraiding him for some trivial thing that he admitted was an error in judgment, but he immediately added, "I am a competent therapist nevertheless." I have quoted this to myself and to others many times, and it may have done more for me than anything else in my therapy, at least so far as my work is concerned.

So why would an unconscious wish to "cure" suddenly come to the fore at this time? Am I perpetuating the old quarrel? Do I need to prove that he was wrong and I was right, and in the most public of all possible ways, in a published book? Well, I have long since learned not to look this kind of gift horse in the mouth, not to reject a good result simply because the motivation for it was not entirely pure, my own motivation or that of others. If anger, so long forgotten or repressed, has come to be expressed as part of the underlying reason for this writing project, so be it—as long as it does not interfere with Martha's therapy. Hence the telephone call, for a hitherto unrecognized factor in the course of therapy must be turned from disadvantage to advantage.

# therapy hour, october 17

**MARTHA:** Your phone call the other morning took a lot of the pressure off.

**ESTHER:** Yes, I hoped it would, because obviously I was pushing for more than. . . . Well, I had not recognized that little piece of unconscious operating.

**MARTHA:** For me, that was a major piece because it is a repetition of an awful lot of my experience —of being expected to perform up to my capacity, to fulfill the teacher's (or later the therapist's) expectations of me. And I was not able to, because other things were happening in my life and I couldn't devote myself to performing the way they wanted me to.

**ESTHER:** Well, that's a terribly important point because it happens to an awful lot of kids. The teacher says, "Look, you've got all this potential"—but the kid is all tangled up with stuff in his family, in his life, and he can't help disappointing the teacher.

**MARTHA:** And coming out of this perfectionistic background of no acceptance, Esther, no acceptance. You have to fight to win some acceptance, and then their game is to snatch it away from you at the very last minute, saying, "No, you're not perfect yet, try again."

**ESTHER:** That must be the way I came on to you: Well, yes, you've done all right so far, but you've got an awful lot further to go.

**MARTHA:** Yes, and it's true. I can see it.

**ESTHER:** Well, that's the trouble. In one sense it is, but in another sense it is not. I don't usually fall into this trap, you understand.

**MARTHA:** I know you don't. Your whole thing is to let the client determine what the meaning of the experience is and what the limits of the experience are.

**ESTHER:** That's right. But I think, just by the writing in itself, I'm pushing. The minute I make a comment, if it's something you yourself haven't already thought of, it's pushing you. And if it's something you thought of but discarded for various reasons, you have to rethink the whole thing, and that's pushing you.

**MARTHA:** You see, most clients aren't exposed to the therapist's view of their therapy, which may be very different from their own. That's very threatening. It exposes negative things in yourself that you haven't even thought about.

**ESTHER:** I still am going to have to write things the way I see them, so what are we going to do about this?

**MARTHA:** I have an enormous tolerance for this—essentially because of my long history of it—you know, of being exposed to so much of this kind of thing. So to some extent I've developed the ability to say, "Well, I can only do what I can do." But when you say something from the therapist's standpoint, even though it may be perfectly true, in a sense you take something away from me, some of the meaning it had for me in real life—like some of the things you said about Father Michaelson.

**ESTHER:** Oh, I can see that. Even though that's exactly what I don't want to do.

**MARTHA:** Absolutely. Unfortunately. It makes me go back and evaluate from—

**ESTHER:** —from the therapist's standpoint. I can really see that, and I can see how terribly disturbing that would be.

## from esther's notebook

There are two ways in which the writing of the book has come to play a tremendous part in Martha's therapy for both of us—ways that I could see in advance only in their faintest outlines [the "dangers and advantages" I mentioned in the Prologue] but that, at this point, make it impossible for me to think of the book dispassionately or objectively. Instead, I am constantly faced with two emotion-laden possibilities, which I think of as "Book as Reward" and "Book as Villain," each version representing one side of my own ambivalence. Book as Reward came to light in full force before Book as Villain began to loom very large.

Martha and I talked one day, very early on, about therapy's being so often expected to make up for everything wrong or missing in real life, past and present, and that, of course, it cannot do this. Therapy can be a thread in one's life, and a very important one, but not the whole fabric of it. Nor can a book be the whole of one's life either, but it can come much closer. And the book quickly did come to have a life of its own, contributing a spur to the course of therapy and the hope of a reward when the course was done.

Rewards have their dangers, too. Although we are told by the people in the field of behavior modification that rewards can be extremely effective, I am dubious about rewards that are not in some way inherent in the behavior itself. Outside rewards can easily come to be so intimately connected with performance that a very strong dependency on them is created. If one comes to depend on rewards from outside oneself, one's motivation from within may thereby be lessened, perhaps even replaced, if the course of events seems to render it superfluous. Rewards can be used to manipulate and to distort human behavior for a variety of purposes, and so the danger to an individual's autonomy, to the whole matter of independence of spirit and of thought, becomes very great. This is not, of course, to say that outer rewards should be entirely dispensed with—who knows what we would bother to do without them—but only that they should be looked at squarely for what they are, since sometimes they may actually be more of a danger than an advantage.

Book as Villain came more slowly into evidence than Book as Reward. I was aware that my therapy "style" was occasionally affected by thoughts about the book during some of our hours, causing me to focus on some concerns for "literary" rather than "therapeutic" reasons. Whenever I recognized that this had happened (I rarely saw it at the moment it was taking place), I let Martha know, but these occasions were rare and there seemed little likelihood of their getting out of hand, because I was very much aware of the danger. The serious danger came from an entirely different direction. It arose out of the fact that although our previous communication and interaction had been entirely in person, there was now a great deal going on through our writing, and everything that Martha and I put down on paper was being drawn into the total content and process of our work together. What it amounted to was that Martha had been switched without warning from one therapeutic approach to an entirely different one, and we really didn't know whether such a change was a good idea. This development was not one that I had anticipated, and I could not see any way of insuring that it would not get out of hand.

My usual style is to do everything I can in a therapy hour to give the client freedom, to enable him to do as much of the therapeutic work as possible without interference from me, to use my interventions to help him control the course of therapy in keeping with shifts and subtle changes of need of which only he can be aware, and not to impose my interpretations, theories, or experiential findings on him. I am not saying that I have no influence on the work done by the client or the conclusions at which he may arrive. On the contrary, I expect in therapy that the client will incorporate something of my thinking and feeling and thus end up with a somewhat different view of self, others, human relationships, and the world in general—and somewhat different ways of handling what comes along in life—just as I expect to incorporate something of his experience and thinking into my own scheme of things. It is a mutual process, the client and I each changing in the course of it.

Every problem in therapy, like every question in real life, is multifaceted; that is, it can be looked at from a wide variety of angles and is open to a wide range of interpretations. There is a multiplicity of potentially useful choices in the course of every therapy hour. The actual choices made will depend on what my client's questions are and on my understanding of their usefulness to the client's own purposes at that time. I do not decide what should be looked at but explore whatever aspects the client brings to the fore. By a process akin to trial and error, with the client's reaction serving as our guide, we settle together on those pieces of the question that seem most useful at that point. The multiplicity of choices is not just a matter of different areas involved, or different forces operating, or even different levels of awareness, understanding, motivation, and so on. It is also a matter of relationship factors between therapist and client, with all the complexities that these bring to any problem. In the course of a therapy hour, all kinds of signals are going back and forth, verbal and nonverbal, conscious and preconscious and unconscious, which contribute to the process of choosing and using this explanation or that, this interpretation or that, this question or that. If I mistakenly pick up on one clue when the client needs to pick up on another, the shift from former to latter may be so automatic and spontaneous that neither of us is aware of the transaction that has taken place.

Yet, when I sit and write my comments on what Martha has written or on what has happened between us, with neither of us consulting the other during the process, we are very far from the immediate, personal communion with one another that we have in therapy hours; we are in quite a different situation entirely. In therapy hours, too, what I say will emerge tentatively, gradually, subject to immediate modification or alteration, depending on the response I hear, see, or sense. In my writing, however, I am making highly artificial selections without any clues from Martha at that point, and what I write becomes typed words on a page of paper, words that remain until they are erased or crossed out. No matter how diffidently I try to put those words together, they are bound to seem like declarations, even judgments.

I find, too, that away from the chastening reality of a live human being sitting there as my point of reference and with that person's reactions as my guide, I am prone to be carried away by theoretical considerations or by speculations that take my fancy. These may not necessarily be related to Martha's therapy at all or, perhaps more accurately, not usefully related at that point. As a consequence, it seems to me that in some instances Martha is being subjected not so much to a different kind of therapy but to poor therapy, and of a sort that in person I would never fall into. But it is a sort, I'm afraid, that is not entirely foreign to what sometimes passes for therapy, for if there is no rapport, and if theory is substituted for the kind of human understanding that comes with rapport, then therapy is being conducted in name only.

I would be inclined to formulate an axiom to some such effect as this: The greater the distance, emotionally speaking, between therapist and client, the greater the possibility of therapeutic error. The actual errors I have fallen into with Martha are proving to be of some value, partly because it has been possible to discuss them almost immediately, in person in an atmosphere of as much emotional harmony as we can bring to it under the circumstances. Because Martha has problems in handling her anger and in trusting anyone, she is going through a veritable ordeal by fire with me, and in the process my own anxiety has mounted. I find myself in a situation for which I am not at all prepared, because I certainly have had neither training nor practice in combining therapy with the writing of a book.

Beyond that, it happens to be a situation that threatens what has been my most vulnerable spot: my fear of anger, of my own as well as that of others. It also puts to the test a great many of my ways of adapting to emotionally fraught encounters, and I wonder whether my adaptations are adequate. I know that many old wounds are being probed, for my dreams, which have been quiescent since the time of my own therapy, have suddenly sprung into vivid and significant life. Could it be that some of the bits and pieces of myself that I put together at earlier times in my life are coming unglued? If so, Book as Villain is giving Book as Reward quite a cementing task to perform. Or can I, in the course of Martha's therapy, achieve a sturdier and healthier putting together of my own identity, along with hers, so that the major contribution of the book for me, as for Martha, will not be as reward but as therapy?

# 8
# Working
# Through

# therapy hour, october 19

**MARTHA:** I have a kind of double bookkeeping system whereby I say, "My home life was totally impossible because my parents were thus and such, and nobody could live sanely under those circumstances." And then I turn around and say, "Well, of course, I have to believe what I just said in order to justify myself, but it wasn't really like that at all; it was really pretty normal, and I'm just telling myself those other things. . . ." But I'm not just telling myself those other things; they were true. Sasha, having just been there on a visit, on her own and without my having described it that way to her, said exactly what I've said to you—that my parents see and believe only what they want to see and believe, regardless of what the real facts may be.

**ESTHER:** So you have outside confirmation. That should help. Sasha sounds as though she has a perceptive, evaluative way of looking at people, which is unusual for an eighteen-year-old.

**MARTHA:** That's one of the bonuses for mothers who have gone through hell. They have children who are way ahead of the average. . . . Something about my relationship with my mother came back to me when Sasha was talking about her visit. My mother will not acknowledge any kind of negative happening. There is no anger. There are no bad feelings. For her, there's only one pattern. She can't say her taste is different from yours, but yours is nevertheless acceptable. She can't say anything about differences of opinion because she would feel she was saying you're outside acceptable limits, and she wouldn't say that to anybody.

**ESTHER:** There's something in there that's been getting in the way of what we're trying to do together. . . . It occurs to me . . . I have been so puzzled by your saying that Jean Dalton was a good therapist—not *in spite of* her saying, in effect, "I don't believe you. There is nothing you can say that will make me believe you," but *because* she said it. I'm beginning to see from your standpoint that that must have been a relief to you. At least there was a certainty in it. She wasn't going to believe a word you said, so you knew exactly where you stood.

**MARTHA:** Exactly. You can't imagine what a relief that was. All my previous therapists had never contradicted me but never believed me either, and that left the whole thing in a big mush. I never knew what was solid and what was not. It never gave me a chance to prove my point to them, because they had never said they doubted anything.

**ESTHER:** Okay, but there's an all-or-none thing in here . . . and that's what I'm afraid is getting in the way, what I'm afraid may happen with us.

329

MARTHA: Yeah—that's the kicker. . . . I wish I could send you to spend a week with my parents.

ESTHER *(laughing):* Then I could understand why you're so . . . Okay, but the all-or-none thing is the danger because, I think—I guess I've said it in a number of different ways—I'm a relativist, and I can't help thinking in part that your problem arises in some way out of your being an absolutist.*

MARTHA: Yes, that's true. I don't think there's much you can do to tinker with that, frankly. It can be mitigated somewhat, but I'm never going to be a relativist. I'm always going to be an absolutist. I just have to learn how not to let it screw up my life. I see the relativist approach for me as a sellout, that I would do something wrong in order to be more comfortable.

ESTHER: But you see what this does . . . I'm trying to think how we can work with this . . . I think you're entitled to have an absolutist position if that's what you need and want.

MARTHA: But I need to have you understand that it's a legitimate philosophical position, not just a neurosis we're going to have to leave alone. It rests also on rational . . .

ESTHER: But you see, if you do that, then you don't leave any room for me.

MARTHA: No, that's not true, that's not true.

ESTHER: But by your terms, I'm not philosophically sound.

MARTHA: No, that isn't true. My absolutism is only for me. One of my absolute principles is, as a matter of fact, self-determination. I would never try to make up anybody's mind.

ESTHER: Okay, but then how can you accept anything I offer you in the way of relativistic ideas?

MARTHA: No, that's not true either. It really isn't.

ESTHER: Then maybe your absolutist position really isn't all that absolute.

MARTHA: It isn't held to absolutely, if you see what I mean.

ESTHER: Because if I were to look at things from an absolutist position, I would have to stop doing therapy, and that I can't do.

MARTHA: No. Of course. But you see, the kind of discomfort it gives you when I reflect on your relativist position is very much akin to the kind of discomfort I feel when you . . .

ESTHER: Yes, we're equally uncomfortable.

MARTHA: We're equally uncomfortable. You're threatened in the same place that I am for the same reason I am.

ESTHER: Yes, because the only way that I can operate in so many things is by way of a relativistic approach. Now, it doesn't mean that I don't have any absolutes at all, but it does mean, for instance, that if I see a little piece of my motivation is ulterior, I will acknowledge it and allow for it, but I will not say that I'm no good, that my entire motivation is tainted and poisoned by this. And I will not look at anybody else that way either.

MARTHA: Yes. Well, I hope I won't either. That's not a point of absolutism I will defend. But there are some principles . . .

ESTHER: I certainly think there are some things that you and I would agree on in the absolute sense. I think we need to clear the air on this because I think there's a danger here.

MARTHA: Well, there's something in relation to my parents. They put me in a position over and over again where they tried to control my choices by making them contingent on the things I wanted. Like I had to pick the dress my mother chose for me because if I didn't pick that dress, I wouldn't get a dress at all. Or like my father, saying to me when I went out to get on my bike to ride on Sunday afternoon, "This is a Sunday. You're not going to leave the house in blue jeans. You either change into a dress or you can't go." And to me, the idea that a dress was more respectful of Sunday than jeans was so infuriating that I said, "Okay, I won't go," and got off the bike and went into the house.

ESTHER: Well, what kind of choice do you think I'm trying to put over on you?

MARTHA: The choice of saying that the fact that Scott was out of his mind had a minimal impact on the marriage.

ESTHER: Where did you get that idea?

MARTHA: That's the way it comes through. I know that isn't what you're saying, but it's what's coming through: not that this is so, even, but I have to be willing to say that this is so. I don't even have to believe it; I just have to be willing to say it. And then we can publish the book and everything will be fine. But if I won't say it, then . . .

ESTHER: Martha, what have I done to deserve this?

MARTHA: This is the content of my anger when I lose my temper.

ESTHER: But I don't understand. What have I ever done to give you the idea that any opinion I express is nonnegotiable?

MARTHA: Nothing. That's strictly a carry-over from other situations. I'm not presenting this as what I think is actually happening. I'm just telling you where a part of my head is.

ESTHER: It seems to me the two things got mixed up together—book and therapy. From that standpoint, it wasn't a good idea, I'm afraid, to try to write a book before the therapy was finished, before you were so solid in your own feeling that you wouldn't be threatened. I wonder if it might be wise to decide now not to try to finish the book until we've gotten that far in therapy. I hate to do that, you know, I think we could finish it somehow. . . .

MARTHA: But you see, you're cutting right into it because my only choice then is not to do what we started to do, not do the book.

ESTHER: Martha, what are you doing to me?

MARTHA: I'm not . . .

ESTHER: You have power over me as well as I over you.

MARTHA: That's what I can't see; that is exactly what I can't see.

ESTHER: You can't see that you have as much power over me as I have over you as far as the book is concerned? For you to say "No, I won't do the book" is going to hurt me just as much as for me to say "No, I won't do the book" is going to hurt you?

MARTHA: I can't see it. I know that it's true, but I can't see it.

ESTHER: Well, it would seem to me that unless you do see it . . . I mean, we have to work on your ability to see this.

MARTHA: Yes, that's exactly what we're doing now. When I see you reacting, I see that it's true, but when I think about it, it doesn't seem to be.

ESTHER: You feel in my power in some way?

MARTHA: Yes. Exactly. But that doesn't have to do with you; it has to do with my mother, really, really, really.

ESTHER: I don't want you to feel in my power, and I don't want to do anything to put you in my power, but we are to some extent in one another's power—and we can't help that.

MARTHA: There's no way around that. No, that's a reality thing, and simply to come to the point where you can see the reality thing solves the problem, if you can just hold on to it long enough. If we can really ride this one through, we will have solved the problem.

ESTHER: Look, I'd like to try to bring something to bear on this. You have influenced everything that I have written. I am prepared to rethink and to rewrite . . .

MARTHA: That's what's going to solve the problem.

ESTHER: And I have done it, you know, over and over and over again.

MARTHA: I know. It's just when I get into this thing that I can't see it, but the longer we stay with it . . . writing the book will solve the problem. When we have gotten through this, we will have solved the problem with my mother. It's just very difficult and dangerous and frightening and painful.

ESTHER: But why should it have to be that bad? It seems to me it's just inherent in the situation that we will have differences, that we will have to resolve them, and that as we resolve them, we will come out with something that is better than anything either you or I can do alone. We will come out with something that is a joint product.

MARTHA: The only reason there is a problem is that I went from my parents, who had absolute control over me, to Scott, who assumed absolute control over me, and he did it because by then I was so taken in that I simply handed it to him.

ESTHER: So I have to help you see that these things, which go all the way back, can be handled.

MARTHA: Yes. In fact, my only models, my only two models of problem-solving were all-or-nothing models, because Scott is, if anything, twice the absolutist I am; and my parents are, if anything, twice the absolutist Scott is.

ESTHER: Then can I, sort of in advance, make a request that you give me the benefit of the doubt?

MARTHA: Sure, that's what therapy is all about.

ESTHER: Okay, then if anything I say or write doesn't seem right to you in some way, it should be understood the minute you hear it or lay eyes on it that it is something for us to discuss.

MARTHA: The only danger in that is that I maintain my double bookkeeping system, which is a danger to me in relation to you, and that is: It's okay for me to see something I disagree with and tell her and we'll straighten it out. But of course she's right all along, because she's the therapist. You know, we'll work it out as best we can, but actually we won't have worked it out at all, because, of course, she was really right all the time.

ESTHER: Well, Martha, that's the other part of this we have to look at. It's not . . . I mean, you have to learn to decide that kind of thing for yourself. There is no rule that of course the other person is always right.

MARTHA: No, I know. Once I bring it to mind, once I realize what I'm doing, this problem is over. It's when I don't realize I'm applying this double-bookkeeping standard that I get so angry, because I feel my whole commitment as a person from this background where nothing nasty was ever said but where plenty of nasty things happened, my whole sense of how the world *has* to go and of how I *have* to live in the world, is to find the realities as quickly as I can and live with them however I can, and know what's really going on. . . . So when I've settled it in a relativistic sort of way, I feel like I've sold out my own basic survival value. Coming from this "see-no-evil" background, my only survival was to say I'll see evil if it's there and deal with it as I can. If I settle it in an inappropriately relativistic fashion, I sell out my own survival.

**ESTHER:** Okay. Then we need to know what inappropriately relativistic fashion you're talking about, because I don't believe in that either.

**MARTHA:** Like saying, all right, I cannot afford to lose you as a therapist.

**ESTHER:** I don't mind if that operates to keep us working on it, but not as a solution. I would not consider that any good at all.

**MARTHA:** Well, I can't afford to lose you as a therapist, but that's not the solution. An inappropriately relativistic solution would be to say: I've got too much invested in the therapy or the book to go with what I really see; therefore, I'll have to make the best of it and say that I see what I don't see.

**ESTHER:** No, I wouldn't accept that either.

**MARTHA:** I know you wouldn't, but I'm capable of doing it, and, of course, if you do it on that basis, it shoots the whole thing down.

**ESTHER:** Yes. Because it becomes false right there.

**MARTHA:** It becomes false and it vitiates the therapy. And also, my anger in the relationship, my anger toward the person who "made me do that," will not let the relationship survive long anyway.

**ESTHER:** Well, I don't want an inappropriately relativistic solution any more than you do.

**MARTHA:** Okay, but the alternative is to go on exploring the problem, which is what we're doing, knowing that my all-or-nothing stance can in reality blow the thing up at any time. It's a terrible danger. Conversely, the fact that I have so much invested in the therapy and in the book motivates me really to explore so as to get out of it alive at the other end, with the relationship intact, without making it inappropriately relativistic. In truth, I have got a lot invested in therapy, in really truth-telling therapy, and not just to publish the book but to publish it the way it really is. That's what motivates me. And I have a lot invested in the relationship with you, you know, aside from the therapy. The time we've spent together has been very happy, not just pleasant but really happy, so I've got a lot invested in the relationship apart from the therapy relationship. I'm motivated to go on in real therapy and find a real answer, a real answer that's neither a sellout nor blowing things up. I've had very little practice in doing that.

**ESTHER:** It's as though the choice has always been between blowing it up and selling out?

MARTHA: That was my choice with my parents, and that was my choice with Scott. At least, that was the only choice I ever found. The only choice I ever knew there was to make with my parents was to sell out, because they would not accept an appropriately relativistic solution. It had to be all or nothing, I either had to buy it or to do without.

The only time I ever remember selling out was in high school. I had a chorus teacher. Then as now, music kept me going and I was singing in the chorus. In class one day the teacher said something about Mozart's "hundred symphonies," and I said, "He only wrote forty-one." She said, "Oh, no, dear," and I said, "Look, I'll prove it." So I went and got the encyclopedia and brought it back and proved it, and then she lost her temper and kicked me out of the chorus for insubordination. The only way I could get back in the chorus was to make a public apology to her, and I had so much invested in my being in the chorus that I did. I saw that she had made a power play. You know, if she had been angry at me when I contradicted her, I would have considered her justified, but she lost her temper only when I was right.

ESTHER: She used her power.

MARTHA: She used her power. As long as she was sure I was wrong, she was all sweetness and light, but the minute I proved that I was right and she was wrong . . .

ESTHER: But you see, the right and wrong, the win and lose business, does not belong between you and me. That's what gets the whole thing off on some kind of tangent we have to get away from in order to get rid of it.

MARTHA: I'm on it by compulsion. I'm on it because I had no choice but to be on it. I'm trying to get off it, and that's why I'm in therapy. But it's difficult and dangerous, and therapy is difficult and dangerous, and exhausting.

ESTHER: I wish that it were not. My hope is that in some way your own self-esteem and self-knowledge will grow so strong that you won't feel so vulnerable, or jeopardized, or whatever. In a way, that is for me the ideal therapy: for you to become that strong.

MARTHA: I'm strong enough to let it happen between us and to examine it without collapsing.

ESTHER: Okay, but what we want is for both of us to win, neither of us to lose.

MARTHA: I believe that this can be done, but it's an act of faith, not an extrapolation from experience. I believe it can be done because I wish to believe in people and not because I've ever seen it successfully done, because it rarely is successfully done.

ESTHER: I think that in some instances it can even be done without any residual anger, but I think we have to face the fact that in any such thing there could be some residual anger.

MARTHA: Yes, right. That's a realistic expectation. I don't want the world to become wonderful; I just want it to become possible.

ESTHER: So when I say that we can both win, that neither of us has to lose, it doesn't mean we can each win 100 percent.

MARTHA: No, I understand that. My Adult is operating on the situation as well as the trapped Child, but there is a trapped Child there, too.

ESTHER: I think you have to know I honestly believe that every time you question something I write or say and I think it through further, I come out with something I think is better than what I started out with and that I feel is a joint product.

MARTHA: This is coming through and it is what saves the situation. It's really coming through.

ESTHER: Could you contemplate something of that sort working the other way around, too? That you would come up with something not the same as what you started with? That would incorporate some of my thinking as well as yours, so it would also be a joint product, but of your making?

MARTHA: Oh, sure, that's what I do. That's what therapy is for.

ESTHER: You've already done it, of course, and that was a purely academic question, but I thought to make it conscious in so many words is probably necessary. Because when it happens that way, it happens pretty painlessly; in other words, you take on some of me and I take on some of you, and we each come out somewhat different.

MARTHA: But I have no license to do therapy with you, if you see what I mean.

ESTHER: No, but you do know from everything I have written and said that I find any true therapy I do with a client is also therapeutic for me, that I learn and get from the person I'm supposed to be helping.

MARTHA: Yes, that's why I'm working with you and not with somebody else.

ESTHER: So if you weren't changing me in some way, the therapy wouldn't be working. It wouldn't be working for you if it weren't working for me.

MARTHA: Right. I know that. You know, I have a lot invested in *real* therapy, not just in reaching an agreed-upon end.

## from esther's notebook

I have a colleague, a member of the staff at the agency where I work, from whom I learned a great deal during the time I was "supervising" her. I trust that she learned some things from me, too, but it is hard for me to imagine what she could have learned from me that would be half as valuable as what I learned from her. It was from her that I learned how to see what was happening in the social work world, the world that had for so long provided me with a resting place, a refuge from the "real" world in which everyone was engaged in a constant struggle with everyone else, not only for survival but for prestige and power and advantage over one another as well. She and I compared notes in a way I had never done with anyone before, at least never with anyone involved in the same work situation with me. I had the opportunity to compare very exactly and quite fully her interpretation of a more-or-less joint reality with mine.

For many years I had been able to insulate myself from the impact of many realities in a professional world in which people were every bit as much engaged in a struggle as those in the outside world. If it was a struggle not so much for actual survival, it was at least one for recognition of the worth and meaning of their own existence to colleagues, to the public, and to themselves. Thus, I could remain insulated because I was living under the sheltering wing of a mother figure, the director of the professional work of the agency. So my safety was guaranteed, not only by the larger framework of professional principles to which we all subscribed but also by her backing such principles to the hilt, which seemed to give them almost the force of absolute law. There was a great deal of security for me in this. I needed that resting place so much that I made no attempt to explore with her the very real differences in theory and practice that probably existed between us within the professional framework to which we were both equally devoted.

I may have done the director an injustice in withholding some of my real thinking and feeling, but it was she who had warned me against the dangers of the eclectic clinic, the dangers of so "relativistic" an atmosphere to one's personal security; and I felt her words told me something about herself: "The eclectic approach is all right for some people, but for people like you and me it is best to remain within a definite, well-spelled-out frame of reference." There was nothing I could say to this, because the possibility of my remaining within such bounds had never existed. I had been outside of such bounds from the day of my birth.

I was born of a Jewish father and a Christian mother, a nonpracticing Jewish father and a nonsectarian Christian mother. My earliest and all my ongoing religious influences were quite heavily weighted on the Christian side, though by default rather than intent. My mother had tried, before either my sister or I was born, to convert to the Jewish faith, but since my father hadn't the slightest interest in such an affiliation she soon gave up and returned to the more *gemütlich* frame of reference of her own heritage. This also was a highly relativistic matter, however, for she was born in Germany of a Catholic father and a Lutheran mother and had come to the United States at the age of sixteen on the strength of the missionary efforts of the Mormon Church. She was befriended by one of its Salt Lake City families and attended its university. Although she dropped out both as a student and as a prospective convert to marry my father, she kept up a long and faithful correspondence with her Mormon "family," all the while dropping in and out of a number of other congenial Christian sects. How could I, who was the daughter of so heterodox a mother and so free-thinking a father (who voted for every third-party candidate who ever ran for office from Theodore Roosevelt on), how could I be anything, ever, but a relativist?

I was also, unfortunately, very insecure, though I think this state was the product of psychological far more than doctrinal uncertainties, and I envied the director her security within her magic circle. But I knew of no way I could get into the kind of circle from which, it seemed to me, I had been excluded from birth. I did, however, value most tremendously the shelter she provided for me within the boundary of her own certainties. When she retired, ill and soon to die, I experienced one of the greatest losses of my life—professional, personal, every possible kind of loss. So I was left with much of my original insecurity, though some had been worked out in therapy, to cope with a changing professional scene in which I was about as well equipped to fend for myself as a newborn baby, both emotionally and practically. For the first time I saw this world as one in which I, like everyone else, must struggle to establish myself—as though all those years under a protective wing had done nothing to establish me as *me,* in my own or anyone else's eyes. I felt there was no longer space for me at my agency, because now that I was free to be my real self, there seemed to be no room for me outside of my accustomed corner.

It was while I was floundering in this welter of uncertainties that a young colleague, new to our staff, asked to be supervised by me—a happening that in itself was a very great gift to me. Although I did not believe in "supervision," I did believe in comparing notes, professionally even more than personally. It was on this basis that she and I began talking together, though she called me her supervisor and I think really thought of me as her supervisor. Where she had gotten her ability to size up situations and people so realistically and to handle herself and her own relationships so wisely, I don't know, though I suspect that her being black had something to do with it. Over and over again, our note-comparing became a learning process for me as we talked of events going on in the agency, in the field of social work, in the world itself. It was not that I wasn't well informed myself, or that there weren't other people on the staff from whom I learned a great deal, too, but the quality of tough-mindedness she combined with warmheartedness seemed to make it possible for her to look at realities of our competitive professional world that I would not have allowed myself to see.*

So in that long process of learning to assert myself, of trying to find ways of making room for myself in a world in which I had hitherto remained safely within my allotted corner, I had something of an expert from whom to gather valuable and probably vital clues. I have never been one to beat my head against stone walls for very long, and now I had someone to help me identify which walls were made of stone (and would never make room for me), a part of my education that seemed not so much to have been missing as to have been dissolved in quantities of idealism, wishful thinking, fantasy, and all those psychological devices whereby good little girls turn themselves into good, feminine, lovable, uncompetitive, certainly "uncastrating"—and ineffectual—women.

One subject that she and I talked about a number of times, because it was a basic bond between us, was the need we both always had to have "a way out," an alternative. If something wasn't working very well, so long as we had somewhere else to go, something else to turn to, we were all right. We made our commitments and we held to them, but some were made as tentative commitments only, deliberately so. Our most basic, definite commitment was always to keep as many doors open as possible. Thus was I once again confirmed in my relativism by my sister—and fellow relativist—under the skin!

## therapy hour, october 26

**MARTHA:** One of the things I've been thinking about in connection with our last hour is that you were just beginning to react emotionally to the crisis we've been through.

**ESTHER:** Oh? What do you mean?

**MARTHA:** You said, for example, "Martha, what have I done to deserve this?" I would have expected that right away.

**ESTHER** *(laughing):* You mean why not sooner?

**MARTHA:** Right. That seemed curious to me. Because for me it's virtually over.

**ESTHER:** Well, I don't think I realized what was happening to our relationship until then.

**MARTHA:** That's it, that's it! Because that's the only place where the crisis really was. . . . I mean,

I've been through many crises in therapy, I've fought about a lot of things, but this was something that threatened the relationship between the two of us and that's why it was so difficult.

ESTHER: Well, I didn't see it as such until the end of the previous hour—the hour before last—so there was no way I could react to the feeling of threat to the relationship. I could see it only as things began to add up that way for me, because I didn't think until then that you could really distrust me or my motives. I thought you would disagree with me and we would have differences that we would have to reconcile, but I didn't recognize that you would bring distrust of me . . .

MARTHA: Distrust is my first reaction.

ESTHER: But that's the last thing that I considered.

MARTHA: That seemed very curious to me because distrust was the emotional tone of my experience, which is why it was so trying. That you didn't see it surprises me.

ESTHER: Well, that's an interesting thing. I don't think I look for that kind of explanation until I have thoroughly explored all the other possible explanations; and in therapy, most often between therapist and client the other explanations take care of it. It's very, very rare after so many hours of therapy together to have the distrust factor enter. I would have expected it, possibly, way back, and I would have thought it through. We would have worked with it then, but it didn't happen then.

MARTHA: Well, distrust can be my reaction at any time. My early experiences were devastating. What I learned . . .

ESTHER: Not only your early experiences, but some of your later experiences.

MARTHA: Right. What I learned is that you can never depend on anybody for anything, literally. That's the main thing I know—that no matter what you seem to have, you may not have.

ESTHER: I sort of knew that about you in regard to your relationships with other people, but I don't think I felt that it operated in your relationship with me, because I would have expected it to have shown itself much sooner. So by the time it happened, I had all kinds of reasons not to recognize . . .

MARTHA: That's true, I think that's very true. That the thing about me, that there is no point at which this possibility . . . I never pass a place where this possibility cannot erupt. I never have, in any relationship.

ESTHER: Well, okay, you distrusted me, it seemed, all of a sudden. Okay, there's always been question in the back of your mind, anyhow. But there always has to be in any relationship between human beings, not question so much as that, after all, you have to take care of your own interests in every relationship. That's what it amounts to, all it really amounts to, pragmatically. So it seemed to me, as I recognized that you were disagreeing so strongly with me in a few things, that these were things we would have to talk through. We would arrive at some answers together that would be a combination of your understanding and my understanding, and we would come out with something better than yours or mine alone.

MARTHA: Well, the way the experience felt for me was that the quality of your position, as you expressed it, was such that I wondered whether this was possible between us in those instances.

ESTHER: Even knowing that I revise and rewrite and reevaluate and change . . .

MARTHA: Well, I want to justify my view, justify the rationality of my view.

ESTHER: I'm perfectly willing to grant you the rationality of your view. What I'm concerned about is our relationship.

MARTHA: Right, but that's what I didn't believe. I want to tell you how it threatened the relationship, threatened my estimation of your good will toward me as being strong enough for me to depend on it. I don't think I'm trying to put you in the wrong. I'm just trying to detail to you the experience I had. When I read your comments on the time that I tried to hospitalize Scott when he was threatening suicide, your comments on it seemed extremely flip to me, as though it had not been an appropriate thing to do under those circumstances.

ESTHER: Martha, that's a misunderstanding.

MARTHA: I know it is, but I'm trying to tell you the experience I had. I'm not giving you an objective view; I'm giving you the most subjective view possible of what happened that I can. So I called you up, thinking maybe you didn't understand why I called the police, maybe you thought I was calling them to break up a domestic brawl, which is something I never would have done and something I couldn't imagine your thinking I would have done. But this seemed to me the only possible explanation for what you'd written, so I called you up and said, "What did you think I wanted the police to do?" And you said, "Oh, haul him off for observation or something," and that struck me as extremely flip, because that's what they do; after all, that's standard operating procedure when they talk somebody down from the bridge.

ESTHER: Martha, I'm sitting here and my heart is just pounding. I'm so afraid of what you're doing, I'm really afraid.

MARTHA: But I'm not doing it now. I did it a month ago.

ESTHER: But it didn't come through to me.

MARTHA: You're having my reaction *then*, the reaction I had a month ago. You're feeling a terrible threat.

ESTHER: Okay, you felt this threatened by me; you felt I was putting you that much in the wrong and that you'd never get out of it again.

MARTHA: Exactly. Right.

ESTHER: And that's what I have the feeling you're doing to me now.

MARTHA: Right.

ESTHER: Well, I have no intention, never did, of putting you that much in the wrong, or for that matter in the wrong at all, but there is no way that I can say something exactly right the first time, or maybe at all. And there's no way that you would feel confident we could work things through to some mutually satisfactory conclusion?

MARTHA: There isn't any. That is what I don't have; no place in me do I have that faith. There's no relationship where it worked for me so that I can reach back and say, "Well, I did it there, so it can be done."

ESTHER: Then this is exactly what you should be bringing here to this relationship, so that in this relationship—now, for the first time—you can have this experience.

MARTHA: Exactly. Right. This is the experience one eventually needs to have with one's parents.

ESTHER: That's right. Absolutely.

MARTHA: Because when you're little, they have to be *all* right; you have to believe they're just superhumanly competent to take care of you. But when you have come out of that child stage, then the next thing you have to have from them, starting maybe at age seven or eight, is the confidence that they will take your view of the situation into consideration. They're still superhumanly able to shake your whole world. If your parents decide that that's the way it's going to be, that's the way it's going to be. And what you need from them is sufficiently disinterested good will for them to take into consideration what you absolutely must have. I mean, there are some basics that a kid really needs. He needs to be treated as a human being, not as a commodity or object; and he must have his feelings and emotional needs taken into consideration in constructing the whole living situation.

ESTHER: I absolutely agree with you.

MARTHA: And if you never get this consideration, the basis of all your other relationships in the world is corrupted. If you go through, then, maybe ten or fifteen years of experiencing yourself as insufficiently interesting or important to have your needs taken into consideration, unless you can find another place where you can do it . . .

ESTHER: This is the place.

MARTHA: This is the place. That's what therapy is about. It's a second chance.

ESTHER: That's right. So we've got to do it.

MARTHA: Oh, we'll do it—we've already done it, you know. The fact that we're still sitting here proves we've already done it. My crisis was over two weeks ago. You're just reacting with fear now. It's already under our belts.

ESTHER: I didn't know how bad it was until it was all over. Martha, that's typical of me, that's what I do. I don't let myself . . . I don't let it hit me until the worst of it is over. And it only began to dawn on me that you had to bring this distrust—it only dawned on me, really, last week—that you had to bring this distrust into the relationship with me, that doing so was the only way you could ever get rid of it.

MARTHA: Sure. Whatever your main conflict is, that's what you have to work on in therapy. The medium is the relationship with the therapist, and unless I really brought it in . . .

ESTHER: You would never have gotten better.

MARTHA: I would never have gotten better. But as a matter of fact, you did rewrite the part.

ESTHER: Oh, hell, I've been rewriting everything from the very beginning.

MARTHA: Yes, but at this point I didn't expect you to, I truly did not expect you would. I know better, but I didn't . . . emotionally I don't know . . .

ESTHER: You know what I think—I think you didn't quite realize that I had a stake in making whatever I wrote the best that I could. And "the best that I could" meant that it had to be based on your understanding as well as mine.

MARTHA: You see, I don't give anybody credit for that.

ESTHER: That was what nobody ever did before.

MARTHA: Right. Well, of course they had, but I had been unable to utilize it; I mean, I've met up with good will, floating through the world . . .

ESTHER: But the point is, you had to trust me in order to let me see the extent of your distrust. That's why it took so long for you to bring out your distrust.

MARTHA: If we had not been writing the book together, I don't think I would ever have gotten it anywhere—from therapy or friendship or . . .

ESTHER: Well, that's probably true, because I wouldn't have gotten in that deep with you. Probably I would have operated the way I did in that first contact, which is what "supportive" therapy is—supporting the strengths and the wisdom, and all that, of the person without . . . and that's usually enough.

MARTHA: Well, it would have been enough in a sense, because I'm still walking around. But to accomplish what we just accomplished . . .

ESTHER: I've kind of wondered—your suggesting the book. You know, unconsciously you may have known that you needed a deeper involvement. . . . No? No, well, you see, I don't think it's necessary to know it consciously. Sometimes one's unconscious is awfully, awfully smart.

MARTHA: That's possible, but I think that's giving my unconscious more credit than it deserves.

ESTHER: I'm willing to give your unconscious quite a lot of credit myself.

MARTHA: Well, I've survived quite a lot.

ESTHER: That's right, that's one of the reasons . . . I think I've given your unconscious a lot of credit all the way along. You know, going back to that long tape we did, I had the feeling that what I was doing then was trying to explain to you what you were doing back there, that I was filling in what I thought were some of the unconscious things operating with you, healthy instincts . . .

MARTHA: That came over very well, and it was quite reassuring.

ESTHER: And I think I was doing that because I felt you had probably not been aware of your healthy instincts, you had not been aware of how healthy your unconscious was in many respects. I think you've always been too quick to recognize what was wrong rather than what was right with you.

MARTHA: I think that's true.

ESTHER: That's why the supportive approach is so useful and sometimes all that is needed, because so many people are so much more aware of what is wrong with them than what is right with them. When they begin to look at what is right with them, what is wrong with them sort of falls by the wayside. It takes care of itself. But that didn't happen with you.

MARTHA: Well, it did to the extent that I was then willing to bring this up—the distrust.

ESTHER: Yes, that's right, of course it did. All right, I mustn't discount that, because all those years of work really built up enough trust in you for you to bring your full distrust to me. Also *(laughing)*, you had to know that I was strong enough to stand it.

MARTHA: Well, it didn't look as though it was easy. And it's a good thing we didn't both react at the same time because it would have been terribly difficult to deal with, much more difficult than it was.

ESTHER: Yes, I think so. I really shudder at what would have happened if we had reacted at the same time.

MARTHA: Well, I think we would still have gotten through it.

ESTHER: But I wonder how much help you do need in recognizing the "rightness," or wisdom, or whatever, of your unconscious, because I think that this is part of the problem. Part of what went wrong in the marriage was that you didn't realize how right you were about a lot of things. If you did, you didn't have the courage to say it to other people because you didn't think you'd be able to put it across.

MARTHA: Both. Both things. The main reason for that is what I was talking about last week when I spoke about double bookkeeping. To go back to the parent-child situation, when I got into the second stage, where I needed to be taken seriously and have my emotional needs as an individual human being met—as well as my survival needs—what I said to myself was: Of course, if I say my parents are wrong, then I'm saying that nobody is in control of the situation, which is terrifying. But if I say that I'm wrong, it wipes me out, I can't survive as me. So I have to say that I'm right in order to survive, but I won't really believe it, because if I say my parents are wrong, as I think they have to be, then nobody is steering the car.

ESTHER: That's terrifying, a very terrifying thing, for a kid.

MARTHA: Either I had to say there was no one in charge and the whole thing was getting off the road, or I had to say that I was wrong. It had to be one way or the other. So I commenced, and have continued to this day, to say, "I'm going to tell myself they're wrong so that I can survive as me, but actually I have to believe that they're right because I have to believe that somebody is in charge."

ESTHER: What a terrible, terrible bind.

MARTHA: It takes a lot of energy.

ESTHER: And you know, I keep feeling that if you had had any real input from other kids, I think you would not have gotten stuck on this thing, because I think that other kids would have reinforced the possibility of differing with your parents, with your being right and their being wrong, but their still being able to steer the car. I keep coming back to the thought that you didn't have any way of testing out the reality of all this, no one with whom to compare notes, and I keep thinking of this as somehow the beginning of everything. Whom could you check anything out with? Not in school, never. A scapegoated kid never has a chance, no chance whatsoever, to compare notes with other kids. Even in college, whom on earth did you have to compare notes with? Not with a bunch of smarties, all competing with one another to put themselves up and everyone else down.

**MARTHA:** Well, I had buddies in the dormitory, and I've done a fair amount of checking since then.

**ESTHER:** And then, of course, the thing that comes through as you wrote your story is how quickly you began to be able to act more and more on what you had already felt and sort of known. At first you sounded pretty helpless, but after that . . .

**MARTHA:** I'm a fast learner, and I think that was the major thing in my survival.

**ESTHER:** Okay, but this was your first opportunity, apparently, to learn that in a relationship both people count. One is not sacrificed to the other. Both can give and take and come up with a solution or compromise that is workable, that may be better than either one of them could possibly have arrived at on his own.

**MARTHA:** Yes. Well, I don't know it thoroughly, but I'm in the process of beginning to learn it, and that's a lot.

**ESTHER:** That's the reason why I've done so much rewriting, not because I was a perfectionist but because I was struggling through to a better understanding and to put that better understanding into better words, into words that would say it more clearly.

**MARTHA:** One of the reasons I'm willing to be exposed as I will be—as I already am—in the book is that it's a way of comparing notes. If you wait until you're twenty to begin the note-comparing that kids have out of the way by the time they get to kindergarten, you have to do it more explicitly and more dangerously. Because the piece of your life that's being exposed by your asking such questions is more crucial to your functioning. I'm willing to expose myself in the book because it will be a note-comparing for readers, and I'm sufficiently confident that these things that seem so bizarre are really not all that bizarre, once you get into the things that really go on in the day-to-day lives of human beings.

**ESTHER:** No, they're not so different, really. It has seemed to me all along that your marriage was comparable to the "alcoholic marriage," in which the woman is willing to make any sacrifice to keep the marriage going, no matter if the man beats her, or whatever. You know, there are some pretty bizarre things going on between alcoholic husbands and women who let themselves be treated that way.

**MARTHA:** But the book is also going to speak to women not married to alcoholics, women with husbands who are just plain ordinary neurotics but who feel quite free to load their neuroses on their wives in the intimacy of the family circle.

**ESTHER:** Yes. All this is terribly important.

MARTHA: Well, this is my neurosis again. It seems to me if something is obvious to me, then it must be obvious to everybody else.

ESTHER: No. There are therapists who don't really know these things either. They don't necessarily hear what is being said, though their hearing may be fine. And you know, I couldn't hear how distrustful you were of me until I could stand it—and I couldn't stand it until you weren't that distrustful of me anymore.

MARTHA: Now, that's very interesting. It's very important for the understanding of how therapy has to be done. People really have to hear each other.


MARTHA: There's nothing much going on. We've worked though the crisis, I think.

ESTHER: A thought that occurred to me as a result of it is that we're demanding nothing less than the best from each other.

MARTHA: Well, I don't know about you, but it's a habit with me.

ESTHER: I think from the standpoint of my work that's actually what therapy is about, in a way, but you don't just plunge in and demand the best the first day.

MARTHA: Right. But I do.

ESTHER: Well, okay, you do. That may be part of what goes wrong sometimes, because very few people will measure up to it. And you know, some quite decent people can't measure up to it. It's that kind of good-but-less-than-perfect-relationship experience that I think was so badly lacking in your earlier days. I'm not sure a person ever gets completely over something that has seriously hurt him, but it can be cut down much closer to comfort.

MARTHA: Yes, where it won't interfere with my daily life. I'm well aware that I don't trust people. I'm hardly conscious of it as I operate day by day. It rarely comes up, but it's there.

ESTHER: Well, I guess I have the feeling that when you find how much more fun and how much more comfortable it is to . . .

MARTHA: Esther, that comes under the heading of selling out for comfort . . . if you sell out the truth . . .

ESTHER: Oh, golly, you always have to put the worst possible interpretation on everything. I'm talking about the Adult; the Adult is not selling out, the Adult is . . . adult.

MARTHA: I understand that, but when my strength is down, the Parent devours the whole personality, the Parent just opens its mouth and swallows everything, and there's nothing left but that God damn rejecting Parent . . . it isn't even the parenting Parent . . .

ESTHER: Well, that's what I mean when I say it's a lot more comfortable and more fun—you know, come on in, the water's fine. I see this as inviting you to allow your Adult to come free. You don't have to be in bondage to your Parent anymore . . . like that period when you were on Atherton Island, you were free of your Parent then.

MARTHA: Yes, that was my first experience with getting free of the Parent, but somehow . . . I feel as though I'll never get free of it by myself; I need an outside view of it. I can take a detached view of many things about myself, but on this . . . because I think if I had even gone into that marriage in better shape, even given everything that was wrong with Scott . . . I don't know whether I'm dreaming or not, it seems to me that in a way I insisted on being treated the way I was. There was a period of months before the pattern was set when something more positive than was done might have been done. I don't know. It's impossible to find out.

ESTHER: Okay. It may be that you might want to try to figure it out sometime, but I don't think it's the most important thing to work on. I think the fact that you can *say* it is terribly important is really terribly important. That's a milestone! But to bother our heads now with whether you could have or couldn't . . .

MARTHA: And you know, I feel guilty about blaming my parents . . .

ESTHER: Well, let's take that word "blame" out if we can, because I don't like it; it's not a useful word. You feel guilty about looking at things in your parents' personalities that affected you adversely. What makes it a sort of scientific pursuit, from my side of the desk, is that we're simply trying to discover what were the things that affected you in ways that were not useful to you, were even actually detrimental. I realize that from your side of the desk it's going to feel just like blame, even with the fancy terms, the scientific terms, I put on it. But I think by talking about it nonjudgmentally, eventually some of what's on this side of the desk will rub off on your side of the desk.

MARTHA: Yes, I think it will. Another component here is that if I blame my parents for the things that went wrong in me, then by the very self-same logic, I'm to blame for whatever went on in my kids, for whatever difficulties they have now.

ESTHER: That's right. You can hang yourself on the same hook, if you want to.

MARTHA: Sasha and I had a lengthy discussion. We were talking about how sensitive our whole family is. She said, "I feel like I've inherited a rare disease that shortens your life, or destroys your life, or vitiates your energy, or whatever." We had started by talking about Benjy, how sensitive he is, and then about how sensitive she herself is, and we'd been through all the bad things. Sasha said, "I can't find any friends that operate at my depth," and I said, "If you want a lover or a friend to match your depth, you're not going to find very many, but there are plenty of good people around. It's just that they're as sensitive and retiring as you are, so it's hard to find them. They're rare. You will find them, but you won't find lots of them." Then later, after the conversation was over, she stuck her head out and said, "Don't you think there's a lot of good things about being the way we are?" and I said, "Sure, lots." I'm working out a lot of things with Sasha.

ESTHER: Aren't you glad that you're able to do this for her? How many parents can do this?

MARTHA: Yes. And Benjy is going great guns. You know, I've got to put something about my kids into the book. I don't know how, I'll have to . . .

ESTHER: About how good they are? Of course, that belongs.

MARTHA: I know it does, but if they object . . .

ESTHER: Well, all right, but somewhere along the line you'll be able to talk with them about it, and you're going to be able to let them read it, and you're going to be able to work out whatever you have to work out.

MARTHA: I think so, probably.


## some ending-up passages, november hours

MARTHA: The people in my unit who scapegoated me are all leaving. One is gone as of today and two will be gone as of next Friday, so things are looking up there. No matter whom they are replaced with, they can't be as bad; they won't be a clique. And you know, as this situation in which I suffered so much disintegrates and I'm the one who's left . . .

ESTHER: Yes, very interesting.

MARTHA: Yes. There were times when the only thing that kept me from asking for a transfer was the fact that they brag about having forced people out of the unit. I was damned if I was going to give them one more satisfaction. I was determined to outlast them.

ESTHER: That's perfectly good motivation.

MARTHA: I stuck in there out of pure spite, and I think I've learned something about myself and something about scapegoating in the process. Their desire to get me was what . . . I was perfectly clear when I went into this unit at work that what they were doing was ridiculous, that it was their standards that were screwy; I had no doubt at all about that. It was their desire to make me miserable that made me miserable. It wasn't anything I did, it was something I was, something in me, my very existence was unacceptable. When they saw there was something they could fasten onto, there was something unusual about me . . . what they were seeing, what it truly was, was my sensitivity. But the other thing that was different about me was that I could see their malice. Most people don't see malice unless it really hits them over the head. And because I see it, I react to it. Most people don't react this way; they just say, "Oh, fuck you!"

ESTHER: Yes. Most kids by the time they get to school have set up defenses against name-calling, and so on. As I recall it, we used to say, "Sticks and stones can break my bones but names can never hurt me." And you know, that helped. We had defenses. I think we learned that in the neighborhood long before we ever got to school, so we came to school with some kind of defense.

MARTHA: Somebody did something in the scapegoating line to me once, and I replied by calling her something, I forget what, and she said, "Sticks and stones, . . ." the whole bit, and I picked up a rock and heaved it at her. I said, "Well, if that's what it takes to hurt you, all right," and I threw the rock at her. She was telling me that the only way she could be hurt was with a stick or a stone, and I literally did it. But that's the total anger, that's where we get into what flared up, the total anger, when I would dynamite any relationship, no matter what, because that's the only recourse I have. Total, insane anger. It was my total anger. I was like a mad creature. I mean, they couldn't believe it; it frightened them.

ESTHER: Sure, that's what is meant by madness.

MARTHA: That's what is meant by madness. And then they really had me, because then I showed I was really crazy.

ESTHER: Yes, I can see how this would be. Actually, though, I think you came out somewhat better than a lot of scapegoated kids because you got angry. I think your anger was a way of saying, "I do not accept your evaluation of me." The kids who really get ruined are the kids who do accept that evaluation. You chose the label "crazy" rather than "no damn good," or whatever it was.

MARTHA: Well, I bought the "no damn good," too, over a period of years. When it kept happening to me, I thought they must have been right.

ESTHER: Okay, you bought a piece of that, but you didn't just settle for that.

MARTHA: I bought a piece of it, so it still happens that my security is the security of isolation, of anger, and that's why I could think of dynamiting the relationship between the two of us. Because when the chips are down, the only place of security is all by yourself, where you've defended yourself with your anger. That's where that position of safety originated; it was the total anger in the face of being scapegoated.

ESTHER: With so little faith in either your ability to struggle through to some position of influence, or even to be heard, so little faith in your ability to get anybody to hear you, . . . it seems to me that this has to tie in with the problem in communication. I think it was more complicated than it seemed originally because you had no faith, you'd lost your faith in the power of communication. It wasn't just that you didn't know how to communicate, or that you assumed other people already knew what you meant, but that you really had lost faith in the power of communication, so why bother to communicate?

MARTHA: Yes. When I lose my temper, when I come to the anger thing, I'm not interested in communicating, I don't care what they think of me.

ESTHER: Nor do you care whether they understand what your point is. So in a way, you give up on communication in both directions. Well, I guess when people get angry enough, that's what always happens. First they don't hear each other, and then they stop trying to get through to each other. That's the end of communication.

ESTHER: It's as though it took me until now to understand intellectually some things that I think I already understood intuitively. It's been a very gradual process.

MARTHA: What strikes me now is that I thought you were so in command of all this material.

ESTHER: Well, I couldn't be in command of things you didn't tell me.

MARTHA: But I thought I had told you. When I'd thrown out three or four hints, I thought you had the whole picture.

ESTHER: Indeed not. All kinds of things that were in your head were not in my head at all. Also, the other part of it was that you would skid away from this material when I'd try to pin you down.

MARTHA: I was afraid you were going to tell me I was all wrong.

ESTHER: And then I began to realize I don't really know exactly what happened in your therapy, how those therapists could have arrived at such conclusions, how on earth a psychiatrist could say to you, "So you see, none of that really happened."

MARTHA: I don't know whether any of them actually said it or whether I so feared it was what they were saying that it was what I heard.

ESTHER: I suspect it was halfway between. I suspect that they came up with very pointed questions or rather skeptical remarks. And I do think some therapists feel it's their job to get clients to look at all the possible negative explanations, to face up to the worst in their unconscious.

MARTHA: Right, that's it. And if you are someone who is already doing this to yourself in spades, you don't need someone to leap on that side of the seesaw.

ESTHER: To make you do it further. Well, I have a hunch . . . therapists differ quite a bit, but the ones who would have the most impact on you are the ones who would arouse the most anger and anxiety. It would seem as though everything that ever happened in your therapy was pretty much like that, but you couldn't have gotten as much better as you have over the years if it had all been bad therapy. I think that along with the bad there was good, and somehow you were able to use the good. Although the bad stayed with you, too, it didn't keep you from using what was good in what they had to offer.

MARTHA: No, I don't think it did, but it increased my anger, and that was the very problem I had to find some way of dealing with. Now I'm sort of pulling myself back together again after this long business of ours of dealing with the anger phenomenon. This last week I have felt a lot better at times, as though a load has rolled off. Incidentally, on this business you wrote about subjecting me to "bad therapy," what I feel is that we've been doing a kind of therapy that nobody has done before, and it's so much more difficult, but I don't feel I've been subjected to "bad therapy."

ESTHER: Well, there's another whole thing. That's the fact that we've had to go through a lot of anger together for you really to assimilate a lot of this past history. One reason you didn't just sit down and tell it to me all the way down the line was that you hadn't really assimilated it yourself. All you could do was live through it, that was all you could do at the time. Then all you could do for a while was to get your head together and your feet on the ground and know the ground was solid, and then. . . . So it all represented a process of assimilation and incorporation of things that you kind of knew all along, but you couldn't really afford to take them out and look at them and put them all together again. So you couldn't very well sit there and tell me: It was this and this and this and this, because you didn't have it all that together in your own thinking.

MARTHA: That's very true, particularly just now when I wrote the section on the sexual relationship between Scott and me. I was really suffering as I wrote. I've held that off most of all because it was really so bad, it was so terrible.

ESTHER: You see, you had to start with what was the safest and easiest, though none of it was really safe and easy. But you used good judgment in doing it that way, whether you thought it all out deliberately that way or not. You know, your unconscious is very intelligent.

MARTHA: I think that's true, and I think if it weren't true, I wouldn't be here.

**ESTHER:** That's right, I think your unconscious saved you all the way along the line. And that means that sometimes you were aware of it and sometimes you weren't, because sometimes the unconscious surfaces and sometimes it doesn't. So all these are things you could hardly put together in a cohesive, coherent, chronological story without a lot of thinking through, reexperiencing, and all of that. . . .

**MARTHA:** Well, it's all part of my communication problem. . . . I think other people know so much more, and I think I've told them . . . like when I threw you those hints.

**ESTHER:** Actually, I was simply taken aback when I saw you had written right at the beginning of your story that you'd thought it all over carefully and decided not to commit Scott. I looked at it and I thought: Now where did that come from? I hadn't even known you'd ever considered it. I thought the only person who had ever regarded Scott as schizophrenic was Meg Goodwin, and that was so much further along. I just didn't have those facts at all.

**MARTHA:** He was visibly psychotic almost without a break for four months.

**ESTHER:** Well, that became very clear eventually. But, of course, I think other things were involved in this, too, things like, bad as it was, you were less scared with Scott than you felt you would be without him—all kinds of very ordinary, everyday considerations, everyday, that is, for a lot of women involved in such a situation.

**MARTHA:** Very true.

**ESTHER:** But I don't think you knew that. You had the feeling that your staying with him showed some of your therapists—maybe it would "prove" to them—that you were as sick as he was. Well, it doesn't prove any such thing.

**MARTHA:** If I was as sick as he was, we'd probably both be dead. We would have starved to death.

**ESTHER:** But I can see that in bringing it out, even to me, you would be conditioned by all those implications from the past . . .

**MARTHA:** Yes, yes, yes!

**ESTHER:** So you couldn't tell me how it was because you didn't dare. If you had told me how it was, I might have reacted the way other people reacted.

**MARTHA:** That's extremely true. And that's one of the reasons I'm willing to expose myself in writing the book, so that other people will have the chance of comparing notes. Because you can't just say to people, ordinarily . . . you know, I've provoked some pretty extreme reactions, like when I once said to people I thought I knew quite well, "My husband at one point used to go down and roll in the crawl space under the house, among the spiders. . . ."

ESTHER: That isn't exactly in the category of polite conversation.

MARTHA: I realized that after I said it, but I had thought these people and I were far beyond the stage of polite conversation. After I'd opened my mouth, I realized that we were still on the polite conversation level and I'd blown it. But there are people who need to hear this kind of thing, who need to know that their own situation isn't the only situation like it in the world; it's not so terrible that they mustn't talk about it—in therapy, that is, not in polite conversation.

ESTHER: And your doing it got put off too long, for all kinds of reasons.

## from esther's notebook (later)

As I work with the transcribed material, reading and typing and editing, I have become aware of an obtuseness on my part, a very peculiar kind of obtuseness, with regard to Martha's assumption that she had told me a great deal more than she actually had. Now that we are no longer working on this material in therapy hours, it has occurred to me that it would only be natural for someone who has had many previous therapists and many different periods of therapy not to remember exactly what was covered with any one therapist at any one time. In other words, there was a perfectly logical, commonsense, ordinary explanation available for the discrepancy between what Martha thought she had told me and what she actually had told me. Then why didn't I think of that possibility when we were in the midst of our misunderstandings and confusions?

Martha does have a remarkably good memory and may be less prone to have lapses of memory than some people, but I was not aware of how very good her memory was until quite far along in her therapy, and only after I had checked it out on many different occasions. So when we were in that period of therapy, the "natural" explanation should certainly have come to mind: Martha couldn't keep exactly straight what she had said to whom over the many years of her therapy. But this thought did not occur to me at all during the hours in which we got into the subject.

Now it seems to me to have been a very good thing that I was so obtuse, for if we had dismissed the matter as "only natural," we would never have been able to make use of it in the many significant ways that we did. Judging from this experience, I think it can be useful to therapy for some things to remain unconscious—at convenient times—a kind of accidental but therapeutic non-attention to an obvious explanation that would not explain the truly important things.

There is a second example in the transcribed material of at least equal importance when I came a little closer to a deliberately planned selectivity of this sort, though primarily an unconscious process was still operating. This was in relation to the matter of Martha calling both Father Michaelson and the police at the point when she was no longer willing to listen passively to Scott's suicide threats. From time to time the thought would momentarily come to my mind that Martha must have had an intuitive recognition that Father Michaelson was a man from whom she could get what she needed, and she may have been just waiting for an opportunity to make a bid for some kind of personal relationship with him. And this "last-straw" situation may have seemed the closest to such an opportunity that she was likely to get! But whenever this thought would come to mind, I was neither with Martha nor with my notebook, and by the time I might have remarked on it or made a note of it, the thought had once again completely slipped away. Had I just once thought of it in a therapy hour, I feel sure that Martha would immediately have agreed, and much of the creative controversy around this episode would never have developed for us to use. (Martha has just now read this and agrees that on some level the intuitive bid for a relationship with Father Michaelson had definitely been operating.)

MARTHA: Another thing I'd like to get into is the whole business of acting out of anger.

ESTHER: Well, I was so thoroughly trained out of acting out my anger that I don't have an instinctive understanding of it . . . and I was trained to be scared of other people's acting out of anger. You know, I think I've done very well with you in that I didn't just run away screaming.

MARTHA: I can see why you would be very frightened of me. I pose a unique threat to you.

ESTHER: You pose a unique threat, period. But you were a particularly therapeutic experience for me, because most of my clients don't have that much need to beat on me. Well, acting out of anger . . .

MARTHA: Okay. My parents pretended never to be angry. One of the things they did to me—not necessarily along this line, but one of the things they did—was to present me with loaded choices, which they then pretended were free choices. One of my acting-out-of-anger patterns is still to do what I did then, and that's to take the loaded choice and to behave to them as though the loaded choice were a free choice. That is, they would say in essence, "You can do this and we'll reward you, or you can do that and we'll punish you, but please feel free to choose." Well, I would take the one for which they would punish me.

ESTHER: You were surely going to get me to do that, too, weren't you?

MARTHA: Uh-huh. Right.

ESTHER: And I guess you got all your previous therapists to punish you?

MARTHA (laughing): I don't know. You did well, let me tell you. From my years of experience, you did extremely well.

ESTHER: But you didn't get them all to . . . actually, Meg Goodwin didn't punish you.

MARTHA: No, but she rewarded me so heavily that I was afraid to get angry at her. . . . Okay. One of the acting-out-of-anger things that I still do is not to take anything nice from or do anything nice for people I'm down on. I want them to know I hate them.

ESTHER: Well, that's very difficult for me to understand. (Laughing) I guess I'll have to work on that.

MARTHA: Yes, it's very difficult for anybody to understand. Once you've really got to me, you're going to get it back in spades the rest of your life. I'll never forgive you, never, never, never, never. I'll never speak to you except on extreme pressure of business. I will thank you very coldly if you do something for me. My hostility is unrelenting. I've been very angry at you, but you ain't seen nothing, just nothing.

ESTHER: Now, why have I deprived myself of this pleasure? It suggests to me the idea of being comfortable about one's death wishes. You know, I can't really be comfortable with them, nor do I feel that I would be able to be happy with what you're describing, yet I think I'm sort of enjoying it vicariously.

MARTHA: I think you are. Other people enjoy my hostility vicariously, too, though I don't do this kind of thing often. The reason it's coming out now is that when these people scapegoated me, they didn't know what they were letting themselves in for.

ESTHER: Well, I'm really trying, you know . . . it's hard for me . . . trying to understand.

MARTHA: You know, I've been surprised . . . I haven't realized that people are so appalled at hostility. Hostility is part of the world. And that anybody would be horrified that I would be deliberately hostile shocked me, because I want to say, "Where have you been?" I'm not hostile often, and everybody who knows me at all well knows that I'm usually a very cheerful and charitable soul, but . . .

ESTHER: You know what I think is operating. Hostility is the next step after anger. I think everyone can somehow understand anger, but then the elaboration of anger, which is hostility . . .

MARTHA: Oh, I'm very elaborated. I never will initiate . . . but if someone takes up arms against me, I'll give it back in spades.


MARTHA: When I finally sat down to figure out just why these women scapegoated me, I had a hard time figuring anything out.

ESTHER: Okay. So you don't really understand people like that. They are so different from you that it's very hard for you, even by a stretch of your imagination, to figure out what they are like or how they would feel.

MARTHA: They think they're dumb, I can see that, but I haven't made them feel inferior. I've gone out of my way to make them feel they know something.

ESTHER: But no matter what you do, there is something in people—and I think it's stronger in some people than in others—there is a feeling of being threatened, a feeling of being inferior, an unbearable kind of comparison that arises when someone else is obviously brighter.

MARTHA: Well, I think I understand that somewhat. I have friends who go to the ballet whenever they want to go to the ballet. Consequently, they've been to the ballet hundreds of times. They consider me their equal, which I am. When you set me down with them to something and we all start equal, my reactions to it are on a par with theirs. But when you need as the basis something you can know only if you've seen a particular ballet performed hundreds of times—you know, how does this performance compare with that one?—and I've only seen it maybe once . . .

ESTHER: You can't compete with that.

MARTHA: You can't. If we were to sit down and talk about survival, how to survive without enough money or enough of anything, I would put *them* in the shade. It's not that I'm not their equal, but it makes me feel very inferior; I feel very uncomfortable. I get very nervous and frightened, and I can see how people must react to me, but it isn't anybody's fault.

ESTHER: It isn't their fault.

MARTHA: It isn't their fault.

ESTHER: That's right, it's nobody's fault. Whatever advantages people have had, unless they've stolen and cheated and lied or whatever to get them, it isn't their fault. They were born with this or that or the other advantage; it wasn't anything they did, yet those are the very things that seem to arouse tremendous resentment or envy.

MARTHA: I've never taken credit for my brains. I know perfectly well that I didn't cause myself to be bright. There's no credit due me for that.

ESTHER: But other people are going to resent it. I know that I'm glad not to be exposed to people who have obvious advantages over me. I stay away from people like that. I don't want to put myself through that kind of thing. Why should I? So I don't.

MARTHA: They make very good ballet-going companions.

MARTHA: There's a new person in the unit, a guy, who is vaguely interesting. He's coming out of a bad divorce, I think. The reason he is interesting is that men, in large groups of women, don't usually say something in defense of men, but he does. He came out yesterday with something about how so many women marry for financial security, sounding really bitter. He says it, the whole thing.*

ESTHER: Yes, that's very interesting. You can learn a lot from a man who comes out in the open with his feelings about the unfairness to the man.

MARTHA: Right. I need to hear that; you never hear that. And from the standpoint of getting a fair hindsight view of Scott, I'm interested in what this man has to say.

MARTHA: I'd like to talk some more about my acting out of anger. It's connected with my original position of isolation. It doesn't matter if I alienate everybody, when the chips are down it really doesn't matter, because my original view of myself is totally isolated. That's where I started from, and that's where I retreat to. I don't have anything to lose, really. I've come to realize over the last few years that it scares the daylights out of everybody.

**ESTHER:** The question that comes to my mind about it . . . I would imagine that for most people there has to be at least some unconscious—if not conscious—guilt about acting out of anger, particularly for someone like you, with your ideals for yourself.

**MARTHA:** It's very unconscious, though.

**ESTHER:** Well, that's why I think it's important, you see, because if there is some unconscious guilt operating, it's very, very deep; it's truly unconscious. And in that case, when all of a sudden you reverse your whole image from the positive to the negative, could it not be that the negative image is then fed not only by all the things that people had done and said to you throughout your past, but also by the unconscious guilt?

**MARTHA:** Yes, that sounds very likely.

**ESTHER:** Which could make the difference, it seems to me. It could account for your continuing to fall back into that negative image when I wouldn't expect you still to be doing it, with the amount of understanding you now have.

**MARTHA:** Yes, I think that's a good point, that there's something extra in there.

**ESTHER:** But if there is this deeply buried kind of unconscious guilt . . . it's the most difficult thing to uproot that I know, it's the toughest to get at. I've had experience with it within myself and also with clients. You know, I think what alerted me to this question about you may be the fact that I've asked myself why I didn't feel guilty about something I would have expected myself to feel guilty about. And what I came up with was that what I felt was shame. I felt shame that I didn't live up to my ideal of myself. I didn't feel guilt.*

**MARTHA:** That sounds very much like me.

**ESTHER:** But I had all those inexplicable symptoms that I was torturing myself with. I had noticed that other people were constantly talking about how guilty they felt about this, that, and the other, so I thought I must have a lot of unconscious guilt. But that wasn't the way it felt. I didn't feel guilty.

**MARTHA:** I think this may be one of the very deep bonds you and I have. I think we have this in common. I think it is a very uncommon phenomenon. Many of my therapists have tried to get me to discuss my guilt and are flummoxed that I don't feel what they expect me to feel. I think this was one reason why they thought me very odd.

**ESTHER:** Well, I didn't think of it as highly unusual until I started to realize that I simply wasn't feeling all the guilt that a lot of other people were constantly feeling. Of course, I was doing everything I was supposed to, the very best I could. I was being "good," that's all I seemed to know how to be at the time. That might account for the fact that I didn't need to feel much guilt, and I think that's the other part of it. And you're that way, too.

So, for example, if 99 percent of the time we're operating on the basis of the very best we can do, then we're maybe 99 percent "good." That leaves 1 percent "not good," and we should be feeling it. But if we're not, that 1 percent gets buried. And if you stockpile 1 percent on 1 percent on 1 percent . . .

MARTHA: Right. You get compound interest on it.

ESTHER: Yes, you get to the point where you think you're never bad. You're always so good that you don't have anything to have guilt feelings about, but this plain isn't true. It's just that we keep up a pretty high average, and we kid ourselves and other people, too.

MARTHA: Yes, but I think the dynamics of the thing are the reverse. I think the reason you and I forced ourselves to do everything right 99 percent of the time if we possibly could was because of the danger of the buried guilt. We knew what the guilt would do to us if we didn't get our 99 percent in.

ESTHER: Oh, yes, we would torture ourselves to death.

MARTHA: And if we found ourselves 5 percent off, we'd be in the soup.

ESTHER: Okay, but you know, this is ridiculous . . . you don't have to do this. It doesn't seem to me that . . . I don't seem to be torturing myself anymore, so it suggests to me that I must not be burying a lot of guilt anymore.

MARTHA: I don't think I'm adding to it now, particularly, except by this acting out of anger.

ESTHER: I'm convinced that on some unconscious level you do have to feel some guilt about your anger. . . . I think you do, because I think it's excessive. If it were only the amount of anger that was needed to accomplish your purpose . . .

MARTHA: Yes, that's it, that's it! The bomb instead of the flyswatter.

MARTHA: One of the things I've been coming to . . . one of the conclusions I'm coming to is that the subject of equality and inequality hasn't been nearly enough explored. I think a lot of marriage dynamics, for example, circle around feelings of inequality.

ESTHER: Oh, yes. Well, I called it competitiveness, but I think inequality is the better word. I think it becomes competitiveness.

MARTHA: Right. I think competitiveness is the result, but I think the name of the problem is inequality. And that's what arouses my hostility, my anger. It's the sense of inequality. I need my anger, I need my rages to equalize things. And I think the thing in me that calls out this response in other people in the first place is the sense of inequality.

I've seen how one of the women at work tries to keep up with some of the conversation that goes on, and it's clear that she'll never make it. I'm finding myself a little sorry for her, even though she was one of those who went along with some of the scapegoating. I've been in circumstances recently where I'm never going to be able to keep up with the people I'm talking to, and I'm beginning to know what it feels like.

And there's a young girl at work, in another unit, who is very beautiful and very bright. She's pursuing a guy in the office who is also being pursued by a dumpy girl who's not very pretty and has an illegitimate baby. The beautiful girl is in terror lest the guy will choose the other girl. She's taken to talking to me at lunch hour; she tells me she feels this other girl is playing dirty pool to get the guy, and it makes her very mad. I said to her, "Imagine what you look like to Bertha. To Bertha, you've got every advantage over her. Why shouldn't she play dirty pool?" So I can see it in other people, and I can see it a little in myself. But it's just at the beginning.

ESTHER: Because you suffered so much on this score without any clues to go by, to tell you what was going wrong.

MARTHA: And it occurs to me now that I have frequently been irritated by people who weren't able to keep up with me on something, but that was before I got into a situation where I wasn't keeping up with the people in it either.

ESTHER: Well, I think that once you get off this hook, you begin to be able to enjoy many more kinds of things and many more kinds of people.

MARTHA: I've always been able to relate on an equality basis to my clients at work, which is a big resting place, I think.

ESTHER: Well, that's probably why you and I are doing the kind of work we're doing. It's as though we have to give the gift of equality—to ourselves and to our clients. I don't quite understand what I mean by that.

MARTHA: Oh, I understand exactly what you mean by that, I think.

ESTHER: Well, I have a fantasy that you're going to take this problem, this question, and you're going to work it out yourself. Now, maybe that's a fantasy and maybe it isn't. But I think this is what I've been waiting for.

## from esther's notebook

How could I have forgotten, when I wrote about my own experiences, that I was in group therapy for about six months before I went to graduate school? I value what I learned in that group very much, and I have shared it with both clients and colleagues many times. I was one of the first to push for group therapy at my agency, and I have conducted quite a few groups of my own. How could I now have left out my own experience with it?

Once again, I seem to have suffered a peculiar kind of obtuseness, for the most important thing that happened to me in group therapy is directly related to a question that lies at the heart of much of Martha's troubles. Yet it did not come to mind at all, neither when I was writing nor in any of our interchanges. Strange, because it so clearly belongs in here somewhere.

I was in a group in which the members were all women, though the therapist was a man. One of the members reminded me of the kind of person whom I had always thought of as "acting superior." I'm sure the exact meaning to me of that phrase shifted somewhat with each different instance of such an encounter. In general, I always felt that the person either just automatically felt superior to me, without giving the matter a thought, or was deliberately trying to make me feel inferior. Whichever it was, I always resented and disliked such people—especially, I think, when they were women—and avoided them as much as possible. But here was one in my therapy group, and there was no way I could avoid *her*.

She represented to me, all rolled up into one, the little girl whose father was a judge and who lived in the beautiful big house on the hill to which I was never invited; the girls who were in social groups that never included me; all the teen-age girls who had nicer clothes than I and were pretty and popular and self-confident, which I was not; all the students who "got ahead" in some way I was afraid to try; and, I think, every woman in my adult life who had any kind of advantage over me whatsoever. But what counted with me the most in the actual therapy group, I'm sure, was the fact that this group member was able to gain and hold the attention of the therapist for long periods of time—which I, quite deliberately, would not try to do. What she said to him came from a context of past and present circumstances equivalent to those of the other "superior" people I had encountered throughout my life. As she went on and on, I found myself growing angrier and angrier. If my reaction was shared by the other members of the group, I was not aware of it, nor was I concerned for them at all. At that point, I was concerned only for me.

On joining the group, I had promised myself that for the first time in my life I would allow myself to say exactly what I thought. I had already found, however, that even here I usually tempered my words somewhat, although now as a free and conscious choice, not as an anxiety-imposed necessity. Whether I felt that this one group member did not deserve such consideration, I don't know, but I found myself finally bursting out to her, "I wish you would stop acting so superior to me all the time!" She stopped short, looked at me silently for a few moments, and then said quietly, "I'm only trying to get admitted to equality."

Martha and I, having completed our project, were talking of other, newer concerns when I finally asked her whether I had ever told her about my experience in group therapy, and I found that I had not. So I told her this story, and when I finished, she said, "That helps me a lot." But she had, of course, already learned to handle the problem without the help of my little story.

The notebook started this way: It usually happens when I like or admire a man that I project onto him, read into his attitude toward me, a dislike of myself. The historical reasons for this are not far to seek; the solution lies far in the future, if anywhere at all. At the time I'm writing about, I was hardly even aware that it was something I was doing.

Okay. Last spring two incidents occurred that set off explosions in my feelings, and they occurred within a week of each other. Both had to do with men I greatly like and admire. In each case, the man moved markedly in my direction, expressing obviously sincere liking and perhaps even admiration. After the second incident, I was plunged into incoherent pain. I cried and cried, I didn't know why. I couldn't get the incidents out of my head; I knew they were the reason, but for God's sake, they were both complimentary. What's to cry?

I was gradually able to tie it into a period in my past life, the period when I was expecting Becky, when I felt that if I could only live without any hope, in true despair, I could manage to function; that it was hope, and the pain of hoping for what I did not and could not have, that was my real enemy.

One morning at work I left my desk and sat in the dark in the women's lounge, crying and crying. Gradually, a couple of sentences of explanation came together in my head. I blew my nose, marched back to my desk, and wrote:

"To be a person who *cannot* be loved is painful but bearable. It is an evil in the natural order, somewhat like a famine or an earthquake. One can grit one's teeth and cope with it, with whatever courage or endurance one can bring to bear. After all, nothing can last forever; bearing with it to the end is not so bad because the end is always inevitable.

"But to be a person who *could* be loved and is not, is unbearable. Then hope becomes an element, and the most painful element. Conflict is constant and excruciating.

"And since love and hope are both qualities that outlast time, one cannot visualize any end at all to the conflict and the pain."

# 9
# Martha's Notebook

After I had written it down, I felt better, as if I were on my way to healing. So I began to write things down in a spiral notebook I keep in my desk.

I found I felt better after I'd written my feelings out, and it had the unexpected effect of making it easier to sit at the typewriter and get the chronological, historical, autobiographical information on paper—one source fed the other.

It had another unexpected benefit. By looking back to entries written in the past, I came to see that a number of emotional states and experiences that I took to be one-of-a-kind happenings when I experienced them are no such thing. They are repeated experiences and occur in observable patterns. To know that brings me much nearer to being able to unknot some of my own emotional tangles.

I think psychotherapy in everyday life is the norm. To work out your own problems in the context of and with the help of your everyday relationships—with friends and relatives and fellow workers—is the normal way to handle crises. You only need professional psychotherapy when that normal pattern for some reason or other breaks down.

Watch it! This is a good one to work on right now because it is active and concerns a new situation but runs precisely parallel to an old habit. Writing a book jointly with Esther: She, of course, agreed to do this before she knew what I could do. I am producing substandard and unusable material for my half of the venture, but she can hardly tell me that. What will she do when she decides she wants out of the project?

Factors in myself tending to mental illness or instability: I'm not sure any amount of love and acceptance would have been enough. Perhaps some children have a need for love so extreme that nothing could ever be enough to fill it. (I think Erik Erikson says something like that about the little autistic girl he discusses in *Childhood and Society*.)

I'm an absolutist and need to test things out to the furthest limit. And I'm extremely sensitive. I don't know what that means exactly, but I think it has something to do with sensory bombardment —with a lot of input, too much hearing, seeing, and so on, registering; and I think it probably has to do with the body itself.

I think intelligence may have been a contributing factor. It makes the normal protections of childhood unavailable to you if you can simply see that the explanations offered to you are not so.

Factors in my family tending to mental illness or instability: My parents don't seem to have been able to manage a planned pregnancy. Annette was conceived out of wedlock. Irene was born thirteen months later. Then, when they were sure that the family was complete, smack in the middle of the depression, there I was.

My mother had a passion for insisting that her fantasies were reality. She insisted for years that both my sisters were redheads and that I had naturally curly hair. To this day she will still tell you what a happy child I was.

My position in the family in respect to our relative ages was a serious handicap. I was six and a half years younger than Irene and seven and a half years younger than Annette. I was, therefore, really the only child in a family of adults, and there were no neighborhood children or children of close friends for me to make common cause with. I was the only person who didn't know the ordinary pieces of information, the basic information, one needs to operate in the world. Much worse, no learning or growing experience of mine was a thrill to anybody else. "The kids" already knew all that. None of my triumphs were triumphs. The thing had already been done, somehow definitively done. It was like being the ten thousandth person to scale Everest.

A difference between Esther and myself that I have been a long time discovering is our attitude toward details. To Esther, they are largely irrelevant. She wants to get to the main points quickly and move on, and when I go into a lot of detail about things that have happened to me, she tends to feel that I'm blocking. To me, any happening is intensely individual and the details provide nuances, shades of feeling that can alter the meaning of a transaction totally. Therefore, I try to give all the details I can, which I think sometimes strikes Esther as a waste of time. For her they are largely irrelevant; for me they're vital.

One of the keys to saner interaction is going to be not having it *matter* so much.

When we first began to work together on the book and began to become, so to speak, more personally acquainted, Esther wondered aloud why she had shared so few details of her own life with me during the course of the therapy. She said that she often says more about herself to clients than she had with me and wondered why.

It seemed to me that her sharing had been on another level and, in a sense, a more profound one. I did not know, for example, how many children she had, but when I asked her if she knew *Let Us Now Praise Famous Men,* her reply that she knew and loved the book, that it had had a profound influence on her, was in a sense a more intense personal fact of her life than more simple and obvious facts might have been.

One of the factors that has been of the most help in the relationship between us has been the sense I have had that because she is a person like me in many important ways, she faces the same problems as she confronts the world. It doesn't matter to me that many of her solutions to the problems are different from my own, or that some of them are only partly successful, or that some of the problems remain unsolved. That other people face the same problems reassures me that the problems are not totally of my own manufacture. That others can solve or at least live with those problems reassures me that I can live with or solve them, too. That's really all the help I need. I can take it from there.

On guardedness—the open or closed stance in regard to the rest of the world: I can't remember when I took up my variation of it—I'm closed on some levels, but mainly very open. I've recently had encounters with a couple of people who in some way really rocked me and started me off on a new line of thinking about self-defense of a certain sort. Both of them struck me as extraordinarily open men, and the absence of the usual barriers told me something about my usual modus operandi that I had never considered before.

For Martin Evans, openness is, I think, a tenet of his own personal metaphysics. (Well, with everyone who lives that way, it's first of all an instinct. What else it is, I'm not sure. I need to talk to a couple of really open players and pick their brains a bit. Which feels as if it might be somewhat of a risky undertaking, for me at least.) Martin, I think, believes in believing, in people being taken on trust, in the creative existential happening. I sense that he is a fellow absolutist and has in mind a sort of ultimate Platonic model that he is pursuing, but it is still at its very deepest level an impersonal thing. The decision he makes to speak to you at the most intimate and personal level either he or you can maintain is not made exactly *despite* the quality with which you answer back, for he is obviously not indifferent to quality and it is apparent that his standards of quality are extremely high. No one will endure lying about his most deeply held values less than Martin. He cares, then, about how well you respond, but his decision to trust you isn't based primarily on *you;* it is based on a very deep sense of the rightness and inevitability of openness itself. That is what gives even a close contact with him a sense of detachment and serenity. I don't know anybody who can bestow a sense of approval the way Martin Evans can. The combination of open stance and high standards makes his rewards very rewarding. You know for sure that he would not lie, but he tells you all the good there is, very directly.

Tim Aaronson is a totally different kettle of fish. My sense of what goes on with him is very different from what I feel goes on with Martin. I felt Aaronson testing first, in very much the way that I test, making a decision and then opening up on his own specific vulnerabilities. I didn't feel I was participating in a general principle. I felt he picks his people, and I got picked.

Martin makes himself vulnerable in the area of values and in self-revelation of how deeply he feels and cares about many things. Aaronson was kidding about a totally different kind of thing—aging and coming death, how men stand toward intelligent women—the kind of thing that if you open your mouth to the wrong people, you stand to get your metaphorical teeth knocked down your throat. (As who should know better than I?) It wasn't that I think he does this rarely. On the contrary, I think he does it often; I just don't think he does it all the time. It came over to me with an impression of great security, as if he were ready to handle whatever came up, even if everybody threw the rules away totally, and I felt that he was not prone to the kind of psychological murder men commit when their backs are to the wall. It is rather dangerous for a man in a room with two intelligent women to talk about men's reactions to intelligent women. It is as delightful as it is surprising to come across somebody who is willing to take that risk with such élan.

Open and closed stance continued—subsection, myself: I am closed about my intellectual and intuitive valuations in the sense that I readily discuss them only with people I have at least some reason to consider my intellectual equals. That, perhaps, doesn't make me many friends. It is with experiences and with feelings that I constantly give myself away with both hands.

The reasoning behind it is that I think the experiential and emotional components of *everybody's* life are just about identical and just about equal. All of us run through the same range of feelings in living out our private lives. Concealing them from each other, not admitting that each of us daily experiences anger, grief, shame, frustration, divides us unnecessarily from one another and causes each of us to believe that only he experiences these things. It is not necessary for any of us to bear the resulting sense of alienation and guilt. I live with my own mouth open, regaling everybody who cares to listen—and a great many who don't—with all the negative and positive details of my chaotic life, and I am very widely believed to be a fool for doing so.

It doesn't seem foolish to me. At the very least, it keeps my head well ventilated. At its very best, it leads very quickly to rapport with enormously diverse people; we may perhaps not have two ideas in common, but we can look at each other and experience a very deep and real bond of human fellowship. That seems to me so great a good that it is worth taking a substantial risk to have it. On those rare occasions when you find that there's intellectual or intuitive parity between you as well, you can find yourself talking really straight to some really fine people with virtually no waste of time or energy. It's a very economical method for making quick, vital human contact. It is not a particularly efficient method. Open people don't exactly grow on trees. I am widely thought a fool, as I said. People tend to feel that self-revelation is done only because you can't help yourself. (I remember explaining to Bette and Tina, who sit behind me at work, that I don't live this way because I'm stupid; I do it because I make a conscious choice to do so. I know Bette feels that these things just slip out without my being able to prevent them and that I don't know why they get me into trouble.)

Beyond the rewards for me, though they are real and substantial, I see an open life-style as a didactic method. My first and last view of myself is as a teacher of sorts (is that common with Open Absolute players, I wonder?). I firmly believe that, screwed up as the human race is, we are meant to live in vital emotional contact with each other and to help and support each other. That would have to mean setting aside petty ideas of our own dignity in order to explore and confirm the dignity of an intensely real brotherhood and partnership with one another. It can begin with me. I'll take the risks and I'll take the consequences.

In the four years after Becky died, four families of very close friends lost children, and each time I went down again to the bottom with the parents, and my own agony was reenacted all over again. Just about nine months after Becky's death, Mark, a bright, happy four-year-old, began to seem listless and ill. A quick diagnosis of leukemia. In less than six weeks, he was dead.

Six months later, Tim, the fifteen-year-old son of friends and neighbors, was killed. He and a buddy sneaked out in the middle of the night and stole a car. The cop who pulled them over inexplicably drew his gun and shot Tim dead.

A year later, eleven-year-old Maria, while at a summer camp, went in over her head to try and save a drowning companion. The other child was saved. Maria drowned.

And last, and closest to home, Rosemary, who had been my foster daughter and my friend, was asphyxiated in her sleep during an epileptic seizure.

In the face of all that pointless and unmerited suffering, there really isn't anything to say. Even "Why?" makes no sense.

Remembered from my work with Dr. Knight: "Martha, there is a quality in some of your actions that for lack of another word I can only call mischief. I hope you will remember how fond the Germans have been of Till Eulenspiegel—ever since they got him safely hanged."

Wrote the Kirkpatrick Hospital section of the book and feel a lot of self-doubt and depression. I still feel that of all of us at that time I was most oriented to the reality situation. I still feel that at the time of Becky's death and my hospitalization, Scott showed his hand most openly. But still I feel a lot of self-doubt and depression.

Childhood dreams remembered: I dreamed these two repeating dreams for years.

1. It is deep winter. The streets are covered with snow and slippery with ice. The State Street bridge over the Mississippi is detached at both ends and steeply arched like a huge steel Japanese moon bridge. It moves back and forth over the river on cable. It is night. I can see the icy river far below. I am on the slippery slope of the bridge, desperately trying not to slide off the open end into the river. My family is there on the bridge. They are trying to push me off.

2. I am on a streetcar, alone among strangers. I am traveling to an unknown destination. I've never been there, and I am not sure where to get off the streetcar, or where to go from there. The ride goes on and on indefinitely; the mood is of intense and concentrated anxiety.

I have had both of those dreams hundreds of times, but neither one, now, for several years.

When I was about eight years old, my sister Annette, who would have been about fifteen, dreamed and related to the family the following:

1. Our mother was insane. She was prowling through the house with a butcher knife trying to find me to kill me. Annette was trying to hide me behind a chair.

2. It was a cold dark day. Annette was standing at the end of a long dock leading far out into a deserted lake. I was in the water, drowning. She was trying to hold me, but I kept slipping through her fingers.

She must have seen fairly clearly that I was in serious danger.

Some exploratory definitions:

*Pragmatic Open-Stance Players.* Ability to make contact across the board, withholding of contact on some occasions. Above all, the belief that they themselves have a right, as good a right as anybody, to define the here-and-now situation according to their own lights. Aristotelians. The Buddha.

*Absolute Open-Stance Players.* Ability to make contact across the board, the feeling that they ought not to make exceptions, a feeling of failure when they do, however reasonably, withhold contact. Belief that the situation is defined elsewhere, not by "the others" but in some kind of Platonic Ideal. Platonists. Jesus.

Open Position: How, when, and why to choose your defenses.

What really saves my family life right now is the unanimity in all our feelings about which goals are most important. It shows up, for example, in our decisions on how the money gets spent. We all agreed that the very last money we had for the month should be spent on the veterinary bill to keep the cat from dying instead of on groceries. (We improvised on what was in the house.) We all agreed that the insurance money from the burglary claim should be spent to replace the stereo that was stolen rather than, for example, for a TV. I think that kind of agreement between parents and teen-age children is relatively rare, and it gives all of us a lot of positive reinforcement, besides saving us all a lot of hassle in our lives together.

My paramount demand of the world is for equality in relationships. I won't tolerate anything else or anything less. I think I suffered a great deal in my childhood from the manifest lack of equality in my family, and it has left me permanently intolerant in any situation in which I feel I'm "not as good as" somebody else or am being underrated in some way. It is the basis of all my hostility dealings with the world, including, but not limited to, my current work situation.

One of the sources of my immense fund of depression and frustration and anger is the feeling that I have been sent out into the world underequipped in numberless ways: I have no money, no training or education except what I've been able to scrape together myself, no time, my health is terrible—yet I feel I'm expected to "produce" on an equal basis with people with none of these problems. For example, my neighbors get upset because I don't keep my yard neat. In actual fact, it is a mess. I don't like to look at it either. I crave absolute respectability with a very great craving!

But all of the neighbors either pay someone to work on their yards, which I can by no means afford to do, or have enough bodily strength to do the work themselves, which I likewise don't have, or at the very least get some enjoyment out of the work itself, which heaven only knows I do not. If their objections ever get verbalized, I could defend myself verbally. However, since they only glare at the weeds on my lawn (my lawn *is* weeds), short of putting up an explanatory billboard, I don't even have a means of defense.

Down with bricks without straw!

Understanding doesn't bring forgiveness; at least it doesn't for me. I can understand why Scott turned out the way he did. I've met his family and heard his childhood stories. I know, too, that he was often in great pain during the time we were married. I know somewhat, too, what forces made my parents, forces in society and in their own families. I know that they were made by circumstances beyond their control and that they often suffered.

But I don't care. They have collectively taken away years of my life that can never be given back to me. That they didn't *intend* that it should be this way matters not at all. Especially, I cannot forgive Scott's very obvious pleasure in constructing the situations that, during our marriage, caused me so much pain. His recognition of the choices involved was obvious, as was the deliberation with which he made the choices. I'm sorry for him, in an abstract sort of way, but I will be infinitely pleased never to see him again.

Similarly, I know that it's silly to blame my sisters for things they did when they were nine or ten years old. Of course they weren't responsible, not in any adult sense of the word. But my sense of alienation, at least from Irene, is unbridgeable. I see my own kids interacting with each other, talking, laughing, giving comfort and support, and all I can think is, "Where was that world, for me?" Intellectually, I can understand. Emotionally, I doubt that I ever will.

I go through the motions of caring about my parents. I know that they care about me as best they can. I care about them as best I can, too. That's just not very much.

There's a great puddle of cold in my very middle, like liquid nitrogen. Everything that comes near it is instantly frozen and instantly fragile, apt to be broken off the minute it is touched.

I realize that from the social point of view, the above is very reprehensible. I should at least be willing to pretend. I don't care about that either. I won't say that I care when I don't. When you finally come to that place inside me, I am cold, cold, cold. And my feelings about being cold are cold.

Dee Proctor (she casts her own small sculpture) told me, "I just bought some silver nuggets, and a friend ripped me off. I'm not closemouthed, I was really excited, and she's my friend. Why did she put me through this? It's not the money I mean. I've got a pay check coming, that's okay. Now I have to learn to be more careful. You don't become a better person that way."

There's a difference, I think, in the ways that Pragmatic and Absolute Open-Stance players behave about love, but I need to explore the heads of some other players before I can put my finger on what it is. All Open players leave themselves open to devastating love experiences. That's what the Closed position is all about, just exactly that, protection against vulnerability in love. But granted the Open position, some people get lacerated less; finding themselves in what might be called the Shakespeare Sonnet position, where all that's left for you is to wish devotedly for the greatest good for the person you love, and very little else (a position where a lot of love goes out and precious little comes in). Some people handle that far better than others. I would like to know why.

I used to handle that one superbly. Now I can't handle it at all. I can't even figure out if it means that I've progressed or regressed. The difference, I think, has to do with being *grounded*. The Absolutist is off the ground, in a sort of mystical state that effectively severs contact with bread-and-butter reality. (I am thinking, for example, of watching Martin Evans conducting the Bach *St. John Passion*. He was very obviously in something closely resembling a mystical state. An immense amount of energy was moving through him, but it was evident that he was not grounded.)

Pragmatic players keep their contact. They sustain as much pain; there's no difference in that. But Open Pragmatists, who stay grounded when the energy—love, music, emotion, whatever—flows through them, seem to me more apt to become damaged in the process, become contaminated with bitterness and fear. It is a much more dangerous position to play from. (But I think their overall aim is not so high as the Absolutists'.)

I think the reason I was better able to work with social workers rather than with therapists with only a psychiatric background is mainly that social workers are more experienced in taking reality situations into account. I think psychiatrists are somewhat more apt to be prisoners of theory.

Transference phenomena: I don't make a classical transference, a dependency relationship, because I never had the original experience with parents and siblings on which that arrangement is modeled. I could never trust my family all that much.

Another trip through the Shakespeare sonnets, enjoying reading them critically, trying to set them in a sequence (not seriously, just as a kind of game). It struck me that of all the hundreds of times I have read them, the only one I can say from memory all the way through is XC . . . "If thou wilt leave me, do not leave me last. . . ." Read, as if for the first time, XXIII, XLIX, LXXIV, all of which speak of endings.

How do people learn to trust one another? The knowledge of the approaching death of love is to me the one factor in any relationship that governs every other factor. And how to brace myself for the end long, long before . . .

Love of beauty for itself alone: A world exists apart from the exigencies of daily living. It is not an inhuman or antihuman world, for its values are drawn from the deepest and most real level of human experience. But it is apart from the uncertainties and pressures of everyday life, a world of order and value. To move in that world refits me again for the struggle that must be made in the day-to-day world. There my courage and faith in the ultimate triumph of humanity are restored. There I can rest, not to hide myself away from the struggle but to renew myself to continue the struggle.

Beauty and order exist apart from me. The muddle I make in my own life cannot destroy nor diminish them, cannot shut me away from them. They are a source of happiness, a happiness that is able to overcome the world of human disorder and sorrow.

There are people who speak of poetry as if it were the antithesis of reality, or at least extraneous to it: "That's poetic, but of course it isn't *true.*" On the contrary, to people who love and understand it, poetry—in fact, art in all its forms—is the essence of reality, the true core of the truth. To understand it is to know the bones, the true internal structure, of the real world.

Esther writes that she does not commit herself to doing therapy with a client until she comes to understand, not the answers, but the basic questions. What are my basic questions in therapy? These, perhaps:

> What level of functioning can I hope to attain?
> How much can I trust "the others"?
> What are the proper uses of my sensitivity?
> How much of my past trouble did I myself cause?

Is it possible for me to change the way I react to others' evaluation of me?

I have just about finished writing the section on Ann's hysterical aphasia and what happened to me then. It was hard to write—I sat at the typewriter and cried and cried. Gradually I've come to see what happened to me then. It was most of all the time when I bought, accepted as real, the whole negative image of myself so lovingly worked at by Scott and my parents before him. And juxtaposed in time, as this writing has been, with the collapse I experienced when I first went into the new unit at work, I see for the first time quite clearly how my "illness," my "breakdowns," come about.

My negative self-image exists partly as a historical accident. Meeting other people or other circumstances at crucial times in my life would have mitigated it. If I had not been born during the depression, my family would have been far gladder to see me. If I had married Dick, who adored me, rather than Scott, who rather noticeably did not, it would have altered things a lot.* If Dorothy Jackson had not been called to jury duty, if the crop of psychiatric residents had been better that year—well, anyway, it exists partly for accidental reasons and partly because I have worked on it myself, as a means of buying love: "I'm not very good, so you don't have to love me very much, only a very little, and you can afford to do *that* much, can't you?" But anyway, for whatever reasons, the negative image exists.

For similar historical and accidental reasons I have at some points in my life, such as at City Mental Hygiene Clinic and Family Guidance Clinic, been urged and encouraged to buy it as reality. So that pattern of thinking, the pathway of logic mixed with feeling, which tells me I'm no good and ought to destroy myself, exists ready-made beforehand at the service of each new emergency.

I have only to set aside the barriers I have erected against that path in my recent years of therapy and successful functioning to find myself once again on the familiar trail. Having it reinforced from outside myself by apparently "uninvolved" people like Dr. Crosby and my unit partners at work is the activating circumstance that destroys my defenses.

Rationally, I know that no one is totally uninvolved, everybody projects somewhat, and my attitude to the world in my everyday life is somewhat striking and flamboyant, enough to draw more than an ordinary amount of projection from others. But my neurosis says that only I am subjective, because I am bad. The others are all good, and objective, and they are trying to tell me something about myself that I need to know and haven't caught onto yet.

I wonder if seeing the form of my own danger this clearly will be of any help in dealing with my collapses as they occur. I don't think I can deactivate the negative image. I'm afraid it's too firmly established for that. I can hope to put an effective stop sign at the entrance to that trail—that's about all.

A memory: Running into the living room on Christmas morning, the year I was four. My sisters were getting a new toboggan; there it was, standing on end up against the wall. On top of it, far out of my reach, was a large brown teddy bear. I held up my arms toward it, at which my parents and sisters all immediately said, "What makes you think it's for you? It's not for you." I was very confused and put my arms down at once, fearing I'd committed yet another faux pas. It seemed unlikely that it was for either of my parents, and my sisters were eleven and twelve and openly scornful of my interest in stuffed toys, but I knew you weren't supposed to ask for something that was somebody else's, or not meant for you.

Being eventually handed the teddy bear did not effectively wipe out the pain and confusion.

Another memory, this time from age eight or nine: The little girl visiting across the street, aged about eleven or twelve, came over one summer morning to find me reading and said to me, "The man who wrote that book got drunk every night. That's a bad book."

I started to cry. I was not confused about the facts; the book was written by a woman; besides, how was this snotty-nosed, illiterate kid going to get accurate information about so august and illustrious a person as the author of a book? What confused me was the barefaced and obvious and unprovoked desire to give me pain. Why?

Because I was open to the point of transparency, and because I reacted not to the act but to the motive behind it, it left me open to the charge of irrationality (all motives being by definition invisible). I was so lonely and deprived that I was close to the edge of unbearable pain. Any small thing, any deliberate cruelty—no matter how small—would reduce me to tears, would send me over the line into behavior not tolerated in the peer world. I had no position of strength from which to retaliate. It was always possible for my tormentors to say with any amount of pious self-justification, "But we didn't *do* anything to her!" (for the teachers were occasionally curious as to why I was weeping uncontrollably—at least until my reputation for being crazy was firmly established). It was perfectly true. They didn't need to do anything. To make obvious their unprovoked desire to give me pain was plenty.

I kept trying and trying to figure out what I had done to make them want to torment me. I came to the conclusion that it wasn't anything I *did;* it was simply how I myself *was.* I was somehow in some obvious fashion despicable. The sugar-sweet, see-no-evil world my family pretended to inhabit did nothing to explain to me that there was such a thing as plain sadism at large in the world. The only response I could make, given what I knew, was to search frantically within myself for the total cause of the problem. And until the end of my marriage at age thirty-two, that was the only response to the phenomenon (repeated a million times by playmates, husband, "friends," family) that I ever made.

Competition hasn't been talked about enough. In married couples, for instance, and between close friends. Between Esther and me? Is competing always as dirty and destructive as we've always thought? Can't it have a benevolent or constructive side?

Basically, all the viable relationships of my life have been built on the sibling model rather than, say, a parental or lover model. It's the only sector of relationships in which I have any reliable experience. Unconsciously, I seem to have the view that those other kinds of relationships are radically different, that how you make them is almost totally different from what I know how to do, and when I try to establish a relationship with a "parent" or a "lover," I flounder hopelessly, shrivel, despair, give up.

But maybe all relationships are made in mainly the same way; maybe I don't have to learn to do something so entirely new after all. The trouble is that when I'm trying to establish bonds with a prospective lover or "parent," it becomes so dreadfully important, I'm so terrified I'll blow it, I'm so sure that this opportunity is my only chance for that kind of love, maybe for the rest of my life, that I try too hard, and of course that does blow it.

It's funny that I have so little faith in the ability of human beings to change their outlook and behavior, when I myself have changed so radically in the course of my own life.

Esther sees my situation at the beginning of that first round of therapy as precarious, as my being in danger of losing everything I had gained. I saw it as looking for a therapist in a calm period when there were few problems so that there would be someone on hand when the next blow fell. I don't think there's as much contradiction there as it seems. It was by far *my* best level of functioning, but in terms of where most people function, it was probably pretty precarious.

On the other hand, she sees me as coming back to therapy this second time in rather good shape, as simply wanting to work on past problems, those of my years of marriage, childhood, and so on. I see myself as having been in extremely shaky shape the second time. My life seemed to be coming unravelled. My migraines had increased to a point where they virtually paralyzed my life: My neurologist had offered to sign for me to draw total disability if I wanted to go that route (I didn't). My family life, with three adolescent children at home, was tense and complicated. And I had suffered, one morning at work, a nervous and physical collapse that wiped me out for twenty-four hours. (That later turned out to be a reaction to an experimental medication I was taking for my migraine, but I had no way of knowing it at the time. All I knew was that I couldn't go on.) I was afraid my ability to handle a full-time job was in question. All in all, I felt I was in a very tenuous and vulnerable state.

I had a vivid and upsetting nightmare last night. It fell into two parts. In the first part, I was living in an apartment in another town with a woman, not my mother, whom in the dream I knew to be my mother, and my father, who was Scott. Scott was insane. He had a kitchen knife. It was the middle of the night and all through the night he kept making suicide attempts, obviously not of a serious nature. At daybreak he came to the bedroom to attempt to stab first my mother and then me. Those attempts were serious.

In the second part of the dream, which followed without transition, I was married to Scott and had a small daughter (Becky?). We were living in the same apartment with a childless couple. The husband was in a state hospital, so the woman was there with us by herself. Scott was obviously insane and overtly homicidal. I decided to commit him after he had made multiple attempts to stab me and the child. After I committed him, I was terrified that he would talk them into releasing him and he would come and murder the child and me. I was making hurried preparations to disappear before that could happen. The other woman was helping me escape. At the end of the dream, Scott was released before I could get away, and the dream ended. I woke in terror, at early daylight.

My unconscious has validated everything I've written. I don't know how it was objectively. I do know exactly how it was for me.

The midwestern injunction, "You mustn't say that, it isn't *nice,*" always made me very angry. It may not be nice, but it is true, interesting, and necessary to be said if the matter in hand is to be discussed in any real relation to the way things move in reality. So it isn't nice, so what?

More difficult: "You mustn't *want* that, it isn't nice." Well, yes. Jim is married, I mustn't sleep with him. So okay, I know I mustn't; he's got his own job to do, it's serious, I mustn't distract him. So I know I mustn't sleep with him. But how come I mustn't want to sleep with him? What's bad about that? It seems to me that some, or even a great deal, of wanting things you can't have is inevitable. It just happens. What can be good or bad about it? If you then put the wanting of those things out of your head because it isn't "nice," how can you have any idea at all what the reality of the situation is like, especially when your own feelings and reactions to a situation are a vital part of the reality of the situation?

Running through my head today: the hair-raising fugue sung by the villagers in *Peter Grimes,* "Him who despises us, we'll destroy." A very perceptive man is Benjamin Britten!

It's impossible to measure or even imagine the part that art in all its forms, but most especially lyric poetry and music, has played in my life. Time and again it has given me the courage to continue the struggle, the refreshment that makes living not just happy but possible at all. Art has given me the capacity to believe that I am not utterly alone, that the world of deep experiences and values is a shared world, that it is not vain to feel and hope and believe as I do —others may experience and believe in that same world.

Yet I realize more and more that these experiences are closed to most of the people around me. Partly, I think, it's because they simply do not move at that depth. But also, someone must clue you in, turn you on, tell you that the world of art exists, and give you some hint as to how it can be reached.

Keeping my ears open among friends and, for example, in Chamber Chorus, I find that the overwhelming number of people I know who value music learned about it in their family; it was part of the normal transmission of cultural values from parent to child. They can't remember, for instance, when they heard their first Bach piece.

That was certainly not the case in my family. My parents value "culture" in general. They know they are supposed to venerate Mozart and Beethoven, so they make a stab at it. They buy an occasional record and listen to it respectfully, but as for the core of the experience—that intense flash of pleasure and recognition and meaning and delight (like having an orgasm in bed with somebody you love)—they haven't a clue; they don't even know it exists.

I was for a long time puzzled about how it was transmitted to me. My sister Annette taught me in my early teens, that much I know beyond any doubt. She spent hours reading poetry with me, listening to music, Beethoven especially. But who taught Annette that it was there?

I have left out of the book one important factor, my relationship with Joe (whom I met after I left Scott). Why? What happened there? I tried to parlay his sexual need into a "love affair" and it didn't work.

Originally assured of his desire to go to bed with me, I began to pour enormous amounts of time and energy into propping him up and helping to stabilize his emotional situation. He was appreciative but very nervous. Both of us then agreed that he "owed" me something in return. We did not agree exactly, however, on what that was. I tried desperately to convince him that he should or did love me with some form of exclusiveness. He refused to be pinned down on what he should give me, what I could count on from him. When I pushed him harder and harder for some form of emotional return, he went to pieces utterly and retaliated with a specifically sexual rejection that damaged me badly, perhaps beyond repair, and cut the connection between us. That relationship took up the vast majority of my time and energy for nearly three years. Its lasting influence on my life has been extremely destructive. Above all, it has kept me from choosing another man. My choices, both of Scott and Joe, have been so destructive to me and above all have gone on for so *long*.

Joe wanted kids very badly and fastened on me as a mother for himself and a potential mother for his kids. Joe's view of women as the "good" sex, i.e., the totally loving, giving, self-sacrificing sex, made him hate himself for being the "bad" sex for whom women must totally sacrifice themselves—but that didn't keep him from piling the whole responsibility of the relationship on me. He simply saw that as being in the nature of things. It was foreordained for him that I take the constructive steps and he take the destructive ones.

One essential reason for my tendency to pick "unavailable" lovers: If they then don't respond much to me, don't move toward me, I can always say it's because they're not free to move, not because they don't really want me.

Nevertheless, I am permanently indebted to Joe for one extremely important thing: I know that he was very attracted to me sexually, and that's been rare indeed in my life (or at least the awareness that somebody is attracted to me is very rare).

There were serious external problems between Joe and me. He was transferred to another city almost immediately after we got together. I saw him only on his rare trips here. I sustained myself between trips with huge amounts of fantasy. When he then showed up and reality didn't match my fantasy (how could it?), I had a hard time handling the less-than-glamorous reality. Nevertheless, I was angry then and still am that his trips to see me were so infrequent. He had much more choice in the matter than he exercised, by a long shot. He chose to go other places, to see other people, but seldom came to see me. It hurt then and it hurts me still.

He told me in many other ways that he was simply unprepared to cope with me. He was habitually late for our meetings, sometimes over an hour late. If I had been any less hung up on him, I would simply have walked out on the whole thing, many times over. One reason that I am so ashamed of the relationship is that, in effect, he told me over and over from the very beginning it was really no go, and I continued to hang on to him for so long, for three long years. I was so hung up that I simply could not find the door. Meanwhile, I couldn't look around for a man with whom things would have been more possible because my emotional investment in Joe was so extreme.

What was the nature of my hang-up with Joe? Through the difficult period of my divorce, I needed somebody to reassure me that anybody could want me, could find me desirable, attractive, lovable. I needed to feel that I had a man, that I was like everybody else. I needed to feel that my need for love and tenderness and sexual gratification was somehow *usual,* that the need could be met in the ordinary world. And Joe was, in fact, a very attractive man. I've never met anyone whose wit and intellect were so closely fitted to mine. Whether we were being funny or serious, somehow we matched each other, and that match was good, vital. I sometimes miss it still.

But he was afraid, and that, somehow, was what did us both in at last. He was afraid of me, of my lack of ordinary "prudence," of my tendency to do what the spirit moves me to do, of my propensity to move by intuition rather than by reason. He was terrified of the vulnerability that comes through love, both in the ordinary sense that if you love someone very much you suffer their pains and losses as your own, and in the specific sense—he knew my vulnerabilities well and feared my deep pull toward self-destruction, feared to become involved as one of the causes of my self-destruction. He said to me once, "I'm always afraid to call your house. I'm afraid they'll tell me that something terrible has happened to you."

Joe was afraid more than anyone I've ever known. If he had been willing to grit his teeth and face his terror, I think things might have come out all right for both of us. But he felt his fear contrasted so strongly with my lack of fear that he experienced my surprise at his inability to face the situation between us as a scalding contempt for his cowardice. He collapsed in self-contempt and panic, and he turned on me with a rejection that broke me where I was most vulnerable. It was all over in an instant, then, but it took me years to work free of my entanglement with him. There are times when I want him, still.

I doubt that the damage will ever entirely heal over. It was as if he were my first lover, my only lover, and there is a sense in which that is true. I was attached to him in a way that I've never been attached to anybody else. He called out my sensuality as no one else ever has. My craving to sleep with him was of the essence, and different from anything I've ever experienced, before or since.

And still, concerning Joe, the same overall feeling of guilt that I feel about Scott: If I was willing to stand for all that, then I totally asked for it and the whole painful business was totally my fault. That's partly true, of course, but for Christ's sake, it's not absolute! But most of all, I'm ashamed of settling for so little when I needed so much.

Writing all that has made me feel very lonely. I need the ongoing comfort and security of a long-term love relationship with an equal. I face as best I can the probability that it is never going to happen to me. I can survive without it, can be comfortable alone, even happy. But I'm periodically painfully lonely.

The one piece of sexual wisdom I have to pass on to my daughters is: Sleep with your equals. Don't bed down with anyone just because you feel sorry for him. Equally, don't accept that kind of favor from anybody else.

It was at the time I split up with Joe that I had the suspected brain tumor. The end of the relationship was plainly at hand. I developed a headache that wouldn't quit. It went on for weeks without a break. I went to bed with it at night and got up with it in the morning—blinding, nonstop pain. After it had gone on for five or six weeks, I made an appointment at the School of Optometry to see if it was because my glasses needed changing. There were no changes in my eyesight, but tests showed I had lost a perceptible amount of peripheral vision in part of the field of vision of one eye. Another test a month later showed that the vision loss had progressed. The test for glaucoma was negative. Possible diagnosis: brain tumor. They made an appointment for me at the Neurology Department of the University Hospital. I was so miserable that I really didn't care one way or the other. A quick death without my even having to make the decision would have solved all my problems. I was prepared to let the whole matter slide.

But the student nurse at the School of Optometry kept calling me several times a week, insisting that I keep the appointment. Clearly she cared, whether I did or not. I changed my mind and kept the appointment. Neurology Department was depressing, long hours of waiting among obviously destitute and moribund patients. EEG, brain scan, X rays, test after test—it dragged on for weeks. I hardly cared. At last the final diagnosis was migraine. The vision loss was from brain cells killed off by constant pressure. I wasn't going to die after all. It was weeks before I realized I was relieved.

My Poor Mad Wife as a marital interaction depends upon a combination of one Open and one Closed player, both of whom appear to be playing from Open positions. (At least to me, paranoid schizophrenia is the epitome, or maybe a parody, of the Closed position.) It takes a paranoid who appears to be sane and open to bring that transaction off.

Open position, an alternative view: Self-revelation is a pathetic testing for acceptance. If I show it all and the world does not land on me, if I'm still allowed to live, then I must not be so bad after all. A great price to pay for such a negligible gain. (I'm really discouraged today!)

Sex-derived models of insanity: My husband was crazy and I said so. He said I was crazy. Everybody believed him and not me.

I think this is deeply related to everybody's unconscious expectations of sanity and insanity in regard to gender. I think that it happens by no means infrequently and causes incalculable misery and injustice. I need to know why it happens.

Just for starters: Women are socially permitted/encouraged to show emotion, though men are not. Insanity is sometimes virtually equated with "excess emotion."

It's hard to keep a unified version of who I am straight in my head. When there's no pressure, I'm okay; but let me get hassled and the negative side of myself starts to show. I can't reconcile what happens with the "official" version of myself that I normally carry around. Maybe I flare up at a client, for instance, or at one of the kids. It doesn't even matter how understandable my loss of temper is, or even how clearly it was provoked. Or suppose I do a slipshod job at work for a few days. My hold on any self-esteem begins to slip. I lose my footing, can't remember that I usually don't lose my temper in those circumstances. I begin to feel that I'm just no damned good.

It is in those moments that the negative feedback I have collected from other people all during my life (and I have treasured up quite a bit of it, believe me, from parents, husband, and various friends who have "only wanted to help"), the bad image of myself I've built up from various sources, comes to the fore and threatens to become my operative image of myself.

The negative self-image is as coherent and unified as the self-image it replaces, and it contains enormously convincing portions of the truth: I am smug, smug and self-satisfied (I'm even writing a book about how good I am); I am capricious and so unobservant of what is going on around me that I will never be able to form an accurate picture of the world. I am operating solely on a very cockeyed notion of what the people around me are really like, so naïve as to be amusing, erratic, self-indulgent, childish beyond belief, living in a world of fantasy.

And, God help me, it's all true.

But it isn't, so to speak, the only thing that's true. As an operating image of myself, it's no good. I become paralyzed by self-contempt and cannot move at all.

I used to cultivate this image of myself, partly in pursuit of humility as a religious ideal and partly because I equated comfort with fantasy and pain with reality. And then, of course, I am an interested party in self-evaluation and you can't trust the evaluation of interested parties. I have every reason to lie to myself about what I am truly like (this argument goes), and no one else has any reason to lie to me on that subject. The truth about oneself inevitably hurts; therefore, the more pain, the more truth.

If I am so rotten, for what reason of my own or anyone else's do I stay alive? The pain of self-hatred is nearly intolerable, and what do I have that I can reasonably offer to anybody else? As soon as the first impression I make on people wears off, they'll see me as I really am and either reject me (painful for me) or be disappointed in me but loyal all the same (equally painful). In fact they will then become my long-suffering husband, children, friends, whom I know I don't deserve to have but cling to out of a selfish fear of being alone.

And that's the path to a nice, juicy suicide, and I traveled along it for quite a little way.

There's something else behind this problem, though, and I think it's this: For some reason I see other people as objective, both about themselves and about me. As I see them from outside themselves, being and behavior are the same thing; others are as they behave, as they appear to me to be, and I am not. I am obliged to push myself to a much higher standard of behavior than I would require of anybody else in order, so to speak, to apologize to the world, to make reparation for being allowed to exist in it at all. I am simply not good enough to be entitled to a natural right to existence.

I woke at daybreak one August day, vaguely conscious that I was uncomfortable and sleeping badly, but I couldn't figure out what the problem was and I quickly fell back to sleep. I woke again at about eight and sat bolt upright, acutely conscious of a sharp, cramping pain in my midsection. I was alone in the house except for fifteen-month-old Peter. I could hear him singing to himself in his crib. Scott must have gotten himself off to work without waking me.

There was the pain again. I put my hand on my by now sizable belly. It was tight and hard. The unborn baby seemed unusually quiet. Come to think of it, I hadn't felt much movement all this last week. The pain again, really hard. I swang my legs over the side of the bed. Peter was calling me to take him to the bathroom. It was time to begin my day.

Pain again. It feels like a labor pain, I thought. There was a gush of warm water from deep inside me. The edge of the bed where I was sitting was soaked. I realized at last what was happening. The baby was coming now. I was having a miscarriage. I didn't want to believe it was true. I took Peter to the bathroom, dressed and fed him as though nothing were the matter. But the cramps by now were too hard and frequent to ignore.

Acceptance of the inevitable brought panic. I was alone in the house with a small child. I had no money, no phone; the doctor at the Public Health Service maternity clinic couldn't be reached even by phone until next Thursday. The buses weren't even running —the transit workers were out on strike. Whom could I call, what should I do? I decided first of all against calling Scott. I needed someone with me who could stay calm in a crisis, and I didn't know what his reaction to this situation would be.

I slipped into my clothes, picked up Peter, and went next door to ask if I could use their phone. I was by this time shaking so hard I could barely dial. I got two wrong numbers before I finally got through to Bob and Ellen Jones. Somewhat incoherently, I conveyed the problem. Bob said, "I'll be right over. Go to bed and stay there. Wait, better call the Medical Association and see if they can send a doctor. But after that, go home and stay quiet."

I called the county Medical Association and told them I was five months pregnant and seemed to be in labor. They promised to send somebody over right away.

I took Peter home, settled him on the bedroom floor with some toys, and lay down on the bed. The cramps by now were regular and heavy. I tried, in between, to feel if the baby was moving, but I couldn't feel anything.

Bob was there in about ten minutes. It was a relief to have someone else there. I told him I'd phoned the doctor and that somebody should be here soon. Desperately, I asked Bob if there were any hope that a baby born this early could possibly live, but I knew before he answered that there was none.

Bob insisted that we call Scott at work and tell him what was happening. I was reluctant but didn't want to explain to an outsider why I didn't want Scott to be there. There was still no sign of the doctor. It was obvious that the baby would soon be born.

At about eleven o'clock, Bob took Peter into the living room and came back to sit with me. After about twenty minutes of fairly hard labor, the baby was born. It was a girl. She was tiny and blue and never moved or made a sound. Bob carried her out into the kitchen and performed an emergency baptism at the kitchen sink. We both knew she was already dead.

Scott arrived soon after. He had walked most of the way from the plant. The buses weren't running, and he had no money for a taxi. There was still no sign of medical help.

The doctor arrived at last, about two-thirty in the afternoon. He examined me perfunctorily, glanced at the baby's body. "Baptize it if you're Catholic. You can get rid of it however you want," he said without interest. "Bury it in the backyard if you want to." He turned back to me. "I'll have to report this to the police, of course," he said, surveying the bare and messy house with a distaste that he made no effort to conceal.

I was puzzled by his remark but not frightened; curious, I asked him why. "Because you did it without a doctor," he said. "As for you, young lady, I doubt you'll ever be able to carry another child." With that crushing blow, he departed.

I was terrified. What had I done that was wrong, why had my baby died? If I truly couldn't have more children, what would I do? The only future I had ever imagined for myself was as the mother of a large and happy family. Why had this happened to me? I cried and cried. Scott buried the tiny body in the backyard. He was grim and silent.

It was late evening before the significance of the doctor's remark about the police finally dawned on me. He had seen how desperately poor we were from the condition of the house, and he thought I had aborted the baby. It seemed to me bitterly ironic that I, who more than anyone I knew was opposed to abortion under almost any circumstances, should be so accused. It was late that night when I finally cried myself to sleep. It was my twenty-first birthday.

I later learned that the doctor was a prominent Catholic, very active in church affairs and charitable activities. One of his charities was to contribute his time free of charge to a maternity clinic for low-income mothers. I learned years later from a friend who was a nurse there that he terrorized the women who came to the clinic, predicting death in childbirth or dead babies to those who didn't follow his instructions to the letter.

I think that the miscarriage was probably caused by malnutrition. When I had gone for my first prenatal-care appointment, I had weighed only 106 pounds—and I'm quite tall. Scott had been extremely ill, in fact had suffered a total breakdown, and at that time hadn't worked for a period of more than four months. We were not eligible for welfare or for unemployment insurance, and there had been very little to eat for quite some time. I had nursed Peter during the first two months of the pregnancy because our food supply was so doubtful. My body just couldn't support all three of us.

I was terrified that I couldn't have another child, and three weeks later I became pregnant again. I had some irregular bleeding all through the early part of the pregnancy. On one occasion I called another doctor, who made a house call. He told me, "We should take you in and scrape you. It'll probably be defective." He then said he wouldn't leave the house until he was paid for the visit on the spot, which I simply could not do.

That problematical embryo was my brilliant and beautiful Ann. I have a fantasy of sending her to his office after she graduates from medical school, with a note to him recalling his advice.

I always have been quite sure that Scott was being hypocritical when he said, on those rare occasions when he was willing to say so, that he loved me. He did just about everything in his power to destroy me, actively choosing each opportunity as it came along. Almost never in all our time together did he show or express that he valued anything I was or did. He was never faithful to me sexually, nor would he behave in the presence of another person as though he were connected with me in any way; people constantly told him during the time we were married that he didn't "behave like a married man." That reaction always made me very proud. It was one of my greatest conscious values as a wife not to put "conventional restrictions" on my husband.

It was rather in the mode of the open marriage of today. The obligation was not reciprocal, however. After all, it is "woman's nature" to crave to be possessed. Only "man's nature" craves freedom.

It certainly seems to me that at that time I was willing to sell myself very cheaply. But there was another very strong element in my attitude, which was simply this: I wanted Scott to value me freely, voluntarily. I wanted his allegiance to come to me as a gift, not an obligation. To me, love that is required is useless. My family gave me that and it was worthless to me.

In looking back from this new perspective provided by the writing of this book, I think that perhaps in his own sense and according to his own lights he may indeed have loved me. For one thing, his sense of connection with other people is very tenuous indeed, very shallow and fragile compared with anybody else's, though he doesn't have enough emotional experience to realize that. Coupled with my very extreme need for emotional reassurance, that's a disaster all by itself.

While we were in conjoint therapy at Family Guidance Clinic, I also came to realize that he has another protective device that simply boggles my mind: He instantly forgets any unpleasant or adverse thing he's ever done. Therefore, there's no connection between incidents, no pattern, no continuity. Each time it happens is the first time it's happened, and for Christ's sake, nobody's perfect, can't he be forgiven just this once? I must be a very cold bitch indeed if I won't forgive him this one transgression.

I found that out in joint therapy. It was one of the most important factors that oriented me toward divorce. It was a defense I would never have been able to overcome, and live with it I could not, because it eliminates for him any sense of responsibility for his own actions. And a sense of responsibility, accountability, is one of the things I most value in people to whom I'm emotionally related.

Responsibility is anathema to Scott. It's what the Mamas of the world want to make you have. You demonstrate your manhood by resisting them, and that, in a nutshell, is what relations between the sexes are all about. Excepting, of course, the Bad Girl who helps you to evade Mama's requirement of responsibility. (It's a slight variation of the common Virgin-Whore dichotomy.)

The secretary who transcribed our "marathon" tape sent it back with a warm personal note saying that working on the tape had been of great personal value for her. She hoped we would publish it, for she thought it would be of value to many women. I am now for the first time entertaining the thought that the book might be *good.* I have had fantasies of the book being successful, but what if it's a really *good* book? I would be so happy.

It was Meg Goodwin who finally got me to apply for state medical assistance and see a doctor for my multitude of physical problems. We always had this myth, Scott and I, of my great health. What that really meant was that I was adept at ignoring pain, stoical rather than healthy. When I finally saw a doctor on a regular basis, we coped with and largely solved a sizable number of medical problems: anemia, a resident staph infection, severe migraine, persistent urinary infection, numerous menstrual problems. Until I began to get better, I didn't even realize I'd been walking around sick for years.

On going to the opera with Pete and Ed: God damn, I have no peers. Pete and Ed are my age or younger. They have important professional work to do, extensive professional qualifications, and professional social status, but mainly they have experience. They've lived in Europe for several years, traveling whenever and wherever they pleased. They can afford good food, wine, clothes, good living in general; their advantage in experience, because of money, status, freedom, is incalculable.

Because of my years of illness, poverty, coping with a bad marriage and all the children's problems as well as my own, my experience of the world, except for survival, at which I am adept, is negligible. I can hardly enter the simplest conversation on any terms of equality. I've been in such a hole that I'll never catch up, no matter how fast I learn. Pete, Ed, and all their friends just make me feel horribly inadequate and self-conscious. It isn't that they look down on me, it's not that at all. They seem, in fact, hardly to be aware of any disparity. But just by being who and what they are, they automatically make me feel like a horrible klutz. God damn!

The most clear sexual message I got from Scott was this: I was not the source of his sexual interest. Other things excited him, fantasy mainly, I suspect. I was simply one of the ways he had of working off the excitement. I was never the one to arouse the interest in the first place. It was very defeating and more than a little degrading.

From the time Peter was a year old until the time of our separation, Scott kept down his contact with the family by the device of working the swing shift at the plant. He always presented this as a regrettable necessity; in actuality he had enough seniority after the first year to choose any shift he wanted but nevertheless continued to choose swing. He went to work around two-thirty in the afternoon, before the kids were home from school, came home about one in the morning, sat up by himself until six or so, then slept until eleven or noon, spending the rest of the time by himself again until leaving for work. He kept the same schedule on weekends, so that he saw very little of the children or me. This went on for fifteen years.

One effect this schedule had was that Scott and I, in the literal meaning of the words, never "went to bed" together. He always came to bed in the early morning when I had been long asleep. Such sexual contact as we had was on that basis, never a very satisfactory one for me because there was virtually no personal emotional contact involved. From my point of view, making "love" on that schedule was quite useless, but it was the only routine that Scott could tolerate. He would climb into bed with an erection, we would have intercourse, he would fall asleep, and that was that. Any attempt at initiating lovemaking on another basis would draw a hostile reply such as, "Why don't you go take a cold shower?" It didn't take me long to quit trying.

At the same time, I thought there was something wrong with me because I didn't enjoy sex. We often seriously discussed my "problem" and I felt I was a very poor excuse for a woman. No wonder he was unfaithful. I didn't know sex wasn't that cold with everybody. How could I? I had had no other experience. Now when I think back, I am furiously angry, more angry than I'll ever be able to express.

Scott's illness broke through into our sexual relations and frightened me. He was impersonal with me in bed, always, and not a little given to trying to act out his more bizarre fantasies, whether they were of any interest to me or not. To do him credit, he tried to control that aspect of himself as much as he could, but the sense of there being no *person* there to relate to me defeated me always. Since I had never slept with anybody else and was faithful to him during our marriage, I had no standard of comparison and blamed myself. In that sense, fidelity served me very badly. When I finally fell in love with someone who liked *me,* I was fine, but that wasn't till after years of self-blame, and it came far too late to save me from permanent hurt.

It seems to me that, to a certain extent, time, money, and energy can be converted into each other. Money can buy other people's time and energy to supplement or substitute for your own. If you have a lot of energy, you can get enough done, moving efficiently, to make up for lack of time. If you have plenty of time, you can work slowly or gradually and don't need so much energy. But if more than one is in short supply, you are in trouble. I'm in trouble.

My overall feeling right now is that, psychologically speaking, there's not enough *space* around me. I'm surrounded by clients at work and children at home. They crowd around me too closely. Yet I can't do an acceptable job either at work or at home unless they *can* come close to me. But my overall reaction as time rolls on is of acute claustrophobia: It's like being stuck between floors in a crowded elevator.

The tapes don't show Esther's contribution to the therapy properly because so much of what she does is conveyed in facial expression and body English rather than words. And what she ironically calls her "brilliant remarks" fill a vital place in the contact for me. I desperately need to know, each minute, that she is tracking with me, that I am making sense that another person can understand. City Mental Hygiene Clinic left its mark on me.

It was the quality of openness that made the singing of the *St. John Passion* the moving experience that it was. Martin's open approach and his conviction that the work has profound human and metaphysical meaning, as well as musical and dramatic meaning, were transferred to all of us very directly. The group was quite open with one another; some of the reservations that people use to defend their highest values somehow got set aside. We were able to perform the work with great conviction, and our sense of unity, which came from our personal commitment to the ideas Martin articulated, affected our music very profoundly.

At the last performance, at the Cathedral, the chorus gave Martin a standing ovation. All of us understood what had made it possible to perform the work on that level. We could not have approached that degree of technical choral excellence without being committed to the interior meaning of the piece. Only that sense of human importance would have made us work with such dedication. All three audiences understood what had made us able to do it. They were able to experience it directly and to participate in the meaning of the work through our conviction, and our conviction was possible mainly because Martin was able to call it forth, to make us trust ourselves and each other and Bach and him and the audience. That's what the standing ovation was about. There was nobody in the whole performing crew of, say, one hundred and fifty people who I felt was on any kind of ego trip at all. That alone makes it an extraordinary experience.

I think that's the power of Open Life Stance at its human best, and an example of what I mean by considering Open Life Stance as a didactic technique. This year's *St. John* was an educational experience for a great many people, maybe thousands.

On Sunday morning, I finished typing out for the book the section on Becky's death. That evening the chorus sang our final performance of the Bach *St. John Passion* at the Cathedral. That night, for the first time, I was able to sing the final chorale, "Ach Herr, Lass dein' lieb' Engelein," through to the end without collapsing into tears. The two events helped each other. Some bad things inside me are beginning to heal over, I think.

When anyone asks me what I did over the weekend or if anything happened during the holidays or my vacation, I invariably reply, "No, nothing happened, it was wonderful." Simple, ordinary, regular, uneventful day-to-day life is such a blessing. I may never get my fill of it.

If a woman reveals her husband's weaknesses to the outside world, she immediately becomes a "castrating bitch," no longer licensed to approve of herself. How come there isn't even a word for the thing a man does to a woman when he in some way sells her out to the malice of the world?

In my relationships with both Scott and Joe, I still believed in the power of my love to overcome all. Love won't overcome psychosis or severe neurosis.

One reason Scott looked so attractive to me when I first met him: I could tell instantly that he was a person who would never be made a scapegoat. I thought I could magically incorporate some of that strength.

Discouraged rainy-day thought: Sometimes I feel like a figment of my own imagination. It seems like almost too much work to keep the whole show in motion.

Until I was about thirty, I played a game—first with my parents and then with my husband—called "Am I Good Enough Yet?" which consisted of my asking the question and getting this reply: "No, not yet. You're still not fulfilling all my needs. Try harder."

So I tried harder and repeated the question, with identical results. I was trying so hard that it never occurred to me to climb off the stick by retorting, "Your needs are based on total fantasy," or "Revise your standards," or yet "How about you meeting a need or two of mine for a change?"

My first move away from this endless cycle was to substitute the standards of the Roman Catholic Church for my husband's standards. Although that at first left me in the hands of confessors hostile to intellectuals and to women, it was a help in that the standards applied to others as well as to myself, and it gave me a chance to compare my behavior with that of others. Also, although it did to some extent play into the demands of my by then morbid perfectionism, it still left me free to choose saner and saner interpreters of the general rules, as I did when I gradually began to work things out.

I am very taken with Eric Berne's notion that you can tell a lot about how an individual conducts his life by asking his favorite fairy tale. For example, he says that the corporate woods are full of Little Red Ridinghoods forever waiting for one seductive wolf after another.

My favorite fairy tale had always been Hans Christian Andersen's story of the wild swans. In that story the youngest sister accepts the task of saving her brothers from the cruel enchantment that has deprived them of their human shape and turned them into wild swans. She must weave each of them a shirt of stinging nettles, and above all, during the time she undertakes the task, she is not to speak. If she should say one word before the task is finished, her brothers' chance of freedom will be ended; they will lose their chance to return to human form forever. She is accused of witchcraft and is going to be burned, but she is faithful and does not defend herself.

But in the fairy tale it all comes out right in the end. Where did I go wrong?

I've been divorced for eight years and I'm just beginning to feel really angry.

I hate Scott, I really hate him. I can remember seeing, and often I can see now, times when he made the *choice* to do the hateful, damaging thing instead of letting the occasion pass. It's seeing him make that choice that makes me hate him.

Also, I'm still afraid of him. He retains some remnant of the only power he ever really had over me: the ability to make me hate myself.

I don't need a therapist to tell me who I am. Ultimately, it's I who decide that for myself. What I need is a therapist who keeps telling me I'm somebody.

Sometimes I feel like a fatherless child.

I was was willing to continue on at Family Guidance Clinic, even though I felt it was an environment very hostile to me, because of one single thing: I felt that the therapists, although they had made a prejudgment concerning my sanity and the trouble in the marriage, were exceedingly honest people. If they ever changed their minds, I felt I could count on them to say so. I didn't believe they'd keep their mouths shut to save face.

There's some negative residue in almost any relationship. There can be things about your closest friends that tend to drive you up the wall. Therapeutic relationships are certainly no exception to the rule. I look back on the work I did with Meg Goodwin with an enormous amount of gratitude, yet my afterthoughts about what we accomplished together are not completely unmitigated by negative considerations.

For one thing, Meg worked hard at convincing me that I was and am schizophrenic. In the long run, I don't believe that's been in my best interest. First off, I don't really think it's true. In my job as a worker in the Aid to the Disabled program, I met a great many schizophrenics and I really don't agree I belong in that category. Meg used to emphasize to me that I mustn't ever try to work outside the home or put myself into any job situation in which I had to deal with people or came under any sort of pressure—kind of ironic when you consider how things finally turned out. Instead, doing a difficult job well has turned out to be one of the main factors on which I've built my self-esteem and, as such, a vital contribution to my growing ability to value myself.

Also, I always felt that Meg, perhaps because of her age but also because of the social circumstances in which she grew up, tended very much to identify her own social values with mental health. She would have expected me to demonstrate my recovery, for example, by wearing white gloves when I go downtown and espousing immaculate housekeeping. It's my feeling that I can continue to wear blue jeans in the "best" stores and coexist with a fair amount of domestic mess, and it's not a reflection on my mental health at all. It only demonstrates that I'm the child of a different time and place, with an alternative notion of what's acceptable.

I was never able to say any of this to Meg. I was too afraid of losing her so-much-needed support. I don't think that's a reflection on her skill as a therapist, though. I just hadn't come far enough along in therapy.

Father Michaelson was more terrified of being "the man who broke up my marriage" than of any other thing. He leaned over backward in the confessional not to give me any advice whatsoever that would cause me to withdraw from my efforts to "make the marriage work" (impossible task). He cultivated his friendship with Scott assiduously, was in fact one of Scott's closest friends. But he broke up my marriage, for all that. It was he who gave me my first standard of comparison: How would someone behave toward me if he loved me? And that in itself finished me with Scott.

Scott took Father Michaelson aside one night and told him, "Martha may have to go back to the hospital. She's really behaving strangely."

Friend of Scott's or no, Father Michaelson was on to him by that time. "What's she doing?" he asked.

"She was talking tonight about going to a movie alone," Scott said, "and you know that's not like her at all."

During that time Father Michaelson told me a dream he had had. He and I were in a bed by our front window; my husband and children were standing around the bed. And we were making love. I told him I'd never been any good in bed for Scott; maybe I wouldn't be for him either. All he said was, "Impossible."

I believed him.

The chief and most useful effect of the second round of therapy has been to reduce Scott to life-size.

For me, courage and generosity are the most important virtues, maybe the only virtues.

I think sexual reciprocity is one of the toughest things to manage, even between reasonably honest and well-intentioned people. Even when there aren't many pitfalls in the relationship, there are plenty of hidden traps within myself.

I remember once remarking to Pete something like, "The thing I really hate about being a woman is that you're physically capable of making love even when you don't want to in the least. It's so unfair. It means you have to make up your mind. I've always envied men in that one respect. They can't do it unless they want to."

He grinned and said, "I've always envied women in that respect. I can think of times when I would have given anything to be able, although I didn't want to at all. The social consequences of my inability were so devastating."

It was one of those moments of shared wry understanding.

It's a pity men and women don't talk together more.

Why do people resent intelligence in others? When I was small, the accusation most commonly hurled at me by my contemporaries was, "You think you're so smart!" (Come to think of it, that's still the most common accusation. It just isn't put into words anymore.) What can I say in reply? Because, as far as the accusation goes, it's perfectly true. I do think I'm smart and, what's more, I'm not even particularly sorry about it. I used to apologize all over the place, falling all over myself to prove that I wasn't intelligent at all and furthermore was really, humbly sorry that it looked that way. I at last quit falling all over myself. It looked gauche and it wasn't even true. It wasn't convincing anybody either.

I don't take credit for my intelligence; Lord knows, it's no doing of mine. It's a given, external attribute, like brown eyes or height, and there's no more credit for having it than there is for having any other such attribute. But I do like having it, do enjoy the experiences in the world that it makes possible for me, and I'll be damned if I can see why I shouldn't. Problem-solving feels good. It's a sensation as exact and distinct and pleasurable as any of the sensual experiences one can have of the world. Why should people who can do it be sorry they can do it or apologize for their ability?

The ability to experience a work of art, although it's not solely a function of intelligence, leans heavily on it and, as our culture is now structured, is an experience much more apt to be available to the "intelligent" or "educated" person. To experience, say, the "Sanctus" of the Verdi *Requiem* or a Shakespeare sonnet or Monet's field of poppies is as keen and intense a pleasure as a sexual experience. It's a simple and complete joy in a sensual experience coupled with the intellectual and intuitive ability to participate in the unique world view of the artist who created the piece. It's very like the direct joy of small children experiencing the world of sound and form and color for the first time. My own life has been changed and renewed and strengthened, times without number, by that experience. I know plenty of other people who can testify to the same. Those are some of the most vital and compelling and exciting and comforting experiences in my life. Then why, in God's name, should I apologize for them?

I don't think the experiences that intelligence makes available to me make me better than anybody else. I don't claim moral or any other kind of superiority because of them. But they are there, they are real, they can't be ignored. Any statement of who I am has to take them into consideration. What's wrong with that?

A present is something somebody gives me because they want me to have it. A favor is something somebody gives me because they think they should. I'll take all the presents I can get, but please don't do me any favors.

I often (usually) think presents are favors.

How do social workers, technicians, psychiatrists, or whatever in an intake position distinguish between a person with relatively weak defenses in a minimal pressure life situation and someone with rather great strengths in a maximal pressure life situation? After all, they can't evaluate the situation itself from their place in the consulting room. And the misestimation of his own life situation is frequently part and parcel of the patient/client's problem/illness. (City Mental Hygiene did me wrong.)

I have learned a great deal about valuing myself as a woman, in the moral or psychological sense, from men. In fact, I think it has been only from men that I've become aware of that valuation, of the existence of that scale of values. Father Michaelson fell in love with me when I called him on that desperate night to try to prevent Scott from killing himself, and his realization of what shit I was prepared to take really blew his mind.

Writers, people like Brecht, especially in *The Caucasian Chalk Circle,* and John Fowles, have been an enormous help because of their ability to construct flawed and sometimes socially inoperable (or nearly so) women, whose loyalty nevertheless is unshakably committed to a "true" scale of values. I'm thinking especially of the disparity between Allison and Nicholas in *The Magus,* of her struggle to get him educated to a more viable form of loving.

My main objection to both Brecht and Fowles, in fact, is that *all* their virtuous characters, or nearly all, are women. Their men make faint attempts at goodness; their women arrived at the goal long before the book started.

I suppose, to be fair, one should balance that off by remembering Aristotle's dictum about not straining the credulity of your audience by depicting, for example, nobility in a woman or a slave. Oh, well.

Heads I win, tails you lose: The first time Scott's friend Lloyd came to dinner with us, Scott started going on about me to Lloyd (in the presence of the children and me, of course), humorously deploring my cooking, housekeeping, personality, competence, and so on, pretty familiar stuff. I had heard it all so often, I was inured. Lloyd turned to me and said, "Why are you letting him do this to you? Tell him to stop."

Scott replied, "She's too honest to want me to lie to her about my feelings about her."

*Why* did I accept those two alternatives, verbal abuse or hypocritical silence, as the only two possibilities?

All of those years, I never *asked* for anything. I did not want to be given something, anything, because I had asked for it. I wanted to be given something, anything, because someone wanted to give it to me.

I may be in for rather a long wait.

I can't make a "proper" transference with a man. Thanks a lot, Daddy.

I have now said to quite a large number of people, "I was supposed to be schizophrenic and incurable. Then I got a divorce and my husband got custody of the mental illness."

The people who have said to me, "I've heard that before; it happens all the time"—Esther, Meg, my neurologist—have mostly been women. Don't the men know? Don't I say it to men?

My past therapists wanted to help me make "realistic" plans for my future: "Don't try to function on a normal level. Don't, for example, try to take a job outside the home in the normal workaday world." But my problem wasn't schizophrenia, as they thought, but inexperience or deprivation or underdevelopment of a sort. And testing myself in new and difficult situations turned out not only *not* to be destructive but just exactly what I most needed to do, and my best kind of learning and growing experience.

I have been really encouraged by several previous therapists to use insights gained in therapy to lacerate myself. They seem to equate that process with "facing the reality of my illness." The more I pleaded guilty to being sick, sick, sick and the cause of all the mess around me, the more they told me what good work I was doing. I wonder why they never noticed that all that good work made me a lot sicker.

My original model of love: selfless devotion to someone who then either dispenses approval or denial. There is no return devotion, no reciprocity.

One of the keys to my "recovery" was learning to recognize in myself states of mind, or moods, or psychological configurations, or whatever you want to call them, as *recurring*. To begin with, I had no notion of what it felt like to be happy. Then when I first experienced it, I figured it was a fluke, that it had happened once or twice but couldn't happen again. I had to learn that I could feel *that* over and over, that it could come back over and over, that it was caused by specific things, and that I could learn to reproduce the conditions myself, could bring about happiness again. It was a great victory to be able to say to myself, "I feel terrible now, but I've felt this way before and it went away. I've been happy before and I'll be happy again."

And that was really all I needed to work on.

A PSYCHODRAMA
*Act One: Scene One*
> ME (infant): I'm hungry.
> PARENTS: Not yet, you don't get hungry till four o'clock and that's not for two hours yet.
> ME: That makes me angry. *(Tears, total uproar.)*
*Scene Two, some months later*
> ME: I'm lonesome.
> PARENTS: If we talk to you, we'll spoil you and you'll be bad.
> ME: That makes me angry. *(Tears, total uproar.)*

*Scene Three, some years later*

ME: I'm angry.

FAMILY: You're so cute when you say that.

ME: I mean it. I hate you all.

FAMILY: We just love the way you stamp your foot when you say that.

ME: Damn it, I'm hungry, lonesome, and angry.

FAMILY: You're so cute.

ME: *(Periodic tears, silent horrendous anger, uproar, headaches.)*

FAMILY: People who stamp their feet and make an uproar for no reason are crazy.

*Act Two: Scene One*

SCOTT: Take care of me *(goes limp)*.

ME: I'm angry. I take care of you, but nobody's taking care of me.

SCOTT: Women are supposed to take care of everybody. Other women don't get angry. If you get angry, you must be crazy.

ME: *(Periodic tears, silent horrendous anger.)*

SCOTT: I told you that you were crazy. See? People who have periodic tears and silent horrendous anger for no reason are crazy.

*Scene Two, some years later*

PSYCHIATRIST ONE (TWO, THREE, FOUR, ETC.): You seem very angry.

ME: Let me tell you about my childhood and my marriage. *(Years of work.)*

PSYCHIATRIST(S) *(in conclusion):* So you see, none of that really happened, did it?

ME: *(Silent horrendous anger, headaches. All work unravelled back to the beginning.)*

*Scene Three*

PSYCHIATRIST FIVE (SIX, ETC.): You seem very angry.

ME: Let me tell you about my childhood and marriage. *(Years of work.)*

PSYCHIATRIST(S) *(in conclusion):* So you see, you had no real reason to be angry, did you?

ME: *(Silent horrendous anger, headaches, total uproar. All work unravelled back to the beginning.)*

*Act Three*

ESTHER: You seem very angry.

ME: How can I trust you enough to tell you how angry I am?

*(Cut to Happy Ending?)*

*Open Life-Style and Sanity:*

I think some of my past therapists have mistaken for insanity my tendency to say what I mean. When I'm working hard in therapy, I tend to speak very intuitively, very metaphorically. Before I learned to test to see if the therapist was tracking with me, I think this was mistaken for schizoid "flight of ideas." I didn't realize that some people don't know how to follow metaphors—especially psychiatrists. How could you become a shrink, or why would you become one, if in your own head or in someone else's you couldn't follow the line of thought as it actually happens (not as it's supposed to happen)?

I know my effort to live with minimum defenses might seem to some people insane. As a matter of fact, I don't think it is. I pursue that life-style with a reason, which I'm happy to discuss with you if you ask. How come my therapists never asked?

On the other hand, when I was in Kirkpatrick Hospital, the staff used to point me out to other patients as an example: Look at her, she's really working hard on her problems, you could do that, too. The other patients didn't understand. They associated sanity with looking cool and walked around the world trying to look as if nothing was the matter. And here I was crying, pacing the floor, talking endlessly about a welter of confused and irrational feelings and impulses—and I was supposed to be an example of a successful attempt at sanity? No thanks!

Yes, but listen, you guys, that's how it's really done. Reality is real, is tough, it doesn't exist in the agreed-upon social order, that myth we all agree on for convenience; equally, it doesn't necessarily demand abandonment of useful conventions if you want to keep them. But you *can* learn to do something else!

The School Problems Clinic, in conjunction with the School Guidance Department and the Special Learning Center, has established a fairly firm diagnosis of neurological handicap for Benjy, as firm as it's ever possible to establish in the absence of demonstrable brain damage. He has a scholarship now at the Special Learning Center. They have alternative methods of teaching reading and writing that bypass the specific area in which each child is handicapped. Benjy is learning fast. He has already come up more than two years in his writing, and he has done even better on his reading scores. His teachers and I are proud of him, and he is justly proud of himself.

In a way, the diagnosis is a great comfort. If there's a specific pinpointable disability, then it lets me off the hook. It isn't just that I've raised him all wrong or made him crazy, as some of the people involved have been quick to state, or at least to imply. It lets Benjy off the hook, too. He has been told that he's lazy, destructive, and, God help us, wicked. Now he's free to realize that it isn't his fault, or indeed anyone's, and can move on to find ways to cope with the problem.

But in another way the diagnosis is a burden, and that's because of Peter. For all during his school years Peter had a problem with reading and especially with writing that was virtually identical to Benjy's. Especially, he couldn't arrange things in sequence. I used to try to help him with his spelling. If you spelled "cat, c-a-t," he would spell it right back to you "cat, c-t-a." Nothing—threats, bribes, pleading, hideous scenes—budged him.

This was before the neurological handicaps were seen in any kind of focus and his I.Q. tested as extremely high, so the school kept telling me, and I eventually believed, that Peter was so emotionally disturbed that he wasn't able to cope with the world at all. I was quick to blame myself. Scott and, to a large extent, the school system were happy to join in the blame. His mother is schizophrenic, you know, so what can you expect? Inevitably, I took some of my fury and terror out on Peter, adding immeasurably to his crushing load. What followed was truancy, misbehavior, self-hatred, and collapse.

Peter worked himself back again almost purely by his own efforts. He himself, after a couple of years of home teaching, found a continuation school in a neighboring town that fostered a learning environment he could handle. He talked the school into taking him, got himself there regularly, and got his high school diploma. He's functioning extremely well now. He's found himself a craftsman's vocation. His work is beautiful and enjoyable; he does it well and it's lucrative. He seems a free and happy person. I know that through it all he never doubted that I love him. But the scars, my God, the scars are there, and they are horrible and so needless. And my scars are there, too, for I feel I failed him when he most needed me. He forgives me, I know, but I wonder if I will ever forgive myself.

Is the antidote to "bad" social contacts, e.g., the abrasive and hostile behavior of my work colleagues or the loaded and inimical relations with some of my clients, to be found in "good," i.e., warm and affectionate contacts, or in solitude—no contacts?

Benjy seems to be coming along. The healthy social experience he is building up in his time at the Special Learning Center, in his judo class, and now in Boys' Chorus is beginning to show. Next month he can try himself out at day camp and maybe overnight camp, too.

I wish Ann would hear whether she got her scholarship. We are all living on tenterhooks.

Until I was in my late twenties, my primary experience in the emotional world was that of being alone. Until then, I was essentially without friends, without human connections. The threat of ending relationships, of noninclusion, of being ostracized, of being made lonely, therefore registers on me now as less of a threat. When I get into a panic situation in social relationships, it's always to that first experience that I instinctively turn. I say to myself, "So what? If they don't include me, even if I lose all my friends, that's where I started out, that's my natural state. I know I can cope with it." When I'm in psychological jeopardy, that isolation seems a state of safety. It's to that that I automatically turn.

I know I've come to a place where some sort of psychological reordering is possible when I get the impulse to move my living room furniture around.

Esther does not consider herself a good teacher and does not like to teach. (My motto is find a head and fill it.) I like to teach.

She is strongly motivated to make a good appearance. I'm really pretty indifferent to appearances.

She was always sure she would find a man who would "understand" her. I have always been sure that I was going to be essentially alone.

Esther believes that she has a right to define or interpret the situation, reality, whatever—at least as good a right as anybody else. I believe that my view is so distorted that anybody else's appraisal is better than mine. My first move in defining reality is to take a consensus of what everybody else thinks.

She is a relativist and a pragmatist. I am a total absolutist. If it's ever right, then it's always right and right to the furthest limit. Hardly anything is sort of right or a little bit good.

I'd rather write. She'd rather rewrite.

Living with my mouth going constantly, Open Life Stance, is my way of comparing notes with the people around me, something I still don't feel I've had sufficient chance to do.

Benjy loves Boys' Chorus. Martin is setting out to train the boys from scratch. Their first performance will be next week, along with the adult chorus; they will sing the chorales with us from Bach Cantatas Nos. 4 and 140. I am so glad they will be starting with music that has meant so much in my own life. The chorale in Cantata No. 140 is the first Bach piece I ever sang.

I'm not a creative writer. I'm a critic, right down to the bone.

Taking Benjy through the Bach cantatas at rehearsal last night, watching him hear his own vocal line in harmony with the other parts, was a great pleasure. I could see he understood what making music is all about; it really turned him on. I can see he might have the makings of a musician. How much am I allowed to push him? Where does teaching stop and manipulating begin?

Reading through the Shakespeare sonnets again. Like the Bach chorales, I never get sick of them. They're like going swimming on a hot, muggy day. Exercise and refreshment, all in one.

A fantasy, like the moldy joke about people who tell jokes by number: a pair of lovers who converse with each other by sonnet number.

One of the main themes in this book is hope: what to hope for, establishing a reasonable hope, or perhaps having sufficient courage to pursue an unreasonable one that is more healing.

Martin Evans at rehearsal last night: "There's nothing else in the world but making music and enjoying nature. That's all there is." I think I would add something about loving and serving other people, but other than that, I agree—that's all there is.

Ann didn't get her scholarship. The financing for Benjy's Special Learning Center semester fell through. The insurance company doesn't want to pay on the burglary claim; they're hinting that we stole the stuff ourselves. Both our cats died of separate forms of cancer—one of leukemia, the other of lung cancer. I am sick to death of living in a bloody soap opera.

Searching through a book for another poem, I ran across this one by Gerard Manley Hopkins, which stopped me dead in my tracks:

> My own heart let me more have pity on: let
> Me live to my sad self hereafter kind,
> Charitable; not live this tormented mind
> With this tormented mind tormenting yet.
> I cast for comfort I can no more get
> By groping round my comfortless, than blind
> Eyes in their dark can day or thirst can find
> Thirst's all-in-all in a world of wet.
>
> Soul, self; come poor Jackself I do advise
> You, jaded, let be; call off thoughts awhile
> Elsewhere; leave comfort root-room; let joy size
> At God knows when to God knows what; whose smile
> 's not wrung, see you, unforseen times rather—as skies
> Between pie mountains—lights a lovely mile.*

After the "crisis" in therapy, the upsurge of anger, distrust, and resentment: I wondered if I couldn't have gotten through this much earlier if I had had the "right" therapist. I decided it wouldn't have been possible. It simply had to take this long for me to trust anybody enough to let her know how little I could trust her—or anyone.

I didn't think I was unhappily married. I thought marriage was an unhappy state.

Creeping up on my migraine problem: The only migraines I had as a child were after prolonged bouts of crying, which I had every so often. Are my present migraines perhaps a substitute for tears? After writing the sections of the book about Becky's death and Ann's hysterical aphasia, over both of which I cried a good deal, I was totally migraine-free for over a week.

My old friend Arlene called last night, after we had been out of contact for almost a year. With almost no preamble, she offered me a very large sum of money. I told her I was just fine, didn't need it. "I really don't want to start that again," was what I in fact said.

After I hung up, I thought, God damn! I could have sent Benjy to Special Learning Center for a year and paid Ann's university tuition with that money. But I knew it was the only thing to do. As I was talking to Arlene, I realized that if I took the money it would automatically renew her demands on me, reinitiate those old scenes of drunken importunity. If I took the money, I could see that I once again wouldn't be able to call my soul my own.

I'm the only person I know who has to beat off large sums of money. And I need it so badly, it really isn't fair.

This isn't a soap opera I'm living—it's an Iris Murdoch novel.

The antidote to the problem of the pain and poison of competitiveness, I'm pretty sure, lies somewhere in the direction of self-acceptance. To wish you were that someone else is but to know and accept the fact that you're not—with a minimum of bitterness or self-recrimination—seems like having made at least a start.

The one central piece of world view that differentiates those people I can basically get along with from those I cannot: the notion that there is somehow, somewhere, one standard pattern by which life ought to be lived. It doesn't matter what the pattern is or even how close it comes to my ideal for my own life. I am just plain allergic to one-pattern people.

I'm starting to move toward people, to want to make new friends, see old ones again, to take the steps necessary to make and preserve friendships. More and more I want to be with other people. My long mood of isolation and resentment seems at last to be wearing off. A more extroverted life pattern seems to be at hand.

The writing of the book intertwined inseparably with therapy. Together they've helped free me from perpetually repeating the past.

# CLOSING
# NOTE
# esther

In choosing names to replace those of the real people about whom we were writing, I had at first suggested for Becky the name of the little girl in the vignette in the Prologue. I had written the story about this child's picture a good many years before, with no use for it in mind at that time. When Martha and I decided to write the book, I dug it out of a bottom drawer because I was seized with the conviction that it was part of our story in some way. I saw many immediate connections: the theme of growth and change in therapy, my identification with my clients in the process, the little girl hidden away beneath the adult exterior of the woman, and so on. There was another connection, however, of which I was not aware until the question of the pseudonym for Martha's child arose.

Most children are attracted to my husband, and I long ago gave up any attempt to compete with him for their affection, so it was a rare and wonderful gift when a child happened to choose me. This had been the case with Elizabeth (and since I am now telling something of her real story, I have given her a psuedonym, too). When the question of a name for a beloved child came up, the name Betty naturally came to my mind, but when I started typing that part of Martha's story, I suddenly remembered that Betty had been in a car accident at an even younger age than Martha's daughter and had hovered between life and death for weeks. Betty's mother, a woman of courage and beauty, had not long before been found to have Hodgkin's disease. She was not one to flinch from bitter truths, and she lived her life for all it was worth for as long as she had left to live, but she was to have no more children. Betty eventually recovered, miraculously it seemed, with no permanent damage of any sort. And so I was able to draw her picture and to follow her progress until the ordinary circumstances of her life took her out of mine. But her picture remains on my wall, and she has never gone as completely out of my life as I thought.

Having remembered Betty's accident, I became uncomfortable about using her name. Martha suggested changing it to Rebecca, a biblical name that had its own dignity and meaning, with the nickname of Becky for purposes of the book. But I realized that I had

418

stumbled upon the real link between the little story I had written so long ago and the story we were writing now—the happenstance of a similar accident to another beloved child. Insight often comes in just such a belated, roundabout discovery of an unconscious emotional connection between two otherwise unrelated facts.

The other connections I had seen were, of course, "real" connections, too, but on the level of rational thought rather than intuitive happening; and they were a *result* rather than a *cause* of my decision to use the story. Thus do we tend to rationalize and to intellectualize emotional experience in order to fit it into our own way of looking at things. But let us not cast aside such mental activity and place value only on the "experiential," for true understanding demands a dual approach.

To understand what has happened from the standpoint of one's heritage, one's life experience, one's situational circumstances, and to understand what is happening in the here and now—and the relationship between the two—can be of immense therapeutic benefit, but without emotional meaning, such understanding would fall short of its goal. Martha did a great deal of intellectual work in the course of her therapy, but when she looks back on it, she *feels* the experience more than she analyzes it. Such an upshot is typical of successful therapy.

Whether we are dealing with a forgotten memory or with repressed feelings, whether we are restoring broken connections or establishing new ones, therapy is a matter of both the mind and the emotions. Neither can get along without the other; both are essential. That is one of the things this book is about.

This book is also about man-woman conflicts as well as one woman's problems. We anticipated that we might be writing a book that would speak to some of the points made by the women's liberation movement. I think we have done so, though not to the extent nor quite in the way we had expected. Certainly we did not present the man's point of view, except perhaps coincidentally. Books need to be written about the unfairnesses to men, but that was not our need.

Martha felt at times that I was asking her to look at things from Scott's point of view, which I never actually did, but I must admit that in one sense she read me correctly. Identified as I was with her and with all women in our shared plight, there was nevertheless a part of me that kept saying somewhere in the back of my mind: But Scott was caught, too, in a trap not of his own making with all the problems life had dealt him, acting out as best he could the man's role foisted upon him by our society.

I think that a woman must arrive at the point where she no longer allows men to victimize her before she can recognize them as fellow victims. They are necessary partners in the changes that must be made in this world if human beings are to survive at all. If we agree with Martha that, beyond the pursuit and enjoyment of beauty in nature and the arts, life also holds the possibility of love and service to others, surely that is a joint goal and not just a matter of the "woman's" role—if men and women are not to live forever alienated from themselves and from each other. And that, too, is what this book is about.

So now I come back from my picture of the girl child to my picture of mother and son—a theme of some relevance to this book also. The relationship between mother and child is the first and the deepest emotional experience a human being is likely to have, and certainly the one most difficult to "outgrow." But husbands are not sons, to be taken care of as though they were children by wives who are mother substitutes. Conversely, women are not children either, to be taken care of and controlled by father figures. Women, like men, may have that deeply rooted, childlike longing for a blissful emotional dependency in which all *their* needs will be met; but this fairy tale is not, alas, an adult possibility, either for men or for women.

Life isn't easy. It is no easier for women than for men. Women are no better equipped, and not necessarily more inclined, to take a parental role with their partners in marriage (or in any other joint endeavor) than are men. Biology is destiny for women only in the sense that they are the childbearing sex—and the child-nurturing sex when it comes to breast-feeding. Beyond that, the gift for nurturance is no doubt divided between the sexes as much according to chance and individual inclination as our society will permit.

Biology is, unfortunately, destiny for both men and women in that both suffer from the aftereffects of the prolonged dependency of their early years. Each must deal with the yearning to go back to that Golden Age—a yearning that disguises itself at times as aspects of the "feminine role," at times as "masculine prerogatives." And society, with the rationalizations and intellectualizations it has developed for fulfilling what it sees as its own function, has compounded the problem. It is to this problem that therapy quite often must address itself.

This book has also been about a discovery that was basic to Martha's therapy: The notion that a woman's femininity, her womanhood, her capacity to love—indeed her very worth as a human being —should be measured by her willingness to sacrifice her own needs to those of men is utter and wicked nonsense. This is a discovery that can be as therapeutic as it is liberating, and it is a discovery shared by a world of women today. If a woman defines herself, judges herself, by anyone's definition or judgment but her own, no matter who the parent figure may be—man or woman, husband or lover, or therapist—she remains as powerless and as vulnerable as a child. Only when liberated from such definitions can women be free to value, let alone to demand for themselves, the psychological and emotional equality that enters into the making of truly equal rights.

Martha's story became a book. Everyone's life is a story and everyone's therapy is a rewriting of that story, whether it is put into a book or not. There are always themes from an earlier drama, acted out in the course of current experiences and present relationships, with the client often placing the therapist in the role of one of the original cast of characters. It is the essence of therapy that the therapist accept no role but his own, the role of professional participant-observer, and examine as objectively as possible whatever personal and subjective reactions arise, those of therapist as well as of client. Thus do therapist and client become collaborators in the reconstruction and revision of a life history.

Martha and I found creative conflict in the experience of collaborating on a book. Others find it elsewhere. There must always be some kind of emotional turmoil if lifelong patterns are to be shaken up and put together in a new and better way, but the conflict need not be with the therapist. It may be with some significant person in the client's everyday life; or it may be an inner conflict, contending forces competing within the client's own personality. There is always likely to be some anger generated in the process. The expression of anger may be essential to communication or it may be a necessary safety valve, but if it goes no further than that, if it turns upon itself and feeds on itself, it can become a crippling obsession or a dangerous addiction. Anger is not a curative agent in itself. Anger becomes creative only when it leads to change or to effective action of some kind.

For me, therapy is always a collaboration. It is the joint product of client and therapist together. But it is a special kind of collaboration, one in which the therapist has the responsibilities as well as the advantages of the professional role. It is a role that requires of the therapist an ability to handle and use his own subjective reactions for the benefit of the client. It is this role that makes the therapy relationship different from any other relationship.

The course of each therapy develops collaboratively as events and relationships unfold. Martha's story is unique, but only in the sense that every life—and every therapy—is unique. So our using this particular example of therapy to convey the meaning of therapy in general proves not to have been much of a paradox after all.

Almost a year has gone by since Esther and I sat across the desk from each other and discussed the writing of a book about therapy. From all that has passed, for good and ill, in that year, we have fashioned this book together. As we have been writing, various friends who volunteered to act as readers and literary guinea pigs for us have read our material as it was written and rewritten. All of them, as they returned chapters to us with comments, have asked, "But what finally happened? Does it have a happy ending?"

It's an important question. And the answer is yes, the ending is a very happy one. But it's an answer that needs a statement of qualification: It's a happy ending to a very human story, and nothing human is perfect.

Of course, in the most concrete and mundane sense, when I consider the ways in which my life has changed and improved since the beginning of the project last year, the ending is very happy indeed. I was, a year ago, in very shaky shape. The happy ending we had reached at the end of the first round of therapy had come all unravelled, and it seemed to me as if all of the work needed to be done all over again.

My family life was tense and complicated. The job with "professional" status, the opportunity to work with people, to bring my own experience of poverty and trouble to a vocation in which it could be useful to other people, which at that time had seemed so marvelous, had turned out to be largely illusory because of the way the Welfare Department is structured and the stringent and illiberal fashion in which the welfare laws are administered. The ability to hold down a nine-to-five job, which seemed so exciting when I contemplated it then, had on the one hand come to be taken for granted and on the other to be threatened by my upsurge of migraines to a point where it was an open question whether I would be able to hang on to any day-to-day job at all. By that time, I felt that if I lost the ability to carry on a full-time job, all my gains in therapy would be put in question. I felt very shaky and vulnerable; the therapy seemed crucial to my survival and very far from an academic review of what had gone before.

# EPILOGUE
# martha

There has been steady change and improvement through this year. The siege of migraine has receded, not totally gone, it's true, but reduced to a livable level and with medication virtually not a problem any longer. As an unexpected side effect from that medical program, I have lost nearly forty pounds and look and feel far better. Although the tensions relating to my job have not been totally resolved, there is some improvement. I am on the list for promotion and have begun to look for a way to combine a return to college for a degree, which seems necessary if I'm going to move ahead in civil service with earning my living and raising a family.

In addition, through the writing of this book combined with my work in therapy, I have come to identify much more with the problems of other women, of all women. I have come to see my troubles, both present and past, as an example of the struggle all of us are making together to clarify our position and to find new and better ways to live our lives. That identification has strengthened me beyond measure, for it makes me in my own eyes no longer crazy, bizarre, the outsider, but a bona fide member of the human race.

I have had a chance in this year of our work together to live through, in a therapeutic and constructive framework, the two nightmare-in-daily-life situations that have haunted me since childhood. When my new unit at work tried to make a scapegoat of me, tried to treat me as if I were the outsider, unacceptable, worthless, I was thrown into a panic, but as I lived out that struggle, day by day, I found that I had gained too much strength for that ever to happen to me again. The scapegoaters ended by looking silly.

And in the flare-up with Esther over the book, I experienced my recurring inability to deal with my own anger. Time after time throughout my life, I've been unable to deal with my own hostility. I have lost friends, have paralyzed my daily life by my inability to handle that anger, which manifests itself as inarticulate rage. This time, with Esther's help, I managed to turn it into articulate rage and at least to live through it, experiencing in the living-through a new piece of information: People around me are willing to enter into give-and-take negotiation. There may be solutions to a quandary that do not demand the ending of all relationships or the sacrificing of one's own integrity.

I don't for a moment think I've seen the last of these problems. I've experienced them a thousand times and doubtless will again, but I think perhaps that now I can experience them with hope, the hope of finding my way through to a better and more constructive resolution of the difficulties involved. I realize, at least, that there can be alternatives to total isolation or total surrender, and that indeed friendships can draw strength, just as therapy can, from even the most serious and deeply held differences of opinion.

Surveying my life from this momentary resting place, I think that the ending to our story is a very happy one. I look around the home I have made and it seems to me a warm and welcoming place. I remember Marian's note when she returned some manuscript pages she had typed: "It really helped me to read that." I think of the client who turned to me as she left the waiting room yesterday and said, "I'm glad it was you who came down to see me today. I feel so much better." I think of standing in a Chamber Chorus performance, digging my toes into the floor and singing Bach with all the love and energy in me. And I think of Peter, secure and happy in his work; of Ann headed for medical school, proud and happy; of Sasha playing her flute, on her way to college, smiling and happy; of Benjy learning, singing, happy.

I realize that this happy ending is not final and for all time. It, too, will come unravelled, will be outgrown, after the nature of all human happy endings, as I move forward and grow and change. And it's the certainty of moving, growing, changing, that makes it a happy ending indeed.

As I look back on all the years of change and struggle, I realize how much help I have received from the people around me. Often they were people who had no "obligation" to me at all. How much I owe to their generosity and support, which I was often even unable to request or to thank them for! It was really freely given when I most needed it. Any victory of mine belongs to all those people. I think that very often the help that they gave me was the result, the end product, of their own victories. And I feel that if their victories could be put at my disposal, mine can be of use to others.

That's what makes me able to say to a really desperate client, a dying alcoholic, a far-gone junkie, "Fight on, hang on, I *know* you can do it!" When I say it, I can feel behind me the number of people who were willing to help me, to hang in and fight for me, to put not just their strengths but their whole human experience at my disposal when my need was most real. I know there must have been others who were willing to help them. I feel most deeply that they are my family, those I have learned from and those who will learn from me.

And I know there is something in all of us greater than the hostility, the destructive urges that we all feel within us, that we all fear, and that threaten to wipe out our species and perhaps our planet. I know that our power of human contact, our love for each other, is stronger than all of them and that together we can all make it into the future.

Yes, there is a very happy ending.

# Notes

PROLOGUE

*page 9*    No one can be entirely "objective." Each person tells a story or reports an event from his own vantage point. Objectivity, as defined in social work terms (from Fern Lowry by way of Helen Harris Perlman), is the therapist's recognition and control of subjectivity. It has nothing to do with coolness, colorlessness, neutrality of emotion. I was rereading Lawrence Durrell's *Alexandria Quartet* around this time and found myself very much taken with the way in which the "truth" is pursued and presented in "a soup-mix recipe," as Durrell puts it in *Balthazar*, "based on the relativity proposition," with information coming to the reader through both subjective and objective presentations. Whatever "truth" we are able to bring to the readers of this book will be very much a "soup mix" of the subjective and the objective, controlled for purposes of therapy.

MARTHA'S STORY

*page 26*    Martha was neither suicidal nor on the verge of a breakdown when I saw her some years later. It is clear that she must have made considerable progress before her contact with me. Had she been in a critical state, I would have wanted some psychiatric participation in the responsibility for her treatment, either directly through referral for evaluation or indirectly through consultation. Her application to the clinic was the appropriate choice for Martha at that time, just as her application to the Family Service Bureau, when neither psychological nor physical survival was any longer in question, was a good choice later.

*page 41*    At the time that Martha wrote this passage, I thought that I and the reader would just have to take on faith that Martha's interpretation of what Scott was doing in the interview was correct since she gave no back-up examples of ways in which he was slanting things. I did not get the significance of his remark to Martha, when they were leaving the office, about her starting to cry. In fact, I assumed there had been some kind of inadvertent error in the writing or typing and added the word "again" to complete what I thought Martha had intended to convey. I was entirely in error on that score, however, as it turned out later—much later—when we were proofreading the final draft of the manuscript. Not only had there been no error made in that passage, but Martha had intended that remark by Scott as her back-up example of the way he operated. This was one of many examples of Martha's taking for granted that everyone would know anything that she might know—but even more, it was an example of my failure to pick up a written clue that I would undoubtedly have picked up in a therapy hour.

*page 45*    There were many such "baby books" in those days, and I will not single out the doctor-author of my particular specimen, for he is long since dead and forgotten. When the tide turned with the publication of Margaret Ribble's *The Rights of Infants* in 1943, Lawrence Kubie's review in *The Psychoanalytic Study of the Child* (Volume I, 1945) epitomized this new approach as "a corrective to an era in which every mother and nurse has been encouraged to attempt to turn an infant into a clockwork mechanism"—a description that echoed my infant son's exact sentiments at the time!

*page 46*  It has been only recently, with the publication of such books as Helene Deutsch's *Confrontations with Myself* and Paul Roazen's *Freud and His Followers,* that I learned something of the personal matters that went into the making of supposedly quite objective theories. (I found myself muttering every now and then, with considerable satisfaction, "So that's where *that* came from!")

*page 55*  By today's perspective, of course, why not "Samoa" (to which Martha refers, page 19)? Or some other place, some other answer? The important distinction, therapeutically speaking, is not whether to have sex or not to have sex, but to recognize that if the choice by therapist and patient is for a sexual relationship, it must be acknowledged as an expression of love in an actual life situation, a choice that terminates therapy, not an act of therapy. Ordinary coincidental social intercourse with a client is difficult enough for a therapist to handle therapeutically. He who claims the ability to handle sexual intercourse for the therapeutic benefit of the client seems to me to be claiming omnipotence; he is likely to be dangerous to himself and others and should be treated accordingly. Father Michaelson did not, of course, have this problem—he was subject to no delusions of grandeur, either as a man or as a counselor. He handled himself with the restraint that his religious duties toward a disaffected couple required, whatever the cost to himself in private suffering.

*page 56*  Here I am making a distinction (on which I elaborate later when the matter comes up in Martha's therapy with me) between family-oriented therapy, which includes or does not include family members, flexibly according to circumstances, and a more rigid total-family-group approach.

*page 119*  At this point, Martha is bringing to bear some evidence that one of Scott's defenses was "forgetting" things that had happened. It was very clear at the time of Becky's accident that his way of dealing with painful reality was almost diametrically opposite to Martha's: Martha insisting that the truth be faced, Scott refusing to face it. A simple matter of one person managing without a defense mechanism to which the other clings, yet this difference that sounds so innocent, just one of many differences among individuals, may have played a major part in turning the marital conflict into a psychosis-breeding, life-and-death battle for both. Witness, to this effect, R. D. Laing, *The Politics of Experience:*

> If Jack succeeds in forgetting something, this is of little use if Jill continues to remind him of it. He must induce her not to do so. The safest way would be not just to make her keep quiet about it, but to induce her to forget it also. Jack may act upon Jill in many ways. He may make her feel guilty for keeping on "bringing it up." He may *invalidate* her experience. This can be done more or less radically. He can indicate merely that it is unimportant or trivial, whereas it is important and significant to her. Going further, he can shift the *modality* of her experience from memory to imagination: "It's all in your imagination." Further still, he can invalidate the *content:* "It never happened that way." Finally, he can

invalidate not only the significance, modality and content, but her very capacity to remember at all, and make her feel guilty for doing so into the bargain.

This is not unusual. People are doing such things to each other all the time. In order for such transpersonal invalidation to work, however, it is advisable to overlay it with a thick patina of mystification. For instance, by denying that this is what one is doing, and further invalidating any perception that it is being done by ascriptions such as "How can you think such a thing?" "You must be paranoid." And so on.

From R. D. Laing, *The Politics of Experience.* Copyright © R. D. Laing 1967. Reprinted by permission of Penguin Books Ltd.

*page 120*    Martha's experience in family therapy illustrates what might be called "the communication fallacy," i.e., the notion that just being able to communicate about something is therapeutic or valuable in itself. Sometimes this is true. But communication can be useless or worse than useless if it's about the wrong thing. In other words, the crux of the matter is what the communication is *about.* For instance, Martha's communicating to Scott the incident of Sasha's hysterical crying served only to give them each something more to be angry about and to defend in the conflict with one another. Granted that it may have been far too late to expect Martha and Scott to focus on the concern and anxiety about Sasha that they both truly felt and to consider what they might together try to do about it. Perhaps it was even too late to attempt some communication about the fact that everything was being drawn into the who-is-right/who-is-wrong battle. But there still might have been some point in questioning whether Sasha's problem was serving as a "red herring" whereby they could postpone communication about the marriage itself and whether it should be continued.

BEGINNING TOGETHER

*Chapter 1 The First Round*

*page 128*    Contrary to masculine folklore, the ex-wife does not "take the man to the cleaners," at least not among people with low or modest incomes; there simply isn't that much money around. From the economic standpoint, Martha did not benefit by the divorce at all. Not only was she worse off financially, but she was also still tied, for the sake of far less income than she had had before, to a man with whom she wanted nothing further to do. It is just such realities that must be taken into account when evaluating the "neurosis" of the wife who stays in a bad marriage. It seems to me that the subject of money has long since displaced that of sex as the major taboo of our society from the standpoint of the confusions and contradictions it occasions within and between human beings. Women often see themselves as remaining in a relationship for reasons of love, and they are often designated psychiatrically as emotionally dependent or even masochistic because they feel guilty or ashamed to admit to their financial motives. Loving, no matter how foolishly, is an acceptable feminine preoccupation, but hardheaded self-interest is not. Yet considering the concrete hardships, physical and economic, in working at a full-time outside job while taking sole care of home and children or, worse yet, of existing on a public assistance grant, there are certainly more compelling reasons for remaining in a bad marriage than those that merit a psychiatric label.

*page 134*   In retrospect, as I wrote this section, it occurred to me that the negative image might have come up in such an overwhelming manner because the positive image did not sufficiently include the normal complement of negative aspects, and Martha might have been experiencing a mounting accumulation of unconscious guilt. Though she had told me about many negative aspects of her behavior, she might have been accepting them on an intellectual level only, ruling them out on an emotional level because they did not come up to the absolute standards of her ego-ideal. The repressed guilt could conceivably come to consciousness in the form of a reinforcement of the earlier arrived at and therefore basically stronger negative image. Martha would then experience this side of her image as the "true self" and the positive image would become the imposter, the "false self" she had tricked me into accepting.

*page 140*   My science-minded son tells me that "luck" is not the proper word to use, that the legitimate, scientific term for what I was talking about is "chance." I agree with him and would like to think I always do use the proper word. But obviously I do not—just as, quite as obviously, I sometimes make mistakes on the appointment cards I give clients. (My sins are finding me out indeed.)

## Chapter 2 Return Engagement

*page 147*   Martha had not entirely given up the role of "good mother." So far as her children were concerned, of course, this was a perfectly valid and necessary function, and she was entirely sincere in performing it. She was sincere in playing this role in other relationships, too, but there it was inappropriate. And it was this role, with its demand that she always please, always serve —whatever her own needs and feelings might be—that was, as much as the current struggle with reality factors, perpetuating the imbalance of giving and getting in her life.

## BOTH SIDES OF THE DESK: THE INTERACTION

## Chapter 3 Remarks by Esther

*page 158*   Although I am prointuition, I am not antiscience and certainly not antiintelligence. Indeed, I am profoundly distrustful of those who advocate in one way or another "thinking with the blood," elevating emotion over reason as an approach to human problems, without any of the protective controls provided by scientifically oriented attempts at objectivity. But I am equally afraid of those who would apply the rigorous technical rules of research from the physical sciences to the study of subjective experiences of human beings, losing sight of their own subjectivity in the process. I hold with C. Wright Mills that scientific techniques are for the purpose of sharpening one's thinking and clarifying one's concepts, a way of disciplining the scientific inquiry—which is itself basically the use of the mind for all it's worth. I believe that any psychotherapy conducted in a spirit of disciplined and imaginative inquiry may qualify as a piece of clinical research even though nothing is being *measured*.

| | |
|---|---|
| *page 163* | Martha has suggested that "when in doubt, take a chance" might be an example of countertransference on my part, for while it is very definitely not my style, it is very much her style. I'm inclined to think she's right. |
| *page 165* | Although we do not recommend marathon sessions, we do recommend extra sessions when the going gets really tough. During October, when our crisis was at its height, we had several extra hours—and needed them! |
| *page 166* | The major problem with the transcriptions proved to be that of reducing them to manageable proportions. Our first editing was for purposes of disguise, focus, and intelligibility. We found ourselves far more literate than we had expected (the presidential tapes were still fresh in our minds), and there were many passages that we used exactly as they had taken place. But we were covering approximately nine months of interviews, averaging one interview a week, and we finally brought ourselves to cut the transcribed material further. |

## Chapter 4 Opening Phase

| | |
|---|---|
| *page 187* | The convention in professional writing calls for the use of the masculine pronoun unless a special point about female clients is being made. When I used the feminine pronoun to designate the client here, I did so not only because of the specific reference to Martha but also because in my experience it has usually been a woman who has had this dangerous pattern. |
| |     The term "scapegoat" originated in the Hebrew custom of turning a goat loose in the wilderness after the high priest symbolically laid the sins of the people on its head. For our purposes, the usual dictionary definition of "one who is made to bear the blame for others or to suffer in their place" is both a little too narrow and too far from the original meaning. The scapegoated child is seen by the other children not only as having all their sins (whose existence within themselves they can deny by deriding that child) but also sometimes as having desirable traits or advantages that they do not have and for which he is envied and resented. It is often such a double burden of "sin" that is laid upon the scapegoated child, for which the actual "sinners" drive him out into the wilderness. |
| *page 193* | As my mind wandered from a topic with which we could not expect to deal adequately, that of psychosomatic symptoms, it made an association (by way of human chagrin at the dilemma of it) to a more productive topic. Thus does the process of free association operate sometimes on the therapist's side of the desk. |

## Chapter 5 Development

| | |
|---|---|
| *page 224* | Sylvia Plath, of course, is not the only poet who expresses awareness of the injustices visited upon women in a world run by men for men. In fact, much of the emotional inspiration for the "women's lib" theme in our discussions came to Martha and me from an anthology of poems by women, *No More Masks!* |

*Chapter 6 Exposition*

*page 253*     I was simply not grasping the fact that here was an example of exactly what had struck me most in another context, that is, the issue of who is to meet whose needs. I didn't recognize it in the lopsided version in which Martha was presenting it because it most often appears in a dual form, each partner accusing the other of not meeting his or her needs. Though Scott wasn't meeting Martha's needs for either practical or emotional support, Martha didn't inject the matter of *her* unmet needs but merely tried to defend herself against Scott's complaints. Interestingly, as Martha's mind wandered from a subject on which I was held up by my failure to make an important connection, she was associating to a very significant connection of her own. Here is an example of free association as it sometimes operates on the client's side of the desk.

*page 283*     Martha suggested here a passage from a sonnet of Gerard Manley Hopkins:

> O, the mind, mind has mountains; cliffs of fall
> Frightful, sheer, no-man fathomed. Hold them cheap
> May who ne'er hung there.

From Sonnet 65, *Poems of Gerard Manley Hopkins,* Third Edition. Copyright 1948 by Oxford University Press, Inc. Reprinted by permission of Oxford University Press.

*page 286*     Otto Rank says somewhere that both the artist and the neurotic have "committed themselves to the pain of separation from the herd, that is, from unreflective incorporation of the views of their society." I see such "commitment" not as a matter of choice but as something thrust upon the individual as much by the characteristics of that society as by the individual's own nature.

*Chapter 7 Crisis*

*page 310*     Martha has been doing a great deal of the analyzing and interpreting for herself and has chosen her own frame of reference: the Bernian terminology of Adult, Child, and Parent to designate the operational parts of the personality. The usefulness of these designations to our work at this point is obvious. Martha has avoided using the Bernian terminology of "game playing," however, which would have been inappropriate to the way in which we were dealing with each other (and, I think, to the level on which we were trying to understand what was happening). Other clients choose from other frames of reference—socioeconomic, political, cultural, or religious, as well as a variety of psychological theories—any and all of which may be suited to their own therapeutic needs.

*page 310*     Martha and I knew, from having shared our mutual enthusiasm for Sayers' *Gaudy Night* quite early in our relationship, that we each valued true detachment very highly, so I was risking a good deal in my intuitive use of the term "pseudo-objective" (a risk that might not be apparent, or even exist, with some other client).

*page 318*     It should be understood, of course, that my view of what took place between us may differ considerably from my psychiatrist's view—each looking at things, in therapy as in life, from a different (and unique) vantage point.

## Chapter 8 Working Through

*page 330*   We did not get into a discussion about actual philosophies of absolutism and relativism or of how such philosophical positions differ—or should be differentiated—from the psychological necessities with which we were here concerned. I was making a back-of-the-head decision against so theoretical an approach at this point.

*page 339*   Probably the most important other learning experience that came to me from within the agency staff at that time was the example of a fellow old-timer. Her humorous acceptance (and use) of her own anger did much to free me and to liberate my anger. Her emotional support throughout did much to prop me up while I was tottering around on my newfound legs.

*page 359*   Once women are in a position to bargain from equal strength, they will have to bargain in earnest and in all honesty. I would think that in the process there would need to be a new look at the contribution of the man who works, whether he likes his job or not, and who takes complete financial responsibility for the family with most or all of the money he earns. (Single working mothers have a double dose of this burden, of course, since they are without a stay-at-home partner as compensation.) The trouble has been that men have tended to assume—and wives have often acquiesced in this—that the man is thereby buying his own dominance and his wife's compliance, if not her actual servitude. Such a "purchase" has not been productive of much human happiness, judging from the bitterness of divorced men as well as of women, and the traditional contract might well be rejected by both sexes. Renegotiation would need to be in the direction of a contract in which no one is exploited, in which the balance of winning and losing and compromising is as equal as possible, and in which men and women can have value for one another as human beings, not as objects to be used.

*page 360*   The distinction between shame and guilt is a matter of such complexity that it deserves far more than a footnote (I would recommend Helen Lynd's *On Shame and the Search for Identity* to begin with). For our purposes here, the important point is that shame arises from awareness of shortcomings (a function of the ego ideal), while guilt arises from awareness of transgressions (a function of the superego, in a narrower sense).

## Chapter 9 Martha's Notebook

*page 379*   Martha recognizes here the significance of those men in her University of Chicago days who sought her out, which Scott so obviously did not (except, perhaps, on some unconscious level), and who might have been able to meet some of her healthy needs—a recognition that was utterly beyond her at the time. The time factor in one's life history can make a tremendous difference in one's ability to deal with life constructively, but unfortunately such timing is not something over which one is likely to have much control. Events that may be traumatic for a child at a particularly vulnerable stage of development may be innocuous or even growth-producing at a later stage. And opportunities that come before a person has arrived at the point of being able to see them, let alone to use them, might as well not exist at all. Opportunity and developmental stage must coincide for a person to make a real choice, and whether or not these do coincide is largely a matter of chance. But out of a failure to recognize this factor arises a whole mythology of the individual's total responsibility for his own fate!

*page 415*     Sonnet 71, *Poems of Gerard Manley Hopkins.* Third Edition. Copyright 1948 by Oxford University Press, Inc. Reprinted by Permission of Oxford University Press.

# Bibliography

Bach, George R. and Wyden, Peter. *The Intimate Enemy.* New York: William Morrow and Company, 1968.

Bernard, Jessie. "The Paradox of the Happy Marriage." In *Woman in Sexist Society,* edited by Vivian Gornick and Barbara K. Moran. New York: Basic Books, 1971.

Berne, Eric. *Games People Play.* New York: Grove Press, 1964.

_____. *Transactional Analysis in Psychotherapy.* New York: Grove Press, 1961.

Coles, Robert. *Migrants, Sharecroppers, Mountaineers: Children of Crisis,* Vol. 2. Boston and Toronto: Little, Brown and Company, 1968.

Deutsch, Helene. *Confrontations with Myself.* New York: W. W. Norton and Company, 1973.

Durrell, Lawrence. *Balthazar.* New York: E. P. Dutton and Company, 1958.

Erikson, Erik H. *Childhood and Society.* New York: W. W. Norton and Company, 1950.

Hartmann, Heinz. *Ego Psychology and the Problem of Adaptation.* Translated by David Rapaport. New York: International Universities Press, 1958.

Hollis, Florence. *Casework—a Psychosocial Therapy.* New York: Random House, 1964.

Hopkins, Gerard Manley. *Poems of Gerard Manley Hopkins.* 3rd ed. New York and London: Oxford University Press, 1948.

Horney, Karen. *The Neurotic Personality of Our Time.* New York: W. W. Norton and Company, 1937.

Howe, Florence, and Bass, Ellen, eds. *No More Masks! An Anthology of Poems by Women.* Garden City, New York: Anchor Press/Doubleday, 1973.

Laing, R. D. *The Politics of Experience.* New York: Pantheon Books, Random House, 1967.

Lynd, Helen Merrell. *On Shame and the Search for Identity.* New York: Harcourt, Brace and World, 1958.

Piaget, Jean. *Six Psychological Studies.* With an Introduction, Notes, and Glossary by David Elkind. Translated by Anita Tenzer. New York: Vintage Books Edition, 1968; copyright Random House, 1967.

Plath, Sylvia. *Ariel.* New York: Harper and Row, 1965.

_____. *The Bell Jar.* New York: Harper and Row, 1971.

*The Psychoanalytic Study of the Child,* Vol. I. New York: International Universities Press, 1945.

Roazen, Paul. *Freud and His Followers.* New York: Alfred A. Knopf, 1975.

Sackheim, Gertrude. *The Practice of Clinical Casework.* New York: Behavioral Publications, 1974.

Saint-Exupery, Antoine de. *The Little Prince.* Translated by Katherine Woods. New York: Harbrace Paperbound Library, Harcourt, Brace and World, 1943, 1971.

Sayers, Dorothy L. *Gaudy Night.* New York: Harper and Row, 1936.

Towle, Charlotte. *Common Human Needs.* New York: National Association of Social Workers, 1965.

Weintraub, Stanley. *Whistler.* New York: Weybright and Talley, 1974.

# Appendix

## Position Statement*

I came to the practice of therapy through the profession of social work, which means that my education, training, and experience incline me always to look at a client's problems within the context of his total life situation. A human being, complicated enough within himself, lives in a most complex environmental network. His emotional and mental condition is the product of social dynamics as well as of psychodynamics, and there is a reciprocal relationship between his physical health and his psychological well-being. Whatever the power of unconscious strivings within an individual, the concrete realities that impinge upon him are powerful, too. And it is by no means only the poor who are subject to the impact of such realities; the middle class does not live in a benign vacuum either.

In recent years attention has increasingly been redirected from a too exclusive preoccupation with inner troubles to an examination of the outer circumstances that help to produce these troubles, yet knowledge of these realities has always been available to any therapist who chose to seek it out. For my awareness of realities I am indebted most of all to the clients I have listened to over the years of my practice. I occasionally wonder if they could possibly have learned as much from me as I have from them. They tell me of other backgrounds, other ways, and the vast array of circumstances different from my own with which people must try to deal. As I listen, I am constantly identifying with and differentiating myself from them and their experiences, and imagining as much as I can what it would be like to be in their shoes.

For me, such listening is a kind of research. If one truly listens to what a client is saying—not for the purpose of pigeonholing him into a diagnostic category or pinning a sociological label on him—one begins to know some of the basic, recurring questions arising out of the human dilemma. What I learn from one client I can often apply to another, though always in a different and individual way. Although the patterns I see may correspond quite closely to textbook material, my understanding does not arise from an acquaintance with concepts as such but from that which comes alive in the interchange between me and the client across the desk from me.

The trouble with intellectual concepts is that they can be put to other than useful uses. Just as outer circumstances can be cited in defense of old patterns and in resistance to new, so can psychoanalytic interpretations be cited to give the appearance of understanding in the absence of true insight. Psychological and sociological hypotheses can be invoked in ritual manner, substituting new rigidities for old; or intellectual formulations can be piled one upon another until the original pursuit of meaning becomes lost in a tangle of fancy phrases.

Understanding, even when achieved, is not in itself enough to effect a "cure." It is necessary, if at all

---

*This statement was written in the spring of 1974, when Martha and I first began to work on the book. It spells out exactly where I was in my professional thinking at that time and is thus the basis on which I proceeded with Martha as I did. In a sense, it is the real beginning of the book.

possible, to help the client change the circumstances that are responsible for his troubles, whether they are within or outside himself. Sometimes change needs to be made only with regard to the family situation; although this is difficult or sometimes impossible without the participation or at least cooperation of other family members, the individual at least has the choice of walking away if all else fails.

Where change must take place within society, it is not that simple. One can opt out of one's community or job or even one's nation, but one cannot take up residence on another planet as yet. If wider social change is required to eliminate or ameliorate problems, concerted action by many people working together may be necessary. Meanwhile, however, understanding can release the client from symptoms that arise from a misconception of the nature of the problem and of where change must take place.

People grow and change in therapy. I grow and change along with my clients. It is my therapy as well as theirs, but I have a responsibility they do not—the responsibility to protect them from anything within me that may be diminishing or damaging to them. This responsibility is a complicated one because it requires me to recognize those emotions—mine and the client's, both loving and hating in nature—that do not arise from the realities of the therapy relationship but are transferred to it from other relationships the client and I have experienced in our lives.

There is an element of relief in recognizing this transference, for I then need not take the kind of responsibility that would be mine if truly the client so loved or so hated me; I am sufficiently weighted down with my real-life obligations on that score. The danger lies in assuming that every response by the client arises from inner transference sources instead of acknowledging the existence of feelings arising out of the current facts of the client-therapist situation.

As therapist, I have the advantage of position over the client because it is he who is in the role of needing and asking for help and I who am in the role of professional helper. There is sometimes the possibility of other advantages in such things as income, education, and status and often now, alas, the chronological one of having lived a good many more years than most of my clients.

In each therapeutic encounter, I not only possess some of these very real advantages but I also have the benefit of the magical powers or other imaginary assets with which the client endows me by way of transference from the powerful figures of his early years. Because what I say or do is bound to carry far more weight with my client, for good or for ill, than it realistically is entitled to do, I must constantly examine and reexamine my own assumptions and attitudes. It would make no sense to put the client once again into the childlike position of having to agree with an "authority" against what may be his own better judgment when one of the goals of therapy is the development of the client's ability to make his own best choices. Besides, there is a good chance that I shall discover something of value to myself if I open my mind sufficiently to the contemplation of possible alternatives. So I deliberately divest myself of such magical power, whatever the real authority I may have through professional competence.

Though I use everything I have learned and experienced from science or the arts or inner personal struggle, I simply do not know what the answers are for my clients. They must find their answers for themselves. But as I come to understand who they are and what they are contending with, I begin to learn a good deal about—and from—their questions. I do not like the term "diagnosis" because it suggests a precision that does not exist. Nevertheless, I do not commit myself to therapy with anyone until I feel I can come to know him in this special way—not his answers, but his questions.

It is the questions people ask—about themselves, about their families, about their world, about life itself—that give me my clues as to how I may be able to help them. Various groupings of questions may correspond rather well with some psychiatric categories, and I then find the use of a psychiatric term a convenient time-saver. But too often the use of the term becomes a substitute for true understanding and I choose to discard it. The diagnostic label does not provide a view of a full-bodied human being in all his own and his world's dimensions but a stick-figure existing if not in an entire void, at least in a mere cardboard world.

The therapeutic journey is traveled by real people in a real world. The client will bring along enough phantom figures of his own that will need to be reduced to life-size; he has no need for the additional fantasies spun by psychiatric nomenclature. A diagnosis can be as stereotyping as a racist slur, and even more dangerously prone to becoming a self-fulfilling prophecy.

I have learned, too, that I must protect my clients from making too quick and total a commitment to other kinds of answers. Those who have managed to survive thus far by selling their souls as prescribed by childhood or adult necessities are all too ready to sell them once again—to a leader, a dogma, an illusion.

As I read the popular psychological literature, I am struck with the tone of evangelism, the conviction of certainty, the breadth of territory staked out by many of the claimants. I have found something of value in all these books and have added bits and pieces of their wisdom to my own to be drawn upon when needed, just as I have added to my collection from a variety of nonpsychological sources (murder mysteries, for instance, and poetry). I am concerned, however, by the effect on troubled people of popular psychology too hastily and uncritically read and of therapeutic endeavors too enthusiastically and thoughtlessly launched, sometimes by professionals as well as nonprofessionals. I have helped pick up the pieces for clients who have gone through a shattering progression from ecstatic conversion to ultimate despair, and I have found many others limping along wearing theoretical shoes that did not fit.

I have never been able to make a total commitment to any one school of thought, but only to that shifting patchwork of thoughts that at any given moment constitutes my own best judgment. I will offer that judgment to my clients when I think it will be helpful, but always with the understanding that different things help different people and that no one way—including my own—is the only way. My clients will have to deal with conflicting theories and philosophies for themselves; whatever faith they choose to live by, metaphysical or psychological, I do not try to make their choice for them.

I am, nevertheless, a person of considerable conviction and hold quite firmly to some beliefs, yet however emphatically I express my point of view, it is simply a statement of position, open to evaluation, revision, or rejection, according to one's own lights. This is not to say that it does not at all matter what one believes, that one position is as valid or useful as another, but only that one must be allowed to make a free choice. To the extent that I make my biases explicit, I can free others to make their own independent judgments. I have but one reservation to such freedom of choice, and that is the therapist's absolute obligation to make his choices within the bounds of professional discipline and informed self-discipline.

My own roots go as deeply into psychoanalytic as into sociological ground. By psychoanalysis I do not mean simply Freudian territory but also that of those many others who have in various ways improved on the original conception. I use the term "improved" with the qualification that I by no means endorse all the modifications and alterations that have been made, though some are truly vital. Whatever the personal feelings Freud had toward followers who so quickly appropriated and reshaped for their own uses the fruits of his discoveries, I believe he would now recognize that their doing so was in itself the greatest honor they could bestow upon him, their precursor in the use of self-exploration as an essential tool in the pursuit of knowledge. I view the various psychoanalytic contributions as classics, just as I do such sociological "greats" as Durkheim, Lasswell, and C. Wright Mills, and such psychological masters as William James, the early Gestaltists, Piaget, and Gordon Allport—and I cannot conceive of a therapy that does not in some way draw upon them.

When it comes to interpretations, however, I find that the interpretation an individual arrives at for himself, it it has emotional meaning for him, may well outweigh in significance whatever the more "correct" interpretation may be. I find it as impossible for me to impose interpretations on a client as it is impossible for me to adopt a theoretical position or a technique that is not congenial to me. It was for this reason that early in the course of my own career I developed a strong preference for consultation over supervision. It was not that my supervisors were arbitrary or domineering—indeed, they were most open-minded and generous-spirited—but I find that the concept of supervision tends to impose an artificially arranged superiority and inferiority of position, creating a barrier between people and discouraging the kind of spontaneous and open communication that is most fruitful.

Two minds are better than one, but only if they are equally free to disagree or to agree. Whether I am consultant or consultee, and whether I am patient or therapist, I need an atmosphere in which it is assumed that each will learn from the other and that differences will be examined not from the standpoint of who is "right" or "wrong," but for their divergent contributions to a broader or deeper understanding of the total situation.

For me, a relationship of equality is in itself therapeutic. More than that, without some feeling of equality I am diminished in humanity, as I am not free to be myself and cannot bring to a situation all that I have to give. I believe this is true for the other person in the situation, too. This is not to say that there must be some kind of exact and complete equality between two people. I do not believe that would be possible, and to pretend to it when it does not, in fact, exist would also diminish our humanity. Philosophically speaking, I suppose I am trying to put into other words what religious people mean by "equality in the sight of God." Practically speaking, I try to find something that I and the other person have in common—and this does not seem to be dependent upon some coincidence of race or class or age or creed—upon which we can begin to build a relationship.

Because of my strong feeling in this matter, I cannot take an approach in therapy not based on recognition of some kind of mutual sharing, both for me and for my client. In so stating my position, I am in no sense denying whatever superiority in training or experience I may have, nor disclaiming any legitimate authority I may derive from my professional role, nor abdicating my responsibility for the client's therapy, to the extent that I have responsibility.

From the psychodynamic standpoint, my approach is one that deals almost entirely in what is known as ego psychology. Transference and countertransference are deliberately maintained at as minimal a level as is feasible but vary somewhat, of course, with the client and the purpose of that client's therapy. In practice, I have found that the more I communicate, even though the nature and purpose of my communication is strictly professional, the mere fact of my communicating helps to keep the transference within bounds. There is something about dead silence that encourages both negative and positive transference feelings, but any kind of responsiveness on my part, verbal or nonverbal, seems to encourage clients to see me more realistically, more as the human being I am, with less and less transference distortion. As I became aware of this, I began to experiment occasionally with revealing more of my personal reactions along with professional ones. Thus far, such sharing has seemed to increase mutual feelings of equality and by my criteria to further the course of therapy.

The sharing of a personal reaction is a most delicate matter, however, far more so than the expounding of a theoretical concept derived from some remote authority. It is a mistaken notion, and probably a presumptuous one, to assume that because of some similarity of experience a therapist automatically understands the meaning of the client's plight. Although there is probably some comfort to the client in hearing "I know what you mean; I was there once myself," there are inevitably aspects of his situation that he knows are peculiarly his own and are not to be understood on the basis of identification alone.

This is where the well-meant efforts of amateurs so often fall short or come to grief. The ex-druguser, for instance, does not necessarily have the key within his own history to free another from similar bondage; to claim that he does may be as false for himself as for the other and therefore potentially harmful to both. Even when in fact there is a coincidence of circumstances and their meanings, there is no reason to deprive the client of the pleasure of making his own discovery. It is as irritating to be told something that one already knows as it is to be told something that just does not happen to be true. Any therapy, professional or not, that is conducted with an air of knowing exactly what the problem is and exactly what to do about it is likely to prove not to be therapy at all.

If such pitfalls are kept in mind, the selective sharing of experiences may provide a safety measure in the course of therapy, with the therapist's personal reaction providing the measuring rod for the client to determine overreactions of his own. Such a safety device is especially useful with clients who are prone to turn their capacity for insight against themselves. Such a client, on discovering his contribution to his own problems, may make use of this knowledge to negate his innermost essential sense of value as a human being. Just to interpret to the client at this point that he is turning his insight against himself is not enough, because he may simply add this observation to his collection of "bad" things about himself to throw into the self-destructive hopper. Each successive interpretation of this sort will add to the collection. Personal communication may then be far more useful than professional comment, for it may provide a basis for identification whereby the client can shift ground from a negative self-image to a positive one.

The actual ongoing relationship between therapist and client is as valid a subject of interest and inquiry as is the client's misperception of it in terms of past experiences. In any case, the therapist cannot escape revealing aspects of his own personality and his own life to the client, whatever his attempts to remain unknown. Just as bias in research must be spelled out in order to allow for it in evaluating results, so must these personal aspects be taken into account as part of the therapeutic process. The client who considers himself to blame for the failure of his life will otherwise be only too likely to blame himself for the failure of his therapy.

The safeguard provided by such sharing between therapist and client can itself be abused, however, if the therapist goes beyond what is necessary to the therapeutic task, but just where the line is to be drawn is a crucial professional question. This is not to say that one can establish a once-and-for-all rule to be applied wholesale (such as complete "transparency" on the part of the therapist), but it is a question the therapist must ask himself with each client, thus bringing intuitive subjective responses into awareness so that they become part of the process of conscious control.

There are other professional questions that occur again and again, questions that periodically receive special attention as this one or that one rediscovers their importance or restates them in a new way. There are many useful restatements of old truths. For instance, the matter of crisis intervention: It has always been clear that when one's world is falling apart, or even when one has simply reached a point where old guideposts no longer serve and old ways of functioning no longer suffice, one has the opportunity to put things together in a different, perhaps more felicitous way. Or the matter of brief treatment: It is quite apparent that helping a client deal with his problems on the level on which he perceives them, superficial though such a course sometimes seems to be, is likely to be the most economical from the standpoint of time and often, certainly from the client's standpoint, the most understandable and productive of results. Deeper understanding is unnecessary if the client is able to achieve his goal without it or the understanding may come of its own accord after the event, because the roots of change lie below surface level and may well bring some deeper feelings to conscious awareness in the process of change.

It seems to me as unreasonable to offer only brief therapeutic encounters as it is to offer only interminable supportive or analytic experiences, or to offer only a group or family approach as it is to treat an individual always as an island unto himself, or to deal only with the here and now as it is to probe invariably into the distant past.

It also seems as unreasonable to speak of mental health only in terms of growth and development as it is to speak of it entirely as a matter of sickness or health. My preference, when there is a choice, is for the former, since growth and development are for me both means and ends in therapy, but this is not to say that the matter of sickness and health is not at issue, too. Anyone suffering from severe psychoneurotic symptoms usually feels very sick indeed, and psychotic symptoms are likely to be even more disabling. There are certainly times when the emotional and mental problems of a client may make it advisable that he literally become a medical patient—that is, he may need medication or hospitalization, services traditionally supplied under medical auspices. So it would not seem unreasonable in some circumstances to use the term "sick."

Unfortunately, if one follows such criteria, one often labels the victim rather than the perpetrator of the stresses and strains that help to precipitate the condition. As the exponents of family therapy have so strongly stated, the "sick" behavior of a child may actually be a healthy effort to escape infection or crippling by destructive family patterns. Marriage counselors frequently experience the phenomenon of having to work with the "wrong partner"—that is, with the one who is willing to come—who is often the more vulnerable because less well defended against emotional reactions but thereby more open to the processes by which growth and development take place.

Because the contribution of the significant others in a client's life may be the factor that pushes him into the patient category, one hesitates to use the label of sickness at all. Nevertheless, the word has its therapeutic value. When even one client hitherto caught in an impossible marriage or affair experiences the tremendous impact of the discovery that what he thought to be love was actually a sickness, a therapist will probably ever after be reluctant to rule out the word sickness entirely.

My opposition to professional jargon is most often directed toward the misuse of a term rather than the term itself, but one's choice of words sometimes reveals attitudes underlying that choice. When workers in the field of mental health speak of "plugging people into delivery systems," for instance, they are diminishing the humanity of those people and of themselves. The social work background from which I came declared its belief in the therapeutic value of respect for the individual and it gave humanitarian considerations precedence over statistical ones. I still choose to be on the side of a continuing faith in the efficacy of treating people like human beings. Plugs are for machines, not for people. And mental health depends far more on the quality of human contact than on the perfection of administrative structure.

It is ironic that one of the old truths needing restatement is that on which the profession of social work was founded: the worth and dignity of the human being, his right to be viewed and treated as an individual, and his right to participate in the necessities of existence and in the conduct of his life as an equal among equals. In the field of public welfare, the increasingly illiberal attitude toward mothers receiving financial aid for their children seems antiwoman as well as antihuman. It is a sad departure from the tradition of a profession once honored for having such leaders as Jane Addams, Bertha Reynolds, and Charlotte Towle.

Through these leaders and those inspired by them, social work for a time seemed to have become the conscience of a nation willing to take upon itself the commitment that no child should suffer by reason of the economic, psychological, or social failings of its elders, and that adults on welfare (whatever their state of grace) should be accorded the same title to humanity as any other adults. From such roots, social workers could not help bringing to their practice of therapy a view of things somewhat different from that prevailing among psychiatrists and psychologists. Though social workers already shared—or quickly borrowed—many of the theoretical tenets of the established psychotherapies and enriched them in turn, they established a psychosocial therapy of their own, which retains a special quality that reflects its own beginnings.

I make no claim to originality. The basic philosophy underlying my practice came to me from the profession of social work, and some of the technical aspects came to me through my training in the psychiatric specialty. What is original with me, as with all experienced practitioners, is primarily a personal style. Psychosocial therapy has a body of knowledge, theoretical and practical, of its own. Innovations by individual practitioners are made within that framework and evaluated by its standards in responsible professional fashion. This book arose in part out of my conviction that psychosocial therapy needs to be better known to the general public so that it will have equal status with other psychotherapies when mental health services are authorized for payment under private and governmental insurance plans.

Social work was originally known as a woman's profession, but men soon came to outnumber women in the top administrative positions. More recently, men seem to be outnumbering women in the influential academic posts as well. Whether as a result of this displacement or other factors, there is now a great push for accountability. This usually means proof of measurable results, but sometimes it also means control by clients over services offered.

Perhaps it will eventually be possible to state in quantitative terms what can now be described only in qualitative terms, but it may be that only the computer, which tabulates such things, will be able to make much use of the results. Meanwhile, I am inclined to think that a process whereby human beings discover and understand and foster in their own ways their desire to improve the quality of their own and others' lives, even though such improvement remains unmeasurable, is already a process in which clients control their own therapeutic destinies. It is about such a process that this book has been written.